Next Year in Jerusalem: Exile and Return in Jewish History

Studies in Jewish Civilization
Volume 30

Proceedings of the Thirtieth Annual
Symposium of the Klutznick Chair
in Jewish Civilization,
the Harris Center for Judaic Studies,
and the Schwalb Center
for Israel and Jewish Studies

October 29–30, 2017

Other volumes in the
Studies in Jewish Civilization Series
Distributed by the Purdue University Press

2010 – Rites of Passage:
How Today's Jews Celebrate, Commemorate, and Commiserate

2011 – Jews and Humor

2012 – Jews in the Gym:
Judaism, Sports, and Athletics

2013 – Fashioning Jews:
Clothing, Culture, and Commerce

2014 – Who Is a Jew?
Reflections on History, Religion, and Culture

2015 – Wealth and Poverty in Jewish Tradition

2016 – Mishpachah:
The Jewish Family in Tradition and in Transition

2017 – *olam ha-zeh v'olam ha-ba*:
This World and the World to Come in Jewish Belief and Practice

2018 – Is Judaism Democratic?
Reflections from Theory and Practice Throughout the Ages

Next Year in Jerusalem: Exile and Return in Jewish History

Studies in Jewish Civilization
Volume 30

Editor:
Leonard J. Greenspoon

The Klutznick Chair in Jewish Civilization

Purdue University Press
West Lafayette, Indiana

Copyright © 2019 by Creighton University
Published by Purdue University Press
All rights reserved
Manufactured in the United States of America

Library of Congress Cataloging-in-Publication Data

Names: Greenspoon, Leonard J. (Leonard Jay), editor.
Title: Next year in Jerusalem : exile and return in Jewish history / Leonard J. Greenspoon.
Description: West Lafayette, Indiana : Purdue University Press, [2019] | Series: Studies in Jewish civilization, 1070-8510 ; volume 30 | Proceedings of the thirtieth annual symposium of the Klutznick Chair in Jewish civilization, the Harris Center for Judaic Studies, and the Schwalb Center for Israel and Jewish Studies, October 30-31, 2016. | Includes bibliographical references.
Identifiers: LCCN 2019032343 (print) | LCCN 2019032344 (ebook) | ISBN 9781557538758 (paperback) | ISBN 9781612496054 (pdf) | ISBN 9781612496047 (epub)
Subjects: LCSH: Jews—History—Babylonian captivity, 598-515 B.C.—Congresses. | Jews—History—586 B.C.-70 A.D.—Congresses. | Zionism and Judaism—Congresses. | Jews—Identity—Congresses. | Jerusalem—In Judaism—Congresses. | Jerusalem—In the Bible—Congresses. | Temple Mount (Jerusalem)—Congresses.
Classification: LCC DS121.65 .N49 2019 (print) | LCC DS121.65 (ebook) | DDC 320.54095694—dc23
LC record available at https://lccn.loc.gov/2019032343
LC ebook record available at https://lccn.loc.gov/2019032344

Cover image: vividvic/iStock/Getty Images Plus via Getty Images

No part of *Studies in Jewish Civilization* (ISSN 1070-8510) volume 30 may be reproduced or transmitted in any form or by any means, electronic or mechanical, including photocopying, recording, or any information storage and retrieval system, without permission in writing from the publisher, except in the case of brief quotations embodied in critical articles and reviews.

Table of Contents

Acknowledgments vii

Editor's Introduction ix

Contributors xv

Place as Real and Imagined in Exile: Jerusalem at the Center of Ezekiel 1
Samuel L. Boyd

"How Deserted Lies the City": Politics and the Trauma of Homelessness
in the Hebrew Bible 29
Dereck Daschke

Exile and Return in the Samaritan Traditions 49
Menahem Mor

The Āl-Yāḫūdu Texts (ca. 572–477 BCE): A New Window into the Life
of the Judean Exilic Community of Babylonia 71
Jean-Philippe Delorme

Karaites and Jerusalem: From Anan ben David to the Karaite Heritage
Center in the Old City 99
Daniel J. Lasker

Jewish Folk Songs: Exile and Return 111
Paula Eisenstein Baker

Is Zionism a Movement of Return? 127
Haim Sperber

The Jew in Situ: Variations of Zionism in Early
Twentieth Century America 135
Judah M. Bernstein

Returning to Jewish Theology: Further Reflections on Franz Rosenzweig 153
Jean Alexrad Cahan

Exile and Return: Indian Jews and the Politics of Homecoming 171
Joseph Hodes

Against the Sabra Current: Hanokh Bartov's *Each Had Six Wings*
and the Embrace of Diasporic Vitality 185
Philip Hollander

Shylock and the *Ghetto*, or East European Jewish Culture
and Israeli Identity 211
Dror Abend-David

Exile and Zionism in the Writings of Rav Shagar 229
Shlomo Abramovich

The Role of the Temple Mount Faithful Movement in Changing
Messianic Religious Zionists' Attitude toward the Temple Mount. 247
Mordechai (Motti) Inbari

Acknowledgments

The 30th Annual Symposium on Jewish Civilization took place on Sunday, October 29, and Monday, October 30, 2017, in Omaha, Nebraska. The title of the symposium, from which this volume also takes its name, was "Next Year in Jerusalem: Exile and Return in Jewish History." All of the essays collected here, with the exception of the ones by Jean Cahan and Shlomo Abramovich, were delivered at the symposium itself.

The academic sponsors of this symposium represent three major educational institutions in Nebraska: Creighton University (the Klutznick Chair in Jewish Civilization, the Kripke Center for the Study of Religion and Society), the University of Nebraska–Lincoln (the Harris Center for Judaic Studies), and the University of Nebraska at Omaha (the Schwalb Center for Israel and Jewish Studies).

As it happens, the topic for the 2017 symposium was suggested by Moshe Gershovich z"l, then director of the Schwalb Center. His all-too-early death deprived us of the active and inspiring participation on his part from which we had benefited in previous years.

In large measure, the symposium owes its success to two groups of dedicated and talented individuals. First are my academic colleagues: Dr. Ronald Simkins (Creighton), Dr. Jean Cahan (University of Nebraska–Lincoln), and and Dr. Curtis Hutt (University of Nebraska at Omaha). Their generosity, individually and collectively, has been exemplary.

The second group consists of administrative assistants, the individuals who really know how to get things done. In this context, I offer sincere expressions of gratitude to Colleen Hastings, who works with the Klutznick Chair and Kripke Center at Creighton, and Kasey De Goey of the Schwalb Center at the University of Nebraska at Omaha.

As many readers of this volume know well, the road from oral presentation to written publication is filled with obstacles. Our path has been inestimably smoothed over through our relationship with the Purdue University Press. For almost a decade we have enjoyed the professional and personable staff of the press, first under the previous director, Charles Watkinson, and now under Justin Race. They have made us feel comfortable in every way, and we look forward to many more years of association with the press.

In addition to the academic and communal organizations mentioned above, this symposium is also generously supported by

The Ike and Roz Friedman Foundation
The Riekes Family
Creighton University Lectures, Films, and Concerts
The Creighton College of Arts and Sciences
The Henry Monsky Lodge of B'nai B'rith
The Drs. Bernard H. and Bruce S. Bloom Memorial Endowment
And others

Leonard J. Greenspoon
Omaha, Nebraska
February 2019
ljgrn@creighton.edu

Editor's Introduction

For the last two decades or so, we have held our annual symposium on the last Sunday and Monday of October. At the conclusion of every year's event—and sometimes even before then—someone asks about the topic for the following year. This is not surprising, since our selection of a different topic for each year is a distinctive feature of our series of symposia—and from my perspective (and not mine alone, I think) a positive characteristic.

So it was that at the end of October 2016, with the twenty-ninth symposium still a vivid memory, I began soliciting ideas for our thirtieth installment from my academic colleagues and interested members of Omaha's Jewish community. My good friend Moshe Gershovich, director of the University of Nebraska at Omaha's Schwalb Center and an active cosponsor of the symposium series, was brimming with enthusiasm as he suggested "Exile and Return."

In this context he was especially interested in the Balfour Declaration, which was promulgated one hundred years earlier in 1917. We talked about Moshe's delivering the keynote address on this topic. Alas, Moshe's death, which was a personal and professional loss to all who knew him, intervened, and he was no longer alive in the fall of 2017.

We did keep alive Moshe's idea for the symposium. Recognizing that we could not find a "substitute" Moshe, as it were, to make a keynote presentation, we went in another direction with a concert by renowned performers Maria Krupoves and Gerard Edery. This was made possible through the generosity of the director of the University of Nebraska–Lincoln's Harris Center, Jean Cahan.

In a sense, then, the symposium and these essays are a tribute to Moshe and his vision. In a larger sense, they also reflect the combined talents and energies of those who participated in this symposium and prepared a publishable written version of their presentations.

Wherever possible, I have arranged the chapters in this volume in chronological order, beginning with the biblical period and continuing until the very recent present. Acknowledging that this is but one way of arranging the rich material this collection contains, I nonetheless offer it as an approach that illuminates and elucidates developments, both interdependent and independent, that occurred over the past two and a half millennia.

The first five essays deal primarily with the distant past, from the sixth century BCE to the sixteenth century CE. Samuel L. Boyd, University of Colorado–Boulder, focuses our attention on "Place as Real and Imagined in Exile: Jerusalem at the Center of Ezekiel." As he shows, geography functions in important ways for exiled communities. In the process, real places (near and far) morph into symbols, and symbolic places are reimagined as real. In his essay, Boyd explores the concept of central place in two ancient documents—the *Mappa Mundi* [Babylonian Map of the World] and the biblical book of Ezekiel—showing how Babylon and Jerusalem function as real and symbolic concepts in each.

Dereck Daschke, Truman State University, also looks at the world of the Bible in his essay "'How Deserted Lies the City': Politics and the Trauma of Homelessness in the Hebrew Bible." He explains that a growing body of biblical scholarship has begun to recognize the central role of the Babylonian exile in the shaping of the Hebrew Bible. In such readings, the exile represents a quintessential occasion of individual and collective trauma. In this vein, Daschke's essay examines the trauma of homelessness as it is expressed in the Hebrew Bible in spiritual and political terms.

Menahem Mor, University of Haifa, was the first holder of the Klutznick Chair at Creighton University. His essay "Exile and Return in the Samaritan Traditions" discusses the Samaritan traditions about their version of exile and return in the various Samaritan Chronicles. In the process, he compares these traditions with parallel Jewish sources, including the historian Josephus, to understand the role of exile and return in the Samaritans' history and the function of Mount Gerizim in these traditions.

Jean-Philippe Delorme, University of Toronto, shows how recently discovered texts help to expand our knowledge of the Babylonian exile. In his essay, titled "The Āl-Yāḫūdu Texts (ca. 572–477 BCE): A New Window into the Life of the Judean Exilic Community of Babylonia," he begins by reminding us that Jewish history has been punctuated by numerous exilic experiences since its beginnings. At its genesis stands the Babylonian exile. Until recently, our understanding of this crucial period has been based principally on secondary sources of debatable accuracy. The recent publication of the Āl-Yāḫūdu texts makes up for these shortcomings. In his presentation, Delorme illustrates the daily reality of the exiles as it is seen through these archives.

Daniel J. Lasker, Ben-Gurion University of the Negev, is the author of the last essay in this section, "Karaites and Jerusalem: From Anan ben David to the Karaite Heritage Center in the Old City." He notes that Jerusalem has always played a special role in Karaite thought and practice. The golden age of Karaism (tenth–eleventh centuries CE) was centered in Jerusalem. Even after the Karaite community was destroyed by the Crusaders, there was almost always a Karaite presence in Jerusalem. In his essay, Lasker explores Karaite history and practice, especially as it is presented at the recently opened Karaite Heritage Center in the city of Jerusalem.

The next four essays cover the period from the second half of the nineteenth century to the early decades of the twentieth century, prior to the founding of the modern State of Israel in 1948. First is "Jewish Folk Songs: Exile and Return" by Paula Eisenstein Baker, adjunct instructor of violoncello and chamber music emerita, University of St. Thomas, Houston, Texas. In her essay, Eisenstein Baker shows how Jewish folk songs, as employed in art music, experienced multiple exiles. By the early 1920s, the Society for Jewish Folk Music in St. Petersburg and its Moscow branch had quit publishing. Their works, with new publishers, were exiled to Berlin and Vienna. Beginning in the mid-1930s, these tunes faced exile again, this time to New York City.

Haim Sperber, Western Galilee College, is next with "Is Zionism a Movement of Return?" In this essay, Sperber supports his claim that the early Zionist movement was a political union of two different movements aiming at two different objectives—re-creating the old kingdom of the Jewish people in the Land of Israel and creating a new political Jewish nation. These two movements reflect two different kinds of nationalism: cultural-ethnical nationalism and cultural-political nationalism. The decision to form a united political organization initially blurred the differences between the two.

Judah M. Bernstein, New York University, turns the focus to the United States in his essay, titled "The Jew in Situ: Variations of Zionism in Early Twentieth Century America." He observes that historians who have studied the early decades of American Zionism (1898–1948) have typically operated with the assumption that for Jews, America was viewed as home and not exile. It is no doubt true that American Zionist leaders seldom called on Jews to migrate. At the same time, as Bernstein shows, this interpretation overlooks the ambivalence felt by a number of influential American Zionist intellectuals about whether to consider America home or exile.

Jean Axelrad Cahan, University of Nebraska–Lincoln, is one of the symposium's cosponsors. In her essay "Returning to Jewish Theology: Further Reflections on Franz Rosenzweig," she is interested in reconsidering some of Rosenzweig's ideas on a possible return to Jewish theology. In the process, she shows that historical and scientific critiques of Judaism constituted a central preoccupation of his. Indeed, Rosenzweig's account of revelation was intended to displace or overcome precisely that kind of critique.

The last five essays cover developments from the early years of the State of Israel to the twenty-first century. Joseph Hodes, Texas Tech University, is the author of the essay "Exile and Return: Indian Jews and the Politics of Homecoming." According to the traditions of the Indian Jewish community the Bene Israel, their founders left the biblical kingdom of Israel and came ashore near present-day Mumbai. They lived peacefully with their Hindu hosts for the next 1,800 years. In his essay, Hodes chronicles Jewish life in India and the multiple exiles and returns the Bene Israel made to the State of Israel in its early years.

Next, Philip Hollander, University of Wisconsin–Madison, looks at literature in "Against the Sabra Current: Hanokh Bartov's *Each Had Six Wings* and the Embrace of Diasporic Vitality." He reminds us that the Israeli Declaration of Independence, drawing on traditional Jewish terminology, voices the State of Israel's commitment to the ingathering of the exiles. Thus, in Israel's first years, its resources were committed to immigrant absorption. This monumental undertaking, however, found limited literary representation. In his presentation, Hollander analyzes Bartov's novel of 1954 as a significant exception to this trend.

In his essay "Shylock and the *Ghetto*, or East European Jewish Culture and Israeli Identity," Dror Abend-David, University of Florida, focuses on the theater. In 1984, Abend-David observes, author Yehushua Sobol brought to stage the play *Ghetto*, which was directed by Gedalya Besser for the Haifa Municipal Theater. In reading this work, Abend-David explores the ghetto as a psychological phenomenon that has been ingrained and perpetuated in modern Jewish culture long after the physical walls of the Jewish ghetto were dismantled. For better or worse, then, the ghetto is an essential part of modern Jewish history.

Shlomo Abramovich, visiting scholar, Beth Israel Synagogue, Omaha, begins his essay "Exile and Zionism in the Writings of Rav Shagar" by pointing out that the term "Zionism" can be understood in many ways. Many Zionist thinkers added to it a negative attitude toward the exile and diaspora. Therefore, finding a Zionist thinker with a positive approach to the exile is exceptional. In his essay, Abramovich presents Rav Shagar's ideas on such an approach and examines his unique position on Zionism.

The last essay in the volume, by Mordechai (Motti) Inbari, University of North Carolina, Pembroke, is titled "The Role of the Temple Mount Faithful Movement in Changing Messianic Religious Zionists' Attitude toward the Temple Mount." As he explains, the rebuilding of the Third Temple is viewed in rabbinic literature as the manifestation of Jewish redemption. The establishment of the State of Israel and the Israeli victory of 1967 gave rise to the view among religious Zionists that the End Days were drawing near. In his presentation, Inbari describes the internal debate within these circles over the question of Jews entering the Temple Mount and presents the religious dynamics that permitted Jews to enter.

Leonard J. Greenspoon

Contributors

Dror Abend-David	Department of Languages, Literatures and Cultures University of Florida 337 Pugh Hall PO Box 115565 Gainesville, FL 32611-5565 da2137@nyu.edu
Shlomo Abramovich	Beth Israel Synagogue 12604 Pacific St. Omaha, NE 68154 shlomo23@gmail.com
Paula Eisenstein Baker	2053 Dryden Road Houston, TX 77030-1205 eisenbak@stthom.edu
Judah M. Bernstein	476 Forest Avenue Teaneck, NJ 07666 yehudambernstein@gmail.com
Samuel L. Boyd	Eaton Humanities 240 Pleasant St. Boulder, CO 80302 samuel.boyd@colorado.edu
Jean Alexrad Cahan	Harris Center for Judaic Studies University of Nebraska–Lincoln Louise Pound Hall 325C 512 N. 12th St. Lincoln, NE 68588-0322 jcahan1@unl.edu
Dereck Daschke	Department of Philosophy & Religion Truman State University 100 E. Normal Kirksville, MO 63501 ddaschke@truman.edu

Jean-Philippe Delorme	Department of Near & Middle Eastern Civilizations University of Toronto 4 Bancroft Avenue, 2nd Floor Toronto, ON, Canada M5S 1C1 jp.delorme@mail.utoronto.ca
Joseph Hodes	Texas Tech University Honors College Room 202B McClellan Hall Lubbock, Texas 79409 j.hodes@ttu.edu
Philip Hollander	860 Van Hise Hall Department of German, Nordic, & Slavic/Center for Jewish Studies 1220 Linden Drive University of Wisconsin–Madison Madison, WI 53706-1558 phollander@wisc.edu
Mordechai (Motti) Inbari	5521 Bridford Pl. Raleigh NC 27613 Mordechai.inbari@uncp.edu
Daniel J. Lasker	Goldstein-Goren Department of Jewish Thought Ben-Gurion University of the Negev POB 653 Beer Sheva Israel lasker@bgu.ac.il

Contributors

Menahem Mor   Department of Jewish History
                     University of Haifa
                     Haifa 3498838
                     Israel
                     mmor@univ.haifa.ac.il

Haim Sperber   Ha-histadrut 9/6
                     Kiriat Yam
                     Israel
                     haims@wgalil.ac.il

Place as Real and Imagined in Exile: Jerusalem at the Center of Ezekiel

Samuel L. Boyd

INTRODUCTION

The narrator of the book of Ecclesiastes, upon reflection of the profound depths of Qoheleth's search for meaning, claimed at the final chapter of the work that "of the making of books, there is no end [עשׂות ספרים הרבה אין קץ]" (Eccl 12:12). A similar statement could be made about the making of maps. As J. Z. Smith states, "map is not territory," and the concept of a place achieves significance through intentional acts of delineating and defining meaning through the organization of space.[1] Given the ever-changing landscape of ideologies, be they imperial, religious, economic, or otherwise, the making of maps seems to have no end. Maps and their representation of the world, whether visual or encoded in rhetoric, can serve as especially important symbols for communities exiled from home. These symbols provide such communities with reference points of lost homelands and real or imagined reflections on the history and configurations of places of perceived origins.

This religious mapmaking has been incredibly important in the history and thought of Judaism, particularly the role of Jerusalem as a central place around which the related concepts of exile and return animated the hopes and imagination of diasporic Jewish life as well as Jewish existence in Israel. According to an influential article by Philip Alexander, it was not until the Hellenistic period, specifically in the book of Jubilees, in the second century BCE that Judaism practiced in earnest such mapmaking and thereby developed the notion of Jerusalem as a central place in cosmic geography generally and the city as the *omphalos* [belly button] of the world specifically.[2]

In this essay, I challenge this notion of the Hellenistic origins of this concept in Judaism, tracing instead the concept of city as center of the world and city as *omphalos*, to the sixth century BCE at least. I do so in order to examine the roots of this concept in ancient Israelite and rabbinic thought and, more importantly for the theme of this symposium, the roots of Jerusalem as a symbol around which to organize the concepts of exile and return. First, I analyze the role of central placement of Babylon in the religious imagination of the seventh and sixth centuries BCE, reflected both in texts and in the famous Babylonian Mappa Mundi (Map of the World).

Second, I examine a similar concept of political center, used for a very different purpose than the Babylonian Map of the World, in the book of Ezekiel, a book written contemporaneous with the Babylonian Mappa Mundi. While Ezekiel, particularly chapters 40–48, has been compared with the Babylonian Map of the World in previous scholarship, scholars have focused on the use of water as mythological boundary making and not, as in this study, on the role of political capitals as centers of the world (see more below).

Understanding the cultural background of this rhetoric in Ezekiel through an analysis of the Mappa Mundi provides a foundation for the manner in which Jerusalem as center would become a vital concept (though used in drastically different ways than in Ezekiel) in Second Temple Jewish and rabbinic thought in both diasporic Jewish communities and those residing in Israel. I examine the ways in which Ezekiel's rhetorical picture of Jerusalem as center was received, adapted, and interpreted to provide a vital symbol for Judaism, offering a sense of hope for return and giving new depths to the phrase "Next Year in Jerusalem." Finally, I conclude with brief thoughts regarding the ways in which this concept of Jerusalem as center of the world and *omphalos* in Judaism also animates the religious thought of other groups attaching themselves to Jewish traditions and places in time, such as Ethiopian Christianity and Jewry.

BABYLON AS CENTER: MESOPOTAMIAN HISTORY, IDEOLOGY, AND THE IMAGE OF STATE CAPITALS

The imperial symbolism of directionality appears already in Sumerian, the first known written language. The word for "north" in Sumerian as a direction was *subartu*, but the scope of this lexeme changed along the lines of the tension between realpolitik and imperial ambition.[3] As Assyriologist Piotr Michalowski states, even at this early stage "geographic terms are not neutral, objective, descriptive indexes of natural landscape, but are subjective and emotionally loaded elements of a semantic subsystem. . . . They were reinvented again and again, played with and reformulated as part of larger semantic schemes. As the mental structure of the world changed some terms encompassed larger or smaller domains or changed reference."[4]

With the founding of Akkade around 2350 BCE, the seat of the Akkadian Empire (often described as the first true empire in world history) established by Sargon the Great, imperial centers would also take on great symbolic significance. The feats of this king lived on in literary and political memory to the point that subsequent kings in the ancient Near East (even non-Mesopotamian rulers such as the Hittites) compared their feats to the magnitude of Sargon's imperial achievements.[5] The historical memory of the third millennium BCE Akkadian Empire appeared in the first-millennium BCE reign of the Sargonid kings in the Neo-Assyrian Empire. These Assyrian rulers enacted the creation of new capitals with particular enthusiasm. With the historical seat and the traditional capital of the empire at Assur, in the ninth century Ashurnasirpal II moved the capital to Kalḫu, also called Nimrud. Sargon II, taking his name in some manner to reflect historical memory and ambition in the wake of Sargon the Great, established a new capital located close to Nineveh called Dur-Šarrukin ("City of Sargon"). Finally, Harran became a sort of capital of the Neo-Assyrian Empire during the final gasp of this kingdom when the last Neo-Assyrian king, Assur-uballit II, abandoned Nineveh to make Harran his stronghold. Harran did not remain capital for long, as forces from Babylon and Media overtook the city in 609 BCE and again, finally, in 605 BCE.

In each case, the newly constructed Assyrian capitals were both pragmatic and symbolic. Changing boundaries of the empire necessitated new, strategic positioning, a reality that many expanding empires have had to face. In the third century CE, when Rome's extent was so great that the traditional seat of the empire was no longer beneficial or central for ruling such a large domain with enemies encroaching in imperial territory, Diocletian changed the imperial geography to reflect this need.[6] Later, Constantine began major construction in Constantinople; while Rome still benefited from imperial building, the new face of Roman interests and religion in Christianity became the motivation for investing in a new capital. The situation was no different in Assyrian times. While Ashurnasirpal gives no motivation for moving the capital to Kalḫu in his inscriptions, Joan and David Oates note that the traditional capital "Assur lay at the southern boundary of rain-fed agricultural land and a more central location would have been both strategically and economically desirable."[7] Kalḫu was just such a central location, which Ashurnasirpal inaugurated as the new capital with much feasting and ceremony. Political factors also contributed, as the elites in Assur had developed enough prestige and wealth to challenge the king and become more independent of the Crown, necessitating a new political center removed from an unreliable aristocracy.

The founding of Dur-Šarrukin as a capital in Sargon II's reign was also highly symbolic and necessary politically. Sargon II was likely a usurper to the throne, and he needed to establish both a sense of connection to the past and a statement of his own unique royal place in the empire. Yet the elites in Kalḫu, despite historically being a home to royal supporters from the days of Ashurnasirpal, had proven hostile to Assur-Nerari V in the eighth century BCE, resulting in the overthrow of Assur-Nerari's rule and the rise of Tiglath-Pileser III. As Karen Radner observes, Tiglath-Pileser III and his successor, Shalmaneser V, had no reason to fear this elite base in Kalḫu, as the aristocracy were the reason for installing Tiglath-Pileser on the throne. The usurper Sargon, however, encountered rebellions in both the peripheries and heartland of his empire upon his ascent to power and therefore had motivation to move the capital away from a city whose elites had already developed a proven track record of deposing kings and installing new ones.[8] The move to Harran, then, entailed another political necessity as a forced move by Assur-uballit II, given the advance of Babylonians and Medes into the Assyrian heartland.

The ideology behind Babylon as a capital was in many ways different from the ideology that formed the underpinning of Assyrian imperial centers. With Assyrian capitals, considerations of the king were foremost. As with the king, so with the capitals. For this reason, the city layouts contained the traditional temples in or near the center, but the royal palaces were near the gates. The king was the first symbol people encountered, and the city thrived or fell depending on royalty.[9] Even from its beginnings, Babylon had a strikingly different ideology as its foundation.[10] Hammurabi, the great Amorite king of the eighteenth century BCE, turned Babylon, previously a humble backwater, into the seat of a major empire. As a religious justification of this upstart political center, Marduk, the patron deity of the city, became the high god of the pantheon, dethroning both Enlil, the high god of the Sumerian pantheon, and Ninurta, the god who held chaos in check, providing world order, duties now ascribed to Marduk.

In order to reinforce Babylon as a capital, the Sumerian and Babylonian model of kingship was emphasized: Marduk was king of the cosmos ruling from Babylon and the earthly king "as representative of secular power, ruled in the shadow of Marduk."[11] The presence or absence of Marduk in the city was such a key idea that the removal of the statue of Marduk by the Elamites and its return perhaps became the basis of mythological reflection encoded in the *Enuma Elish*, though debates about the dating of this epic remain.[12] Even into the time of Cyrus, the idea of Marduk in Babylon—and the importance of the idea of divine dwelling therein—became the basis for the rhetoric of Achaemenid expansion into southern Mesopotamia in the sixth century BCE, as attested in the Cyrus Cylinder.

The focus on Marduk as king of the cosmos explains a number of features of Babylonian thought. For example, the phrase "king of kings" was used in Egyptian and Assyrian inscriptions for both kings and gods. In Neo-Babylonian, however, the phrase was applied exclusively to Marduk and never to Neo-Babylonian kings.[13] This focus on Marduk as king also explains the ideology behind Marduk's temple, Esagil, and ziggurat. Power resided so firmly with Marduk in Babylon that his ziggurat Etemenanki was seen as the "counterpart of the heavenly sanctuary Ešarra," the latter term referring to a vault in the sky that housed a divine sanctuary.[14] This cosmic centering was enshrined in the epic of creation, the *Enuma Elish*, where "the gods built the Esagil temple as terrestrial image of the Apsu," which was the underground abode where Ea, Marduk's father, lived.[15] As Paul-Alain Beaulieu points out, even seventh-century Assyrian kings such as Esarhaddon expressed conviction of this cosmic centrality of Babylon. Esarhaddon, who along with Ashurbanipal rebuilt much of the city after Sennacherib destroyed it in 689 BCE, "proclaims the Esagil temple as 'the palace of the gods, the mirror image of the Apsu, the counterpart of Ešarra, and the replica of the constellation of the Field."[16] As Beaulieu argues, this later phrase was the expression of a conviction that this constellation formed an approximate square, providing a celestial apologetic for claiming that the Esagil, also an approximate square, was indeed the center of the cosmos.[17]

Though the North and South Palaces in Babylon were located near the entrance to the city at the Ishtar gate, reflecting an Assyrian (and non–southern Mesopotamian) layout, Nebuchadnezzar interpreted the placement of these royal abodes in distinctly Babylonian terms. Their locations were about not royal ideology but rather self-effacement and not competing with the center of imperial and mythological imagination, namely the cult complexes of Marduk. In other words, Esagila, the temple of Marduk, was the focus on the meeting of Heaven and Earth in Babylon ideologically as the center of the cosmos. Indeed, "later speculation viewed the ziggurat Etemenanki as counterpart of the heavenly sanctuary Ešarra, confirming the role of Babylon as nodal center of the axis joining the underground world to the firmament."[18]

In remarkably visual fashion, the Mappa Mundi combines the rhetoric of empire and symbolic significance of directionality with the ideology of Babylon as cosmic center, though the map itself came from Borsippa.[19]

While other maps existed in the ancient Near East, none combine the world scope, ideology of directionality, and rhetoric of center as does the Babylonian Map of the World. The dates of the map range from the ninth century BCE as the earliest possible point of creation of the document to the sixth century BCE at the height of the Neo-Babylonian Empire. The best argument

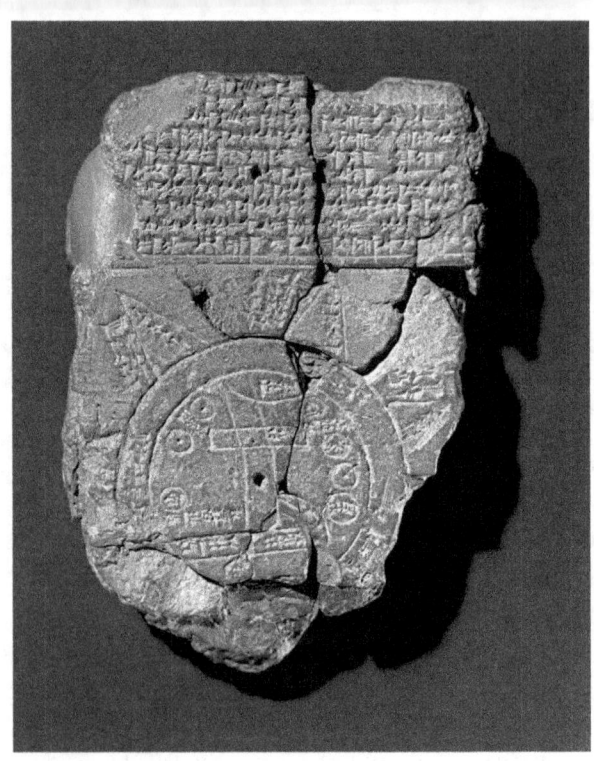

Mappa Mundi: Obverse only, with Finkel's join of the northeast nagû. Courtesy of British Museum.

for dating is in the seventh and sixth centuries, particularly given that prior to this period Babylon was a backwater memory of a once great capital and was particularly in no position to claim world-capital status during the reign of Sennacherib, who destroyed much of Babylon.[20] Only during the reigns of Esarhaddon and Ashurbanipal did the city begin to emerge again as an important cultural and religious center.[21] Yet in neither of these cases did Babylon function as a center in the ways in which the Babylonian Map of the World reflects a global reordering (or as Wayne Horowitz calls it, a "Mesopotamian cosmic geography") around the city.

What allowed such a radical reorientation of the world around this ascendant city? The text surrounding the map presents historical memory and new imperial ambitions. This text uses script on the obverse reminiscent of second-millennium Babylonian, a period in time—until the Hittites sacked Babylon in 1595 BCE—when this southern Mesopotamian empire loomed large in the political and cultural spheres of the ancient Near East. While the expansive empire of the Babylonians in the second millennium was confined mostly to Hammurabi's reign (much of the territory was lost during the reign of Šamsu-Iluna, Hammurabi's son), Babylon remained a powerful political base and symbol. Moreover, the prestige of the Babylonian sphere transferred into literature and the ideology of writing inasmuch as the Standard Babylonian dialect became the means of literary production, so much so that Neo-Assyrian kings adopted it in their royal inscriptions (with the recognizable Assyrianisms present as well). The writing on the reverse of the Mappa Mundi orthographically matches first-millennium conventions. Add other linguistic clues, such as the semantics of *nagû* as a far-off region (a semantic range that appears only in Neo-Babylonian texts, whereas Neo-Assyrian texts refer to administrative regions such as Judah as a *nagû*), and it becomes clear that the final version of the map is from the late seventh or sixth centuries BCE. The combination of second- and first-millennium orthography and language, then, functions as a way to recast memory of the second-millennium glory days but for a Neo-Babylonian audience.[22]

The ideology of Babylon as cosmic center, so different than Assyrian capitals, is what allowed Babylon as an idea to survive its destruction (whereas the destruction of Assyrian capitals meant the "abandonment of its cities and the end of [their] cuneiform documentation").[23] This ideology allowed Babylon to live on as an idea, becoming the planned capital of Alexander's empire and where Alexander died. Traces of the intellectual life of southern Mesopotamia, centered on Babylonian learning, thrived in the Hellenistic period, and the population of the region remained consistent until the Seleucids, when at last the attention toward the maintenance of the city architecturally, culturally, and financially shifted away from Babylon and toward the new capital, Seleucia-on-the-Tigris.[24] The symbol and ideology behind Babylon persisted, however, as evidenced in the application of the name "Babylon" and all it entailed as far as memory of politics, culture, and religious perception to Rome in Jewish literature after the destruction of the temple in 70 CE.[25]

This examination of Babylon as a world and cosmic center as represented in the ideology apparent in the Mappa Mundi has significance for understanding the role of Jerusalem in Ezekiel, a document roughly contemporaneous with the Babylonian Map of the World. In comparison with other ancient Near Eastern cultures, Babylon and Jerusalem shared similar ideologies of the symbolic value of the respective cities. The connection between ideology behind these cities and the concept of the city as cosmic *center* would allow both Babylon and Jerusalem to thrive as symbols even after their destructions and the displacement of local native rulers and dynasties. These elements examined above regarding the symbolic and central values of Babylon will be analyzed in the next section in relation to Jerusalem as a foundation for how these categories were then transformed in the rabbinic imagination.[26]

JERUSALEM AS CENTER: EZEKIEL AND PROPHETIC RHETORIC

The reception of Babylonian culture and ideas in Ezekiel has become a particularly active area in research as of late. The publication of the al-Yahudu tablets, which for the first time offer a window into the everyday lives of the Judean exiles in Babylon, includes mention of the place-name "River Chebar," known also from the book of Ezekiel as the place where the prophet received his visions in Babylon.[27] These tablets, along with the book of Ezekiel, give glimpses into how Judeans engaged in Babylonian society in a manner that few other sources, including other biblical texts, offer. Whereas the al-Yahudu tablets reveal the ways in which Judeans engaged in economic and legal affairs, aspects of the book of Ezekiel show deeper interactions with Babylonian culture. Beyond borrowings from Akkadian that display some knowledge of economic affairs as well as facility with Akkadian scribal education, parts of the book also contain references to literary and scribal traditions reserved normally for the highest levels of scribal education.[28]

Many of these traces of Babylonian knowledge become more apparent as the various translations, or versions, of the book have been explored or, in other cases, as difficult phrases become emended based on solid text-critical principles, after which the relationship to Mesopotamian intellectual culture becomes clearer. Regarding the second, Avi Winitzer has shown that the difficult phrasing in Ezekiel 28:13 תפיך ונקביך, when considering many of the other elements of the chapter in Ezekiel that function as intertexts with the Epic of Gilgamesh, may provide evidence of explicit citation of the Mesopotamian epic.[29] When understood in light of Akkadian text citation, the phrase in Hebrew would mean "your tablets; your Depths" or, slightly emended, "the tablets of your Depths."[30] The Neo-Assyrian title by which this epic was known was *ša naqba īmuru*, or "he who saw the depths." In this manner, Ezekiel 28:13 provides a specific sort of citation peculiar to traditions in cuneiform scholarship, displaying Ezekiel's participation in that sector of society.[31]

In similar fashion, Jonathan Stökl has discovered traces of the Maqlû incantation ritual in phrasing in Ezekiel 13.[32] Should Stökl's proposal be accepted, it is a significant step toward understanding the manner in which Ezekiel was versed in Mesopotamian literary traditions directly as a trained scribe in Babylon. Petra Gesche's study of cuneiform curriculum indicates that incantation texts such as the Maqlû series were taught only at the highest levels of scribal training.³³ Ezekiel's reference to this text series would then demonstrate, like the citation of the Epic of Gilgamesh, that Ezekiel was trained at a high level, if not the highest, within Babylonian scholarship.

Regarding the value of the versions of this text, as Winitzer has argued, the scene in Ezekiel 4 in which the prophet lies on his left- and right-hand side for a number of days to enact in ritual the years of judgment proclaimed on Israel and Judah respectively is best understood in the Greek translation, or Septuagint.³⁴ In this version of the text, the prophet does not lie on his left side for 390 days (or, with Winitzer, the left side is not indicated explicitly, the 390 days being the total days converted to years for both sides) but instead does so for 190 days for both nations (as also indicated in the Septuagint for Ezekiel 4:9). Here, the Septuagint reads the Hebrew אני נתתי לך את־שני עונם as a reference to the guilt of the two nations (with the understanding that Hebrew שני is, instead of "years," a form of the number two). So the Greek reads καὶ ἐγὼ δέδωκά σοι τὰς δύο ἀδικίας, "and I have appointed for you their two iniquities." If the number of days converted to years for Judah is 40, as stated in both the Hebrew and Greek of Ezekiel 4:6, then by subtraction the number of days converted into years for Israel is 150. The use of the two numbers, 150 and 40, has significance in biblical mythology and the numerological importance of total destruction of the world in the flood narratives in Genesis 6–9. Additionally, both numbers have symbolic significance and relevance within the world of cuneiform scholarship of ancient Mesopotamia, used here, if the Greek numbers represent the original reading in Ezekiel 4, to communicate the destruction of Israel and Judah.³⁵

The role of Jerusalem as a central place and the Babylonian background of this concept also lend to the prophetic rhetoric of destruction in Ezekiel 5. Given the examples above in which Ezekiel participates in Babylonian intellectual culture, the probability that other shared concepts reflect contact with Babylonian thought increases, even if the detection of contact with specific texts necessarily remains elusive. In Ezekiel 5:1–4, the prophet enacts a ritual analogy involving shaving his beard, performing different acts to the hair in correlation to different acts of devastation that Jerusalem will face. As an anchor to the likelihood that this passage has a connection to Mesopotamian thought, the word for "razor," גלב, is possibly a loan from Akkadian.³⁶ That the prophet, then, in Ezekiel 5:5 describes a geographical landscape in which Jerusalem is placed in center perhaps offers further evidence of a thematic, ideological connection to the idea of a central place as explored above concerning

Babylon, though Ezekiel uses the concept in this verse for a different effect. Ezekiel 5:5 states: כה אמר אדני יהוה זאת ירושלם בתוך הגוים שמתיה וסביבותיה ארצות, "Thus says the Lord GOD: this is Jerusalem, in the midst of nations I have placed her, and the countries are around her."

Here the prophet recalls a geographic mythology of the capital city as the center of the world, in a very similar manner as Babylon functions in rhetoric and visual fashion in the Babylonian Mappa Mundi. Both cities, Jerusalem and Babylon, served as real and symbolic centers, around which real and mythic historical narratives emerged. In the case of Babylon, these symbols and myths converged to justify the resurgence of an empire that had a glorious past, most notably in the second-millennium Amorite dynasty that preexisted but came into full effect under Hammurabi. By the eighth and especially seventh centuries BCE, Babylon had become a backwater. The reemergence of southern Mesopotamia as a powerhouse in the late seventh and sixth centuries witnessed ways to harness memories of the power of Babylon for the current political moment, such as the central placement of capital in the Mappa Mundi. In converse fashion, the placement of Jerusalem in the center of the world had a different effect. Here, the capital of Judah was positioned in the middle of Earth to display divine wrath, bringing about the downfall that Babylon's central placement reversed.

Yet the ideology behind Babylon as a capital was more than central placement. It also involved, as shown above, a cosmological alignment whereby the divine realm was positioned directly above the earthly templates. In a manner, then, Babylon functioned as a meeting place between Heaven and Earth, even if such a meeting place did not function exactly as some historians of religion have posited. Likewise, in Ezekiel Jerusalem not only sits in the midst of nations but also exists as a navel of Earth in similar manner as Babylonian mythology. For example, Ezekiel 38:12 states that לשלל שלל ולבז בז להשיב ידך על־חרבות נושבת ואל־עם מאסף מגוים עשה מקנה וקנין ישבי על־טבור הארץ, "To seize spoil and to carry off plunder, to turn your hand against the waste places which are being inhabited, and to the people gathered from the nations, who have acquired livestock and goods, who dwell at the navel of the earth." The phrasing טבור הארץ has occasioned much debate. It appears only once more in the Hebrew Bible, in Judges 9:37: ויסף עוד געל לדבר ויאמר הנה־עם יורדים מעם טבור הארץ וראש־אחד בא מדרך אלון מעוננים, "Gaal spoke again, saying 'Look, people are coming down from the center/navel of the land, and one company is coming from the direction of the Diviner's Oak.'"

In both passages, Shemaryahu Talmon found nonmythological meaning behind the expression טבור הארץ.[37] In each case, the terms refer to topographical, not cosmological, parts of the passages. In Judges, Gaal spies riders coming from high parts of the mountains to lower parts, referred to as טבור הארץ and אלון מעוננים, respectively.[38] Likewise, in explicating his method to seek first internal clues within a passage and then within biblical rhetoric, only later seeking external material for comparison, Talmon claims that no mythology lies behind Ezekiel 38:12. After providing intricate form-critical analysis, isolating Ezekiel 38:10–14 as a unit, Talmon argues that the phrase in Ezekiel 38:12 functions as a place of secure dwelling. This interpretation is supported by the importance of ישב as a leitmotif, highlighting the deliverance and security. For Talmon, the fact that such deliverance includes life with "those who have acquired livestock" [עשה מקנה in Ezek 38:12] means that the further description of where this dwelling occurs [על־טבור הארץ] must be able to accommodate such livestock. After examining other biblical passages where such activity occurs in relative safety (Ezek 28:25–26; Jer 49:31–32; 1 Chr 4:40), Talmon concludes that the phrase in Ezekiel 38:12, as in Judges, must refer to a topographical, not mythological, feature and certainly a feature not connected with the top of a mountain as mythic *omphaloi* often are.

Some of Talmon's methodological principles, especially to seek information elsewhere in the Bible first before resorting to comparative evidence from outside Israel, flatten the diversity and complexities inherent in biblical studies. The Bible does not speak with one voice, nor was it written from one perspective and one locale. For example, is it self-evident that Ezekiel 5:5 and 38:12, after rightly examining the units on their own terms, should be compared first with other biblical passages, when the book, at least a large core, was written in Babylon? What context counts, and is genre part of context and a determining (or at least informing) factor for deciding which texts count as a basis for comparison? Ezekiel is prophetic (in which case rare words are intentionally employed) and contains elements of apocalyptic, or at least protoapocalyptic (in which case mythic terms abound). Indeed, Ezekiel 38–39 and the battle with Gog and Magog are such prophetic and nascently apocalyptic literature.[39] To treat them as nonmythological and nonsymbolic, then, may be as undisciplined methodologically, if not more so, as resorting too soon to external evidence.[40] Talmon appeals to phrases of open and secure settlement in Judges and 1 Chronicles 4:40 for understanding Ezekiel, yet the Mappa Mundi is closer in time and place in terms of composition to Ezekiel.[41]

If Ezekiel 5:5 and 38:12 represent imaginings of Jerusalem for prophetic rhetoric of punishment, the moving boundaries of Ezekiel's vision of restoration in chapters 40–48 provide a view toward a different conception of Jerusalem as center. Much as Babylon could live on as an idea after its destruction, so too could Jerusalem survive prophetic condemnation and destruction by the Babylonians in the prophetic visions of restoration. Scholars have long noted the manner in which the tribal allotments in Ezekiel 40–48 differ greatly from those elsewhere in the Hebrew Bible. For starters, there are no Transjordanian tribes in Ezekiel's vision. Instead, all the tribes of Israel have territory on the same western side of the Jordan, showing the manner in which, as Rachael Havrelock has argued, the Jordan functioned as a watery boundary.[42] The effect of such a rearrangement is to place Judah and Jerusalem in it in a more central place in terms of the north-to-south arrangement. In the book of Joshua, Judah and Simeon are the farthest tribes in the south. In Ezekiel's vision, Gad, Zebulun, Isaachar, Simeon, and Benjamin occupy the southernmost territories. In the middle of the allotment are the holy district and Judah, with Reuben, Ephraim, Manasseh, Naphtali, Asher, and Dan lying to the north.[43]

Yet Walther Zimmerli and Talmon have argued against this conception, claiming, rightly, that Jerusalem is not precisely placed centrally in Ezekiel's new vision.[44] Given the additional allotment of a holy district to the twelve tribes, a total of thirteen spaces, in equal portion, comprise the land in Ezekiel 48. By definition, the seventh space occupies the center. Five tribes live in the southern portion, and Jerusalem, residing in the sixth, is therefore one allotment away from the central portion, which belongs to Judah. Yet this scheme may still reveal an impulse toward the centralization of Jerusalem not only by comparison with the book of Joshua (in which case Judah and Jerusalem are relatively positioned much more toward the south) but also by nature of prophetic rhetoric.

Prophetic denunciation often has a geographic aspect relative to the prophetic audience. For example, scholars have long recognized the manner in which Amos crafts his oracles against the nations geographically in a swirling effect, addressing nations at first farther away, only to circle in tighter and tighter on the central target of prophetic rage, namely Israel.[45] Israel therefore forms the center of these oracles geographically in Amos 1–2. In similar fashion, though somewhat reverse in movement, Ezekiel 25:1 begins Ezekiel's oracles against the nations, starting with the nations closest to the prophet's intended audience, and then moves farther away until arriving at Egypt in Ezekiel 29–32. Rhetorically, geography becomes relative to the prophetic audience, which is Judah in the book of Ezekiel.[46] It makes sense, given the target audience and given their interest in Ezekiel's vision of restoration, that Judah would occupy the central allotment. In light of a special portion for a holy district that contains the temple, Jerusalem by definition has to be in the holy district. Since Jerusalem was historically in Judah, these two allotments—Judah and the holy district—necessarily have to be conjoined in the new map. With Ezekiel's audience as center, the holy district will inevitably be one spot away, but it too partakes of this ideology.

Even the vision for the new temple reflects this centralizing impulse. Scholars have long observed the differences between Ezekiel's temple and the sacrifices that happen there and the precepts mentioned in Leviticus. The story of Hananiah ben Hezekiah is instructive. According to *b. Shabbat* 13b, Hananiah used three hundred barrels of oil to keep his lamp light while he attempted to reconcile the legal contradictions between Ezekiel and the Torah. Yet some of the unique features of Ezekiel's temple become intelligible when set in a Babylonian context. As Shalom Holtz and Tova Ganzel have argued, the manner in which space functions in Babylonian temples and Ezekiel's temple displays a shared concern for preserving sanctity and holiness. As Holtz and Ganzel claim, in this respect Ezekiel may not be borrowing from a specific text or tradition, much like Ezekiel very likely does not have the Mappa Mundi specifically in mind when constructing Jerusalem as center.

Nonetheless, the Babylonian context can provide a shared priority of perception, from which useful comparison arises. In both Ezekiel's complex and Babylonian temples, a shared perception exists for keeping the consecrated and unconsecrated distinct.[47] According to Ganzel and Holtz, this concern explains Ezekiel's focus on "walls, gates, and courtyards." In the middle of the temple space was the inner courtyard, where only the Zadokites, the holiest of the priests according to Ezekiel 44, could enter. Judah, Jerusalem, and the temple occupied central place in Ezekiel's configuration, and the inner sanctum occupied the central place of the latter. Ezekiel's configuration of space, Jerusalem, and the temple, then, prefigures, or perhaps draws the map for, the later interpretation found in the *Tanhuma Leviticus*, discussed more below.

In this section, I have argued that Ezekiel's concept of Jerusalem as center participates in Babylonian ideology, the context in which the prophet claims to exist. The shared concepts between Babylon as center and *omphalos* and Jerusalem as center and *omphalos* both give expression to reflection about the cosmic nature of cities as capitals but in different directions. For Babylon the city was ascendant, recalling former glory to be relived. The concept of

Jerusalem as center in Ezekiel functioned as a rhetorical device to evoke punishment and restoration. The image as reflected in this prophetic book survived and took on new forms, particularly in the image in rabbinic circles of Jerusalem as center, where the concept became a central point in the identity of exile and return.

THE MAKING OF MAPS AND LEGACIES OF IDENTITY: SECOND TEMPLE AND RABBINIC RECEPTIONS OF JERUSALEM AS CENTER

The concept of Jerusalem as center as expressed in Ezekiel had a vibrant afterlife in Second Temple Jewish and rabbinic thought. It was during this time, according to Alexander, that the concept of Jerusalem as *omphalos* and cosmic center began in Judaism, though I hope to have shown that Ezekiel, steeped in Babylonian thought, gave expression to the idea already in the sixth century BCE.[48] Here the difference of perception regarding intellectual lineage is also apparent, as Alexander argues that the T-O maps of medieval times were based on Hellenistic models as apparent in Jubilees, whereas Assyriologists such as Irving Finkel lay the intellectual foundations for such medieval maps further back in time in the Babylonian Mappa Mundi.[49]

After Ezekiel, the next attested belief in the concept of Jerusalem as center and *omphalos* appears in the books of 1 Enoch and Jubilees. In many places, 1 Enoch functioned as the source for parts of Jubilees, though the language of Jerusalem as center is not as explicit in 1 Enoch 26:1–2 as it would be later in Jubilees, and a direct connection is difficult to establish.[50] 1 Enoch 26:1–2 reads as follows: "And from here, I went to the midst of the earth, and I saw a blessed and well-watered place, which had trees which had branches that would remain and that blossom from a tree that had been cut. And from here I saw a holy mountain, and under the mountain water from the direction of the east, and it flowed toward the south." While Zion, Eden, and Sinai are not mentioned by name, each in some manner finds evocation in the description of the middle of Earth, an area latter contrasted with a cursed valley (1 Enoch 27:1).[51]

If Ezekiel provides an example of imagining Jerusalem in certain mythic and ideological ways in exile, then Jubilees, which reflects on the concept of Jerusalem as center in more explicit and more sustained terms than 1 Enoch, provides evidence of continued reflection on Jerusalem's cosmic place, though Jubilees does so in return. Most scholars accept that the author wrote Jubilees in or around Jerusalem, though the date of authorship is a much more debated

Place as Real and Imagined in Exile 15

issue.⁵² The concept of Zion as cosmic center takes a few forms in this book, and related issues such as the role of sanctification and sacrifice lend to the validity of Jerusalem as real and imagined from this vantage point of return. For example, Jubilees 4:26 states that "Because there are four places on the earth that belong to the Lord: the garden of Eden; the mountain of the east,⁵³ this mountain, the one you are on today, namely Sinai, and mount Zion [that] will be sanctified in the new creation for the sanctification of the earth. On account of this, the earth will be sanctified from all sin and from all uncleanness into the generation of eternity."

The context of this passage pertains to Enoch's removal from humanity, a story told laconically in Genesis 5:23–24 that spun off a myriad of apocalyptic Second Temple Jewish retellings of the life of Enoch. That Jubilees connects Enoch and Eden with the flood and that Enoch's fate is connected specifically with the deluge have fascinating resonance both with biblical rhetoric and with a theory that some scholars connect to an even more ancient flood story than those that exist in Genesis 6–9. The only two biblical characters who are said to have walked with God [using the *hitpael* of הלך, the preposition את, and the word—including the definite article—האלהים] are Enoch and Noah. That these two figures, then, would be the focus of speculation in Jubilees regarding the survival of the flood makes complete sense. In fact, because flood mythologies in the ancient Near East often entailed not simply the survival of the flood hero but also the hero's subsequent divinization, habitation with the divine, or at least immortality, some scholars see in the Enoch story a character who may originally have been connected to a flood narrative. Such a connection would make sense of Enoch's assumption into the divine realm as well as of the uncannily similar phrasing of both Noah and Enoch "walking with God."⁵⁴

More significant for the issue of place, pilgrimage, and the symbol of Zion as a destination of return is the language of sanctification. In this manner, even before the flood (and certainly before entrance in the land, as the narrative fiction of Jubilees has the angel speaking these words to Moses) Zion becomes the object of reflection for sanctification. As the concept of place becomes flexible, though, the originally four distinct places belonging to God in Jubilees become conflated as two locations are identified in Jewish mythological geography. This conflation appears in *Genesis Rabbah*, a fifth or sixth century CE rabbinic commentary on Genesis [בראשית]. According to Jubilees 4:25, Enoch burns incense in a sanctuary in Eden, in similar manner as Zion occupies the place of sanctification, offering, and incense sacrifice in the First Temple complex.

The connection in rabbinic interpretation and imagination becomes further solidified when the substance from which mankind was created and the substance from which altars were made are lexically related. For example, in the commentary on Genesis 2:7, which states that וייצר יהוה אלהים את־האדם עפר מן האדמה, the rabbis claim in *Genesis Rabbah* 14:8 ר' ברכיה ור' חלבו בשם ר' שמואל הזקן ממקום כפרתו נברא היך מה דאת אמר מזבח אדמה תעשה לי (שמות כ כד) אמר הקב"ה הריני בוראו ממקום כפרתו והלווי יעמוד: "From the ground Rabbi Berekiah and Rabbi Helbo, in the name of Rabbi Samuel the elder (say): From the place of his atonement he was created. As you have read, 'An earthen altar you shall make for me' (Exod 20:24). The Holy One, Blessed be He, said 'Behold, I will create him from the place of his atonement, and may it be that he endures!'"

Many fascinating issues come to the fore when considering this rabbinic connection between the place of mankind's creation and the place of atonement. Indeed, from the perspective of the critical study of the Hebrew Bible, Exodus 20:24 constituted one of the first cruxes of interpretation in Julius Wellhausen's *Prolegomena to the History of Israel* as a justification for his construction of the religious history of ancient Israel.[55] In particular, the phrase quoted in *Genesis Rabbah* 14:8 from Exodus is part of a larger description of where God permits the building of altars, a description that includes both earthen altars and altars of unhewn stone. Exodus 20:24, then, in classical critical scholarship of the Hebrew Bible, acknowledges the existence of multiple sites of worship, an allowance at odds with Leviticus 17 and, most importantly for Exodus 20:24, Deuteronomy 12. Deuteronomy 12 plays with the lexemes of the altar law in Exodus 20:22–24, displaying ancient modes of citation.[56] This lexical overlap, while in Deuteronomy 12 perhaps originally meant to correct, supplement, or dislodge the religious vision of Exodus 20:24, also functioned as the basis for reading the passages together. In this reading strategy, then, the place of atonement in Exodus 20:24, constructed from the ground, is identified with במקום אשר יבחר יהוה, in Deuteronomy 12:14, the place that God will choose, understood to be Jerusalem.

According to Jubilees 4:26, there are four places that belong to the divine. Likewise, according to Jubilees 8:12, the land belonging to God's chosen people reflected, in some manner, the divine possession as well. Jubilees 8:12 reads as follows: "And the lot of Shem emerged from the book (to be) in the midst of the earth, which he would possess for his inheritance and for his sons to eternal generations." The divine ownership of place, and particularly the places Eden, Sinai, and Zion/Jerusalem, meant that in some manner they reciprocated each other. This reciprocal relationship was in some sense temporal, as Eden was the dwelling place with humanity before the expulsion from the garden (and with Enoch through the flood), Sinai was then the dwelling place of God with Moses and Israel for the revelation of the law, and Jerusalem was then the place that God would dwell, with Israel formed as a state.

Such holy characteristics meant that each occupied the center of a chosen realm (such as Sinai at the center of the desert and Jerusalem the center of the world), but such forces drawing them together conceptually also required them to face one another, to be related and placed in circular fashion as if looking toward another central area. For example, Jubilees 8:19 states that "And he [Noah] knew that the Garden of Eden (is) the holy of holies, and the dwelling of the Lord, and (that) mount Sinai (is) in the midst of the desert, and (that) mount Zion (is) in the midst of the navel/middle/center of the earth. The three of them—each facing the other [lit. this one the opposite of this one]—were created as holy places."

The converging ideological maps of Ezekiel, created in the context of Babylonian ideology, and Jubilees come to the fore in the *Tanhuma Leviticus*. In this passage, the idea of Jerusalem as center of the world receives its most explicit expression: "As this navel/highest part in the center of a man, so Eretz Israel is the navel of the world, as it is written, 'those who dwell at the navel of the earth' (Ezek 38:12). Eretz Israel dwells at the center of the world, and Jerusalem at the center of Eretz Israel, and the temple at the center of Jerusalem, and the *heikhal* at the center of the temple, and the ark at the center of the *heikhal*, and the *even shətiyyah*, before the *heikhal*, from which the world was founded."[57] Alexander notes that here, as in other rabbinic texts, Jerusalem "has vertical as well as horizontal centrality: it is the focal point of different, superimposed planes."

Above Jerusalem is the heavenly temple, and below it is Gehenna. The *even shətiyyah* represents either the founding stone or the weaving stone (in the sense of weaving as an act of creation); in either case it was thought to hold back the waters of the underworld that could undo creation. As Alexander claims, these traditions of the centrality of Jerusalem in rabbinic sources are found in Babylonian texts, but many if not all of the traditions can also be traced back to Palestinian authorities. Alexander argues that the reasons for this tradition of Jerusalem as center and *omphalos* may have been the result of anti-Roman polemic or may have been the attempt of Palestinian sages to "highlight the primacy of Jerusalem" in the face of the rise of the Babylonian academies.[58]

In either case, the superimposed plane of Jerusalem was not an innovation or a *novum*, as Babylon in the sixth century BCE shared a similar ideology of place, argued above in the first section of this essay.⁵⁹ This rabbinic conception of space, then, could be argued to have ancient roots, much older than Alexander recognized. As for the reasons behind the interest in this ideology of Jerusalem in rabbinic sources, Alexander is correct not to opt for an either/or solution; indeed, both anti-Roman polemic and inner-Jewish debates could be involved. Yet it is notable that even though Babylonian legal tradition gained higher authority in the Talmud Bavli, the notion of Jerusalem as center and *omphalos*, as promoted by Palestinian authorities, remained a vital part of Jewish identity both in Israel and in exile. Perhaps one reason for this enduring legacy of Jerusalem in rabbinic sources is the rhetoric of the Palestinian sages. What gave this rhetoric persuasive power, as in the *Tanhuma Leviticus*, was its ability to be grounded in the biblical text itself, not as an entirely foreign imposition on a biblical passage but rather as a fuller expression of the ideology already apparent in Ezekiel for new historical periods.⁶⁰

CONCLUSION: JERUSALEM AS CENTER AND *OMPHALOS* AND THE ROLE OF PILGRIMAGE IN EXILE AND RETURN

In this essay, I have argued that Ezekiel developed a sense of place with respect to Jerusalem. His concept of Jerusalem as center had a Babylonian context, and from that context the prophet imagined a real place but one that was cosmically centered in order to present a vision of judgment as well as redemption. The malleable nature of Jerusalem as the center of the world took on new significance in the return to the land, as evidenced in the book of Jubilees and perhaps bolstered by Hasmonean political ambition, though the relationship between Jubilees and the ideology behind the Maccabean rule is a debated topic.⁶¹

The nature of Jerusalem imagined as a central place thus served communities in exile in imagining home as well as communities that experienced the return.⁶² Jerusalem as destination, forming a geographically cosmic pull toward the city as a center as if by centripetal force, would have importance for a variety of Jewish and Christian communities alike, perhaps most emphatically for Ethiopian Jews and Christians.⁶³ These Jews and Christians made regular pilgrimages, three times a year, to Jerusalem until the conflict in the Crusades cut off their pilgrimage route.⁶⁴ As a response, King Lalibella of the Zagwe dynasty built his own version of Jerusalem in Ethiopia, marking each of the most holy sites in Israel with a church constructed into the ground and connected by a waterway called "the Jordan River." This example in Ethiopia shows yet again the enduring value of making maps and the ways that place, especially Jerusalem, functions as real and imagined in both exile and return. As if further proof for the elasticity of place is needed, you can see these rock-cut churches for yourself by checking into a room at Hotel Jerusalem in Lalibela, Ethiopia, where rooms go for $45 a night.

ACKNOWLEDGMENTS

I would like to thank Liane Feldman for reading this essay and providing comments on style and substance. All remaining errors are mine alone.

NOTES

1. J. Z. Smith, "Map Is Not Territory," in *Map Is Not Territory: Studies in the History of Religion* (Chicago: University of Chicago Press, 1993), 289–309. Note especially the terms "locative map" and "imperial figure" in Smith's discussion as relates to the following discussion of mapmaking and its central place in Jewish thought.

2. Philip S. Alexander, "Jerusalem as the 'Omphalos' of the World: On the History of a Geographical Concept," *Judaism* 46 (1997): 147, 152–53. See also the other articles in this edition of the journal, which explore similar concepts of centrality and city as *omphalos* related to Mecca. On the issue of the center of the world generally in antiquity, see more recently the excellent survey and analyses in Jennifer Finn, "The Center of the Earth in Ancient Thought," *Journal of Ancient Near Eastern History* 4 (2018): 177–209.

3. In this sense, the lexeme came to refer both to Subarians and became the general term of "slave," a case in which the semantic domain of a word in the earliest attested language in writing already contains elements of contact, directionality, ideology, and conquest. See William W. Hallo, "Slaves and Strangers," in *He Has Opened Nisaba's House of Learning: Studies in Honor of Åke Waldemar Sjöberg on the Occasion of his 89th Birthday on August 1st 2013* (Cuneiform Monographs 46; ed. Leonhard Sassmannshausen; Boston: Brill, 2014), 57–58.

4. Piotr Michalowski, "Sumer Dreams of Subartu: Politics and Geographical Imagination," in *Languages and Cultures in Contact: At the Crossroads of Civilizations in the Syro-Mesopotamian Realm: Proceedings of the 42nd RAI* (Orientalia Lovaniensia analecta 96), ed. K. van Lerberghe and G. Voet (Leuven: Peeters, 1999), 305. See also Piotr Michalowski, "Mental Maps and Ideology: Observations on Subartu," in *The Origins of Cities in Dry-Farming Syria and Mesopotamia in the Third Millennium B.C.*, ed. H. Weiss (Guilford, CT: Four Quarters), 129–56.

5. See, for example, Hattusili's boasts about crossing the Euphrates and making great conquests, just like Sargon, except that Hattusili inflicted more damage. Trevor Bryce, *Kingdom of the Hittites* (New York: Oxford University Press, 2005), 78, 83.

6. On the religious reflex of this imperial restructuring in Judaism, see Peter Schäefer, *The Jewish Jesus: How Judaism and Christianity Shaped Each Other* (Princeton, NJ: Princeton University Press, 2012), 11, 16, 33–34, and 206–7.

7. Joan and David Oates, *Nimrud: An Assyrian Imperial City Revealed* (London: British Schools of Archaeology in Iraq, 2001), 15–16.

8. Karen Radner, "The Assur-Nineveh-Arbela Triangle: Central Assyria in the Neo-Assyrian Period," in *Between the Cultures: The Central Tigris Region from the 3rd to the 1st Millennium* BC, Heidelberger Studien zum Alten Orient 14, ed. Peter A. Miglus and Simone Mühl (Heidelberg: Heidelberger Orientverlag, 2011), 325–27.

9. For the ideology behind the architecture of Late Assyrian palaces, see David Kertai, *The Architecture of Late Assyrian Royal Palaces* (New York: Oxford University Press, 2015), 102–3.

10. Even in view of these differences, similar underpinnings and ideologies connect Assyrian thought and the seventh- or sixth-century BCE Babylonian Mappa Mundi. The Mappa Mundi is discussed more below. For more on the Assyrian ideology connected to this map, see Beate Pongratz-Leisten, *Religion and Ideology in Assyria,* Studies in Ancient Near Eastern Records 6 (Boston: DeGruyter, 2015), 191–97.

11. Paul-Alain Beaulieu, "Nebuchadnezzar's Babylon as World Capital," *Journal for the Canadian Society of Mesopotamian Studies* 3 (2008): 10.

12. The date of the epic of creation has been a debated topic in Assyriology for some time, and the literature is vast. Some scholars date the Enūma Eliš as early as Hammurabi of Babylon's reign, though most opt for a later date. For the dating of the epic as stemming from the return of the statue of Marduk, see W. G. Lambert, "The Reign of Nebuchadnezzar I: A Turning Point in the History of Ancient Mesopotamian Religion," in *The Seed of Wisdom: Essays in Honor of T. J. Meek,* ed. W. S. McCullough (Toronto: University of Toronto Press, 1964), 6. For the role of divine presence and absence in religious and political thought in the ancient Near East and the Bible, see John F. Kutsko, *Between Heaven and Earth: Divine Presence and Absence in the Book of Ezekiel,* Biblical and Judaic Studies 7 (Winona Lake, IN: Eisenbrauns, 2000).

13. See Samuel L. Boyd, "A Brief History of the Title 'King of Kings.'" in *"Like 'Ilu Are You Wise": Studies in Northwest Semitic Languages and Literatures in Honor of Dennis G. Pardee,* ed. H. H. Hardy II, Joseph Lam, and Eric D. Reymond (Chicago: Oriental Institute Press, forthcoming).

14. Beaulieu, "Nebuchadnezzar's Babylon as World Capital," 10.

15. Ibid.

16. Ibid., citing Andrew George, "E-sangil and E-temen-anki, the Archetypal Cult-Centre," in *Babylon: Focus mesopotamischer Geschichte, Wiege früher Gelehrsamkeit, Mythos in der Moderne,* ed. J. Renger (Berlin: Deutschen-Orient Gesellschaft, 1999), 67.

17. J. Z. Smith is correct to question the *Weltberg* hypothesis of the Pan-Babylonian school and Eliade's construction of the "center" as a religious concept, a hypothesis that

connected the notion of cosmic mountain and temple as *axis mundi*. See in particular Smith's analysis in the first chapter of *To Take Place: Toward Theory in Ritual*, Chicago Studies in the History of Judaism (Chicago: University of Chicago Press, 1987). In Eliade's system, a critique of the *Weltberg* means a corresponding critique of the related notion of temple as center, and as Smith argues, such a pattern cannot be applied universally to the comparative study of religions. Yet despite this critique, and viewed outside of the Pan-Babylonian and *Weltberg* hypothesis, it is clear that the temple in Babylon had a function as a cosmic center, even as Babylon itself topographically was (and still is) very much at sea level and on the alluvial plains between the Tigris and the Euphrates. Indeed, the seeds of this ideology appear even in Neo-Assyrian times. As Smith claims, "the language of 'center' is preeminently political and only secondarily cosmological. It is a vocabulary that stems, primarily, from archaic ideologies of kingship and the royal function. In any particular tradition, it may or may not be tied to cosmological and cosmogonic myths" (Smith, *To Take Place*, 17). In the case of Assyria and Babylon, both politics and cosmology play a part, and in each case it is difficult if not impossible to separate the two factors. For the relatedness of these concepts in Mesopotamia, see Mario Liverani, *Assyria: The Imperial Mission*, Mesopotamian Civilizations 20 (Winona Lake, IN: Eisenbrauns, 2017). See more below on the Babylonian Mappa Mundi.

18. Beaulieu, "Nebuchadnezzar's Babylon as World Capital," 10. In this sense, Shemaryahu Talmon's hesitance in finding the notion of a "navel" in ancient Near Eastern thought is appropriate insofar as it critiques Eliade's flawed categories for studying the history of religions, but his caution seems centered on the observation that the texts in which the "link between the heavens and the earth" do not contain the word *abbunatu*. Shemaryahu Talmon, "The 'Navel of the Earth' and the Comparative Method," in *Literary Studies in the Hebrew Bible: Form and Content, Collected Studies* (Jerusalem: Magness, 1993), 54. Here is it worth observing that the lexeme may not appear, but the concept can still be present.

19. That a map with Babylonian ideology would be discovered in Borsippa makes sense. Borsippa was considered a lesser sibling city to Babylon. Nabu, Marduk's son, was the patron deity of Borsippa, and in a variety of ways Borsippa supported Babylonian imperial ambitions.

20. John Brinkman, *Prelude to Empire: Babylonian Society and Politics, 747–626 B.C.*, Occasional Publications of the Babylonian Fund 7 (Philadelphia: University Museum Press, 1984).

21. The fact that Neo-Assyrian kings were responsible for rebuilding much of Babylon accounts for two innovations of Babylonian city layout as compared to other cities in the south in the Sumerian and Babylon spheres: the rectilinear layout of the city and royal palaces at the gate and not at the center of the city. These features are consistent with Assyrian city planning and royal ideology, but other than Borsippa (the sibling city of Babylon), they are idiosyncratic in the Sumerian and Babylonian contexts. In Ur, for example, the temple and ziggurat of the moon god Nanna-Su'en occupied the center of the city, and the palace of the kings of the third dynasty of Ur "stands very much in the shadow of the

temple complex" (Beaulieu, "Nebuchadnezzar's Babylon as World Capital," 8). The placement of the North Palace in Babylon (where the famed and perhaps mythological Hanging Gardens of Babylon once stood according to Greek sources) in the city-gate complex reflected Assyrian conventions but received a uniquely Babylonian interpretation of the king, in self-effacing style, preventing his royal complex from competing in any way with that of Marduk's in the city center. See the quotations of the court documents of Nebuchadnezzar in Beaulieu, "Nebuchadnezzar's Babylon as World Capital," 7–8.

22. Irving Finkel claims that the ideographic character of orthography in the first twelve lines fits well with the preference of the first millennium BCE generally and the sixth century BCE specifically. That the spelling conventions of the rest of the document differ from the first twelve lines and that these spellings are syllabic ("a style abhorred in first millennium manuscripts"), among other things, indicates to Finkel that the descriptions of the world after the first twelve lines derive from the second millennium BCE generally and most likely from the Old Babylonian period. The first twelve lines (Horowitz counts eleven), in which many mythic elements appear, are also distinct from the following description by a dividing line that the scribe inserted. In any event, the scribe clearly indicates that his version was itself copied from an older text [*ki-ma la-bi-ri-i-šu ša-ṭi-ir-ma ba-r(i)*, "copied according to its old exemplar and collated"]. See Finkel, *The Ark before Noah* (London: Hodder & Stoughton, 2014), 267–69. For a text edition and translation, see Wayne Horowitz, *Mesopotamian Cosmic Geography*, Mesopotamian Civilizations 8 (Winona Lake, IN: Eisenbrauns, 1998), 20–42.

23. Beaulieu, "Nebuchadnezzar's Babylon as World Capital," 11.

24. Ibid., 10–11. See also Amelie Kuhrt and Susan Sherwin-White, "Aspects of Seleucid Royal Ideology: The Cylinder of Antiochus I from Borsippa," *Journal of Hellenic Studies* 112 (1991): 71–86; Goldstein, "Late Babylonian Letters on Collecting Tablets and the Hellenistic Background—A Suggestion," *Journal of Near Eastern Studies* 69 (2010): 199–207.

25. See, e.g., 1 Peter 5:13 and the application of "Babylon" to Rome (also showing that Peter could not have written 1 Peter, or at least this portion of the epistles, since Peter probably died around 65 CE during the reign of Nero when Rome destroyed Jerusalem, thereby meriting the connection to Babylon in 70 CE).

26. As discussed below, whether or not Ezekiel displays elements of myth around the issue of Jerusalem as a central place is a debated topic. It is clear, whatever the case with Ezekiel, that the rabbinic inheritance of biblical myth involved at times further myth making. See Michael Fishbane, *Biblical Myth and Rabbinic Mythmaking* (New York: Oxford University Press, 2003).

27. See Laurie E. Pearce and Cornelia Wunsch, *Documents of Judean Exiles and West Semites in Babylon in the Collection of David Sofer*, Cornell University Studies in Assyriology and Sumerology 28 (Bethesda, MD: CDL Press, 2014). See also many of the publications of Laurie Pearce examining scribalism, West Semites, and texts in the Neo-Babylonian and Achaemenid periods. While the Murašu archive provided evidence of Jewish life, such

evidence is indirect, as these documents are about the lives of Jewish merchants but do not contain firsthand accounts.

28. For possible though by no means certain pathways between Babylonian thought and Judean scribes focusing on avenues of social contact between Judeans and Babylonians, see Caroline Waerzeggers, "Locating Contact in the Babylonian Exile: Some Reflections on Tracing Judean-Babylonian Encounters in Cuneiform Texts," in *Encounters by the Rivers of Babylon: Scholarly Conversations between Jews, Iranians and Babylonians in Antiquity*, Texts und Studien zum antiken Judentum 160, ed. Uri Gabbay and Shai Secunda (Tübingen: Mohr Siebeck, 2014), 131–46.

29. Abraham Winitzer, "Assyriology and Jewish Studies in Tel Aviv: Ezekiel among the Babylonian *Literati*," in *Encounters by the Rivers of Babylon: Scholarly Conversations between Jews, Iranians and Babylonians in Antiquity*, 199–200.

30. Ibid., 199.

31. See Winitzer's discussion of the manner in which the Epic of Gilgamesh cites an older text and myth called the Cuthean Legend of Narām-Sîn through the use of the phrase *tupšenna petē-ma* [open the tablet], which would match Ezekiel's putative citation of Gilgamesh perfectly. Ibid., 200–204.

32. See Jonathan Stökl, "The מתנבאות in Ezekiel 13 Reconsidered," *Journal of Biblical Literature* 132 (2013): 61–76; Jonathan Stökl, "'A Youth without Blemish, Handsome, Proficient in all Wisdom, Knowledgeable and Intelligent': Ezekiel's Access to Babylonian Culture," in *Exile and Return: The Babylonian Context*, Beihefte zur Zeitschrift für die alttestamentliche Wissenschaft 478 (Boston: DeGruyter, 2015), 249.

33. Petra D. Gesche, *Schulunterricht in Babylonien im ersten Jahrtausend v. Chr.*, Alter Orient und Altes Testament 275 (Münster: Ugarit-Verlag, 2000). See Stökl's discussion of her work in connection to Ezekiel's access to Mesopotamian scribal education, "'A Youth without Blemish, Handsome, Proficient in all Wisdom, Knowledgeable and Intelligent,'" 230–32.

34. Winitzer, "Assyriology and Jewish Studies in Tel Aviv," 170–71.

35. For much more and convincing discussion on the Mesopotamian math involved, see Winitzer, "Assyriology and Jewish Studies in Tel Aviv," 170–74.

36. David Vanderhooft, "Ezekiel in and on Babylon," *Transeuphratène* 46 (2014): 112.

37. Shemaryahu Talmon, "The 'Navel of the Earth' and the Comparative Method," in *Literary Studies in the Hebrew Bible: Form and Content, Collected Studies* (Jerusalem: Magnes, 1993), 58–73.

38. As Bodi points out, if the Diviner's Oak reference is to a specific, perhaps cultic and mythic, point of origin for the attack, by parallel, against Talmon, the reference to the navel of Earth could have in view a specific, cultically significant, and possibly mythically oriented place-name. The areas of attack here are around Shechem and Mount Gerizim, and the latter would, in Samaritan tradition, become known as the cosmic "navel of the

world." See Daniel Bodi, *The Book of Ezekiel and the Poem of Erra,* Orbis biblicus et Orientalis 104 (Freiburg: Vandenhoeck & Ruprecht, 1991), 219–20.

39. See Frederick Murphy, who identifies protoapocalyptic elements in Ezekiel, specifically Ezekiel 38–39, in *Apocalypticism in the Bible and Its World* (Grand Rapids, MI: Baker Academic, 2012), 48–49). See also his discussion of Gog and Magog in the War Rule at Qumran (*Apocalypticism in the Bible and Its World,* 217–18).

40. Bodi, *The Book of Ezekiel and the Poem of Erra,* 223–24. Bodi also analyzes the poem of Erra, an eighth- or seventh-century BCE document that precedes the composition of Ezekiel by a generation or so. See, however, the mixed reviews of Bodi's work in J. N. Postgate, "Review: The Book of Ezekiel and the Poem of Erra," *Vetus Testamentum* 43 (1993): 137; Winitzer, "Assyriology and Jewish Studies in Tel Aviv," 181n83.

41. Talmon, in this article, rightly argues against the *Weltberg* hypothesis in the history of religions, and he is right that *abbunatu* in Akkadian does not have mythic power like *omphalos* in Greek. The concept, however, existed in Babylonian thought, as argued above. Perhaps the differing Babylonian topography (at sea level, part of the alluvial plains) from Jerusalem (settled in the Judean hill country) could easily have given different expressions to the same concept. Hence, טבור in Hebrew as navel is the operative metaphor, where Sumerian DUR gives a similar expression, but the word for "belly button" in Akkadian that would connote a rising, hilly place does not have such mythic overtones and usages.

42. See Rachel Havrelock, "The Two Maps of Israel's Land," *Journal of Biblical Literature* (2007): 649–67; Rachel Havrelock, *River Jordan: The Mythology of a Dividing Line* (Chicago: University of Chicago Press, 2011).

43. For a map of this layout, see Stephen L. Cook, *Ezekiel 38–48,* Anchor Bible 22B (New Haven, CT: Yale University Press, 2018), 266.

44. Talmon, "The 'Navel of the Earth' and the Comparative Method," 59. See also Talmon's citation of Zimmerli in this discussion.

45. See John H. Hayes, "Amos's Oracles against the Nations (1:2–2:16)," *Review and Expositor* 92 (1995): 163.

46. Ezekiel 4:6, 8:1, 8:17, 9:9, 21:20, 25:3, 25:8, 25:12, 27:17, 37:16, 37:19.

47. See Ezekiel 42:20. See also Shalom Holtz and Tova Ganzel, "Ezekiel's Temple in Babylonian Context," *Vetus Testamentum* 64 (2014): 225. For their citation of Waerzeggers, who claims that the Ezida temple in Borsippa had a courtyard that "established an invisible line of division in the organization of space . . . as this was the area where the distinction between the initiated and the uninitiated crystallized. Only those who were deemed qualified were allowed to enter the courtyard to participate in its busy ritual program," see Shalom Holtz and Tova Ganzel, *The Ezida Temple of Borsippa: Priesthood, Cult, Archives,* Achaemenid History 15 (Leiden: Nederlands Instituut voor het Nabije Oosten, 2010), 11.

48. Seeligmann previously argued for the Hellenistic period as the origin of this concept in Jewish thought. I. L. "Jerusalem in Jewish-Hellenistic Thought," in *Judea and Jerusalem*

(Jerusalem: Israel Exploration Society), 192–208. In addition to some of the texts cited in the body of this paper, Talmon cites the following: 1 Enoch 90:26, where, like Gehinnom in Rabbinic literature and, for different effect, the Apsu in Mesopotamian literature, Gehinnom is an abyss in the midst of Earth; Philo mentions the belief that Jerusalem was the center of the world (in his *Embassy to Gaius* 37.294); Hecataeus of Abdera mentions the centrality of the temple within the land of Judea (as cited in Josephus, *Against Apion* 1.197); in *Jewish Wars*, Josephus claims that Jerusalem is the *omphalos* of the country, though as Talmon indicates it is difficult to discern whether or not country [αρῶχ] refers to Judea or the world; in *b. Meg.* 6a, Tiberias and טבור are paired as puns; in *b. Sanh.* 37a the rabbis use Song 7:3 [שררך אגן הסהר, "your navel is a round bowl"] to refer to the Sanhedrin who sit at the center of the world. For these citations, see Talmon, "The 'Navel of the Earth' and the Comparative Method," 55–57.

49. Finkel, *The Ark before Noah*, 295–96.

50. For an excellent study on the manner in which Jubilees borrowed from Enoch, see Michael Segal, *The Book of Jubilees: Rewritten Bible, Redaction, Ideology and Theology*, Supplements for the Study of Judaism 117 (Boston: Brill, 2007), 109–37. For the relationship between 1 Enoch and Jubilees in the flood narratives, see also Samuel Boyd, "The Flood and the Problem of Being an Omnivore," *Journal for the Study of the Old Testament* (forthcoming). See also Hans Debel, "The Flood from Ancient Mesopotamia to Qumran: Transformations in a Literary Chain of Tradition," in *Insights into Editing in the Hebrew Bible and the Ancient Near East: What Does Documented Evidence Tell Us about the Transmission of Authoritative Texts?*, Contributions to Biblical Exegesis and Theology 84, ed. Reinhard Müller and Juha Pakkala (Bristol, CT: Peeters, 2017), 139–43.

51. See Alexander, "Jerusalem as 'Omphalos' of the World," 152.

52. James L. Kugel, *A Walk through Jubilees: Studies in the Book of Jubilees and the World of Its Creation*, Supplements to the Journal for the Study of Judaism 156 (Boston: Brill, 2012), 4.

53. James VanderKam has a very informative commentary on this section. He observes that "The Syriac has «mountain of the Garden of Eden [= Paradise] which may well be original." For more of his commentary on this passage, see VanderKam, *The Book of Jubilees*, Corpus Scriptorum Christianorum Orientalium 511 (Lovanii: E. Peeters, 1989), 29.

54. See John Day, "The Flood and the Ten Antediluvian Figures in Berossus and in the Priestly Source in Genesis," in *On Stone and Scroll: Essays in Honour of Graham Ivor Davies*, Beihefte zur Zeitschrift für die alttestamentliche Wissenschaft 420 (Boston: DeGruyter, 2011), 218.

55. Julius Wellhausen, *Prolegomena to the History of Israel*, trans. J. Sutherland Black and Allan Menzies (Atlanta: Scholars Press, 1994), 39–75.

56. See Bernard Levinson's use of Seidel's Law and his use of it with respect to Deuteronomy 12 in *Deuteronomy and the Hermeneutics of Legal Innovation* (New York: Oxford University Press, 1997), 18, esp. note 51, 35, and elsewhere.

57. Ecclesiastes 2:5. See Alexei M. Sivertsev, *Judaism and Imperial Ideology in Late Antiquity* (New York: Cambridge University Press, 2011), 67–68.

58. Alexander, "Jerusalem as the 'Omphalos'" of the World," 156–57.

59. The lines of transmission between ancient Near Eastern and specifically ancient Babylonian thought on the one hand and rabbinic thought on the other have been fertile areas of research. The separation in time between the two bodies of literature amounts to a few hundred years. As Yohanan Muffs claims, rabbinic and biblical covenant grants differ so much that the latter could not have been the source for the former. The similarity between rabbinic and Akkadian sources then suggests that it was borrowed (a) "from an Aramaic reworking of Akkadian material, (b) from an independent Greek source, or (c) from a Greek source that derived the institution from an Akkadian source found in some Aramaic form." Yohanan Muffs, *Love & Joy: Law, Language, and Religion in Ancient Israel* (Cambridge, MA: Harvard University Press, 1992), 162. As Muffs has also shown, Akkadian loanwords entered into the Aramaic lexicon and influenced much later Aramaic texts, such as Akkadian *eṭir* [(payment) received], which appears in Aramaic papyri from Elephantine in the fifth century and then also in the Talmudic איטרא (or עיטרא). This Talmudic word was a mystery before Muffs noticed the connections, and the fact that the lexeme appeared in passages dealing with exchanges bolstered his case. See also Michael Sokoloff, "New Akkadian Loanwords in Jewish Babylonian Aramaic," in *An Experienced Scribe Who Neglects Nothing: Ancient Near Eastern Studies in Honor of Jacob Klein*, ed. Yitschak Sefati et al. (Bethesda, MD: CDL Press, 2005), 575–86. For the connection between ancient Babylonian cuneiform law and rabbinic law (without corresponding laws from the Bible), see Samuel Greengus, *Laws in the Bible and in Early Rabbinic Collections: The Legal Legacy of the Ancient Near East* (Eugene, OR: Cascade Books, 2011). See also Irving Finkel, "Remarks on Cuneiform Scholarship and the Babylonian Talmud," in *Encounters by the Rivers of Babylon: Scholarly Conversations Between Jews, Iranians and Babylonians in Antiquity,* 307–16.

60. For more rabbinic references to the idea of Jerusalem as the center of the world, see also the *Midrash Tehillim* 91:7; *Midrash Aggadah* to Leviticus 19:23; *Lekach Tov* to Song of Songs 7:3; *Bereshit Rabbati* 28:22; *Sekhel Tov* to Genesis 30:13. For these references, see Miryam T. Brand, "1 Enoch," in *Outside the Bible: Ancient Jewish Writings Related to Scripture,* ed. Louis H. Feldman, James L. Kugel, and Lawrence H. Schiffman (Philadelphia: Jewish Publication Society, 2013), 1449n84.

61. For a Hasmonean context of Jubilees, see Alexander, "Jerusalem as the 'Omphalos' of the World," 149–51. For a dating of Jubilees prior to the Hasmonean revolt, prior to 175 BCE, see Kugel, *A Walk through Jubilees,* 348–49.

62. Note, for example, the description of Jerusalem in the *Letter of Aristeas,* line 83, in which Aristeas, joined by Demetrius the librarian of Alexandria, journeyed from Egypt to Jerusalem to meet Eleazar, the high priest. In describing the journey, a pilgrimage-type of narrative ensues in the letter, including a general description of the land. Aristeas recounts that νὴληψύ ϛυορὸ 'πὲ νωίαδυο'Ι ϛηλὸ ϛῆτ νηνέμιεκ νησέμ νιλόπ νὴτ νεμῦορωεθέ

νισατάνά νὴτ ςοτνοχε̃ [We beheld the city, lying in the midst of the whole of Judea upon a mountain having high extension (or, having great height)].

63. Ethiopian Christians have been called the most "Jewish" version of Christianity. "It must be appreciated that those forms of Judaism and Christianity which were found in south-west Arabia at that time were not only imbued with a markedly oriental ceremonial, but their general Semitic character, the circumstances of their development as well as their entire religious, historical, and emotional atmosphere, rendered them much closer and more akin to each other than is the case with their westernized counterparts." Edward Ullendorff, *Ethiopia and the Bible,* Schweich Lectures (London: Oxford University Press, 1968), 22). See Ullendorff, *Ethiopia and the Bible,* generally for the ways in which Ethiopic Christianity contains similarities with Jewish rituals and beliefs. For his own experiences and reminiscences in Jerusalem and Eritrea and for how these experiences unpack the ways in which Ethiopic Christians and Jews understand their relation to Jerusalem, see also Edwaard Ullendorff, *The Two Zions: Reminiscences of Jerusalem and Ethiopia* (New York: Oxford University Press).

64. For more on imagined geography in Late Antiquity, see Scott Fitzgerald Johnson, *Literary Territories: Cartographical Thinking in Late Antiquity* (New York: Oxford University Press, 2016). See especially this work for a brief but illuminating discussion regarding the manner in which the sixth-century CE Madaba Map provided a visual correspondence to Eusebius's topographical work called the *Onamasticon* (*Literary Territories*, 33).

"How Deserted Lies the City": Politics and the Trauma of Homelessness in the Hebrew Bible

Dereck Daschke

For a full millennium in Europe, with frightening regularity, Jews of the diaspora were subject to all manner of political restrictions on their ability to live, work, and worship in their adopted countries. This domestic insecurity would be punctuated with frightening regularity, with entire Jewish populations being expelled from this place or that, leaving behind all but what they could carry and sometimes not even that. They would have to start again in a new place, with no guarantee that the same fate would not befall their children or their children's children. The rise of political tolerance of non-Christian religions in the Modern Age was supposed to have finally put an end to this horrific pattern, but eighty some years ago in Germany, and eventually through most of Europe, Jews watched helplessly as a new political regime deprived them of their rights as citizens, then their homes, and ultimately their lives.

The Holocaust ostensibly represents an incontrovertible beacon that should forever protect Jews and every other vulnerable population from threats of systemic oppression, loss of rights, and even genocide. Yet on a global scale human communities today seem less safe from the trauma of dislocation stemming from a nation's politics than at any time since World War II. Not only are antisemitic attacks on the rise in Europe, the United States, and the Middle East, but around the world the overall displacement of persons has reached epidemic proportions, with 65.6 million people, or 1 in every 110 people in the world, "forced from their homes by violence, war and persecution"—a record high.[1] Whether people are forced to leave their home, leave as an act of desperation, or feel as if their home has left them, a state of homelessness can be the result of larger political forces out of their control. Homelessness of any sort is a truly traumatic experience, but because it is a phenomenon that arises at the nexus of power, community, and identity, it is an enlightening lens through which to view certain aspects of the Jewish experience, in particular those of the Hebrew Bible that echo the impact of the Babylonian exile.

TRAUMA AND HOMELESSNESS

When we speak of trauma, we can be speaking of a wound to the body, lingering psychological distress, a disruptive upheaval of social norms and functioning, or some combination of these together. How is it that one concept can apply equally well in three distinctly different contexts—or, better, be the concept that allows the damage in one realm to be related to and understood in terms of the others? How might we conceive of trauma so that the qualities that tie body, mind, and community together are brought to the fore? Sociologist Kai Erikson's trenchant examination of the interrelationship among trauma, disaster, and community in *A New Species of Trouble: The Human Experience of Modern Disasters* provides this description: "Trauma is generally taken to mean a blow to the tissues of the body—or, more frequently now, to the structures of the mind—that results in injury or some other disturbance. Something alien breaks in on you, smashing through whatever barriers your mind has set up as a line of defense. It invades you, possesses you, takes you over, becomes a dominating feature of your interior landscape, and in the process threatens to drain you and leave you empty."[2] The most immediately striking thing about this description is how spatial its metaphors are, as though trauma takes place in an actual place, even if any specific injury might refer to a body, a brain, or a society. Even though Erikson rightly notes that the original use of the term in the modern context was biological, more typically now we understand the injury to be to the way a person (or a group of people) experience the world—the world as a physical place where one lives but cannot do so safely any longer.

Trauma is something "alien," Erikson says; it "breaks in on you," it smashes your barriers, invades you, possesses you, and dominates your "interior landscape," where it threatens to "leave you empty."[3] Elsewhere, he says, a "true home ... is an extension of the individuals who live in it, a part of themselves. ... People need location almost as much as they need shelter, for sense of place is one of the ways they connect to the larger human community. ... That is the geography of self." Clearly, Erikson sees trauma as akin to an attack on one's home, one severe enough to leave you homeless. When "that combined sense of dwelling and location ... is missing, one is deprived of a measure of personhood. That, too, is the geography of self."[4]

Bessel van der Kolk, a physician and trauma researcher, concurs from the medical and psychological points of view as well: Trauma is at the same time a loss of one's connection to one's body and to oneself.[5] Trauma makes you an alien in your own home, not just socially but also in body and mind. Of course, our bodies *are* our homes. They are our first home—or second, if we count our mothers' bodies. Every description of the meaning of home can be applied to the meaning of our bodies. And whatever the source or type of injury, at some level trauma is always stored in the body, and therefore one needs a body to work out trauma.[6] At the same time, moving outward rather than inward, "home" also signifies the entire world around us and all that we come to know and believe about it as it relates to our existence. We can call this our *Weltanschauung* [worldview], but for the purposes of this essay the concept is best conveyed by the "assumptive world" as introduced by Colin Murray Parkes and incorporated into a theory of trauma by Ronnie Janoff-Bulmann.[7]

Jeffrey Kaplan begins his collection exploring trauma through this lens: "The assumptive world concept refers to the assumptions or beliefs that ground, secure, or orient people, that give a sense of meaning, reality, or purpose to life."[8] In a later chapter, he explicitly ties the idea of the assumptive world to an underlying sense of safety, specifically the safety of self: "The ground on which we live and stake our existence is presumed. . . . When I lose my assumptive world, my self, which is normally presumed to be, is annihilated. . . . To the extent the self ceases to be safe, it ceases to be."[9] Kaplan even extends the implications of the assumptive world—and threats to it—to the metaphysical and spiritual: "The assumptive world provides cover for the soul. Traumatic loss is violation of the soul's cover. . . . Traumatic violation is unholy. . . . The horrifics of defilement, sacrificial self-loathing, or traumatic exposure to violence obliterate sacred cover."[10] Where the biblical texts lay bare the trauma of the loss not just of a home but also of a sacred home, Kaplan's description of the "traumatic violation" as "unholy" or the "obliteration" of "sacred cover" seems particularly apt.

Notably, Kaplan's explication of the assumptive world is nearly as spatial and locative in its metaphors as Erikson's, speaking of it as "the ground on which we live" and a "cover for the soul," the loss of which results in "traumatic exposure to violence." To lose one's "cover for the soul" is to be exposed, defenseless, vulnerable to violence, and shamed, a set of experiences also associated with homelessness—and with exile.[11] Erikson states that "the sense of being despised and rejected and set apart as loathsome—'contaminated' might even be the right word—is a palpable part of the world of the homeless."[12] So too can the same be said of the world of the exiles as expressed in the literature of the Hebrew Bible, and thus it offers a lens through which to view this literature and perhaps the Bible as a whole.

One of the most immediate symptoms of a traumatic wound is for it to be so overwhelming as to resist articulation into the basic narrative of one's life experience. In fact, when this happens, some aspects of the trauma defy language and cannot be remembered in conventional ways. Trauma can thus be assimilated only by placing it in symbolic sequence, like a story, poem, liturgical prayer, or some other kind of structured language. Making pictures, erecting spaces, and creating other kinds of symbolic constructions can work as well. Literary critic Ronald Granofsky describes narratives he calls "trauma novels" as a "resymbolizing" of the trauma—that is, they reinscribe meaning into the events that caused the trauma.[13] It is one contention of this essay that the Hebrew Scriptures represent such resymbolizing narratives inasmuch as their writing, redacting, compilation, and preservation are, in degrees large and small, the product of forces resulting from the Babylonian conquest and exile. The resymbolizing presented by the particular texts most directly confronting the traumas wrought by the Babylonians appears to represent effective efforts to contend with the destructive impact of a powerful political entity upon a sacred homeland.

HOMELESSNESS, TRAUMA, AND THE BABYLONIAN EXILE

Currently, a strong body of scholarship has cast not only specific books but also the entirety of the TaNaKh itself in light of the demands of the Jewish people in the wake of the exile—before, during, and after.[14] Whether it is the emergence of the Deuteronomistic history and Mosaic narrative as the unifying theodicy that explains how history went so wrong, the preservation of the Nevi'im (Prophets) as the retroactive moral conscience of wounded people, or any other number of fragments of poems, prayers, laments, oracles, short stories, philosophical treatises, or theological assertions, in this picture of the Hebrew Scriptures the exile is the "grand unifying theory" that makes it more than the sum of its parts, the historical sun whose gravity binds together the diverse ideological systems expressed in the twenty-four books of the Hebrew Bible. That is to say, at its core, the Hebrew Bible is an extended response to the trauma of the exile; even more specifically, in form, function, and content, the echoes of the loss of Zion as the "master symbol" of Jewish life, qua temple and homeland, reverberate throughout its pages. The destruction of Jerusalem represents the loss of the covenantal symbols in the Jewish "assumptive world": the Promised Land, the Davidic Kingship, and the temple.

To be sure, the temple, as "Zion," is a metonym that encompasses all of those symbols and more. It is the Jewish people and their home; even more, it is Beit HaMikdash, the Holy House, the earthly residence of the presence of the Lord (1 Kgs 6:11–13). The Judeans so trusted in the sanctity of "the Lord's house" that they believed that its inviolability kept them and the city safe from attack, a position that the prophet Jeremiah mocks by mimicking people reflexively babbling about "The Temple of the Lord! The Temple of the Lord! The Temple of the Lord!" in response to prophetic warnings (Jer 7:4).

As such, telling its tragic tale is both the expression of and the solution to experienced trauma. The dispiriting conditions of homelessness are expressed throughout the narratives of the Bible. Crucially, in relating the events and moral failures that lead up to exile, the Hebrew Bible simultaneously lays the groundwork to make itself the Jews' new home in exile—as the "home" of the Law. Even after many of the major issues that the exile raises are resolved in the Second Temple period, this paradigm is reproduced in later traumatic challenges to home, as under the Hellenists in the books of Daniel and Maccabees, or under the Romans, as in the apocalypses of 4 Ezra, 2 Baruch—or Christianity. Prior to the fall of the Second Temple (and thus essentially a second exile), the issue is not physical displacement rather but social and even spiritual displacement. That is, home has left its inhabitants. They are aliens in their own country, strangers in their own strange land.

THE POLITICS OF HOMELESSNESS IN THE TORAH

It is worth lingering a moment on the implications of this last point, as it drives home an often overlooked reality of the myriad ways the exile impacted and even brought into being Judaism as we know it today. Arguably, Judaism was birthed in the trauma of the exile, which is to say, it was born homeless. Moreover, that trauma was inflicted within the very specific political arena of several centuries of ancient Near Eastern imperial history. Then as now, people do not become homeless in a vacuum, and the pain does not become "trauma" outside of a context of social relationships, power dynamics, and authoritative policies of some sort. Homelessness and its effects come into being by choices that are made and not made, by people both in and out of power. As Erikson puts it, "Homelessness is the cost we are willing for one portion of the population to pay in the hopes of benefitting another. It is a matter of policy."[15]

Where there is policy, there is politics; where there is politics, there is power; and where there is power, there is the potential for injury and suffering. Homelessness, in all the senses of which this essay will address, is but one manifestation of this relationship between politics and trauma, and on the world stage of imperial designs and military campaigns, it is so obvious and ubiquitous as to be virtually overlooked. This essay contends, though, that significant parts of the theological record we call the Hebrew Bible captures the specific deep-seated pain associated with homelessness, and thus it becomes a means by which to understand these texts better.

This essay assumes Harold Lasswell's broad but intuitive and inclusive observation that politics is "who gets what, when, how."[16] This definition, as sparse as it is, has the benefit of working on either side of power divides. That is, it recognizes that politics is also about who does not get "what" they want (because someone else got it), who never gets it (thus "when" never comes), and the variety of forms "how" must take on—because "how" is about strategies of power. Many strategies of power may leave traumatic consequences in their wake, both intentionally and unintentionally. However, in many ways, effective responses to trauma involve creating new strategies for reconceiving that power and its effects, even if retroactively.

This essay will use such a lens to examine places where the Hebrew Scriptures confront the traumatic legacy of the politics that brought it into being, both to honor the wound and express the pain still being felt but also to create a space where the healing process will result in heartier, more resilient people. Therefore, this essay will assume that the Scriptures examined are not morbid or melancholic relics of a traumatic past but instead are a vibrant, living record of the successful process of transforming trauma into a new, if still emerging, whole. Irene Smith Landsman notes that psychological research indicates a "paradox of good outcomes" resulting from trauma; despite all the damage that it does, trauma often also makes people more resilient, allows them to find life more meaningful, and enables them to value important relationships more. The Hebrew Bible and its legacy may just be the ultimate example of this paradox of trauma.[17]

Confronting the Hebrew Scriptures again with a perspective informed by exile, politics, homelessness and their resultant and often intergenerational traumas, the way these themes are bred in the bones of the Bible, as it were, is unmistakable. From a biblical point of view, the very first story, the expulsion from Eden, is nothing if not the first narrative of human homelessness and the traumas that ensue. And lest the politics that spur the inciting incident be forgotten, one must recall not only the authoritative rule structure imposed on Adam and Eve concerning the Tree of Knowledge but also God's unnerving confession that "'the man has become like one of us, knowing good and bad, what if he should stretch out his hand and take also from the tree of life and eat, and live forever!' So the Lord God banished him from the garden of Eden, to till the soil from which he was taken" (Gen 2:22–23).[18] In light of Lasswell's definition, the implicit politics of paradise are palpable: There is a clear "what" that is restricted, and violation of that policy is enforced powerfully. As it happens, adherence to the divine directive not to eat from the Tree of the Knowledge of Good and Evil was a precondition for calling Eden "home"; thus, with the expulsion, everywhere on Earth outside of the garden now represents homelessness—an existential condition that some Jews (and Christians) would say persists until the Messianic age and the coming of God's Kingdom on Earth.

The major narrative of Genesis that follows the Fall story, the episode of Noah and the Flood, in essence is also a story of losing one's home by dint of power brought to bear on those who got what they wanted, how they wanted, and when they wanted in illegitimate ways. In this case, "home" was the earth itself—the very place that became home after the expulsion from Eden—and the enforcement of moral law resulted in the near-complete annihilation of all living creatures.[19]

The Jewish story per se begins just a few chapters later with Abraham, né Abram, whose name change is part and parcel of the covenant that God grants him, which brings both the concept of the Chosen People and the Promised Land into being. From the very start, then, the quintessential Jewish covenant involves the promise of a homeland—but also from the very start, the foreknowledge that possession of that homeland would be deferred. Abraham is portrayed as rootless if not exactly homeless, moving from Ur to Harrah to Canaan to Egypt and back to Canaan. Seeking to bury his wife Sarah in Canaan, he states to the Hittites, "I am a resident alien among you; sell me a burial site among you" (Gen 23:4).

From Abraham down his line, from one generation to the next, readers encounter one deception or dirty trick after another, culminating in the assault and sale into bondage in Egypt of Abraham's great-grandson, Joseph, by his own brothers (Gen 37). A dream prophesied the brothers' subjugation to Joseph, and thus his siblings acted to avoid powerlessness and disenfranchisement. There is also an element of family politics in the fact that the brothers knew that their father, Jacob, loved Joseph more. One can only imagine how traumatic an experience this betrayal must have been for Joseph, especially when he is later thrown in prison on false charges. Yet he is spared the deleterious effects of his situation because of God's interventions, ones that eventually allow him to gain great political power in his new country. So when a famine drives the brothers themselves into Egypt, recapitulating Abraham's earlier dislocation, the prophecy is fulfilled—though the brothers too are spared the worst consequences of their homelessness because of Joseph's political status.

Of course, all of this narrative place-setting leads inevitably to the story of the return back to Canaan to finally fulfill the Abrahamic promise and make a homeland for his descendants. Unsurprisingly by now, the Moses narrative, too, is replete with dislocations, expulsions, and other jarring disruptions of "home" for Moses, starting with his journey from a Hebrew home in slavery to a home in the center of Egyptian political power. Subsequently, he became a fugitive after killing an overseer in defense of a (fellow) Hebrew and recognizing that he could never return to the home he knew. Then he memorialized his alien status in Midian by giving his son the name "Gershom," a reference to his being a "stranger in a foreign land" (Exod 2:22). Later he wandered with the Israelites for forty years before reaching the Promised Land, where God, by an arguably cruel and tragic command, forbade him from entering before his death. The entire Mosaic storyline can be seen as an extended meditation on a situation of chronic homelessness brought about by traumatizing politics, first for Bene Israel, after the death of Joseph gave way to a series of bad conditions and worse pharaohs, and second, experienced and borne by Moses himself.

Apart from the thematic resonance of the central myths of the Jewish origin stories, the Hebrew Scriptures preserve texts understood by most readers, religious and scholarly alike, to be actual responses to the devastation of the exile. Chief among these, depicting the sentiments of those either left behind in the devastated land of Judah or carted off to Babylon as human booty and slaves, are the books of Lamentations and Ezekiel as well as Psalm 137, all of which certainly exhibit the immediate impact of imperial politics and the trauma of homelessness.

PSALM 137

One of the most famous verses of all the Psalms is the opening of 137, a crie de coeur over the loss of Jerusalem as a geographic place, as a home, framed specifically by emphasizing dislocation in another place. Psalm 137 is remarkably real-worldly in its clear-eyed acknowledgment of the traumatic events that brought the Judeans to this foreign land, beginning with the almost documentary-like description of the humiliation heaped on them by their captors, which added insult to injury. As brutal and painful as the scenario depicted in Psalm 137 is, it seems to grapple with the harsh realities endured by the exiles as exactly that, harsh realities. To begin, literally, "by the rivers of Babylon" is a very real-world statement of fact, which sets the tone for the poem as a whole:

> By the rivers of Babylon, there we sat, sat and wept, as we thought
>   of Zion.
> There on the poplars we hung up our lyres,
> for our captors asked us there for songs,
> our tormentors, for amusement, "Sing us one of the songs of Zion."
> How can we sing a song of the Lord on alien soil?
> If I forget you, O Jerusalem, let my right hand wither;
> Let my tongue stick to my palate if I cease to think of you,
> if I do not keep Jerusalem in my memory even at my happiest hour.
> Remember, O Lord, against the Edomites the day of Jerusalem's fall;
> how they cried, "Strip her, strip her to her very foundations!"
> Fair Babylon, you predator,
> A blessing on him who repays you in kind what you have inflicted
>   on us;
> A blessing on him who seizes your babies and dashes them against
>   the rocks.

A critical portion of this short lament is devoted to the concern that the exiles will forget their home, Jerusalem. There are repeated calls to keep Jerusalem in memory, creating social conditions that should prevent its memory either from being repressed, thus giving into the worst effects of the injury, or from legitimately being forgotten, as though its loss were inconsequential. Intriguingly, in verse 6 the speaker calls on himself—and presumably the other exiles—to remember the city "even at my happiest hour," suggesting a turn of fortunes that will require preserving the memory of the city's tragic end and not just their home in its glory days.[20] From the perspective of a trauma reading, this entire poem could be understood as instructions to the exiled population on how to mitigate the damage done by the violent and humiliating loss of its homeland by keeping real-world events from becoming overwhelming, despite how painful they are. That is, the psalm models how not to lose the narrative of one's own history, and what resymbolization there is appears as a hope that the conquerors will someday experience the same pain they have inflicted.

Notably, the two images that are not specifically about the loss of one place while sitting helpless, vulnerable, and exposed in another are about injuries inflicted on bodies. First, the consequence of forgetting Jerusalem will be a hand's loss of ability. The construction of verse 5 is strange in Hebrew and in English. Historically, most translations have understood the verse to read something like "may my hand forget"—variously, forget "its skill" or "its cunning." The fact that the text is not clear what the hand is forgetting is part of the problem. "How can hands forget?" asks Bob Becking.[21] Thus, some biblical scholars, including those behind the Jewish Publication Society's translation above, emend škḥ [to forget] to tšḥk [to wither], as in "may my right hand wither." In the context of the effect of trauma on the body, either reading is intriguing. While describing a body part as "forgetting" may be unusual, the inability to perform some well-learned task in the wake of trauma does fit the psychosomatic symptomology as traumatic amnesia; ordinary actions or well-rehearsed public performances may be experienced as "blocked" or "forgotten," as though the body has lost its muscle memory.

In the context of Psalm 137, the phrase would likely refer to the inability to perform music, with one's hands literally embodying the inability to remember Jerusalem. The traumatic suppression of the memory of home is expressed physically in the loss of skill in the hands that once used to play the music from home. By the same token, the other reading, "wither" for "forget," provides a bodily reaction in parallel with the inability to speak of the next verse (or perhaps sing, given the immediate textual context), suggesting an even more crippling psychosomatic expression of the trauma.[22] Just as the Judean body politic has been withered and crippled and will be more so if it forgets its home and all it once stood for, so too may their hands be palsied, unable to work, let alone rebuild, if that connection to Jerusalem is permanently severed.

The other image is of "dashing" the infants of "Fair Babylon" (literally, "Daughter of Babylon") against rocks, "in kind what you have inflicted on us." This horrific picture captures a real-world aspect of the brutality of war and the way that vulnerable women, children, and families are targeted by invading armies in efforts to demoralize the resisting population into submission.[23] It also suggests that apart from watching their city fall to ruin, this injury is the one that most lingers in the memories—and the bodies—of the exiles, such that it will be the first act (re)visited upon Babylon when the time comes. In reversing the roles of the conquest's victims and perpetrators, Psalm 137 appears to be resymbolizing the exile within the sacred record of the Judeans.

Of the two excurses into body imagery, one insightfully posits the (psychosomatic) damage if the memory is forgotten, and the other posits a relatable revenge fantasy against those responsible for their suffering. Their captors' mocking calls for joyous songs of Jerusalem suggest ongoing humiliation; the power and politics leading up to this particular scene are strongly implied. Psalm 137 therefore speaks forthrightly to the immediate pain and disorientation of the exiles and presents images of some of the horrors of the war that can be resolved only in the future when the political stakes have reversed. There is still hope here, even as these exiles deal with their situation as exactly what it is, a heartbreaking but temporary blow—schadenfreude in Babylon reaping what it has sown is on the horizon somewhere.

THE BOOK OF EZEKIEL

An even more heart-wrenching case than Psalm 137, if such a thing is possible, is found in perhaps the quintessential picture of the trauma of exile, the book of Ezekiel. In earlier work, the present author has addressed trauma in Ezekiel as reflecting the condition once known as melancholia, understood by Sigmund Freud to be a state of being overwhelmed by loss and therefore unable to let go of the reality that was now gone.[24] More recently, Ruth Poser sets forth perhaps the hallmark reading in her contribution to *The Bible through the Lens of Trauma*.[25] Therefore, this essay will limit itself to highlighting a few lines of thought relevant to the current discussion.

Just as in Psalm 137, the book of Ezekiel immediately frames its key figure's present alienation from place as a result of exile. But rather than the real-world reportage that marks the psalm, Ezekiel and the book's audience are swept into the most incredible, astounding, surreal visionary experience imaginable. This is the return of God after five years with no contact with his people in exile. Yet God appears to Ezekiel not to deliver good news but instead to affix blame on the exiles for their own predicament, due to the religious corruption that it presents as being deeply rooted even into the priesthood and temple practice. Indeed, in the course of the first half of the book, the entire lauded history of Israel and Judah is transformed into a horror show of betrayal, degeneration, and faithlessness.

From the perspective of trauma literature, two noteworthy therapeutic moves seem to be happening simultaneously. First, this tragedy has now become part and parcel of a story that has existed from Israel's origins, doing the narrative work required to comprehend the incomprehensible.[26] Second, psychological research shows that trauma victims who express a certain degree of self-blame (even when definitively not at all responsible for their injuries) exhibit better overall coping mechanisms in the long run. Demonstrating an internal locus of control, even when it means accepting responsibility for things that are objectively not one's fault, seems to be a more adaptive healing strategy than blaming others, even if warranted.[27] Notably, the blame in the book of Ezekiel is squarely fixed not on the Babylonians or on God but instead on the exiles themselves, including the prophet, and the entire sad lineage that preceded them.

Like Psalm 137, the book of Ezekiel expresses the impact of exile in two vivid ways through bodies. Ezekiel turns his own actual body into a stage for performing a series of bizarre and often denigrating sign acts, starting with rendering the prophet mute—literally exhibiting the "cleaving of the tongue to the roof of the mouth" defended against in Psalm 137—except when he speaks as the prophet of the Lord (Ezek 3:26). These jarring rituals mark a moment when the text demonstrates collective, psychological, and bodily trauma simultaneously.[28] And yet, many of the actions allude specifically to the political situation that gave rise to the trauma in the first place—chapter 4 is a full-on recapitulation of the siege of Jerusalem, wherein Ezekiel, as the Babylonian army, first attacks a block of clay and then bears the weight of sin for Israel and Judah collectively for 430 days.

Later the symbolic embodiment of trauma takes an entirely different form in the graphic depictions of Jerusalem as a faithless, promiscuous wife. But as Poser indicates, "the text exonerates Jerusalem to some extent: the biography of the city-as-woman in Ezekiel 16 portrays her as of low birth and the daughter of wicked parents who left their infant daughter to die.... Such a depiction... absolves her of responsibility: if she is incapable of remaining faithful, it is because of the maltreatment she suffered earlier."[29] Be that as it may, the choice to portray the city as unfaithful is at the same time an only slightly veiled critique of a national policy of political and military alliances that also facilitated polytheistic intrusions into the monarchal and priestly operations of Judah, Jerusalem, and the temple.

The ultimate connection among wives, Jerusalem, and detrimental imperial relations is solidified when the death of Ezekiel's wife in chapter 24 foreshadows the fall of the actual temple to Babylonian forces. These depictions of the destruction of Jerusalem in the book of Ezekiel all find it necessary to capture, one way or another, three key aspects of the situation: the physical destruction of the city and the land; the painful experience that the loss inflicted on the community, usually represented by forms of exposure, humiliation, and bodily abuse; and, though not referenced as directly, a clear allusion to the political facts of exile. Any torments they suffer are the product of the homelessness brought about by the successful political strategies of the

Babylonians and just as much by the unsuccessful political strategies of the Judean leadership.

As I have argued elsewhere, the concerns of the book of Ezekiel begin to pivot after the physical temple finally falls in chapter 33, and from there on the concern with restoration becomes more and more prominent.[30] The remaining chapters contain the evocative New Heart passage (36), the depiction of national resurrection in the form of dry bones that regain bodies (37), the bloody revenge fantasy against Magog (38–39), and ultimately the detailed appearance of the New Jerusalem (40–48). This final vision imagines, in very concrete terms, the return of the Jewish home and all of its concomitant political and religious facets, right down to the very name of the place: *Yahweh Šammah* [Yahweh Is There].

In the first two of these passages, the trauma of exile is worked out within the framework of bodily healing. In the Magog apocalypse, as in Psalm 137, what had been inflicted on Judean bodies is now wrought against the wicked perpetrators, thereby creating the conditions for Judah to be restored. Poser argues convincingly that the entire Gog-Magog narrative is a therapeutic recapitulation of exilic history.[31] Both the political situation and the damage inflicted have been reversed. Having restored the body politic with new bodies, recovered a "new self" with a new heart, and then reclaimed the homeland in a new telling of the Babylonian conquest, the space has been prepared—narratively, first, but then emotionally, spiritually, and politically—to go home. Suffice it to say, to promise that the future consecrated house of God and land of the Jewish people will restore the entire original religio-political apparatus of the Israelites, while at the same time becoming ascendant over the other nations of Earth, directly resolves the trauma brought about by imperial politics and the homelessness they cause by reversing both in an idealized and wholly restorative way.[32]

THE BOOK OF LAMENTATIONS

But what about that actual physical place, that home that was lost, that city that lay in ruins? Do the emotional and political visions of the exiles mesh with the realities of the land they imagine being restored to? The book of 2 Chronicles paints the picture of a Judah devoid of Jews, who were carried into exile to be subject to redeeming punishment for seventy years. The book of Ezra presents the place to which the exiles return as rife with foreigners and mixed marriages, essentially perpetuating the original unfaithfulness believed to have caused the exile in the first place.[33] Even as the depiction in Ezra contradicts the statement in 2 Chronicles on the face of it, one might argue that it is a distinction without a difference; if those who remained in the land did not change their ways in light of the devastation all around them, then Judah was empty of redeemable Jews, at least until the exiles returned and Ezra reinstated (or, more likely, instated broadly for the first time) a political code of conduct reflecting Mosaic Law and monotheism.[34]

The viewpoint of Judah being an "empty land" over centuries became standard for the Jewish community and, later, biblical scholars. But this stance has been fairly conclusively challenged over the last few decades, giving way to an understanding that this biblical construction reflects a political strategy of the returning exiles themselves, one infused with the Deuteronomist narrative that allows the Hebrew Scriptures to cohere as a response to exile.[35] By the same token, it allowed the exilic community to make meaningful sense of the devastating losses they suffered. The stance thereby emerges from the traumatic events in a position to build a new world from them, with the Bible as their chief instrument.

To be sure, one book, the book of Lamentations, resists either picture of the Judean landscape after 587 BCE. An eloquent and heartbreaking poem, in Hebrew it is titled '*Êykhôh*, named for its first word, traditionally rendered in English as the question "How?" but carrying the meaning of the interjection of despair "Alas!" (or, as frequently exclaimed in Yiddish, "Oy!"). But as the English name suggests, it captures the pain of the loss of Jerusalem every bit as acutely as Psalm 137 but does it from the point of view of people who have lost their home without leaving it.[36] Even without being removed from the land, the eradication of the other Zionistic aspects of day-to-day life, not to mention the long-term reduction to subsistence living among the ruins in the aftermath of war, would have transformed the sacred space of the Promised Land into an alien presence in its own right—a promise withdrawn. Like Adam and Eve, they were cast out of paradise; like Noah, they were unmoored after an apocalypse; like Moses, they were out of place in a strange land. But it was their home that left them. Would the trauma of homelessness present itself in the literature in the same way as it did among the exiles? Would the politics of the situation linger in the background or emerge more profoundly?

Like the other literature of the displaced examined above, Lamentations establishes place and then contrasts it with assumed normal conditions: "Alas! Lonely sits the city once great with people! She that was great among nations is become like a widow; the princess among the states is become a thrall"

(Lam 1:1). Throughout, the injurious effects are presented as the direct result of the successful imperial campaign: "My children are forlorn, for the foe has prevailed" (Lam 1:16). Yet chapter 2 is almost entirely a catalog of the ways in which the homeland of the Jews was rendered uninhabitable, not by the Babylonians, but by God.[37] In fact, verses 4 and 5 explicitly call or compare God to an enemy, just after alluding to how God allowed the approach of the invading forces. "The Lord has acted like a foe, he has laid waste Israel, laid waste all her citadels, destroyed her strongholds. He has increased within Fair Judah mourning and moaning" (Lam 2:5).

As in the book of Ezekiel, the city becomes personified as a traumatized woman, though in this case, first as a widow and then, through most of the rest of the poem, as "Daughter" (literally *bat*; rendered as "fair" in this translation) Zion. "Fair Princess Daughter" Zion is vilified along the same lines as the faithless wife in Ezekiel, blaming her sins for her lowly state. God acts like an abuser and an abandoner, intentionally humiliating his "daughter" in public for all the world to see (Lam 1:8–9, 13–17).[38]

Chapter 2 moves back and forth from clear-eyed assessment of the damage to the homeland to the emotional and bodily effects that damage has had on the people there and on "Daughter Jerusalem" herself, culminating in the telling but despairing "Your ruin is as vast as the sea: Who can heal you?" (Lam 2:13b). The way that trauma of the loss of the Jewish homeland becomes embodied by Jerusalem here underscores that the witnessing of the destruction of the city and the subsequent deathly tribulations of the populace are every bit as painful as those of their exilic counterparts—and perhaps even more so; maybe the deep, ruinous wound cannot be healed.[39]

In fact, the juxtaposition of Daughter Zion's violation both with the people's suffering, especially that of mothers and children, and with the physical destruction of the city draws the reader to a stark conclusion: The city of Zion itself is just as homeless and traumatized as the people who once inhabited it. This depiction of Daughter Zion literally expresses the people's trauma in her body, which signifies both the physical place and the collective social body. At the same time, as the symbol of the complete loss of the assumptive word that the devastation of the communal Yahwistic institutions and symbols represents, her character conveys the corresponding dimensions of trauma in mind and spirit.[40]

Chapters 4 and 5 thoroughly depict the before and after of life in Judah following the fall of Jerusalem. The sentiment of homelessness within one's own homeland is stated most starkly in chapter 5: "Our heritage has passed to aliens, our homes to strangers" (Lam 5:2). Graphic depictions of wartime strife abound, especially in the many allusions to hunger and the desperation with which people search for food, including the humiliating bargains they are forced to strike with their oppressors simply to survive: "We must pay to drink our own water, obtain our own kindling at a price.... We hold out a hand to Egypt; to Assyria, for our fill of bread.... We get our bread at the peril of our lives, because of the sword of the wilderness" (Lam 5:4, 6, 9). This last line in particular ties the threat of hunger to the military threat that continues because of the political realities of imperial domination. But nothing comes close to conjuring the horrors of their new life like the references to mothers cooking their children to eat them, perversely reversing the natural order wherein mothers feed their children to give them life (Lam 2:20, 4:10).[41] This single image manages to combine and exceed the dreadful memories of hunger and murdered children inscribed in Psalm 137.

But unlike that psalm or the second half of Ezekiel, Lamentations does not relieve the symptoms of the trauma it depicts, with the exception of a brief turn toward the future and the hope for restoration and revenge in chapter 3 (vv. 55–66). Even the final verses of the book are forlorn and pleading rather than hopeful: "Why have You forgotten us utterly, forsaken us for all time? Take us back, O Lord, to Yourself, and let us come back; renew our days as of old! For truly, You have rejected us, bitterly raged against us" (Lam 5:20–22).

The difference in these outlooks may very well lie in the political perspectives in which they are couched. In exile, under the yoke of a foreign power in a foreign land, the only immediate hope would have been to throw off that empire, return to Judah, and restore the land, redeeming the Jewish people in the process. But while Psalm 137 places the blame firmly on the conquering empire and Ezekiel places it on the Jewish people and the exiles, Lamentations attributes the powerful force that has devastated the lives of the Jews and rendered them homeless to God himself. Now that the Babylonians have left, the Judeans' only available response is to address their pain to God in the most direct way possible—and yet, God remains silent and unmoved.[42] Hence, the people structure their pain as a lament and offer it as a vehicle to elicit God's response. The community hopes for governance from God because they formulated their grief in a prayer, which they believed made it undeniably matter to him.[43] Any response to the trauma by God would necessarily address the politics that had most immediately, in a this-worldly sense, inflicted the injuries and suffering on the people.

CONCLUSION: COMING HOME IN THE HEBREW SCRIPTURES

With the compilation of the Torah in exile and subsequently the TaNaKh in diaspora, "home" as master symbol existed more in the Bible than it did on Earth. The promise of a return to the Promised Land grew out of the idea of place that thrived in the text. But the need for a return—and its constant deferral into the future—directly results from the political realities of the times. The remarkable thing is that despite a biblical narrative, a name, a mythos, and a historical identity all rooted in the traumatic loss of their homeland, the Jewish people as a whole do not present themselves as essentially traumatized. In fact, their great gifts to the world—in religion and spirituality, the social and physical sciences, medicine, education, government, literature and the other arts—show them to be in the business of *tikkun olam* [mending the world], a phrase that itself comes from the Kabbalistic story of a trauma in the very fabric of the cosmos.

There can be no doubt that this legacy originates in the Hebrew Bible. Though a product of an intensely traumatic period for the Jews, it honestly records but also transforms that trauma into the platform for a new community, offering a new home and a new politics that resist the string of losses, wounds, and attacks on Jewish selves that history has had in store for them.

NOTES

1. Charlotte Edmond, "The Number of Displaced People in the World Just Hit a Record High," *World Economic Forum*, June 20, 2017, https://www.weforum.org/agenda/2017/06/there-are-now-more-refugees-than-the-entire-population-of-the-uk.

2. Kai Erikson, *A New Species of Trouble: The Human Experience of Modern Disasters* (New York: Norton, 1994), 228.

3. Erikson, *A New Species*, 228.

4. Ibid., 159.

5. Bessel van der Kolk, *The Body Keeps the Score* (New York: Viking, 2014), 12–14, 87–102.

6. Ibid., 89–95.

7. Colin Murray Parkes, "Psycho-Social Transition: A Field of Study," *Social Science and Medicine* 5 (1971): 101–15; Colin Murray Parks, "Bereavement as a Psychosocial Transition: Processes of Adaptation to Change," *Journal of Social Issues* 44, no. 3 (1988): 53–65; Ronnie Janoff-Bulman, *Shattered Assumptions: Towards a New Psychology of*

Trauma (New York: Free Press, 1992); Jeffrey Kauffman, "Introduction," in *Loss of the Assumptive World: A Theory of Traumatic Loss,* ed. Jeffrey Kauffman (New York: Brunner-Routledge, 2002), 1–3.

8. Kauffman, "Introduction," 1.

9. Jeffrey Kauffman, "Safety and the Assumptive Word: A Theory of Traumatic Loss," in *Loss of the Assumptive World,* 209.

10. Ibid., 210–11.

11. One homeless person whose struggles Erikson documents says, "To me, one of the basic fundamentals of life is having a roof over your head. . . . So there's panic and fear, a sense of disbelief. It just doesn't seem possible, yet there you are dealing with it. A nightmare!" (*A New Species,* 174).

12. Erikson, *A New Species,* 175–76.

13. Ronald Granofsky, *The Trauma Novel* (Bern: Peter Lang, 1995), 6–7, cited in Ruth Poser, "No Words: The Book of Ezekiel as Trauma Literature and a Response to Exile," in *The Bible through the Lens of Trauma,* ed. Elizabeth Boase and Christopher Frechette (Atlanta: Society of Biblical Literature Press, 2016), 40.

14. On the collecting, editing, and writing of the biblical corpus as a response to the exile, see John Bright, *A History of Israel,* 3rd ed. (Philadelphia: Westminster, 1981), 333, 350, as one early statement of this scholarly consensus, and Jill Middlemas, *The Templeless Age* (Louisville, KY: Westminster John Knox, 2007), as one relatively current, thoroughgoing reconsideration and explication of the evidence and its implications for understanding the Hebrew Bible.

15. Erikson, *A New Species,* 168.

16. Harold Lasswell, *Politics: Who Gets What, When, How* (New York: Whittlesey House, McGraw-Hill, 1936).

17. Irene Smith Landsman, "Crises of Meaning in Trauma and Loss," in *Loss of the Assumptive World: A Theory of Traumatic Loss,* ed. Jeffrey Kauffman (New York: Brunner-Routledge, 2002), 25.

18. All biblical quotations are from Adele Berlin and Marc Zevi Brettler, eds, *The Jewish Study Bible,* 2nd ed. (New York: Oxford University Press, 2014).

19. Perhaps Noah's drunken state described in Genesis 9:21 can be interpreted as trying to manage the long-term trauma that results from witnessing and surviving a forty-day apocalypse. The story of the Tower of Babel may also presage some of the Flood story's themes of global homelessness as a result of humans' illegitimate use of power to get what they want.

20. According to some traditions, the breaking of the glass at a Jewish wedding ceremony also intentionally incorporates, in the midst of great joy, the recollection of the destruction of Jerusalem (Berlin and Brettler, *The Jewish Study Bible,* 1424).

21. Bob Becking, "Does Exile Equal Suffering? A Fresh Look at Psalm 137," in *Exile and Suffering*, ed. Bob Becking and Dirk Human (Leiden: Brill, 2009), 193.

22. Ibid.

23. Boyd Seevers, *Warfare in the Old Testament* (Grand Rapids, MI: Kregel, 2013), 256. For other examples of this tactic in the Bible, see 2 Kings 8:12; Isaiah 13:16; Nahum 3:10.

24. Dereck Daschke, "Desolate among Them: Loss, Fantasy, and Recovery in the Book of Ezekiel," *American Imago* 56 (1999): 105–32; Dereck Daschke, *City of Ruins: Mourning Jerusalem through Jewish Apocalypse* (Leiden: Brill, 2010), 61–102.

25. Poser, "No Words," 27–48.

26. Ibid., 33; Daschke, *City of Ruins*, 84–85, 98–99.

27. Janoff-Bulman posits two different kinds of self-blame, characterological and behavioral, and observes that when a victim blames the injury on specific actions rather than one's attributes as a person, it "helps restore a sense of control and may be adaptive in this way" (Landsman, "Crises of Meaning in Trauma and Loss," 16–17). On the subject of the book of Lamentations and self-blame, see Christopher Frechette, "Daughter Babylon Raped and Bereaved (Isaiah 47): Symbolic Violence and Meaning-Making in Recovery from Trauma," in *The Bible through the Lens of Trauma*, 79.

28. Ezekiel exemplifies the continuing loyalty to God's commands of the exiles, but I have argued elsewhere (Daschke, *City of Ruins*, 70–81) that these violent, morbid sign acts represent a melancholic turning of his rage at God against himself. In another context, van der Kolk (*The Body Keeps the Score*, 133–34) observes that "The price of this loyalty is unbearable feelings of loneliness, despair, and the inevitable rage of helplessness. Rage that has nowhere to go is redirected against the self, in the form of depression, self-hatred, and self-destructive actions. One of my patients told me, 'It's like hating your home. . . .' Nothing feels safe—least of all your own body." Especially considering Ezekiel's vision of the angels destroying the temple in chapters 8–9, van der Kolk's observation seems entirely relevant to the prophet of the exile.

29. Poser, "No Words," 33.

30. Daschke, *City of Ruins*, 92–102.

31. Poser, "No Words," 38.

32. Daschke, *City of Ruins*, 97–102.

33. Jill Middlemas, *The Troubles of Templeless Judah* (New York: Oxford University Press, 2005), 7–8.

34. Morton Smith, *Palestinian Parties and Politics That Shaped the Old Testament* (London: SCM, 1987), 81–85.

35. Even more than thirty years ago, John Bright was able to write in *A History of Israel* that "the popular notion of a total deportation which left the land empty and void is erroneous and to be discarded" (344).

36. Though it is very likely that the composer of this poem and much of his audience did actually lose their homes in or around Jerusalem in the onslaught against the city. Bright, *A History of Israel*, 344; Berlin and Brettler, *The Jewish Study Bible*, 1581.

37. Berlin and Brettler, *The Jewish Study Bible*, 1582.

38. Middlemas, *The Troubles of Templeless Judah*, 188, 190.

39. Boyd Seevers's presentation of the Babylonian conquest of Judah graphically depicts the systematic decimation of the city and its institutional structures as the dismemberment of a body, with the temple and royal palaces the "heart and vital organs" of the nation (*Warfare in the Old Testament*, 257–58).

40. Berlin and Brettler (*The Jewish Study Bible*, 1582) state that Lamentations may have been ritually recited at the ruins of the temple, bringing the literary home as traumatized body into alignment with the actual traumatized home, thus resymbolizing it and the Jews' own physical, traumatized bodies through scripture.

41. Ibid., 1589. Perhaps there is even an unconscious perversion of the idea of the mother as "first home," as the children return to their mothers' bodies dead, the home that gave them life becoming their graves.

42. Ibid., 1582.

43. Middlemas, *The Troubles of Templeless Judah*, 224–27.

Exile and Return in the Samaritan Traditions

Menahem Mor

In 2017 there were 805 Samaritans living in Israel, 418 of them in the city of Holon with Israeli citizenship and 387 in Kiryat Luza, a village on Mount Gerizim in the West Bank under the Palestinian Authority, which is under Israeli security control. The inhabitants of Kiryat Luza also have Israeli citizenship, but since this village is connected with the municipal area of Nablus (Shechem), its inhabitants have Palestinian citizenship as well.

The Samaritans, who call themselves "Shomrim" [Keepers of the Torah], reject their definition by others as a community and define themselves as an ancient people and as a unique religious-ethnic group that constitutes a direct continuation of the Children of Israel. This claim of the Samaritans is the main issue in the debate concerning their origins, which will be dealt with later on in this essay.[1] The essay is part of an extended project, The Samaritan's History in Ancient Times: Samaritan Chronicles versus Non-Samaritan Sources.

One of the characteristics of the Samaritans is the fact that they live only in Israel, especially on Mount Gerizim in the village of Kiryat Luza and in the city of Holon in Israel. In their opinion, in order to be an Israeli of the Samaritan community, one of the most important identifiers is "settlement in the Land of Israel and never leaving it." Therefore, "for them, one who lives outside the Land of Israel cannot be considered as an Israeli Samaritan."[2] On the face of it, in the absence of a "Samaritan diaspora," the subject of my essay is impossible. However, when I began my research on the Samaritan diaspora, it became clear that in course of time a Samaritan diaspora had indeed existed; it had been created for political or economic reasons.[3] Samaritan communities were scattered in various places such as Egypt[4] (Alexandria[5] and Cairo[6]), Sicily,[7] Delos,[8] Thessaloniki,[9] and Damascus.[10]

My essay focuses on exile and return in ancient Israel and Judah during the periods described in Jewish, Assyrian, Babylonian, and Samaritan sources. I compare the different sources and try through them to understand the Samaritan question. During the history of Israel and Judah, a number of expulsions of the people of Israel and Judah occurred.

THE ASSYRIAN EXILE

The exile of the inhabitants of the northern Kingdom of Israel and the inhabitants in Transjordan had already begun in 733 BCE, during the reign of the Assyrian king Tiglath-Pileser III (745–727 BCE). This king developed the method of a two-way mass exile, a policy that gave the Assyrians advantages in their control over the foreign peoples they had conquered through a demographic transference that created loyalties and commitments toward the conqueror.[11]

According to 2 Kings 15:29, Tiglath-Pileser III captured these regions: Galilee, the land of Naphtali, and the Gilad in Transjordan. In his annals, he reported that 13,250 captives were deported from these areas.[12]

In the year 725 BCE Shalmaneser V, king of Assyria (727–722 BCE), began a siege of the city of Shomron that ended three years later during the reign of his heir, Sargon II (722–705 BCE) with the total destruction of the northern kingdom in 722 BCE during the reign of Hoshea, the last Israelite king.

After Sargon's destruction and elimination of the northern kingdom, he exiled the tribes of Israel to Assyria. The Bible says of the Israelite deportation: "The king of Assyria captured Samaria, he exiled Israel to Assyria" (2 Kgs 17: 5–6). "And he carried Israel away into Assyria, and placed them in Halah and in Habor by the river of Gozan, and in the cities of the Medes" (2 Kgs 17:18).[13]

The campaign of Sargon II against the countries that rebelled against Assyria is reported on the walls of the royal palace in Dur-Sharrukin (=Khorsabad),[14] where it is written in the Khorsabad Summary Inscription that "I besieged and captured Samaria. I took as spoil 27,290 [or 27,280] people who lived there; I organized (a contingent of) 200 [or 50] of their chariots and I instructed the rest of them in correct conduct.[15] I appointed my eunuch over them and imposed upon them a tribute of the former king."

The Calah Summary Inscription added that Sargon II exiled "the rest of them and I settled in Assyria," and he "resettled Samaria more densely than before and brought there people from the lands of my conquest."[16] In light of this, only 27,900 people were taken as exiles by Sargon. In addition, we mentioned the 13,250 who were exiled earlier from the Galilee without listing the number of exiles from the eastern side of the Jordan River. If Sargon II had really expelled all the local population, "the rest," he would certainly have boasted of it in his records, which would have added glory and prestige to him as an imperial leader.[17]

These facts stand behind the research assumptions that deal with the Assyrian exile, which claim that a significant part of the inhabitants of the former northern kingdom were not exiled but remained in their places of residence. Support for this assumption can be derived from biblical testimony concerning the conduct of the kings of Judah after the destruction of Shomron and the expulsion of its inhabitants.

There are two accounts in the Bible after the destruction of Shomron about the marriage of kings of Judah with women from regions that once belonged to the northern kingdom.

One of them highlights diplomatic marriages. Manasseh (698–642 BCE) married Meshullemeth, daughter of Haruz, from Jotbah (2 Kgs 21:19). The place is identified with Yotva (Yodfat) in the Lower Galilee, north of the Beit Netofa Valley. Josiah married Zebida, daughter of Pedaiah, from Rumah (2 Kgs 23:36), identified with Rumi in the Lower Galilee.

Through these diplomatic marriages the kings of Judah wished to link prominent families still living in the Galilee with the House of David through family ties and thus connect the Israelite population that remained in the area of the northern kingdom with the Kingdom of Judah.

Two religious reforms were carried out by the kings of Judah after the destruction of the northern kingdom. Both were an attempt to include the Israelite population remaining in the north with these activities.

2 Chronicles 30 describes the Passover celebration of Hezekiah, king of Judah (698–727 BCE). He invited the inhabitants of the former Kingdom of Israel to celebrate Passover in Jerusalem. Hezekiah sent word to all Israel and Judah "and also wrote letters to Ephraim and Manasseh, inviting them to come to the temple of the LORD in Jerusalem and celebrate the Passover to the LORD, the God of Israel" (2 Chron 30:1). They decided to send a proclamation "throughout Israel, from Beersheba to Dan" (2 Chron 30:5). The couriers went from "town to town in Ephraim and Manasseh, as far as Zebulun" (2 Chron 30:10). Some of the people scorned and ridiculed them. "Nevertheless, some from Asher, Manasseh and Zebulun humbled themselves and went to Jerusalem" (2 Chron 30:11). In order to allow a significant number of them who were not purified to participate in the feast in its proper time, the date was postponed for a month, and most of the celebrants who came "were from Ephraim, Manasseh, Issachar and Zebulun" (2 Chron 30:18). "When all this had ended, the Israelites who were there went out to the towns of Judah, smashed the sacred stones and cut down the Asherah poles. They destroyed the high places and the altars throughout Judah and Benjamin and in Ephraim and Manasseh. After they had destroyed all of them, the Israelites returned to their own towns and to their own property" (2 Chron 31:1).

Josiah, King of Judah (640–609 BCE), in his religious reforms after the discovery of the "Book of the Law of the Lord that had been given through Moses," intended them mainly as a struggle against the cult of high places in order to bring about a unified cult in Jerusalem. Within the framework of this struggle, he also included the areas of the northern kingdom in which a remnant was still residing: "In the towns of Manasseh, Ephraim and Simeon, as far as Naphtali, and in the ruins around them, he tore down the altars and the Asherah poles and crushed the idols to powder and cut to pieces all the incense altars throughout Israel. Then he went back to Jerusalem" (2 Chron 34: 6–7). "They went to Hilkiah the high priest and gave him the money that had been brought into the temple of God, which the Levites who were the gatekeepers had collected from the people of Manasseh, Ephraim and the entire remnant of Israel and from all the people of Judah and Benjamin and the inhabitants of Jerusalem" (2 Chron 34:9).

The various verses in connection with these reforms therefore indicate that most of the autochthonic population of the northern kingdom was not exiled. Many of the indigenous Israelite residents remained on their land, and Hezekiah and Josiah hoped to incorporate them into their kingdom. The Calah Summary Inscription reads "I resettled Samaria more densely than before (and) brought there people from the lands of my conquest."[18]

In 2 Kings it is told that the Assyrians settled exiles from Babylon, Cuthah, Ava, Hamath, and Sepharvaim in Samaria, without mentioning their numbers: "And the king of Assyria brought men from Babylon, and from Cuthah, and from Ava, and from Hamath, and from Sepharvaim, and placed them in the cities of Samaria instead of the children of Israel: and they possessed Samaria, and dwelt in the cities thereof" (2 Kgs 17:24). According to Haim Tadmor, this verse sums up two deportations to the Land of Israel: the first in 720 BCE, when the Assyrians transferred exiles from Ava, Hamath, and Sepharvaim to Samaria, and the second of uncertain date when exiles were brought from Babylon and Cuthah. In his opinion, this second exile can be dated to 689 BCE, to the period of King Sennacherib (705–680 BCE) after the destruction of the city of Babylon, or to 648 BCE, when Ashurbanipal suppressed the uprising in Babylon.[19] The transfer of Arab tribes to Samaria by Sargon in 716 BCE is described in this way: "The Tamudi [Iba]didi |Marsimani Ḫayappâ, the far-off Arabs ... I exiled their remnant (and) settled (them), in Samaria."[20]

Ezra 4:2 refers to another expulsion to Israel. This verse mentions the name of Assyrian king Esarhaddon (681–669 BCE) as the one who transferred exiles into the area of Samaria. This exile can be dated to 671 or 669 BCE during the campaigns of Esarhaddon in Egypt.[21]

In Ezra 4:9–10 there is a reference to the deportees of various peoples to Samaria in the reign of Osnappar, who should apparently be identified with Ashurbanipal (669–627 BCE). Osnappar transferred inhabitants from Babylon, Arach, and Susa either in 648 BCE after suppressing the uprising in Babylon or in 646 BCE after he destroyed Ealam and Susa.[22]

These testimonies show that the Assyrians gave great importance to the province of Samaria as an administrative center in the western part of the empire, and the transference of exiles carried out between 720 and 646 BCE to the Samarian area was meant to strengthen this center. Since the testimonies do not indicate the number of exiles brought over during these years, the matter is subject to estimates and suppositions based on other facts, which in themselves arouse many difficulties. However, the fact that only about 50,000 people were exiled from the northern kingdom, together with the figures from the Assyrian records that mention the exile from certain cities with low numbers of 625 to 656 people from every city,[23] leads to the reasonable conclusion that the number of new inhabitants settled in the province of Samaria was not much greater than the number of people who had been exiled from it.

The estimation of the number of those exiled from Samaria and the assessment of the number of new inhabitants are directly connected with the question concerning the origin of the Samaritans. If we say that the Assyrians exiled most of the population of the Kingdom of Israel, then after 720 BCE most of the population in the province of Samaria consisted of those exiles transferred there by the Assyrians. Therefore, those who make this assumption also claim that the Samaritans are the descendants of foreign pagan inhabitants who were settled in Samaria, adopted the belief in the God of Israel, and were later called Samaritans. On the other hand, if there was no mass exile of the Israelites and most of the inhabitants of the northern kingdom remained in their ancient settlements, the foreigners brought by the Assyrians were a relatively small percentage of the local population and therefore did not have any influence on them. This claim has led some scholars to regard the Samaritans as the descendants and the continuance of the former population in the Kingdom of Israel.

Both of these contradictory assumptions on the origin of the Samaritans ignore the new demographic realities that occurred in the Land of Israel—without any relation to the assumption that most of the inhabitants of the former Kingdom of Israel were exiled from their country or the supposition that only some of them were exiled and that most of them remained in the country. Either way, there was a different situation, with new inhabitants settling in the province of Samaria. Even if their number was not large, they influenced their surroundings, since this was why the Assyrians brought them there. The discussion of the origin of the Samaritans must therefore take into consideration the new situation that was created in the area of Samaria.[24]

Assyrian sources indicate an additional deportation during the reign of King Sennacherib (705–681 BCE). In the campaign, dated to 701 BCE, against the uprising coalition of Syrian and Phoenician kings headed by King Hezekiah of Judah, Sennacherib locked up Hezekiah within Jerusalem: he "besieged forty-six of his fortified walled cities and surrounding smaller towns, which were without number.... Sennacherib, king of Assyria, marched against all the fortified towns of Judah and seized them.... The King took 200,150 people young and old, male and female, horses, mules, donkeys, camels, cattle and sheep, without number and counted them as spoil."[25]

The number 200,150 from Judah is an exaggerated amount of deportees; it is out of proportion to the size of the total population in Judah.[26] According to Bustenai Oded, this large number is the invention of the author. By citing the outsized number of deportees, he is coping with the fact that the king did not conquer Jerusalem and was not able to deport its population.[27]

THE BABYLONIAN EXILE

In contrast to the Assyrians, the strategy of the Babylonian deportation[28] was a one-way policy that included mainly the various levels of the aristocracy and craftsmen in the conquered country, while the lower classes remained behind.[29] Royalty, aristocracy, priestly families, and craftsmen were deported from Judea to Babylon and held there under conditions of captivity in Babylon.

The rest of the deportees were considered as having the Shushanu status. In this status they worked for a number of years on leased lands that belonged to the Babylonians. These lands were later given to them as their property. This status allowed the deportees freedom of movement, social mobility, and the preservation of their ethnic solidarity.[30]

Partial information is available regarding the places in which the exiles settled: Babylon, Sippar, Uruk, Nippur, Āl-Yāḫūdu.[31] In the book of Ezekiel, two geographical locations are mentioned for the places where the exiles resided: 'Nar Kabari and Tel Aviv (Til-Abubi). The books of Ezra and Nehemiah mention Telharsa, Telmelah, Cherub, Addan, and Immer.[32]

According to both the description in the Bible and to historical analysis on the basis of Babylonian records and archaeological excavations, the exile of the inhabitants of Judah to Babylon was conducted in a number of stages or expulsions. These deportations are dated to 597 BCE for the first, with others dated to 587/586 BCE and 582/581 BCE, respectively.

The exile of Jehoiachin and the deportation of 597 BCE. Nebuchadnezzar II, king of Babylon (605–562 BCE), invaded Judah, and Jehoiakim, king of Judah (608–598), became his vassal. After three years, following Jehoiakim's disloyalty, Nebuchadnezzar sent his army against Judah. When Jehoiakim died, his son Jehoiachin succeeded him as king (2 Kgs 24:1–8).[33] After a short reign of three months, Jehoiachin surrendered to Nebuchadnezzar II. Jehoiachin was exiled to Babylon and was replaced by his uncle[34] Mattaniah, whose name was changed to Zedekiah (2 Kgs 24:8–19).

These stormy events described in the Bible are confirmed through the Babylonian Chronicles, the royal Babylonian records that were used for the kings of Babylon. They describe in one sentence the main events of that year.

In Tablet No. 5 in the sentence for the seventh year of Nebuchadnezzar II (597 BCE), it is written that "In the seventh year (of Nebuchadnezzar) in the month Chislev (Nov/Dec) the king of Babylon assembled his army, and after he had invaded the land of Hatti (Syria/Palestine) he laid siege to the city of Judah. On the second day of the month of Adar (16 March) he conquered the city and took the king (Jeconiah) prisoner. He installed in his place a king (Zedekiah) of his own choice, and after he had received rich tribute, he set forth to Babylon."[35]

2 Kings 24:14 reported a total deportation from Jerusalem—"He carried all Jerusalem into exile"—and enumerated the different expatriates from Judah: "King Jehoiachin, his family: mother and wives; his officials and prominent people all were exiled to Babylon" (2 Kgs 24:15). Nebuchadnezzar "exiled all the ministers, all the fighting men, and all the skilled workers and artisans—a total of ten thousand deportees" (2 Kgs 24:14).

In addition, "he took captive to Babylon the entire force of seven thousand fighting men, strong and fit for war, and a thousand skilled workers, craftsmen and metal smiths" (2 Kgs 24:16). Nebuchadnezzar took Jehoiachin captive to Babylon and also took from Jerusalem to Babylon the king's mother, his wives, his officials, and the prominent people of the land. Without pointing out the number of people left in Jerusalem, 2 Kings emphasized that Nebuchadnezzar left a limited size of its population, only the poorest of the land (2 Kgs 24:14).[36]

Jeremiah, summing up the deportations during the reign of Nebuchadnezzar, stated in general, "So Judah went into captivity, away from her land"

(Jer 52:27). Later, he listed the number of people Nebuchadnezzar carried into exile. For the first deportation, during the seventh year of the king, he counted only 3,023 exiled Jews (Jer 52:28).

The exile after the destruction of the Temple in 587 BCE. In addition to the destruction of Jerusalem and the burning of the temple (2 Kgs 25: 8–10), Nebuzaradan, commander of the imperial guard, an official of the king of Babylon, completed the plans of Nebuchadnezzar II by exiling the king, Zedekiah, together with the other people who remained in the city, along with the rest of the populace and those who had deserted to the king of Babylon, leaving behind in Judah the poor people of the land to work in the vineyards and fields (2 Kgs 25:11–12).[37]

Nebuzaradan arrested some higher-position holders and took them to the king in Riblah, where they were executed by the king. Among them were Seraiah the chief priest, Zephaniah the priest next in rank, and the three doorkeepers as well as an officer in charge of the fighting men and five royal advisers. Nebuzaradan also took the secretary, who was the chief officer in charge of conscripting the people of the land, and sixty of the conscripts who were found in the city (2 Kgs 25:18–21).

Again in a general statement, 2 Kings argued "So Judah went into captivity, away from her land." But the biblical text continues by stating that Nebuchadnezzar had left people behind in Judah, and for them he appointed Gedaliah, son of Ahikam, to be over them (2 Kgs 25:22).

The exile after the assassination of Gedaliah son of Ahikam (582 BCE). Jeremiah, in his summation list of deportees exiled during the reign of Nebuchadnezzar, argued that in the twenty-third year, 582 BCE, 745 Jews were taken into exile by Nebuzaradan, the commander of the imperial guard (Jer 52:30). The background of this deportation is related to the anti-Babylonian uprising headed by Ishmael ben Nethaniah, a member of the royal house of David, in cooperation with Baalis, king of the Ammonites,[38] against Gedaliah ben Ahikam, who was appointed by the Babylonians as the governor of Judah. Gedaliah was murdered by the rebels.

Ishmael also killed all the men of Judah who supported Gedaliah and were with him at Mizpah as well as the Babylonian soldiers who were there (Jer 41–43). As a result, some of the rebels fled to Egypt (2 Kgs 25:26), and others were exiled by Nebuzaradan.

Jeremiah lists the numbers of exiles carried in the three deportations dated to Nebuchadnezzar's reign: "In the seventh year, 3,023 Jews; in the eighteenth year, 832 people from Jerusalem; and in his twenty-third year, 745

Jews taken into exile by Nebuzaradan the commander of the imperial guard." He sums up by saying that there were 4,600 people in all.[39]

These low figures for the total number of expatriates in the exiles in Judah contradict the claims "So Judah went into captivity, away from her land" (2 Kgs 25: 21) and "He carried into exile to Babylon the remnant, who escaped from the sword, and they became servants to him and his successors until the kingdom of Persia came to power" (2 Chron 36:20). This conflict raises many questions focused around the subject named "The Empty Land" or "The Total Exile."[40]

At this stage I want to point out that in the descriptions of the exiles from Judah to Babylon, neither the Samaritans nor the population of the former Kingdom of Israel are mentioned at all. In 539 BCE Babylon was conquered by the Persians headed by Cyrus, king of Persia. Unlike Assyria and Babylon, they took a different approach toward their conquered subjects. They preferred to send the exiles back to their previous home countries together with their possessions and the plunder taken from them in the past and to help them to restore their political and religious centers as a means to ensure their loyalty to the Persian kingdom.

The declaration of King Cyrus to the Jewish exiles in Babylon was the first step in the return to Zion and the rebuilding of the Second Temple, which was dedicated in 516 BCE. In view of the economic and religious crisis in Judah during the fifth century BCE, the kings of Persia continued to support the returned exiles. Ezra the Scribe was sent by the king to solve the various difficulties, and later Nehemiah was sent to complete the work of Ezra and to restore Jerusalem.

Ezra 2 lists in detail the people who returned from the captivity of the exiles whom Nebuchadnezzar, king of Babylon, had taken to Babylon. They returned to Jerusalem and Judah, each of them to their own towns (Ezra 2:1). Ezra 2:64–65 sums up the list: "The whole company numbered 42,360, besides their 7,337 male and female slaves; and they also had 200 male and female singers."[41]

We shall now turn to the description of the above events in the major Samaritan Chronicles that are conveyed in the history of the community:[42] (1) *Tulida*, or the Genealogy;[43] (2) the Samaritan Book of Joshua;[44] (3) Abu l' Fath; and (4) Adler-Séligsohn.[45] The main difficulties in using the Samaritan chronicles as historical sources are their late composition and their legendary parts. Some of them were written between the twelfth and fourteenth centuries, relating events dated hundreds of years earlier, and some continued to be written afterward, describing events of their own time.[46]

The *Tulida*, for example, was written in Hebrew by Elazar the priest in 1346, and in later periods it continued to be written and to document the history of the Samaritans until the year 1856.[47] The Samaritan Book of Joshua was written in Arabic, with its first part in the year 1362 and its last part in the year 1513. Its final chapters deal with the events of the Samaritans during the periods of Nebuchadnezzar, Alexander the Great, Hadrian, and other emperors until the days of the Christian emperors.

Abu l' Fath, Ibn Abi al-Hasan al-Samiri al-Danafi, was a fourteenth-century chronicler. His main work, the *Kitab al-Ta'rikh*, a chronicle of the fourteenth century written in Arabic, describes the history of the Samaritans until the year 756. The *Adler Chronicle*, written in Hebrew, describes the history of the Samaritans until 1899.

The main question in regard to the authenticity of the chronicles is whether the parts that are similar to biblical stories or to Talmudic sources are proof of their antiquity or their originality and whether it is possible through them to reconstruct the history of the community.

Adolph Büchler, for example, in his research on the Samaritan Book of Joshua, chapter 47, which is centered on the Samaritans and Hadrian in the second century CE, opposed the main claims for negating the value of this chronicle. In his opinion, despite the late date of the chronicle, we have to examine whether it is completely composed of legendary material without any basis or historical value or perhaps whether some of the descriptions in it at least preserve a reliable historical kernel that allows us to provide more serious consideration to this type of source.[48]

Another perplexity that arises from a study of the chronicles is related to the fact that although the Samaritans recognized and accepted only the Pentateuch and the book of Joshua in the Samaritan version, the chronicles made use of the books of the prophets and, heaven forfend, even of the writings of their archenemy, Josephus Flavius.

James Montgomery, one of the pioneers of Samaritan studies, examined the chronicles and rejected them as historical sources. He argued that they "Add nothing to our scanty knowledge" and that at the most they are "ecclesiastical annals, framed upon a theological scheme of history and with the desire to edify."[49] In contrast to this extreme criticism of the chronicles, Paul Stenhouse a decade ago defended in general the importance of the chronicles and in particular that of the *Kitab al Tarik*.[50]

Despite the profound critique of the authenticity and credibility of the Samaritan Chronicles, Benyamim Tzedaka, a Samaritan from Holon, has recently composed a *Chronicle of the History of the Israelite-Samaritan People*, based primarily on Samaritan sources. The chronicle is written in Hebrew with the vocabulary of the Samaritan Pentateuch.[51]

The Samaritan chronicles review the various exiles and present significant differences between them and the descriptions in the Bible and other sources. I shall briefly summarize the deportations in the late Samaritan sources and examine how these sources adjusted their description to the Samaritan beliefs and attitudes.

The Assyrian exile as testified in the Bible, mainly in 2 Kings 17, raises major difficulties among the Samaritans. The biblical description mentions a "total" expulsion in which the Assyrians make a two-way exchange, leaving the northern kingdom "empty" of its Israelite population and replacing them with people from various places in the Assyrian Empire. One of these places, named Cuthah, is the source for the negative tone of the name "Cuthim," used for the Samaritans by their opponents; this term, with its pejorative connotations, connects the Samaritan community with their possible non-Israelite origins.

Although we can learn from additional biblical and Assyrian sources that some of the population of the northern kingdom was not exiled but remained in the territory of the kingdom under Assyrian rule, the Assyrian chronicles, as we have seen above, present the events of 745–722 BCE in a slightly different manner. They note the conquests of Tiglath-Pileser III and the exile to Assyria of all the Israelites residing in the northern parts of the Kingdom of Israel. They describe Hoshea ben Elah and the reactions of the Assyrians to the contacts between Hoshea and the king of Egypt, Osorkon IV (=So, 730–715/13 BCE).[52] This was interpreted as a rebellion against Assyria and led to a three-year siege of the city of Shomron and the elimination of the northern kingdom and the capital city of Samaria.

For this essay, I shall focus my discussion and arguments mainly on the Samaritan Book of Joshua, chapter 45: "The History of Bokhtonassur (Nebuchadnezzar), the king of el-Mausil (Mosul)."[53] The Samaritan Book of Joshua in chapters 43–44 describes the history of the premonarchic religious center in Shiloh in the eleventh century BCE, under the leadership of Eli, son of Yafni the priest, who is called the "erring man who was envious of the descendant of Finhas the Imam."[54]

The chronological order of the next chapters of the chronicle is unexpected. Chapter 45 deals with Nebuchadnezzar II, who lived in the seventh–sixth centuries BCE. Chapter 46 describes Alexander the Great, the hero of the fourth century BCE, and chapter 47 focuses on the Roman emperor Hadrian, who lived in the second century CE.

Actually, in a chronicle named the "Book of Joshua," the main subjects should be related to the entrance to the land, its occupation, and the settling process. The exceptions in the Samaritan Joshua are very challenging. The more important question is not about the episodes of history that the chronicle cited but rather those stories that were omitted.

The Samaritan Chronicles mostly ignore the Assyrian exiles of the years 721–701 BCE, trying (as discussed above) to separate the Samaritans from the events in the northern kingdom, Israel, apart from some events during these years that support the Samaritan traditions. Therefore, for them the first exile is related to Nebuchadnezzar II, king of Babylon (605–562 BCE), whose name in Jewish history symbolizes the destruction of Jerusalem and the temple and the deportation of the Judean religious and military leadership and its elite to Babylonia.[55] The events in Jerusalem are described in length, since it was an occasion for them to illustrate the destruction of the city el Quds [Jerusalem], the annihilation of its inhabitants, and the peak event of it: the burning of the edifice that was built by King Solomon.

Following the events in Judah, the chronicles shift their description to the north, which is called "our country." The story gets a twist: the chronicles present a Samaritan exile, when the king forced them to leave their places in seven days. "Thereupon he took to goading the people and driving them out unto every country." And "the children of Israel, who now got to the most remote parts of the world, scattered and dispersed throughout the regions east and west." The Samaritan Book of Joshua mentions here that king Nebuchadnezzar II "brought people from el-Furs [Persia] and settled them in this country, the home of the children of Israel." These exiles are mentioned later as those who were driven out from the land.

These descriptions raise some historical questions. First, the dating of the first Samaritan exile is problematical. Nebuchadnezzar II ruled for almost 130 years after the major exile of people from the northern kingdom in 720 BCE. Second, according to biblical and other external sources, Nebuchadnezzar II had no interest in the territory that the Samaritans called "our country." Third, the Babylonians did not use two-way deportations. Therefore, speaking of the above-mentioned Persian deportees as people who were settled in the north is probably the author's imagination based on his knowledge of 2 Kings 17:18–24.

The next verses of the chapter bring together some topics connected with the Samaritans "return" and "restoration." "And God shall scatter thee among all people, from the one end of the earth even unto the other end of the earth" (Deut 28: 64). In the framework of the account of the return and restoration, the author includes letters written by the Persian exiles living in the Samaritan territory, complaining to the king that "The earth is refusing her crops and fruits; for when the fruit promised well, the destroying blight would waste it."

The book of Joshua ignored the episode about the lions and its ending and the aftermath described in 2 Kings 17:25–40 about the lions sent by God that attacked the new population in Samaria, since they did not worship him. In the biblical version, when the Assyrian king heard about the attacking lion, he ordered that a captive Israelite priest who originated from Samaria be sent to teach the new exiles the local religious customs and how to worship God in order to stop the outbreak.

Nevertheless, although the new settlers worshipped the God of Israel, they continued to serve their own gods in accordance with the customs of the nations from which they had been brought: "They would not listen, however, but persisted in their former practices. Even while these people were worshiping the Lord, they were serving their idols. To this day, their children and grandchildren continue to do as their ancestors did" (2 Kgs 17:40–41).

In their version of the book of Joshua, the Samaritans initiated the request for the king's help regarding the drought in their country. The king consulted the Samaritan leaders in exile, who connected the situation in their homeland with their removal and the abandonment in it of the service of their God. They asked him to return them to their land so they could serve God on the Holy Mount. Here again the author of the chronicle is rejecting any ties between them and the "newcomers" brought by the Assyrians to Samaria.

King Nebuchadnezzar II responded to their request and declared, "Go and build the house of thy Lord and offer up the offerings, and serve your Lord as was your custom, and I will assist you." Is this a Nebuchadnezzar II declaration? Can we consider the Babylonian king as an earlier Cyrus?

Cyrus's declaration to the Jews in Babylon represented the general policy of the Persian Empire toward its subjects, most of whom were exiled by the Babylonians. This broad policy was also approved in the Cyrus Cylinder[56] as it applied to the subject nations in order to obtain their loyalty and faithfulness and the cooperation of their religious leadership. This was achieved by allowing the subject nations to return to their homelands, restore the temples that were destroyed by the Babylonians, and take with them all the articles belonging to the temples that were plundered by the Babylonians. However, Cyrus did not expel his subjects, and the return to the homeland was done voluntarily. Those who preferred to stay in Babylon could stay, but they had to support the returnees with silver and gold, with goods and livestock, and with freewill offerings for the temple of God in Jerusalem.

In the cylinder and in the biblical declaration, Cyrus appears as divine messenger: "The great lord Marduk rejoiced in my deeds. Kindly he blessed me, Cyrus, the king, his worshipper, Cambyses, the offspring of my loins, and all of my troops, so that we could go about in peace and well-being." In the Bible, "The Lord, the God of heaven, has given me all the kingdoms of the earth and he has appointed me to build a temple for him at Jerusalem in Judah" (Ezra 1:2; Ezra 2; see also 2 Chronicles 36:23).

Comparing the two declarations creates some major difficulties. The Babylonians used to deport those conquered by them to Babylon. They used to exile the elite of the occupied population in order to exploit their expertise and left behind only the poor population. There is not a single shred of evidence that the Babylonian kings ever permitted exiles to return to their homelands.

The author of the Samaritan Book of Joshua turns King Nebuchadnezzar II into God's messenger, adopting some characteristics of the biblical story about Cyrus and relating them to Nebuchadnezzar II. Though he did not initiate the return of the Samaritan exiles to Shechem, as Cyrus did with the Judeans, he accepted their request to return in order to save their fields.

The author added some details, such as the Samaritans asking the king for letters to all the Samaritan exiles to allow all the deportees to return together to their land. In his letters, the king permitted the expatriates to return to their homeland with his support. He allowed them to return to their holy place, build it up, and sacrifice to God.

In contrast to Cyrus, the Babylonian king urged all of them to assemble their wives and children, take their belongings with them, and leave quickly in order to serve their god who is "Mighty and Powerful."

Unexpectedly, the chronicle also mentioned that among the Samaritan returnees there were also descendants of Judah from the exile to Babylon. According to the chronicle, these Judeans made a proposal to the Samaritans: "We will unite all of us and go to el-Quds [Jerusalem], and build it up, and we will be one word and one soul." But the descendants of Aaron and Joseph, the Samaritans, rejected the proposal and said to them "No, on the contrary, we will go up to the Mount of Blessing and build up the holy place, and we will be one soul and one word."

The author of the Samaritan Book of Joshua based this on a clash dated to 538–521 BCE described in Ezra 4. In this incident, the people who did not leave the land as well as those who were exiled to Samaria by Esarhaddon, king of Assyria, in the mid-seventh century BCE requested the leaders of the return to Zion to let them participate in building the temple in Jerusalem. Their request was rejected, with the argument that "You have no part with us in building a temple to our God. We alone [יחד] will build" (Ezra 4:3).

The interference of these people caused a delay in building the temple during the reign of Cyrus until the days of King Darius I, when the Jews were permitted by the king in 521 BCE to begin the building of the temple in Jerusalem.

The chronicle made use of the story in the book of Ezra but changed the role of its heroes. In the chronicle the Jews were the ones who caused the dispute between the Samaritans and Jews about which site is holier according to the prophet Moses, whether it was Mount Gerizim, the Mount of Blessing, or Jerusalem. And they continued the dispute until it became necessary for the intervention of the king. Zerubbabel and Sanballat came before the king and argued against each other concerning the question of the holiest site: was it Mount Gerizim or Beit el-Muqaddas [Jerusalem]?

The two based their claims on their holy books. The Samaritans centered their arguments on the book of Musa [Moses], in which it is said that the holy and proper place is the Blessed Mount Gerizim. Zerubbabel, on the other hand, relied, according to the Samaritan Book of Joshua, on certain books written after the days of Musa,[57] which designated Beit el-Muqaddas [Jerusalem] as the holy place. Sanballat the Levite argued that Zerubbabel's books were a lie and a fraud. In order to prove this accusation, he asked the king to allow him to throw the books into the fire to see which of them would be burned up.

The king permitted Sanballat to throw the books of Zerubbabel into the fire, and he did so, and they burned up. Zerubbabel, on the other hand, refused to throw the Samaritan book into fire, saying "My books are mine alone, but the Holy Book belongs both to him and to me."

Zerubbabel's refusal was interpreted by the king as fear that his books were false, and he was afraid that Sanballat's book would not burn. However, since Zerubabbel was afraid that the king would put him to death, he took the book and threw it into the fire. The book jumped out of the fire. He cast the book once again, and it was not affected by the fire in the least. The third time he took the book and spat on a paragraph and cast it into the fire, and the place that he had been spat on burned, and then the book sprang out into the bosom of the king. The king then decided in favor of the Samaritan's book.

The king immediately became angry at the children of Yehudah, and right away he put to death 36 souls of those who were present. As for Sanballat and the Samaritans, they were honored by the king, and their leaders were promoted. The king sent them away with the whole multitude of Israel who returned from the exile, and their number was 300,000 men.

The author of the chronicle "purified" the existence of the Persian exiles. According to him, "The king sent unto all the Persians who had taken up residence in their assigned land and removed them from it to their own country." The Samaritans entered into their assigned land, which is their holy place. And they built the sacred apparatus, similar to that which was in the former temple, and offered up a large number of offerings.[58]

Reviewing the dispute between the two recalls the arguments between Jews and Samaritans in Egypt during the Ptolemaic period about the rightful temple. Was the Samaritan author familiar with Josephus's descriptions in *Jewish Antiquities* 12.7–10, 13.74–79?[59] Another question relating to the chronicle concerns the return of the Samaritans to the Samaria region and the building of a sacred apparatus similar to that which was in the former temple. Could this have been evidence that there was a temple on Mount Gerizim?[60]

To sum up, what can be learned from the differences between the biblical sources and the Samaritan chronicles? The writers of the chronicles had to cope mainly with 2 Kings 17, which was perceived as testimony to the origins of the Samaritan community. In order to reject the biblical description, they had to create a different exile, diaspora, and return. On the one hand, they broke off any connection between the Samaritan community and the population that had been exiled from the northern kingdom and never returned, whose places of settlement are unknown. On the other hand, they distanced themselves from the peoples who had been brought by the Assyrians to Samaria and to the area of the northern kingdom after its destruction.

The writers of the chronicles preferred to describe the expulsion twice, the first time in relation to the destruction of Shomron and the second time in relation to the destruction of Jerusalem. On both occasions they return to the area of Mount Gerizim, the first time after seventy-two years and the second time after sixty-five years. On this occasion, 300,000 exiles returned to the Land of Israel.

This is an impossible number, considering the known figures for all the Assyrian and Babylonian exiles. The exaggeration is again intended to break off any connection with the foreign population brought by the Assyrians after the destruction of Shomron, since whatever the number might be, they were still the main population in the area. Besides this, the second exile does not make sense, since the Babylonian king Nebuchadnezzar had no interest at all in the former northern kingdom; therefore, to link his name with the exile of hundreds of thousands from its area is incomprehensible.

These remarks and the matters we dealt with above oblige us to reject some of the descriptions in the chronicles and return to the question of the origin of the Samaritan community through a discussion of what happened to the Israelite population that remained in the northern kingdom and the foreign population brought by the Assyrians into the area of the northern kingdom.

NOTES

1. Gary N. Knoppers, "Cutheans or Children of Jacob? The Issue of Samaritan Origins in 2 Kings 17," in *Reflection and Refraction: Studies in Biblical Historiography in Honour of A. Graeme Auld*, ed. R. Rezetko, T. H. Lim, W. B. Aucker (Leiden: Brill, 2007), 223–39; Gary N. Knoppers, "Samaritan Conceptions of Jewish Origins and Jewish Conceptions of Samaritan Origins: Any Common Ground?," in *Die Samaritaner und die Bible Historische und Literarische Wechselwirkungen zwischen biblischen und samaritanischen Traditionen* [*The Samaritans and the Bible: Historical and Literary Interactions between Biblical and Samaritan Traditions*], ed. J. Frey, U. Schattner-Rieser, K. Schmid; Berlin: De Gruyter, 2012), 81–118; Reinhard Pummer, "Samaritanism: A Jewish Sect or an Independent Form of Yahwism?," in *Samaritans: Past and Present; Current Studies*, ed. M. Mor and F. V. Reiterer (Berlin: De Gruyter, 2010), 1–24.

2. *A. B. Samaritan News* 605 (1994): 18.

3. Alan David Crown, "The Samaritan Diaspora," in *The Samaritans*, ed. Alan David Crown (Tübingen: J. C. B. Mohr, 1989), 195–217; Martina Böhm, "Samaritanische Diaspora im Imperium Romanum bis 200 n. Chr.," in *Juden, Christen, Heiden? Religiöse Inklusion und Exklusion in Kleinasien bis Decius*, ed. S. Alkier and H. Lippi (Tübingen: Mohr Siebeck, 2018), 171–96.

4. Reinhard Pummer, "The Samaritans in Egypt," in *Etudes sémitiques et samaritaines, offertes à Jean Margain*, ed. C.-B. Amphoux, A. Frey, and U. Schattner-Rieser (Lausanne: du Zèbre, 1998), 213–32; Orsolina Montevecchi, "Samaria e Samaritani in Egitto," *Aegyptus* 76, nos. 1–2 (1996): 81–92.

5. See Josephus, *Jewish Antiquities*, 13:74–79.

6. Arutiun Sizefrovich Zhamkochian, "Samaritans in Cairo: An Extinct Community Underestimated," in *Samaritan Researches: Proceedings of the Congress of the Société d'Études Samaritaines*, V [Milan, 1996] and of the Special Section of the ICANAS Congress [Budapest, 1997], ed. V. Morabito, A. D. Crown, and L. Davey (Sydney: Mandelbaum, 2000), 1.48–1.50.

7. Vittorio Morabito, "The Samaritans in Sicily and the Inscription in a Probable Synagogue in Syracuse," in *New Samaritan Studies of the Société d'Études Samaritaines*,

Vols. 3–4, *Proceedings of the Congresses of Oxford 1990 and Paris 1992: Essays in Honour of G. D. Sixdenier*, ed. A. D. Crown and L. Davey (Sydney: Mandelbaum, 1995), 237–58.

8. Philippe Brueneau, "'Les Israelites de Delos' et la Juiverie Delienne," *Bulletin de Correspondance Hellenique* 106 (1982): 465–504; Thomas A. Kraabel, "New Evidence of the Samaritan Diaspora Has Been Found on Delos," *Biblical Archaeologist* 47, no. 1 (1984): 44–46; Michael L. White, "The Delos Synagogue Revisited: Recent Fieldwork in the Graeco-Roman Diaspora," *Harvard Theological Review* 80 (1987): 133–60; Monika Trümper, "The Oldest Original Synagogue Building in the Diaspora: The Delos Synagogue Reconsidered," *Hesperia* 73 (2004): 513–98; Lidia Matassa, "Unravelling the Myth of the Synagogue on Delos," *Bulletin of the Anglo-Israel Archaeological Society* 25 (2007): 81–115; Magnar Kartveit, "Samaritan Self-Consciousness in the First Half of the Second Century B.C.E. in Light of the Inscriptions from Mount Gerizim and Delos," *Journal for the Study of Judaism in the Persian, Hellenistic and Roman Period* 45, nos. 4–5 (2014): 449–70.

9. Baruch Lifshitz and Jacob Schiby, "Une synagogue samaritaine à Thessalonique,"*Revue Biblique* 75 (1968): 368–78; Jacob Schibi, "A Samaritan Community in Thessaloniki" [Hebrew], *Zion* 42, nos. 1–2 (1977): 103–9.

10. Reinhard Pummer, "The Samaritans in Damascus," in *Samaritan: Hebrew and Aramaic Studies Presented to Professor Abraham Tal*, ed. M. Bar-Asher and M. Florentin (Jerusalem: Bialik Institute, 2005), 53–76.

11. Bustenay Oded, *Mass Deportation and Deportees in the Neo-Assyrian Empire* (Wiesbaden: Reichert, 1979); Bustenay Oded, *The Early History of the Babylonian Exile (8th–6th Centuries B.C.E.)* [Hebrew] (Haifa: Pardes Publishing House, 2010); Nadav Na'aman, "Population Changes in Palestine following Assyrian Deportations," in Nadav Na'aman, *Ancient Israel and Its Neighbors: Interaction and Counteraction; Collected Essays*, Vol. 1 (Winona Lake, IN: Eisenbrauns, 2005), 200–219.

12. Mordechai Cogan, *The Ranging Torrent: Historical Inscriptions from Assyria and Babylonia relating to Ancient Israel*, 2nd updated and expanded edition (Jerusalem: Carta, 2013). See also Mordechai Cogan, *Bound for Exile: Israelites and Judeans under Imperial Yoke: Documents from Assyria and Babylonia* (Jerusalem: Carta, 2015), 83–85, no. 4.10.

13. *2 Kings* 17:1–6; Cogan, *The Raging Torrent*, 89–90.

14. Andreas Fuchs, *Die Inschriften Sargons II. aus Khorsabad* (Göttingen: Cuvillier, 1994).

15. Cogan, *The Raging Torrent*, 90–92; Cogan, *Bound for Exile*, 42–43.

16. Cogan, *The Raging Torrent*, 96–99.

17. Haim Tadmor, "The Campaigns of Sargon II of Assur: A Chronological-Historical Study," in *"With My Many Chariots I Have Gone Up the Heights of Mountains": Historical and Literary Studies on Ancient Mesopotamia and Israel*, ed. M. Cogan (Jerusalem: Israel Exploration Society, 2011), 239–319; Amitai Baruchi-Unna and Mordechai Cogan, "The Cylinder Inscription of Sargon II from Khorsabad: Re-Examined in Light of a New Manuscript in the Israel Museum, Jerusalem" [Hebrew], *Beth Mikra* 62, no. 1 (2017): 16–40.

18. Cogan, *The Raging Torrent*, 96.

19. Tadmor, "Campaigns of Sargon II."

20. Cogan, *The Raging Torrent*, 99–104, Text 5.03, The Cylinder Inscription No.1: "Tamudi Ibadidi Marsimani Ḫayappâa, and whose remainder I transferred and set down in the land of Bit-Humria."

21. Israel Eph'al, "Esarhaddon, Egypt, and Shubria: Politics and Propaganda," *Journal of Cuneiform Studies* 57 (2005): 99–111; Mordechai Cogan, "For We, Like You, Worship Your God: Three Biblical Portrayals of Samaritan Origins," *Vetus Testamentum* 38, no. 3 (1988): 286–92; Zvi Ron, "The First Confrontation with the Samaritans (Ezra 4)," *Jewish Bible Quarterly* 43, no. 2 (2015): 117–21.

22. Cogan, *The Raging Torrent*, 99, 175–76.

23. Ibid., 83–84, No. 4.10.

24. Nadav Na'aman, "Population Changes in Palestine Following Assyrian Deportations," in Nadav Na'aman, *Ancient Israel and Its Neighbors: Interaction and Counteraction: Collected Essays,* Vol. 1 (Winona Lake, IN: Eisenbrauns, 2005), 200–219.

25. Cogan, *The Raging Torrent*, 121, No 6.01: The *Rassam Cylinder*, lines 49–54. See 2 Kings 18:13: "Now in the fourteenth year of king Hezekiah did Sennacherib king of Assyria come up against all the fenced cities of Judah, and took them."

26. Oded Borowski, "Sennacherib in Judah: The Devastating Consequences of an Assyrian Military Campaign," *Eretz-Israel: Archaeological, Historical and Geographical Studies* 33 (2018): 33–40; Mordechai Cogan, "Cross-Examining the Assyrian Witnesses to Sennacherib's Third Campaign: Assessing the Limits of Historical Reconstruction," in *Sennacherib at the Gates of Jerusalem: Story, History and Historiography*, ed. I. Kalimi and S. Richardson (Leiden: Brill, 2014), 51–74; David Ussishkin, "Sennacherib's Campaign to Judah: The Archaeological Perspective with an Emphasis on Lachish and Jerusalem," in *Sennacherib at the Gates of Jerusalem: Story, History and Historiography*, 75–103.

27. See Oded, *The Early History of the Babylonian Exile*, 31 n20. See also Ziony Zevit, "Implicit Population Figures and Historical Sense: What Happened to 200,150 Judahites in 701 BCE?," in *Confronting the Past: Archaeological and Historical Essays on Ancient Israel in Honor of William G. Dever,* ed. S. Gitin, J. E. Wright, and J. P. Dessel (Winona Lake, IN: Eisenbrauns, 2006), 359–66; Frederick Mario Fales, "The Road to Judah: 701 B.C.E. in the Context of Sennacherib's Political-Military Strategy," in *Sennacherib at the Gates of Jerusalem,* 223–48.

28. For extensive studies on the Babylonian exile, see Rainer Albertz, *Israel in Exile: The History and Literature of the Sixth Century B.C.E.,* trans. David Green (Atlanta: Society of Biblical Literature, 2003); Oded Lipschitz, *The Fall and Rise of Jerusalem: Judah under Babylonian Rule* (Winona Lake, IN: Eisenbrauns, 2005); Oded, *The Early History of the Babylonian Exile*; Avraham Faust, *Judah in the Neo-Babylonian Period: The Archaeology of Desolation* (Atlanta: Society of Biblical Literature, 2012); Tero Alstola, "Judeans in Babylonia: A Study of Deportees in the Sixth and Fifth Centuries BCE," PhD diss., University of Helsinki, 2018.

29. David S. Vanderhooft, "Babylonian Strategies of Imperial Control in the West: Royal Practice and Rhetoric," in *Judah and the Judeans in the Neo-Babylonian Period*, ed. O. Lipschits and J. Blenkinsopp (Winona Lake, IN: Eisenbrauns, 2003), 235–62; Francis Joannès and André Lemaire, "Trois tablettes cunéiformes à onomastique ouest-sémitique (collection Sh. Moussaïeff)," *Transeuphratène* 17 (1999): 17–34.

30. Laurie E. Pearce, "'Judean': A Special Status in Neo-Babylonian and Achemenid Babylonia?," in *Judah and the Judeans in the Achaemenid Period: Negotiating Identity in an International Context*, ed. Oded Lipschits, Gary N. Knoppers, and Manfred Oeming (Winona Lake, IN: Eisenbrauns, 2011), 267–77.

31. See the essay in this volume by Jean-Philippe Delorme. For the documents, see Laurie Pearce and Cornelia Wunsch, *Documents of Judean Exiles and West Semites in Babylonia in the Collection of David Sofer* (Bethesda, MD: CDL Press, 2014). See also Wayne Horowitz et al., *By the Rivers of Babylon: Cuneiform Documents from the Beginnings of the Babylonian Diaspora* (Jerusalem: Museum of the Biblical Land, Israel Exploration Society, 2015).

32. Bustenay Oded, "The Beginning of the Babylonian Diaspora: Organization and Economy," in *Studies in the History and Culture of the Jews in Babylonia: Proceedings of the Second International Congress for Babylonian Jewry Research (June 1998)*, ed. Y. Avishur and Z. Yehuda (Or-Yehuda: Babylonian Jewry Heritage Center, 2002), 121–35.

33. See 2 Chronicles 36:6–10. Jehoiakim was taken as a captive to Babylon, and his son Jehoiachin was his heir and successor in Judah.

34. 2 Chronicles 36:10: "his brother."

35. No 24 WA21946, The Babylonian Chronicles, The British Museum; ABC 5 (Jerusalem Chronicle); Jona Lendering, Livius.org, retrieved May 31, 2017; Kirk A. Grayson, *Assyrian and Babylonian Chronicles* (Locust Valley: J. J. Augustin, 1975); Jean-Jacques Glassner and Benjamin Read Foster, *Mesopotamian Chronicles*) Leiden: Brill, 2004): "(11) In the seventh year [598/597] in the month of Kislev (November/December), the king of Akkad mustered his troops, and marched to the Hatti-land. (12) He besieged the city Judah and in the month of Addaru (February/March) on the second day [February/March 597] he seized the city. He took the king captive [Jehoiachin; cf. Jeremish 2 52:28–30; King 24.8–17 (13)]. He appointed there a king after his own heart. He imposed heavy tribute and took to Babylon."

36. See also Jeremiah 24:1, 27:20, 29:2.

37. See Jeremiah 39:10: "But Nebuzaradan the commander of the guard left behind in the land of Judah some of the poor people, who owned nothing; and at that time he gave them vineyards and fields."

38. Bob Becking, "Ballis the King of the Ammonites: An Epigraphical Note on Jeremiah 40:14," *Journal of Semitic Studies* 38, no. 1 (1993): 15–24.

39. For a discussion on the difficulties related to the numbers of deportees, see Albertz, *Israel in Exile*, 81–90.

40. We are unable to deal with these important issues here. See Hans M. Barstad, *The Myth of the Empty Land: A Study in the History and Archaeology of Judah during the "Exilic" Period* (Oslo: Scandinavian University Press, 1996); "The Myth of the Empty Land Revisited," Part 1 in *Judah and the Judeans in the Neo-Babylonian Period*, ed. O. Lipschits and J. Blenkinsopp (Winona Lake, IN: Eisenbrauns, 2003), 3–89.

41. Nehemiah 7:6: "These are the people of the province who came up from the captivity of the exiles whom Nebuchadnezzar king of Babylon had taken captive and they returned to Jerusalem and Judah, each to his own town." And Nehemiah 7:66: "The whole company numbered 42,360, besides their 7,337 male and female slaves; and they also had 245 male and female singers."

42. Paul Stenhouse, "Samaritan Chronicles," in *The Samaritans*, ed. Alan D. Crown (Tübingen: J. C. B. Mohr, 1989), 218–65; John Bowman, *Samaritan Documents Relating to Their History, Religion and Life*, trans. and ed. J. Bowman (Pittsburgh: Pickwick. 1977); Robert T. Anderson and Terry Giles, *Tradition Kept: The Literature of the Samaritans* (Peabody: Hendrickson Publisher 2005).

43. Mosheh Florenṭin, *The Tulida: A Samaritan Chronicle; Text, Translation Commentary* [Hebrew] (Jerusalem: Yitzhak Ben Zvi. 1999); John Bowman, *Transcript of the Original Text of the Samaritan Chronicle Tolidah* (Leeds, UK: University of Leeds, 1954).

44. Oliver Turnbull Crane, *The Samaritan Chronicle, or the Book of Joshua, the Son of Nun* (New York: John B. Alden, 1890); T. W. J. Juynboll, *Chronicon samaritanum* (Leiden: S. & J. Luchtmans, 1848); Theodor Willem Johann Juynboll, *Chronicon Samaritanum, arabice conscriptur cui titulus est Liber Josuae* [Arabic and Latin] (Lugdunum Batavorum: Luchtmans, 1848).

45. Elkan Nathan Adler and Max Séligsohn, "Une nouvelle chronique samaritaine," *Revue des études juives* 44 (1902): 118–222; 45 (1902): 70–98, 160, 223–54; 46 (1903): 123–46.

46. Stenhouse, "Samaritan Chronicles," 11.

47. Florenṭin, *The Tulida*, 39.

48. Adolph Büchler, "The Samaritans Participation in the Bar Kokhba Revolt." The article was first published in the Hungarian journal *Magyar-Szido Szemle* 14 (1897): 36–47. It was later translated and republished in Hebrew in the collection edited by Aharon Oppenheimer, *The Bar Kokhba Revolt: Collection of Articles* (Jerusalem: Shazar Center, 1980), 115–21.

49. James Alan Montgomery, *The Samaritans, the Earliest Jewish Sect: Their History, Theology and Literature* (1907; reprint, Eugene, OR: Wipf and Stock, 2006), 311: "The inspired traditions of the ignorant and debased community have preserved just such legends as please the ecclesiastical appetite of a provincial sect whose life was intentionally lived apart from the world. Indeed we must bear in mind that what we posses are ecclesiastical annals, framed upon a theological scheme of history and with the desire to edify;

hence not to expect history in our sense of the word. When at last the keen Arabic spirit of historical research infected the Samaritans, so worthy and honest a chronicler as Abul Fath had little more to build upon than a residuum of inane traditions."

50. See Paul Stenhouse, "Surviving Samaritan Literature and the Sources of Abu 'l-Fath's Chronicle," in *Samaritan, Hebrew and Aramaic Studies Presented to Professor Abraham Tal*, ed. M. Bar-Asher and M. Florentin (Jerusalem: Bialik Institute, 2005), 105–45.

51. Benyamim Tzedaka, *Chronicle of the History of the Israelite-Samaritan People Based on Their Own Sources: From the Entrance of the People of Israel to the Land of Canaan until 2015 CE [3654 Years]* [Hebrew] (Holon: A. B. Institute of Samaritan Studies Press, 2016).

52. 2 Kings 17:4: "But the king of Assyria discovered that Hoshea was a traitor, for he had sent envoys to So, king of Egypt, and he no longer paid tribute to the king of Assyria, as he had done year by year. Therefore Shalmaneser seized him and put him in prison."

53. See note 47 above. I used Crane's English translation.

54. The events are described in 1 Samuel 2–4.

55. In the chronicles, Nebuchadnezzar II, king of Babylon, is a king of the Persians. See *The Samaritan Book of Joshua*, chap. 45.

56. A new translation of the Cyrus Cylinder, by Piotr Michalowski, was published in Mark Chavalas, ed., *Historical Sources in Translation: The Ancient Near East* (Williston, VT: Blackwell, 2006), 428–29, reproduced with the permission of the authors and publisher. Collection online, The Cyrus Cylinder, Museum number 90920; See: Irving Finkel, ed., *The Cyrus Cylinder, The King of Persia's Proclamation from Ancient Babylon* (London: I. B. Tauris, 2013).

57. The author of the Samaritan Book of Joshua is describing here an anachronistic interpretation that the Samaritans accepted only the five books of the Torah, while the Jews accepted the Tanach (the entire Bible—the Pentateuch, Prophets, and Hagiographa).

58. See Anderson and Giles, *Tradition Kept*, 129–31. See also Stenhouse, "Samaritan Chronicles," 85–93; Anderson and Giles, *Tradition Kept*, 164–68. The meeting was in Haran, and the king was Surdi. The leaders who met the king were Sanballat the Levite, the Samaritan leader, and Zerubabel, the Judean leader (Anderson and Giles, *Tradition Kept*, 231–32). The people who were left were exiled to the cities of Babylon (Anderson and Giles, *Tradition Kept*, 232–34; Bowman, *Samaritan Documents*, 99–100).

59. Reinhard Pummer, *The Samaritans in Flavius Josephus* (Tübingen: Mohr Siebeck, 2009), 179–99. Pummer argues that what we have before us is a "combination of the accounts in the letter of Aristeas and in Josephus with the outcome reserved."

60. On the question of the existence of a Samaritan Temple, see Reinhard Pummer, "Was There an Altar or a Temple in the Sacred Precinct on Mt. Gerizim?," *Journal for the Study of Judaism in the Persian, Hellenistic and Roman Period* 47, no. 1 (2016): 1–21.

The Āl-Yāḫūdu Texts (ca. 572–477 BCE): A New Window into the Life of the Judean Exilic Community of Babylonia

Jean-Philippe Delorme

Exilic experiences epitomize life-changing moments for both individuals and larger communities, as they radically disturb the collective consciousness of displaced populations and represent major historical junctures that introduce extensive sociocultural adjustments. Precarious economic conditions and a minority status impel exilic communities to become more inclusive and to integrate into the host culture in order to survive. While this greatly facilitates their survival, it also exposes their culture and identity to foreign influences, as both will gradually begin to change. Jewish history provides a wealth of material for investigating the effects of exilic experiences. Although its course is punctuated by numerous such events from which to choose, none had more impact than the Babylonian exile (ca. 597 and 586 BCE). The beginning of the era of Babylonian captivity brought the curtain down on the First Temple period (ca. 1200–586 BCE) and triggered reflections and adjustments that led to the creation and/or growing importance of several constitutive aspects of modern-day Judaism (e.g., diasporas, Sabbath, synagogue, circumcision). For D. Smith-Christopher, "the specific Babylonian exile must be appreciated as both a historical human disaster and a disaster that gave rise to a variety of social and religious responses with significant social and religious consequences."[1]

The effects of the Babylonian exile are far-reaching and considerably reconfigured the prevailing social order. New figures of authority (i.e., prophets, elders, priests) superseded former traditional leadership, while kinship became an important social structural anchor that contributed to the safeguarding of religious and cultural traditions. Contacts with foreigners were intensified and predisposed the exilic community to assimilation, even though deportees now consciously felt that they belonged to a distinctive group (i.e., Judean) and explicitly manifested their belonging.[2] The Babylonian exile thus established the necessary conditions that triggered extensive reforms, especially in regard to social, cultural, and religious traditions.

Scholarly discussion of this period continues to focus on its consequences and often neglects other areas of investigation. The available sources rarely offer insights into other subjects, which significantly restrict the orientation of academic research. Some of these sources are also of doubtful historical reliability (i.e., the books of Ezekiel, Jeremiah, Ezra, and Nehemiah), while others postdate by more than a hundred years the beginning of the exilic period (e.g., Murašu texts, ca. 454–404 BCE).[3] In sum, scholarly reconstructions exclusively rely on biblical evidence of debatable accuracy and on a generalization of conditions prevailing later in Jewish history.

The recent publication of the Āl-Yāḫūdu texts directly answers to these shortcomings by allowing research into the daily reality of Judean deportees as well as by reducing the chronological gap between the beginning of the exilic period in 597 BCE and our first textual witness to about twenty-five years.[4] The evidence gathered from this new corpus contradicts previous assertions concerning the conditions under which the Babylonian exilic community lived and compels us to readjust our vision of this crucial period. Deportees were in fact able to live a quiet and undisturbed life in southern Babylonia, while Judean identity thrived and prospered. Three facts explain why and how the Babylonian exilic community was able to retain its ties with previous forms of identity as well as to perpetuate them over time. First, Babylonian deportation and economic policies favored the survival of small ethnic communities. Second, the names of the small settlements created for the sole purpose of accommodating deported communities acted as mementos of their respective histories and contributed to the survival of their former identity. Third, personal names/onomastic evidence demonstrate that the site of Āl-Yāḫūdu was inhabited mostly by Judean individuals and that Judean culture was flourishing in southern Babylonia.

THE ARCHIVE

The Āl-Yāḫūdu texts are part of a group of unprovenanced cuneiform tablets belonging to the private collection of David Sofer, published in 2014 by Laurie E. Pearce and Cornelia Wunsch.[5] This group of cuneiform tablets comprises three distinct private archives that amount to a total of 103 economic texts dated to the Neo-Babylonian and Achaemenid periods (ca. 572–477 BCE). The three private archives are that of Aḫīqam of Āl-Yāḫūdu (52.4%, 54 tablets),[6] Aḫīqar of Bīt-Našar (45.6%, 47 tablets),[7] and the royal official Zababa-šarru-uṣur from Bīt-Abī-râm (2%, 2 tablets).[8]

The precise location of these three settlements remains unknown, but circumstantial evidence favors the region of Nippur, east and southeast of Babylon

The Āl-Yāḫūdu Texts (ca. 572–477 BCE)   73

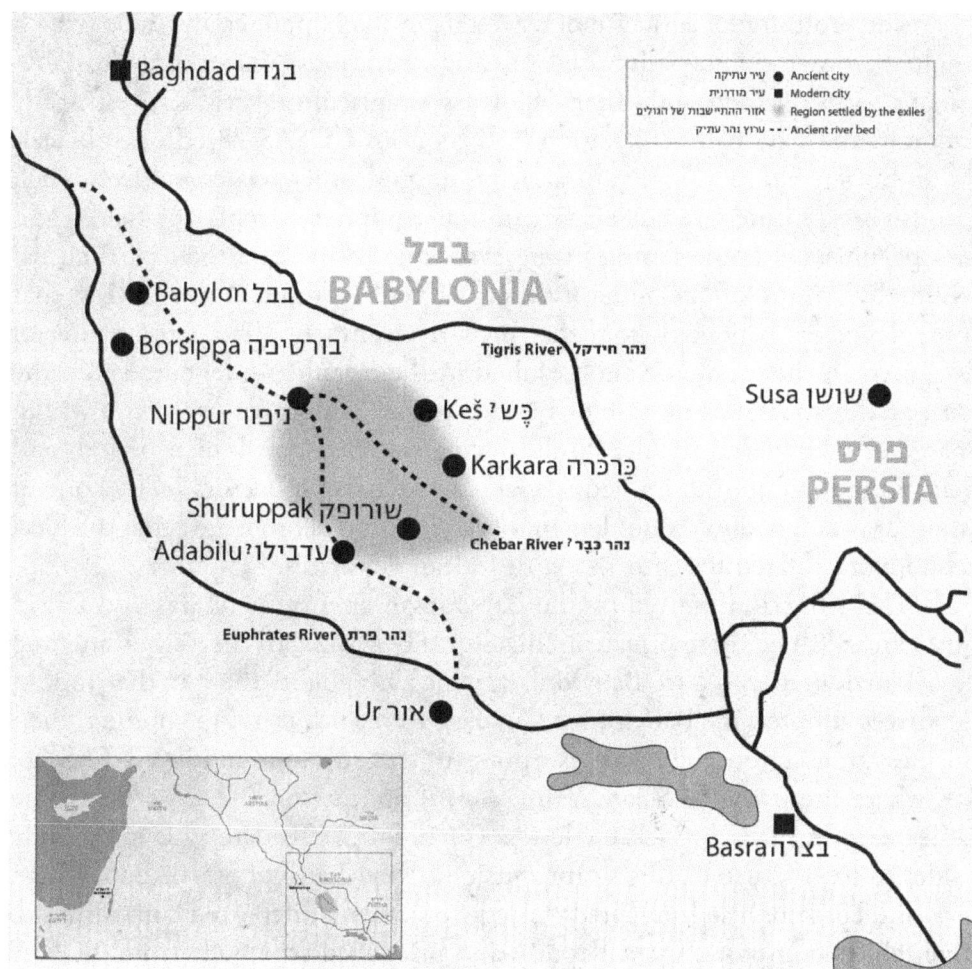

Figure 4.1 Map of southern Mesopotamia with focus on the region likely settled by Judean exiles. Courtesy of the Bible Lands Museum Jerusalem. The map is displayed in the exhibition *Jerusalem in Babylon* at the Bible Lands Museum Jerusalem. A virtual tour of the exhibition is available at http://www.blmj.org/.

between the Tigris and the southern marshlands (Figure 4.1).[9] Nippur served as an Assyrian outpost in Babylonia during the last years of the Neo-Assyrian Empire and was one of the last southern cities to submit to Nabopolassar (ca. 622–620 BCE), the first Chaldean king.[10] There ensued a voluntary negligence of this area, especially in the early years of the Neo-Babylonian Empire.[11] This may have led to a state of decrepitude, which Chaldean kings eventually tried to counter with the settlement of foreigners/exiles in the countryside and their inclusion into the land-for-service/bow fief system [*bīt azanni/bīt qašti*].[12]

The profusion of agricultural real estate in the Nippur countryside, which resulted from the above-discussed historic conditions, did encourage Babylonians to use Judean and other deportees as agricultural workers, especially for grain and date palm cultivation.[13] Texts from CUSAS 28 reflect this reality and often mention agricultural activities and other related subjects, such as business ventures, rental of agricultural equipment, rental of fields, and *ilku* payments.[14] Some families were even able to increase their patrimonial wealth by means of the intensification of cereal production, showing that some deportees benefited from their new environment. The participation of foreigners in the local economy resulted in their gradual integration into the local administration. The case of Bēl-šarru-uṣur/Yāhû-šarru-uṣur, who was in charge of a bow land in Āl-Yāhūdu during the Neo-Babylonian period, and that of the three Judean individuals who acted as tax collectors [*dēkû*], one of whom was assigned to the settlement of Āl-Yāhūdu, demonstrate that the local economy facilitated the integration of Judean deportees.[15]

The attraction exerted by the Babylonian environment was also felt in other areas.[16] The three private archives of CUSAS 28 are all written in good Neo-Babylonian and Late Babylonian, which highlights the fact that Judean deportees adopted the Babylonian language to record, if not to conduct, their business transactions. The sole exception to this rule is found in CUSAS 28: 10, where the name of Šalam-Yāhû [*šlmyh*] appears on the left edge of the tablet written in Paleo-Hebrew letters (Figure 4.2). To date, this is the only evidence for the use of this script outside of the Land of Israel. Babylonian laws and customs also integrated the legal practices of deported communities. Two tablets composed in Āl-Yāhūdu and published separately from CUSAS 28 display a rigid adherence to the Babylonian model. The inheritance division between the sons of Aḥīqam and the marriage contract of Nanaya-kānat

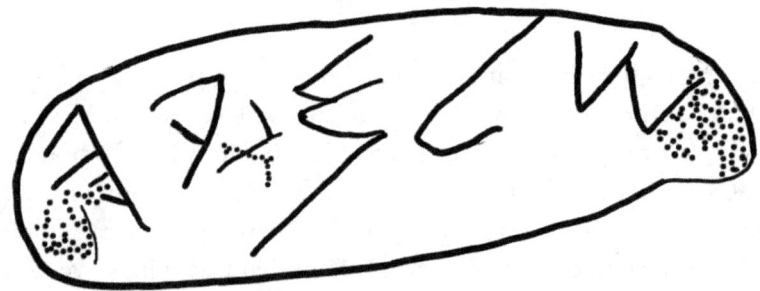

Figure 4.2 Paleo-Hebrew Script on CUSAS 28: 10. Credit Laurie E. Pearce.

are both couched in and respect local Babylonian legal customs for their respective matter.[17]

The attraction wielded by Babylonian culture on the Judean exilic community was indeed strong and unconscious. Despite evidence of early integration, especially in the economic realm, the inhabitants of Āl-Yāḫūdu were able to maintain their own identity and strengthen their attachment to their distinctive culture. As curious as it may sound, Babylonian deportation policies were directly responsible for establishing the necessary conditions for the survival of Judean identity in southern Babylonia.

DEPORTATION POLICIES AND THEIR IMPACT ON THE FATE OF THE JUDEAN EXILIC COMMUNITY

The deportation of conquered populations has a long history in the ancient Near East. This practice started to gain in popularity over the course of the Neo-Assyrian period, especially under the reigns of Tiglath-Pileser III (744–727 BCE), Sargon II (721–705 BCE), and Sennacherib (704–681 BCE).[18] Assyrians were particularly fond of two-way deportations, which became one of the hallmarks of this period. Two-way deportation entails the removal of a group from its homeland while another group is simultaneously brought in to ensure that newly acquired territories remain loyal, seamlessly integrate into the Assyrian provincial system, and contribute to the economic prosperity of the empire. Deported populations were relocated either in major urban centers of the Assyrian heartland (Aššur, Calaḫ, Nineveh, Dur-Šarrukin), in peripheral regions, or along the frontier.[19] Assyrians never built new settlements to accommodate the arrival of foreigners, even though these groups may have contributed and been used to revitalize devastated and abandoned areas.[20]

Neo-Assyrian administration used deportations as a tool to meet the following goals: (1) to punish rebellion, (2) to weaken centers of resistance, (3) to ensure the loyalty of deportees, (4) for military conscription, (5) as a source of craftsmen and laborers, (6) to populate urban centers and strategic sites, and (7) to help repopulate abandoned and devastated regions.[21] Deportees represented an abundant workforce free of any charge, and the vast majority were used either for agricultural work to meet the increasing demands of a fast-growing empire or as forced manual labor in the numerous colossal building projects of Assyrian kings.[22] Only a select few served in the military or acted as royal officials.

In 720 BCE Assyrian forces captured Samaria, the capital of the Kingdom of Israel, and deported a large portion of its population.[23] If the numbers

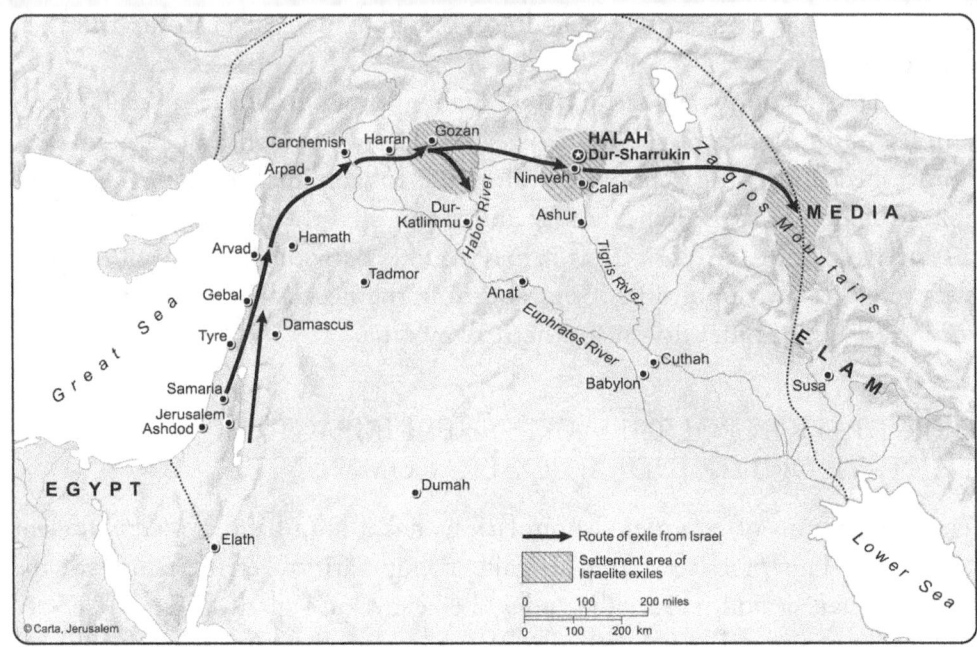

Figure 4.3 The Israelite exile of 720 BCE. Mordechai Cogan, *Bound for Exile*. Map courtesy of Carta Jerusalem.

preserved in the inscriptions of Sargon II are accurate, about 27,290 individuals were taken away.[24] 2 Kings 17:6 and 18:11 state that Israelites made the journey to Assyria, where they were resettled in Halah, on the Habor—the river of Gozan—and in the cities of Media.[25] 2 Kings 17:24 adds that people of Babylon, Cutha, Avva, Hamath, and Sepharvaim made the reverse journey to Samaria. Biblical evidence thus confirms the aims and nature of Assyrian deportation policies, since Israelites were relocated in major urban centers (Calaḫ), in the periphery (Habor and Gozan), and in frontier zones (Media), while diverse foreign populations were brought in to pacify the region (Figure 4.3). Israelite deportees were employed as agricultural workers or forced laborers, with limited integration into the military and the royal court.[26] With the passing of time, Israelites gradually assimilated to Assyrian culture and eventually vanished by the end of the Neo-Assyrian period.[27]

Neo-Babylonian deportation policies adopted the same rationale as the Assyrians, albeit with one key difference: two-way deportation was never enforced.[28] Babylonians were never interested in investing in newly conquered territories or in the elaboration of a vast provincial system. The complete destruction of Ashkelon on the Philistine coast by the armies of Nebuchadnezzar II in 603 BCE should be interpreted as concrete evidence of their lack of interest in the southern Levant.[29] Deportees therefore exclusively took the direction of Babylonia, where they were settled in specific enclaves, especially in the region south of Babylon. Nebuchadnezzar II's ambition to transform Babylon into the capital of the world may perhaps explain this new orientation.[30]

Exiles were therefore brought to Babylonia principally to be employed as agricultural workers to stimulate the local economy. The former status of the region of Nippur (i.e., relative abandonment) rendered the area most attractive, as it became one of the main recipients of the influx of deportees. Evidence for the presence of Judean exiles does locate them in Babylonia, as they appear in texts from Babylon, Uruk, Sippar, Borsippa, and in the vicinity of Nippur (i.e., Āl-Yāḫūdu).[31] The names of several toponyms in the latter region confirm the existence and the presence of deported communities, as they are composed either of foreign idioms (e.g., Āl-Yāḫūdu, Bīt-Našar), the words *galû/galūtu* [exiles or exile], or ethnic names of deported communities (e.g., Arbāya, Ṣurrāya [Arabs, Tyrians]).[32]

The establishment of these villages as an answer to the poor state of the local economy had as an indirect result the creation of isolated ethnic enclaves, which in turn encouraged the survival of foreign cultural hubs in southern Babylonia. The example of the village of Āl-Yāḫūdu illustrates the impact of Babylonian economic policies for the survival of foreign communities in Babylonia. Not only did the names of these settlements echo a past of political and cultural independence, they also reflected the origins and cultures of their respective inhabitants.

ĀL-YAḪŪDU AS AN ANCIENT "LIEU DE MÉMOIRE"

Numerous villages located in the environs of Nippur owed their existence to Neo-Babylonian deportation and economic policies. The sites of Ālu ša Arbāya, Ālu ša Nērabāya, Bīt-Ṣurāya, Bīt-Tabalāya, Āl-Miṣirāya, and Ḫazatu represent, respectively, communities of Arab, Neirabite, Tyrian, Tabalite, Egyptian, and Gazaite deportees.[33] Their appearances in Neo-Babylonian documents postdate the conquest of their respective homelands, which confirms that they are indeed new settlements located in southern Babylonia and not in their country of origin.[34] For instance, the settlement of Āl-Yāḫūdu is first mentioned in a document dated to 572 BCE, which is fourteen years after the second large deportation that followed the destruction of the temple of Jerusalem in 586 BCE.

While the names of these settlements seem rather trivial at first glance, especially when investigating the impact of the exilic period upon the various deported communities, they in fact conceal invaluable information for understanding the dynamics of identity in imperial context. These names fit into two distinct categories: (1) geographical designations based on the name of the country or the city of origin of the deported communities (e.g., Ḫazatu = Gaza) and (2) ethnic designations that added the gentilic ending (-āya) to the geographical name (e.g., Āl-Miṣirāya = City of the Egyptians). Knowing who is responsible for the nomenclature of these sites has important implications for the question at hand. Ethnic designations make sense only from the perspective of the Babylonian administration, as they simply sought to identify the inhabitants for taxation purposes. On the other hand, geographical designations reflect the traditions of deported communities. The reference to their country/city of origin established a tangible link with their homeland while inhabiting a foreign country and confirms that they were able to maintain some form of autonomy, which allowed them to preserve their respective traditions.

The original ethnic name of a handful of sites was converted to a geographical designation, as exemplified by the village of Āl-Yāḫūdu.[35] This site is first attested under the ethnic designation of Ālu ša Yāḫūdāya [town/city of the Judeans] in two texts dated to 572 (CUSAS 28: 1) and 567 BCE (BaAr 6: 1).[36] Its substitution by Āl-Yāḫūdu [town of Judah] was effective at the latest in the first year of Amēl-Marduk, 561 BCE (CUSAS 28: 6), the date of its first secure attestation. Every subsequent mention systematically uses the geographical designation. Yet this change may have been initiated some years earlier, as the orthography of Āl-Yāḫūdu also appears in CUSAS 28: 2, whose date is missing. Internal prosopographical evidence favors the reign of Nebuchadnezzar II (604–562 BCE), most probably between his thirty-third and forty-second years (ca. 572–563 BCE).[37] The pledge clause of the contract in CUSAS 28: 2 may mention the second month of the year (Aiāru [April/May]), a favorable period for the settlement or renewal of debts since it coincides with the harvest of barley. If so, the first occurrence of Āl-Yāḫūdu would date to 563 BCE, the last complete year of the reign of Nebuchadnezzar II.[38]

The complete abandonment of Ālu ša Yāḫūdāya and its systematic replacement by Āl-Yāḫūdu is highly unusual. The fragmentary nature of our sources does not allow definite answers to this historical problem, although some scenarios are more likely than others. One obvious proposition is that no precise reason stood behind this change, which could have been the result of scribal idiosyncrasies. The same movement from ethnic to geographical designations is attested for other foreign toponyms of the region of Nippur. A settlement known as Ālu ša Nērabāya [town/city of the Nerabites] is first mentioned in ca. 540 BCE and soon after changed to Ālu Nēreb [town/city of Nerab], around 530 BCE.[39] These changes were nevertheless far from being systematically applied to the villages inhabited by foreign communities in southern Babylonia. The town of Āl-Miṣirāya [city of the Egyptians] reveals the absence of any overarching logic that would explain the substitution of ethnic designations for geographical names. This settlement is continuously known through its ethnic label, and this from the time of its first attestation in the reign of Nabonidus (547 BCE) to that of its last under Darius I (510 BCE).

A consideration of the scribes responsible for the composition of the tablets of Āl-Yāḫūdu provides a different outlook on this question. CUSAS 28: 1 is written by Nabû-na'id, son of Nabû-zēru-iqīša, who also wrote tablets Numbers 3, 4, and 10, albeit under the name of Nabû-nāṣir.[40] Nabû-na'id/Nabû-nāṣir is the only scribe who used both the ethnic and geographical names of Āl-Yāḫūdu. His writing was consistent, limiting the usage of Ālu ša Yāḫūdāya to the period before 563–561 BCE and only switching to Āl-Yāḫūdu for the period after. The sharp temporal delimitation separating both designations in local scribal conventions underlines a deliberate and intentional change in the name of this settlement, which at the same time negates the possibility for any unmotivated modification.

Therefore, Neo-Babylonian authorities could have altered the name of these settlements due to perceived similarities with other Levantine states that were incorporated into their empire. Several of these small political entities developed under the city-state model, which consists of a large urban center controlling its immediate vicinity. The Phoenician cities of Tyre and Sidon as well as the Philistine cities of Ashkelon and Gaza were conquered by Babylonian forces, and all functioned under the city-state model. Hence, Babylonian authorities could have imposed the name of Āl-Yāḫūdu to the settlement of Judean deportees in southern Babylonia simply by conceiving Judah and Jerusalem as a single reality.[41] The reference to Jerusalem as Āl-Yāḫūdu in a Babylonian chronicle that describes the Babylonian invasion of 597 BCE has led André Lemaire and Francis Joannès to claim that the Babylonian settlement of Āl-Yāḫūdu represents a "new Jerusalem."[42] However, the growing evidence for the composition of this chronicle in the Persian period should caution us against the equation Āl-Yāḫūdu = Jerusalem. The direction of the influence might have gone the other way; that is, the name of the Babylonian settlement might have influenced the one given to the Judean capital in the chronicle.[43]

The release of Jehoiachin from captivity in the accession year of Amēl-Marduk (ca. 562 BCE), mentioned in 2 Kings 25:27, provides an additional context for the interpretation of the shift in the names of Āl-Yāḫūdu.⁴⁴ The geographical designation first appears between 563 and 561 BCE, which coincides with his release.⁴⁵ Ration lists uncovered in the palace of Nebuchadnezzar II in Babylon indicate that Jehoiachin retained his official title of king of Judah [LUGAL *ša* ᴷᵁᴿ *ya-ḫu-du*] in captivity and that he was still considered its legitimate ruler in the eyes of the Babylonians.⁴⁶ Thus, once he was freed, the political term of Judah could be reinstated. His release was an event of great importance for Judean deportees, and the change to Āl-Yāḫūdu could symbolize the emergent hopes for a national revival associated with his liberation.⁴⁷

There is one additional aspect to the names of these toponyms that must be briefly discussed, one that has greater implications than the responsibility for naming these sites and the significance of the shift in designations. These toponyms were far from meaningless, as they acted as mementos to their inhabitants and were instrumental in the conservation of their collective memory as well as their identity away from their homeland. The name of Āl-Yāḫūdu directly points back to an era of national and political independence prior to the events of 597 and 586 BCE, symbolizing Judean history and its landscape. This association could have easily lost its value for the exiles with the succession of generations as well as with the growing desire and need to assimilate. Individuals born in Babylonia had no attachments whatsoever to Judah, but the name of their village reminded them of their origin. Perhaps originally unintentional, the name of Āl-Yāḫūdu contributed to the survival of their collective memory and was one of the repositories of their history, an ancient *lieu de mémoire* [site/place of memory].⁴⁸

PERSONAL NAMES AND JUDEAN IDENTITY IN EXILE

Onomastic evidence is among the most underestimated and neglected aspects of historical research on ancient societies. In regard to the Āl-Yāḫūdu texts, it offers the most profitable avenue of investigation, as it offers the basis for identifying individuals as Judeans as well as for reconstructing the sociocultural dynamics that prevailed within this settlement. Ran Zadok has proposed three criteria to establish the Judean origin of an individual based on onomastic evidence: 1) Yahwistic theophoric names, 2) other non-Yahwistic Jewish names (e.g., Šabbātay, Ḥaggay), and 3) probable Jewish names based on genealogy or historical circumstances.⁴⁹ Yahwistic theophoric names are

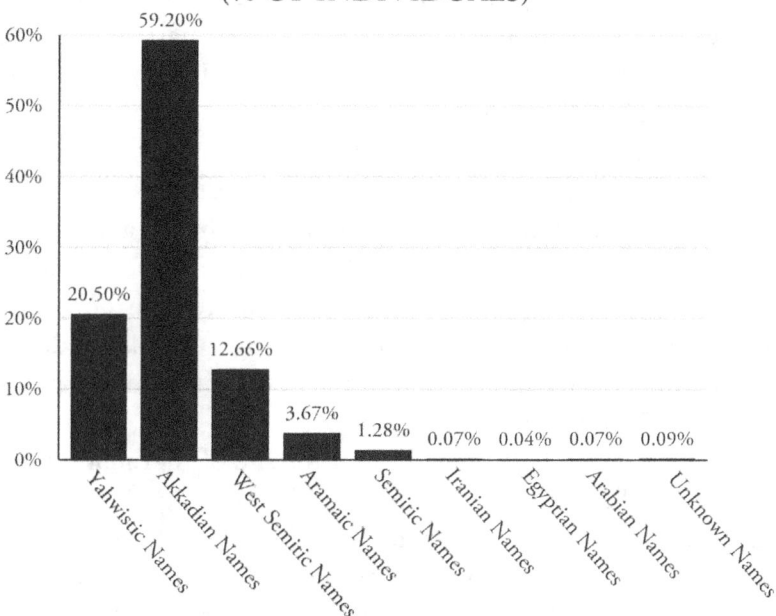

Figure 4.4 Onomastic Evidence in the CUSAS 28 Corpus.⁵³

an exclusive feature of Judean/Israelite onomastica and are the sole criterion by which we can undoubtedly establish the Judean/Israelite background of an individual, as they are the sole populations to have worshipped Yahweh. These names comprise two elements: a verbal predicate and the name of the Judean deity, Yahweh. For example, the name Rapā-Yāma is made up of the verb רפא [to heal] followed by the Yahwistic theophoric element, -Yāma, and translates as "Yahweh healed." The verb and the theophoric element can stand at either the beginning or end of the name, although the position of the latter will influence its orthography in Neo-Babylonian texts. "Yāḫû-" is usually found in initial position, while "-Yāma" appears predominantly at the end.⁵⁰

The onomastic evidence of the CUSAS 28 corpus, both as a whole and within the archives of Aḫīqam of Āl-Yāḫūdu, Aḫīqar of Bīt-Našar, and Zababa-šarru-uṣur from Bīt-Abī-râm, highlights the special character of the settlement of Āl-Yāḫūdu (Figure 4.4). Babylonian names account for the overwhelming majority of the onomastic evidence (57.9% to 60.6% of all individuals) in the CUSAS 28 corpus, which fits the pattern observed for other private archives from southern Babylonia. For instance, Babylonian names represent two-thirds of the evidence in the Murašu texts, dated to the second half of the fifth century BCE.[51] However, the proportion of Yahwistic names in the entire CUSAS 28 corpus is unusually high (20.5%, or 176 of 857 individuals) and does diverge from known patterns of onomastic representation of foreign communities in the various textual records of Babylonia, where they are at best marginally represented. In contrast, Yahwistic names barely appear in the Murašu texts (1.4%, or 36 of 2,500 names) as well as in the archive of Aḥīqar of Bīt-Našar (6.1%, or 17 of 280 individuals, Table 1).[52] Judean deportees are concentrated in the settlement of Āl-Yāḫūdu, as more than 90% of the Yahwistic names found in the CUSAS 28 corpus appear in the archive of Aḥīqam (159 of 176 individuals). They represent more than a quarter of individuals mentioned in this archive (28.5%, or 159 of 557 individuals), while Babylonian names hardly account for more than half of the data (49.7–50.8%, or 277–283 of 557 individuals, Table 2).

The prevalence of Judean individuals at the site of Āl-Yāḫūdu is essentially of greater intensity. Several texts from the archive of Aḥīqam specify that they were written in Āl-Yāḫūdu, and an emphasis on these texts allows for an improved approximation of the sociocultural dynamics prevailing in this settlement (Table 3). The percentage of Yahwistic names now rises to about 38% of individuals (118 of 313), whereas Babylonian names considerably decrease (42.5–43.45%, or 133–136 of 313 individuals). Yahwistic theophoric names even came to surpass local onomastic forms over the course of the Achaemenid period (42.4%, or 56 of 132 individuals, vs. 39.4%, or 52 of 132 individuals).[54] This phenomenon has never been observed for any other ethnic community living in Babylonia. Even Aramaic names never came to represent more than 25% of the onomastic evidence in any given corpus, although they did represent one of the dominant ethnic groups of Babylonia by the early sixth century BCE.[55] The conclusion seems clear: the village of Āl-Yāḫūdu was a thriving and prosperous center for Judean identity in Babylonia during the exilic and postexilic periods.[56]

Almost every individual who appears in the CUSAS 28 corpus is identified with the name of his father (e.g., Šamā-Yāma, son of Naḥim-Yāma [CUSAS 28: 21 obv. 6–7]), composing specific name pairs. These offer a diachronic perspective of the composition of the population living in Āl-Yāḫūdu as well as of the extent of the influence of Babylonian culture.[57] For the sake of convenience, the son will be referred as the first member of name pairs, while the father stands for the second member. Yahwistic names are particularly popular for the first member of name pairs in texts written in Āl-Yāḫūdu, representing 47.2% (17 of 36 individuals) and 42.4% (56 of 132 individuals) of individuals in the Neo-Babylonian and Achaemenid periods, respectively.[58]

Table 1. Onomastic Evidence per Individual from the Archive of Aḥīqar of Bīt-Našar (CUSAS 28: 55–101)

		Yahwistic	Akkadian	West Semitic	Aramaic	Semitic	Iranian	Egyptian	Arabian	Unknown	Totals
Neo-Babylonian Period	Father	1	15–16	2	0	0	0	0	0	0	18
		5.6%	83.3–88.9%	11.1%	—	—	—	—	—	—	
	Son/Daughter	0	13–14	3	2	0	0	0	0	0	18
		—	72.2–77.8%	16.7%	11.1%	—	—	—	—	—	
Subtotals		1	28–30	5	2	0	0	0	0	0	36
		2.8%	77.8–83.3%	13.9%	5.6%	—	—	—	—	—	
Achaemenid Period	Father	6	76–82	12–18	4	2	1	0	1	1	112
		5.4%	67.9–73.2%	10.7–16.1%	3.6%	1.8%	0.9%	—	0.9%	0.9%	
	Son/Daughter	10	94–103	13–20	3–5	1	0	0	0	2	132
		7.6%	71.2–78%	9.8–15.1%	2.3–3.8%	0.7%	—	—	—	1.5%	
Subtotals		16	170–185	25–38	7–9	3	1	0	1	3	244
		6.5%	69.7–75.8%	10.2–15.6%	2.8–3.7%	1.2%	0.4%	—	0.4%	1.2%	
TOTALS		17	198–215	30–43	9–11	3	1	0	1	3	280
		6.1%	70.7–76.8%	10.7–15.3%	3.2–3.9%	1.1%	0.3%	—	0.3%	1.1%	

Table 2. Onomactic Evidence per Individual from the Archive of Aḥīqam of Āl-Yāḫūdu (CUSAS 28: 1–54)

		Yahwistic	Akkadian	West Semitic	Aramaic	Semitic	Iranian	Egyptian	Arabian	Unknown	Totals
Neo-Babylonian Period	Father	10 23.8%	23 54.7%	5 11.9%	1 2.4%	1 2.4%	1 2.4%	0 —	0 —	1 2.4%	42
	Son/daughter	19 41.3%	20–22 43.5–47.8%	3–5 6.5–10.8%	1 2.2%	0 —	1 2.2%	0 —	0 —	0 —	46
Subtotals		29 33%	43–45 48.8–51.1%	8–10 9.1–11.4%	2 2.3%	1 1.1%	2 2.3%	0 —	0 —	1 1.1%	88
Achaemenid Period	Father	52 24.4%	109–113 51.2–53%	32–36 15–17%	9–10 4.2–4.7%	2 1%	0 —	1–2 0.5–1%	3 1.4%	0 —	213
	Son/daughter	78 30.5%	125 48.8%	28 11%	10 4%	4 1.6%	3 1.2%	2 0.8%	2 0.8%	4 1.6%	256
Subtotals		130 27.7%	234–238 49.9–50.7%	60–64 12.8–13.6%	19–20 2.1–4.3%	6 1.3%	3 0.6%	3–4 0.6–0.9%	5 1.2%	4 0.9%	469
TOTALS		159 28.5%	277–283 49.7–50.8%	68–74 12.2–13.3%	21–22 3.8–3.9%	7 1.3%	5 0.9%	3–4 0.5–0.7%	5 0.9%	5 0.9%	557

Table 3. Onomastic Evidence Per Individual from Texts Written in Āl-Yāḫūdu
(CUSAS 28: 1–7, 10–11, 14–15, 19–22, 24–25, 29–40, 42–44, 46)

		Yahwistic	Akkadian	West Semitic	Aramaic	Semitic	Iranian	Egyptian	Arabian	Unknown	Totals
Neo-Babylonian Period	Father	10 28.6%	19 54.3%	4 11.4%	— —	1 2.9%	— —	— —	— —	1 2.9%	35
	Son/Daughter	17 47.2%	16–17 44.4–47.2%	2–3 5.5–8.3%	— —	— —	— —	— —	— —	— —	36
Subtotals		27 38%	35–36 49.3–50.7%	6–7 8.4–9.8%	— —	1 1.4%	— —	— —	— —	1 1.4%	71
Achaemenid Period	Father	35 31.8%	46–48 41.8–43.6%	18–20 16.4–18.2%	4 3.6%	— —	— —	2 1.8%	1 0.9%	— —	110
	Son/Daughter	56 42.4%	52 39.4%	15 11.4%	2 1.5%	2 1.5%	— —	— —	2 1.5%	3 2.3%	132
Subtotals		91 37.6%	98–100 40.5–41.3%	33–35 13.6–14.5%	6 2.5%	2 0.8%	— —	2 0.8%	3 1.2%	3 1.2%	242
TOTALS		118 37.7%	133–136 42.5–43.4%	39–42 12.5–13.4%	6 1.9%	3 0.9%	— —	2 0.6%	3 0.9%	4 1.3%	313

They are, however, considerably less common for the second member of name pairs, with 28.6% (10 of 35 individuals) and 31.8% (35 of 110 individuals) of the onomastic data for this assumed generation in both historical periods. The significant decline between the first member of name pairs in the Neo-Babylonian period (47.2%) and the second member of name pairs in the Achaemenid period (31.8%) may have been the result of the growing assimilation of Judean deportees. Nonetheless, the great discrepancy of texts between the two periods (Neo-Babylonian = 8 texts vs. Achaemenid = 26 texts) should call for caution.

On the whole, generational onomastic trends substantiate the impression of the growing popularity of Yahwistic names among the Judean exilic community (Figure 4.5). They steadily increase from the Neo-Babylonian period to the early Achaemenid period (552–532 BCE), that is, from 26.3% of individuals presumably born between 612 and 592 BCE to 43.7% of individuals born between 552 and 532 BCE.[59] In contrast, Babylonian names considerably decline after the generation of 592–572 BCE (55.7% to 36.75%). The peak in popularity of Yahwistic names for the population of Āl-Yāḫūdu is contemporaneous with the emergent movement of a national revival that promoted the return to the Land of Israel during the late Neo-Babylonian and early Achaemenid periods. Generational onomastic trends thus confirm the existence of a strong and flourishing Judean community in Babylonia, which was able to avoid assimilation by positioning Yahwism at the very center of its identity.

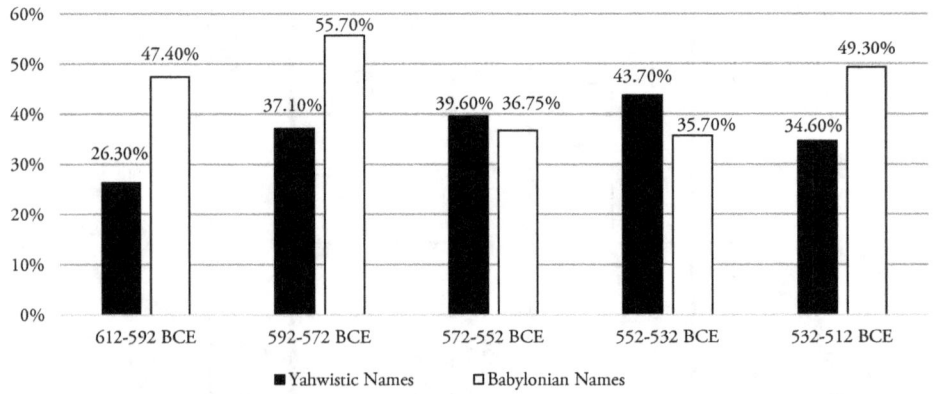

Figure 4.5 Yahwistic Names per Generation in Texts Written in Āl-Yāḫūdu.

The Āl-Yāḫūdu Texts (ca. 572–477 BCE) 87

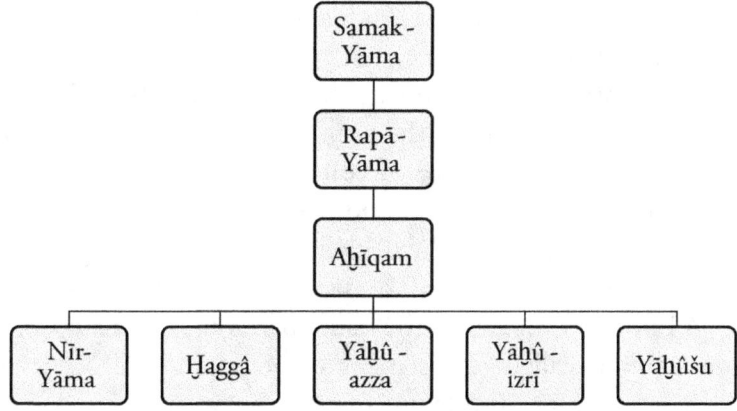

Figure 4.6 The Genealogy of Aḫīqam.

The family tree of Aḫīqam of Āl-Yāḫūdu concretely exemplifies the extent of the influence exerted by Babylonian culture and society upon successive generations of Judean deportees (Figure 4.6). Among the four generations that can be reconstructed from the texts in CUSAS 28, only the third (Aḫīqam) generation and one member of the fourth (Ḫaggâ) generation bear non-Yahwistic names of West Semitic origin. Aḫīqam was probably born in the mid Neo-Babylonian period (ca. 572–552 BCE) and is part of the observable decrease of Yahwistic names for the second member of name pairs in the Achaemenid period.[60] Their return in force in the fourth generation parallels their resurgence in popularity for the first member of name pairs during the same period or that of the generation of 552–532 BCE. The increasing number of Yahwistic names mirrors the growing importance of Yahwism for the identity of the exilic community, the more so as we move closer to the period of the return to the Land of Israel (530s BCE).

Despite this portrait of a thriving Judean community, instances of deliberate assimilation to Babylonian society do exist. Very few cases of a father with a Judean name whose son bears a non-Judean name are attested among the various name pairs from the Neo-Babylonian period in the settlement of Āl-Yāḫūdu.[61] They do, however, drastically increase during the Achaemenid period.[62] Since the majority of these names are of West Semitic affiliation, they may not necessarily express a move away from Judean naming practices and culture but instead may convey a dissociation from Yahwism. The opposite situation, father with non-Judean name and son with Judean name, is well attested in both periods.[63] Some of these fathers bore Akkadian names, which demonstrates that deliberate attempts to integrate into the dominant culture did not hinder the perpetuation of Judean traditions over successive generations.

Whereas extensive assimilation never occurred, Babylonian culture did have a hold on a small portion of the population. The case of Bēl-šarru-uṣur, son of Nubâ, unveils the existence of cultural hybridity in Āl-Yāḫūdu. This individual appears in CUSAS 28: 2 and 3 under the *Beamtennamen* [courtier names] onomastic pattern, which likely exposes his integration into the local Babylonian administration.[64] The same individual is also mentioned in CUSAS 28: 4 but this time under the name of Yāḫû-šarru-uṣur, son of Nubâ. This phenomenon is called replacement orthography and occurs when the theophoric element varies in different instances of a single individual's name. In the present case, the name of the Judean deity, Yahweh, replaced that of the head of the Babylonian pantheon, Bēl/Marduk.[65] According to Laurie E. Pearce, this individual wished to integrate into the royal administration and thus adopted the appropriate Babylonian name pattern, while the Yahwistic form was reinstated in another context to respect the traditions of the exilic community.[66]

Cultural hybridity is also reflected by hybrid names found in the corpus of Āl-Yāḫūdu. Hybrid names are composed of elements from two different languages and embody a form of bilateral cultural assimilation. For example, the name Išši-Yāma is composed of the Yahwistic theophoric element and an Akkadian verbal predicate, the verb *našû* [to elevate]. Whether this name should be interpreted as a calque translation [i.e., translation into the equivalent form of the host language] of the name Yarīm-Yāma/*yrmyh(w)* [Yahweh is exalted/elevated] or simply as an Akkadian phonetic representation of the Hebrew root ישע [to deliver, save] is difficult to determine.[67] The evidence from the various renderings of this root in the names of Uššuḫ-Yāma, Amuš-Yāma, and Amušeḫ shows that Babylonian scribes usually rendered the Hebrew ʿayin with a *ḫeth*, hence supporting the first scenario.[68] In spite of the few cases of cultural hybridity encountered in the settlement of Āl-Yāḫūdu, assimilation was extremely limited and confined to individuals who deliberately tried to integrate Babylonian society.[69]

CONCLUSION

Previous interpretations of the Babylonian exile usually convey the image of a devastating period in Jewish history.[70] This event radically altered the life of thousands of Judeans and left marks of great depth in their collective consciousness. The recent publication of the Āl-Yāḫūdu texts enhances our understanding of this period and calls for a revision of received historical reconstructions. These texts confirm that Judean exiles were in fact living a peaceful and quiet life in southern Babylonia, while some even integrated into the Babylonian and Persian administrations and/or increased their personal wealth and social positions.

Texts from Āl-Yāḫūdu offer valuable insights into the sociocultural dynamics that prevailed within the Babylonian exilic community. Judean culture and identity were maintained throughout this period, although they were substantially modified. The present study has demonstrated the quintessential role played by the Babylonians in establishing the necessary conditions for the survival of foreign collective identities in Babylonia. As opposed to the Assyrians, the Babylonians promoted the creation of small settlements for deported communities in the Nippur countryside in order to revitalize the local economy. This policy indirectly encouraged the formation of isolated ethnic hubs, which in turn favored the development and survival of various foreign cultures. The names given to these small villages concretely symbolized a past of political independence and contributed to the perpetuation of their collective consciousness. These toponyms represented real *lieu de mémoire*, which instituted an indelible bond between their inhabitants and their past.

Finally, onomastic evidence reveals the importance of Yahwism for Judean identity throughout the Neo-Babylonian and Achaemenid periods. Yahwistic theophoric names steadily increase over time and eventually account for the majority of individuals in the site of Āl-Yāḫūdu during the late Neo-Babylonian period, a phenomenon that is unattested in any other Babylonian archive (see Tables 1, 2, and 3). This upsurge coincides with the growing popularity of a movement that advocates a return of Judean deportees to their homeland toward the end of the Neo-Babylonian and the early Achaemenid periods. The weakening of Neo-Babylonian power and the rise of Cyrus late in the reign of Nabonidus led to the emergence of nationalist movements among the various Babylonian diasporas, particularly in the Judean Babylonian community. Yahwistic names became the primary identity marker due to their connection with a unique aspect of Judean culture: the worship of Yahweh. They also express nascent national sentiments in the settlement of Āl-Yāḫūdu. While "a rereading of the Babylonian period of exile can be shown to demonstrate the development of a new creative energy in a challenging, pluralistic context outside of the natal homeland,"[71] this new vitality crystallized in a small village known as the city of Judah, Āl-Yāḫūdu.

ACKNOWLEDGMENTS

I would like to thank Paul-Alain Beaulieu and Robert D. Holmstedt for their comments on an earlier draft of this essay. I would also like to thank Laurie E. Pearce, the Bible Land Museum, and Carta Jerusalem for providing images that significantly enhance the quality of this work. Finally, the vital work of Leonard J. Greenspoon cannot go unmentioned as well as that of the staff involved in the organization of the symposium and, evidently, the editorial staff of Purdue University Press.

NOTES

1. D. Smith-Christopher, *A Biblical Theology of Exile,* Overtures to Biblical Theology (Minneapolis: Fortress, 2002), 6.

2. For a full discussion, see Rainer Albertz, "More and Less Than a Myth: Reality and Significance of Exile for the Political, Social, and Religious History of Judah," in *By the Irrigation Canals of Babylon: Approaches to the Study of the Exile,* Library of Hebrew Bible and Old Testament Studies 56, ed. John J. Ahn and Jill A. Middlemas (New York: T & T Clark, 2012), 27–32; Rainer Albertz, *Israel in Exile: The History and Literature of the Sixth Century B.C.E.,* Studies in Biblical Literature 3, trans. D. Green (Atlanta: Society of Biblical Literature, 2003), 132–38.

3. For the Murašu archive, see Veysel Donbaz and Matthew W. Stolper, *Istanbul Murašû Texts* (Istanbul: Nederlands Historisch-Archaeologisch Instituut te Istanbul, 1997); Matthew W. Stolper, *Entrepreneurs and Empire: The Murašû Archive, the Murašû Firm, and Persian Rule in Babylonia* (Istanbul: Nederlands Historisch-Archaeologisch Instituut, 1985). The sole contemporary sources available are the Babylonian ration lists from the palace of Nebuchadnezzar II in Babylon dated to circa 594–576 BCE. For this corpus, see Ernst F. Weidner, "Jojachin, König von Juda, in Babylonischen Keilschrifttexten," in *Mélanges syriens offerts à Monsieur René Dussaud: Secrétaire perpétuel de l'Académie des inscriptions et belles-lettres, ed. ses amis et élèves,* Vol. 2 (Paris: Librairie orientaliste Paul Geuthner, 1939), 922–28.

4. The earliest text from Āl-Yāḫūdu is dated to 572 BCE.

5. Laurie E. Pearce and Cornelia Wunsch, *Documents of Judean Exiles and West Semites in Babylonia in the Collection of David Sofer,* Cornell University Studies in Assyriology and Sumerology 28 (Bethesda, MA: CDL Press, 2014) [hereafter CUSAS 28]. Additional texts will be published by Cornelia Wunsch under the title *Judeans by the Waters of Babylon: New Historical Evidence in Cuneiform Sources from Rural Babylonia in the Scøhyen Collection,* Babylonische Archive 6; with contributions by L. E. Pearce (Dresden: Islet, forthcoming) [hereafter BaAr 6].

6. For additional texts written in Āl-Yāḫūdu, see Kathleen Abraham, "West Semitic and Judean Brides in Cuneiform Sources from the Sixth Century BCE—New Evidence

from a Marriage Contract from Al-Yahudu," *Archiv für Orientforschung* 5 (2005–2006): 198–219; Kathleen Abraham, "An Inheritance Division among Judeans in Babylonia from the Early Persian Period (from the Moussaieff Tablet Collection)," in *New Seals and Inscriptions, Hebrew, Idumean, and Cuneiform,* Hebrew Bible Monographs 8, ed. Meir Lubetski (Sheffield: Sheffield Phoenix Press, 2007), 206–21; Francis Joannès and André Lemaire, "Trois tablettes cunéiformes à onomastique ouest-sémitique," *Transeuphratène* 17 (1999): 17–27; W. G. Lambert, "A Document from a Community of Exiles," in *New Seals and Inscriptions,* 201–5.

7. See Joannès and Lemaire, "Trois tablettes cunéiformes à onomastique ouest-sémitique," 27–30, for an additional text from Bīt-Našar.

8. For other texts belonging to the same archive, see Francis Joannès and André Lemaire, "Contrats babyloniens d'époque achéménide du Bît-Abî-Râm avec épigraphe araméenne," *Revue assyriologique* 90 (1996): 41–60.

9. Laurie E. Pearce, "Identifying Judeans and Judean Identity in the Babylonian Evidence," in *Exile and Return: The Babylonian Context,* Beiheifte zur Zeitschrift für die alttestamentliche Wissenschaft 478, ed. J. Stökl and C. Waerzeggers (Berlin: De Gruyter, 2015), 9–12; CUSAS 28: p. 7; Cornelia Wunsch, "Glimpses on the Lives of Deportees in Rural Babylonia," in *Arameans, Chaldeans, and Arabs in Babylonia in Palestine in the First Millennium B.C.,* Leipziger altorientalistische Studien 3, ed. Angelika Berjelung and Michael P. Streck (Harrasowitz Verlag: Wiesbaden, 2013), 251. For a reconstruction of the landscape of the Nippur region in the Neo-Babylonian and Achaemenid periods, see Ran Zadok, "The Nippur Region during the Late Assyrian, Chaldean and Achaemenian Periods Chiefly according to Written Sources," *Israel Oriental Studies* 8 (1978): 266–332.

10. Israel Eph'al, "On the Political and Social Organization of the Jews in the Babylonian Exile," in *XXI. Deutscher Orientalistentag vom 24. bis 29. März 1980 in Berlin,* ed. F. Steppat (Wiesbaden: Steiner, 1983), 109. For the beginnings of Babylonian control in the regions of Uruk and Nippur, see Paul-Alain Beaulieu, "The Fourth Year of Hostilities in the Land," *Baghdader Mittelungen* 28 (1997): 367–94.

11. None of the many building projects mentioned in Neo-Babylonian royal inscriptions refer to Nippur. See Rocío Da Riva, *The Neo-Babylonian Royal Inscriptions: An Introduction,* Guides to the Mesopotamian Textual Record 4 (Ugarit-Verlag: Münster, 2008), 60n201; Laurie E. Pearce, "Continuity and Normality in Sources Relating to the Judean Exile," *Hebrew Bible and Ancient Israel* 3 (2014): 173nn34, 35.

12. Israel Eph'al had foreseen the existence of this phenomenon forty years ago. Israel Eph'al, "The Western Minorities in Babylonia in the 6th–5th Centuries B.C.: Maintenance and Cohesion," *Orientalia* 47 (1978): 74–90. For a thorough discussion of Babylonian economy, see Michael Jursa, *Aspects of the Economic History of Babylonia in the First Millennium BC: Economic Geography, Economic Mentalities, Agriculture, the Use of Money and the Problem of Economic Growth,* Alter Orient und Altes Testament 377, with contributions by J. Hackl et al. (Münster: Ugarit-Verlag, 2010). *Bīt azanni* is a rare variant of the more common designation of *bīt qašti*. See CUSAS 28: pp. 100–1.

13. Wunsch, "Glimpses on the Lives of Deportees in Rural Babylonia," 254.

14. *Ilkum* is a general term designating the obligations/taxes owed by the field tenant to the royal administration. These could take the form of either military services or agricultural taxes.

15. CUSAS 28: 2 obv. 6–8. This individual is also known as Yāḫû-šarru-uṣur in CUSAS 28: 4 obv. 2. For the tax collectors, see CUSAS 28: 12 obv. 6–7, 83 obv. 5–6; and Joannès and Lemaire, "Contrats babyloniens d'époque achémnide du Bît-Abî-Râm avec épigraphe araméenne," text no. 9. For a discussion on this issue, see Pearce, "Continuity and Normality in Sources Relating to the Judean Exile," 175–76.

16. For other areas of influence during the exilic period, see Madhavi Nevander, "Picking Up the Pieces of the Little Prince: Refractions of Neo-Babylonian Kingship Ideology in Ezekiel 40–48?," in *Exile and Return*, 268–91; Jonathan Stökl, "'A Youth without Blemish, Handsome, Proficient in all Wisdom, Knowledgeable and Intelligent': Ezekiel's Access to Babylonian Culture," in *Exile and Return*, 223–52; Caroline Waerzeggers, "Locating Contact in the Babylonian Exile: Some Reflections on Tracing Judean-Babylonian Encounters in Cuneiform Texts," in *Encounters by the Rivers of Babylon: Scholarly Conversations between Jews, Iranians and Babylonians in Antiquity*, Texts and Studies in Ancient Judaism 160, ed. Uri Gabbay and Shai Secunda (Tübingen: Mohr Siebeck, 2014), 131–46.

17. For the inheritance division, see Abraham, "An Inheritance Division among Judeans in Babylonia from the Early Persian Period," 206–21; for the marriage contract, see Abraham, "West Semitic and Judean Brides in Cuneiform Sources from the Sixth Century BCE," 198–219.

18. Bustenay Oded, *Mass Deportations and Deportees in the Neo-Assyrian Empire* (Wiesbaden: Reichert, 1979), 21.

19. Ibid., 28–29.

20. According to Oded, Assyrians "tended to maintain the community framework of the deportees by transporting and resettling them in groups." Although communities/families were often deported together, Assyrians never resettled them in specific enclaves created for their sole needs. Ibid., 22–24, 67–69.

21. Ibid., 44–69.

22. For a discussion on slavery and deportees in the Neo-Assyrian Empire, see Heather D. Baker, "Slavery and Personhood in the Neo-Assyrian Empire," in *On Human Bondage: After Slavery and Social Death*, Ancient World: Comparative Histories, ed. John Bodel and Walter Scheidel (London: Wiley-Blackwell, 2016), 19. For a discussion of slavery in link to Israelite deportees, see Oded, *Mass Deportations and Deportees in the Neo-Assyrian Empire*, 91–97, 104–14.

23. For an overview of the deportations that affected the Kingdom of Israel, see K. Lawson Younger Jr., "The Deportations of the Israelites," *Journal of Biblical Literature* 117 (1998): 201–27; Bob Becking, *The Fall of Samaria: An Historical and Archaeological Study*, Studies in the History of the Ancient Near East 2 (Leiden: E. J. Brill, 1992), 61–94.

24. According to the royal inscriptions of Sargon II, between 27,290 people plus 50 chariots and 27,280 people plus 200 chariots were deported. For the variations between the versions, see Andreas Fuchs, *Die Inschriften Sargons II. aus Khorsabad* (Göttingen: Cuvillier, 1994), Prunk no. 24, 197; Becking, *The Fall of Samaria*, 25–33.

25. For a discussion of the fate of Israelite deportees, see Becking, *The Fall of Samaria*, 62–72; Mordechai Cogan, *Bound for Exile. Israelites and Judeans under Imperial Yoke: Documents from Assyria and Babylonia* (Jerusalem: Carta, 2013), 35–53; Bustenay Oded, "The Settlements of the Israelite and Judean Exiles in Mesopotamia in the Eighth–Sixth Centuries BCE," in *Studies in Historical Geography and Biblical Historiography: Presented to Zecharia Kallai*, Supplements to Vetus Testamentum 81, ed. Gershon Galil and Moshe Weinfeld (Leiden: Brill, 2000), 92–99. For the presence of Israelites in Media, see Gerson Galil, "Israelite Exiles in Media: A New Look at ND 2443+," *Vetus Testamentum* 59 (2009): 71–79.

26. For a general discussion on the use of Israelite deportees, see Bustenay Oded, "Observations on the Israelite/Judean Exile in Mesopotamia during the Eighth–Sixth Centuries BCE," in *Immigration and Emigration within the Ancient Near East: Festschrift E. Lipiński*, Orientalia Lovaniensia Analecta 65, ed. K. van Lerberghe and A. Schoors (Leuven: Uitgeverij Peeters en Departement Oriëntalistiek, 1995), 205–9; Younger, "The Deportations of the Israelites," 219–24. For the chariot troops of Samaria, see Becking, *The Fall of Samaria*, 74; Cogan, *Bound for Exile*, text no. 2.02; Stephanie Dalley, "Foreign Chariotry and Cavalry in the Armies of Tiglath-Pileser III and Sargon II," *Iraq* 47 (1985): 31–36. For the royal court, see Dalley, "Foreign Chariotry and Cavalry in the Armies," 41; Younger, "The Deportations of the Israelites," 220–21.

27. Zadok has recently concluded on the basis of onomastic evidence that Israelite deportees completely integrated into Assyrian society. The adoption of Assyrian and Aramaic names by the second generation of exiles highlights this phenomenon. See Ran Zadok, "Israelites and Judaeans in the Neo-Assyrian Documentation (732–602 B.C.E.): An Overview of the Sources and a Socio-Historical Assessment," *Bulletin of the American Schools of Oriental Research* 374 (2015): 174–75.

28. David S. Vanderhooft, *The Neo-Babylonian Empire and Babylon in the Latter Prophets*, Harvard Semitic Museum Monographs 59 (Atlanta: Scholar Press, 1999), 110–12; Wunsch, "Glimpses on the Lives of Deportees in Rural Babylonia," 252.

29. For Ashkelon, see Lawrence E. Stager, "Ashkelon and the Archaeology of Destruction," *Eretz Israel* 25 (1996): 61–74. For an overview of the interest of Babylon in the southern Levant, see Erasmus Gaß, "Nebukadnezzar ante portas—Zu den babylonischen Interessen in der südlichen Levante," *Zeitschrift für die Alttestamentliche Wissenschaft* 128 (2016): 247–66.

30. Paul-Alain Beaulieu, "Nebuchadnezzar's Babylon as World Capital," *Canadian Society for Mesopotamian Studies—Journal* 3 (2008): 5–12; Vanderhooft, *The Neo-Babylonian Empire and Babylon in the Latter Prophets*, 112.

31. For a general outlook, see Oded, "The Settlements of the Israelite," 99–102. For Babylon, see Weidner, "Jojachin, König von Juda, in Babylonischen Keilschrifttexten,"

922–28. For Sippar, see Yigal Bloch, "Judeans in Sippar and Susa during the First Century of the Babylonian Exile: Assimilation and Perseverance under Babylonian and Achaemenid Rule," *Journal of Ancient Near Eastern History* 1 (2014): 127–35; Michael Jursa, "Eine Familie von Königskaufleuten judäischer Herkunft," *Nouvelles assyriologiques brèves et utilitaires* 2 (2007): 23. The account found in 2 Kings 24:15–16, 21 does not specify the destination(s) of deportees, solely mentioning Babylonia or its capital, Babylon.

32. For an outlook of the settlements in this region, see Zadok, "The Nippur Region." See also Eph'al, "The Western Minorities in Babylonia in the 6th–5th Centuries B.C."; Vanderhooft, *The Neo-Babylonian Empire and Babylon in the Latter Prophets*, 111. For the toponyms ^{URU}*galūtu* and ^{URU}*galīya*, see Ran Zadok, *Geographical Names according to New- and Late-Babylonian Texts*, Répertoire géographique des textes cunéiformes 8 (Wiesbaden: L. Reichert, 1985), 137 [hereafter RGTC 8].

33. Gentilics (i.e., ethnic names) are often attached to the pattern URU ša X [city of X] or É ša X [house of X], with the exception of the Egyptian example above. For the location of these settlements, see RGTC 8: pp. 9, 18, 104, 107, 158, 229–30; Zadok, "The Nippur Region." For a discussion of this phenomenon, see M. A. Dandamayev, "Twin Towns and Ethnic Minorities in First-Millennium Babylonia," in *Commerce and Monetary Systems in the Ancient World: Means of Transmission and Cultural Interaction; Proceedings of the Fifth Annual Symposium of the Assyrian and Babylonian Intellectual Heritage Project Held in Innsbruck, Austria, October 3rd–8th 2002*, Melammu Symposia 5, Oriens et Occidens 6, ed. Robert Rollinger et al. (Stuttgart: Steiner, 2004), 138–42; Eph'al, "The Western Minorities in Babylonia in the 6th–5th Centuries B.C.," 80–83.

34. The only exception is the city of Ṣurru, which was initially located in Babylonia by Francis Joannès ("La localisation de Ṣurru à l'époque néo-babylonienne," *Semitica* 32 [1982]: 35–43, and "Trois textes de Ṣurru à l'époque néo-babylonienne," *Revue assyriologique* 81 [1987]: 147–58). For the revised understanding as the Phoenician city of Tyre, see Caroline van der Brugge and Christine Kleber, "The Empire of Trade and the Empires of Force: Tyre in the Neo-Assyrian and Neo-Babylonian Periods," in *Dynamics of Production in the Ancient Near East, 1300–500 BC*, ed. Juan Carlos Moreno García (Oxford, UK: Oxbow, 2016), 197–99; Stefan Zawadzki, "The Chronology of Tyrian History in the Neo-Babylonian Period," *Altorientalische Forschungen* 42 (2015): 278–79.

35. Laurie E. Pearce, "'Judean': A Special Status in Neo-Babylonian and Achaemenid Babylonia," in *Judah and the Judeans in the Achaemenid Period—Negotiating Identity in an International Context*, ed. O. Lipschits, G. N. Knoppers, and M. Oeming (Winona Lake, IN: Eisenbrauns, 2011), 270; Pearce, "Continuity and Normality in Sources Relating to the Judean Exile," 168; Pearce, "Identifying Judeans and Judean Identity in the Babylonian Evidence," 13–15. The alleged similarity advanced for the site of Ālu ša Arbāya is doubtful in light of the error in vocalization associated with the toponym of ^{uru}Arbā. All of its attestations should be rendered as Ālu Arbāya. See RGTC 8: 9, 28.

36. CUSAS 28: 1 rev. 16 = URU šá ^{lú}*ia-u-ḫu-du-a-a*; BaAr 6: 1:14 = URU ^{lú}*iaʾ-{da}-ḫu-du-a-a*.

37. CUSAS 28: p. 101.

38. The name of the year or month is missing from the lower edge of CUSAS 28: 2. See CUSAS 28: p. 101.

39. For the attestations of this settlement, see RGTC 8: pp. 18, 238; Eph'al, "The Western Minorities in Babylonia in the 6th–5th Centuries B.C.," 84–87. The date of the earliest attestation of the orthography Ālu Nēreb is unknown, but the tablet was written during the reign of Nabonidus (555–539 BCE). See P. Dhorme, "Les tablettes babyloniennes de Neirab," *Revue d'assyriologie et d'archéologie orientale* 25 (1928): 53–82; for the earliest attestation of Ālu Nēreb, see text no. 19: 7.

40. CUSAS 28: 1 rev. 15, 3 rev. 12, 4 rev. 16, 10 rev. 15. This individual took the name of Nabû-na'id during the reign of Nebuchadnezzar II and changed once his namesake (Nabû-na'id/Nabonidus) became king of Babylon in 555 BCE. For this practice, see CUSAS 28: p. 99n15.

41. The presence of both city and country determinatives in front of the names of Tyre, Sidon, and Ashkelon in Neo-Babylonian texts may show that Babylonians were indeed drawing such analogies. See RGTC 8: pp. 183, 279, 281.

42. For the Babylonian chronicle, see A. K. Grayson, *Assyrian and Babylonian Chronicles*, Text from Cuneiform Sources 5 (Locust Valley: J. J. Augustin, 1975), text no. 5 rev. 12–13. For the proposal of a "new Jerusalem," see Joannès and Lemaire, "Trois tablettes cunéiformes à onomastique ouest-sémitique," 24–25.

43. For the date of the composition of the Babylonian chronicles, see Caroline Waerzeggers, "The Babylonian Chronicles: Classification and Provenance," *Journal of Near Eastern Studies* 71 (2012): 285–98.

44. Note Finkel's proposal that Amēl-Marduk and Jehoiachin may have been imprisoned together. Irving L. Finkel, "The Lament of Nabû-šuma-ukîn," in *Babylon: Focus mesopotamischer Geschichte, Wiege früher Gelehrsamkeit, Mythos in der Moderne; 2. Internationales Colloquium der Deutschen Orient-Gesellschaft 24.–26. März 1998 in Berlin*, Colloquien der Deutchen Orient-Gesellschaft 2, ed. Johannes Renger (Saarbrücker: Saarbrücker Druckerei und Verlag, 1999), 337.

45. That a coregency existed late in the reign of Nebuchadnezzar II seems to be confirmed by the first datum for the reign of Amēl-Marduk (2nd day/9th month/562 BCE) and the last of Nebuchadnezzar II (8th day/10th month/562 BCE). See M. P. Streck, "Nebukadnezar II. A," *Reallexicon der Assyriologie* 9 (1998): 199.

46. For this group of texts, see Weidner, "Jojachin, König von Juda, in Babylonischen Keilschrifttexten," 922–28.

47. For the ideological trends in exile in link with the figure of Jehoiachin, see Albertz, *Israel in Exile*, 102–4, 109–10; Israel Eph'al, "The Babylonian Exile: The Survival of a National Minority in a Culturally Foreign Milieu," in *Gründungsfeier am 16. Dezember 2005*, ed. Reinhard G. Kratz (Göttingen: Centrum Orbis Orientalis, 2005), 23.

48. While the present case differs slightly from the concept developed by Pierre Nora in that it was not created for reasons of remembrance, the site of Āl-Yāḫūdu eventually became a vehicle for Judean memory. This was done in conjunction with other social projects, such as the exilic edition of the Deuteronomistic History. For the concept of the *lieu de mémoire* [site of memory], see Pierre Nora, "Entre mémoire et histoire: La problématique des lieux," in *Les lieux de mémoire*, Vol. 1, *La république*, NRF, with the collaboration of Charles-Robert Ageron et al. (Paris: Gallimard, 1984-), XVII–XLII.

49. Ran Zadok, *The Jews in Babylonia during the Chaldean and Achaemenian Periods*, Vol. 3 (Israel: Haifa University Press, 1979), 7–34. The second and third criteria are problematic. Non-Yahwistic Jewish names can appear in other West Semitic dialects and could reflect a foreign origin, especially in the absence of genealogical or historical evidence to prove the contrary. On the other hand, genealogical history may not necessarily reflect the identity of the name bearer.

50. For a review of the orthographies of the Yahwistic element in CUSAS 28, see CUSAS 28: pp. 19–26.

51. Matthew W. Stolper, "Archive of Murashû," *Anchor Bible Dictionary* 4 (1992): 928.

52. For the Murašu texts, see Zadok, *The Jews in Babylonia during the Chaldean and Achaemenian Periods*, 78.

53. The percentage expresses the frequency of onomastic forms per individual. For example, if an individual known as Bārīk-Yāma is mentioned five times in the corpus, these five attestations are counted as one instance of a Yahwistic name since they refer to the same individual.

54. Although Zadok's conclusion concerns the proportion of Yahwistic names in Israelite and Judean onomastica, our conclusion concords with the prevalence of this name form in Judean onomastics (50.63% in local epigraphic sources before 701 BCE vs. 63.63% in Assyrian sources dated between 700 and 602 BCE). See Zadok, "Israelites and Judaeans in the Neo-Assyrian Documentation," 162–63. Mitka Golub's study of the epigraphic evidence also supports this picture. Mitka Golub, "The Distribution of Personal Names in the Land of Israel and Transjordan during the Iron II Period," *Journal of the American Oriental Society* 134 (2014): 631–33, and Table 4.

55. Among native Babylonians and Chaldeans, which represented the majority. Stolper, "Archive of Murashû," 928.

56. Paul-Alain Beaulieu has claimed that "'Yahwism' did not constitute the main referent of identity" for Judeans exiles, especially in light of the abundance of non-Yahwistic and foreign names among the deportees ("Yahwistic Names in Light of Late Babylonian Onomastics," in *Judah and the Judeans in the Achaemenid Period*, 259). The situation encountered in Āl-Yāḫūdu nuances this impression, although several Judeans did adopt local Babylonian and West Semitic (Aramaic) names. For the influence exerted by the Aramaic language on the Judean community of Babylonia, see Ran Zadok, "Yamu-iziri

the Summoner of Yahūdu and Aramaic Linguistic Interference," *Nouvelles assyriologiques brèves et utilitaires* 3 (2015): 142–44; Eph'al, "The Babylonian Exile," 24.

57. John J. Ahn has called for the integration of generational differences in research dealing with the exilic period ("Forced Migrations Guiding the Exile: Demarcating 597, 587, and 582 B.C.E.," in *By the Irrigation Canals of Babylon*, 177–80), as there are important differences in coping with this event between generations.

58. The evidence from Sippar shows that royal merchants tended to assimilate to local culture after two generations, while foreign onomastic forms were preserved in the names of the courtiers of Susa (Bloch, "Judeans in Sippar and Susa during the First Century of the Babylonian Exile," 127–41; Jursa, "Eine Familie von Königskaufleuten judäischer Herkunft," 23). Zadok also noted an increase in Yahwistic name for the second generation of Jewish individuals in the Murašu corpus (*The Jews in Babylonia*, 84).

59. Our method of investigation represented generations by a twenty-year range, beginning with the earliest text dated to 572 BCE (CUSAS 28: 1). Names are associated with four date ranges: 572–552 BCE, 552–532 BCE, 532–512 BCE, and 512–492 BCE. Fathers mentioned within one of these specific date ranges are presumed to have been born at least forty years earlier, while twenty years were assumed for the sons. The following generations are thus hypothesized: 612–592 BCE, 592–572 BCE, 572–552 BCE, 552–532 BCE, and 532–512 BCE.

60. Aḫīqam is first attested in CUSAS 28: 12, dated to 533 BCE.

61. The two cases are Bēl-šarru-uṣur, son of Nubâ (CUSAS 28: 2, 3) and [Ṭā]b-šalam, son of Šalam-Yāma (CUSAS 28: 5).

62. The following are Aḫīqam, son of Yāḫû-šūrī (CUSAS 28: 13); Aḫīqam, son of Rapā-Yāma (CUSAS 28: 12, 13); [Badabarr]â, son of Ṣapa-Yāma (CUSAS 28: 39); Ḫiqammu, son of Rapā-Yāma (CUSAS 28: 14, 17); Pakkâ, son of Maqin-Yāma (CUSAS 28: 15); Ḫaggâ, son of Mataniā (CUSAS 28: 37); Ḫanan, son of Azar-Yāma (CUSAS 28: 37); Šalāmān, son of Rapā-Yāma (CUSAS 28: 20); Maltēma, son of Zakar-Yāma (CUSAS 28: 23); Rīmūt, son of Šamā-Yāma (CUSAS 28: 43); and Šullumu, son of Yaḫû-li-ia (CUSAS 28: 44).

63. Neo-Babylonian period: Ṣidqī-Yāma, son of Šillimu (CUSAS 28: 2, 3, 4, 5, 6, 9); [. . .]-Yāma, son of Ḫubaba (CUSAS 28: 2); Gadal-Yāma, son of Šallamu (CUSAS 28: 6); Šalam-Yāma, son of Ṭāb-šalam (CUSAS 28: 3); Ṭūb-Yāma, son of Mukkêa (CUSAS 28: 8); Dalā-Yāma, son of Ilī-šu (CUSAS 28: 10); Šikin-Yāma, son of Ilī-šu (CUSAS 28: 10); and Šikin-Yāma, son of Ḫinnannu (CUSAS 28: 5). Achaemenid period: Yaḫû-e-DIR, son of Ṭāb-šalam (CUSAS 28: 12); Nīr-Yāma, son of Aḫīqam (CUSAS 28: 24, 25, 26, 27, 32, 37, 45, 46); Rapā-Yāma, son of Išê-il (CUSAS 28: 50); Šalam-Yāma, son of Agguru (CUSAS 28: 33); [Abdi]-Yāḫû, son of Nabaḫa (CUSAS 28: 14, 15); Abdi-Yāḫû, son of Ṣalamā (CUSAS 28: 15); Abdi-Yāḫû, son of Kīnâ (CUSAS 28: 15); Iššûa, son of Nabû-ēṭir (CUSAS 28: 40); Šalam-Yāma, son of Malēšu (CUSAS 28: 16 A & B); Qad/ṭa--Yāma, son of Buluqâ (CUSAS 28: 23); Banā-Yāma, son of Il(u)-dū-šu (CUSAS 28: 29);

Matan-[Yāma], son of Malēšu (CUSAS 28: 35); Kīn-Yāma, son of Šili[. . .] (CUSAS 28: 35); Yāḫû-azar, son of Aḫīqam (CUSAS 28: 30); Azar-Yāma, son of Ilta-r[âma?] (CUSAS 28: 30); Šilim-Yāma, son of Malēšu (CUSAS 28: 30); Rupuni-Yāma, son of Qazizi (CUSAS 28: 44); Yāḫû-azza, son of Aḫīqam (CUSAS 28: 45); Yāḫû-izrī, son of Aḫīqam (CUSAS 28: 45); Yāḫûšū, son of Aḫīqam (CUSAS 28: 45); and Mataniā, son of Šiltā (CUSAS 28: 52).

64. The name form DN-šarru-uṣur [DN = Divine Name] expressed loyalty to the ruler and was especially popular among individuals who occupied an administrative position or had social connections. For a discussion of this name pattern, see Bloch, "Judeans in Sippar and Susa during the First Century of the Babylonian Exile," 135–36; CUSAS 28: p. 101.

65. The inclusion of foreign deities into Babylonian onomastic patterns is extremely rare. Arameans and other foreign groups often included Babylonian deities into their own onomastic pattern, while Babylonians never did the same. Rare cases of integration of foreign deities usually meant that they were integrated into the Babylonian pantheon. I would like to thank Professor Paul-Alain Beaulieu for bringing this to my attention.

66. Pearce, "Identifying Judeans and Judean Identity in the Babylonian Evidence," 26–27. The present case might be similar to that of the scribe Nabû-na'id/Nabû-nāṣir. Here, the change was prompted by the emergence of the vice-regent and son of Nabonidus, Belshazzar (Bēl-šarru-uṣur), as the adjustment to Yāḫû-šarru-uṣur took place early in the reign of Nabonidus (ca. 550 BCE).

67. CUSAS 28: p. 61.

68. For a discussion of these names, see CUSAS 28: 36 rev. 14 and BaAr 6: 10 rev. 20; CUSAS 28: 34 obv. 6 and BaAr 6: 3 obv. 4. See also CUSAS 28: pp. 39, 88.

69. Ran Zadok's observation on Aramaic linguistic interference in the name of Yāḫû-i/edir is another reflection of the exchanges taking place between various cultures present in southern Babylonia ("Yamu-iziri the Summoner of Yahūdu and Aramaic Linguistic Interference," 142–43).

70. Robin Cohen, *Global Diasporas: An Introduction*, 2nd ed. (London: Routledge, 2008), 22–23.

71. Ibid., 23.

Karaites and Jerusalem: From Anan ben David to the Karaite Heritage Center in the Old City

Daniel J. Lasker

THE FIRST KARAITES IN JERUSALEM: MOURNERS FOR ZION

It is often said that the Karaites were the first Zionists. Although there were always Jews in the Land of Israel from the destruction of the Second Temple (70 CE) through the present, and although there were always Jews who left their different diasporas to come to the Land of Israel for the purpose of settling there, the first organized attempt at a massive Jewish return to the Holy Land after 70 CE began in the late ninth century with the arrival of Daniel al-Qumisi, a Karaite Jew from Persia (today's Iran). It appears that quite a number of early Karaites were from Persia, which may help explain how Karaism developed as an expression of opposition to the imposition of Babylonian rabbinic hegemony over far-flung Jewish communities, communities that had their own ways of interpreting the Torah and their own customs.[1] Al-Qumisi advocated that other Jews follow his lead and immigrate to the Land of Israel. He even had a practical plan: each community should send five representatives along with their means of support.[2]

We do not know how successful al-Qumisi's detailed plan was, but many Karaites must have followed his lead. By the mid-tenth century, there was a flourishing Karaite community in the Land of Israel centered in Jerusalem and Ramle, which at the time was the capital of the Arabic military district of Palestine [*jund Filastin*]. It may very well be that it was in the Land of Israel that the Karaites became familiar with writings of Second Temple non-Pharisaic groups, which could explain the similarities between Karaism and the religion of the Dead Sea Covenanters of the Scrolls. How Karaites became familiar with the scrolls is still a matter of dispute, but the Karaite presence in the Land of Israel is certainly part of the story.[3]

It was also in the Land of Israel that Karaism as we know it developed and became crystalized. Since the new religion was still somewhat in its infancy, its adherents needed to work out the legal, theological, and exegetical issues that would determine the direction of the community. In the Land of Israel, Karaites rose to the challenge and were responsible for producing significant literary works in the fields of law, biblical exegesis, theology, polemics, and grammar. For a relatively small community, the number of important Karaite scholars is remarkable. Although the names of these Karaite savants, such as Yefet ben Eli the exegete, Joseph al-Baṣir the theologian and legalist, and Abū al-Faraj Hārūn the grammarian, are hardly household words today, their intellectual accomplishments were quite impressive, and they made a significant impact on Rabbanite (or rabbinic) Judaism as well as on Karaism. As a result of their accomplishments, the tenth and eleventh centuries are known as the golden age of Karaism. By the time of the destruction of the Jewish communities in the Land of Israel at the end of eleventh century, Karaism had become fully established as an alternate form of the Jewish religion.[4]

The golden age Karaites were important not only for their distinctive religious practices and their intellectual achievements. A central feature of their belief system was their identification with the Mourners for Zion, a group marked by ascetic practices and a special liturgy employed in the hope of bringing about the Messianic redemption. Although not all Karaites were Mourners, and perhaps not all Mourners were Karaites, the idea that immigration to the Land of Israel could contribute to the termination of the diaspora for all Jews was uniquely identified with the Karaites.[5] These Karaites in the Land of Israel devoted themselves assiduously to bringing the Messiah, and they gave it their best shot—they foreswore meat and wine, dressed themselves in sackcloth, and spent their days and nights in prayers in order to bring the Messiah who would rebuild the temple, but nothing happened. Eventually the Karaites themselves grew weary of this special mourning. Even before the Crusaders (instead of the Messiah) arrived in Jerusalem in 1099, the Mourners for Zion movement had been weakened considerably.[6] Nonetheless, the centrality of Jerusalem in Karaite thought and the idea of mourning for Zion did not disappear entirely, and over the course of Karaite history to this very day one can discern the special place that the Land of Israel in general and the city of Jerusalem in particular has had in Karaite thought.[7]

ANAN BEN DAVID

Mention should be made of Anan ben David, whose name appears in the title of this essay. Contrary to popular wisdom, the eighth-century Anan was the founder not of Karaism but instead of Ananism. Furthermore, the famous story of Anan's revolt against rabbinic Judaism because he was not appointed exilarch of Babylonian Jewry (in present-day Iraq) has at best only a tenuous relation to the historical facts. Ananites and Karaites coalesced a few hundred years after Anan's life, and only then was he considered a founder of Karaism.

In addition, Anan himself was part of the Babylonian rabbinic hierarchy with his own unconventional ideas, and we have no proof that he had any particular connection to the Land of Israel.

When Land of Israel Karaites adopted Anan as one of their own, they also attributed to him their attachment to the Land of Israel. Thus, they believed that after he was released from prison, where he was held on trumped-up charges at the behest of his Rabbanite enemies, Anan left Babylonia, came to the Land of Israel, and established what is now the oldest extant synagogue in Jerusalem, which is located on Karaite Street in the Jewish Quarter of the Old City.

Karaite Street, Old City, Jerusalem.

Sign for the Anan ben David Karaite Synagogue, Old City, Jerusalem.

Anan ben David Karaite Synagogue, Old City, Jerusalem, Entrance.

Anan ben David Karaite Synagogue, Old City, Jerusalem, Interior. Courtesy of the Karaite Heritage Center. Photographer: Avi Yefet.

The modern-day Karaite Heritage Center in Jerusalem, discussed below, is adjacent to the synagogue that the Karaites attribute to Anan. But, just as Anan was not a Karaite, he was also not a Mourner of Zion, and there is no reason to think that he was ever in the Land of Israel, let alone in the synagogue that now bears his name.[8]

KARAITES MOVE ON

After the destruction of Karaite life in the Land of Israel, the next major Karaite center was in Byzantium, most notably in the capital city Constantinople. The first outstanding personality of that community was a local resident who, in the first half of the eleventh century, left home to study with Karaite sages in the Land of Israel and Egypt. He was Tobias ben Moses, who in the Land of Israel was known as Tobias the Mourner or Tobias the Pious, but back home he was Tobias the Translator because of his renderings of the classical Judaeo-Arabic texts of the Land of Israel into Hebrew for the Byzantine community. Mourning for Zion outside of Zion did not seem to make much sense, so Tobias may have dropped not only the appellation "the Mourner" but also mourning itself. Nevertheless, the most prominent Byzantine Karaite of the twelfth century, Judah Hadassi, called himself "the Mourner" and advocated mourning practices in his theological and legal compendium. He realized, however, that most of his coreligionists would not be able to abide by his suggested regimen, so he did not try to impose it.

Hadassi mentions Jerusalem quite a number of times in his magnum opus, *Eshkol ha-kofer* [Cluster of Henna Blossoms], especially in terms of his eschatological vision of what would happen with the coming of the Messiah. Hadassi was one of the first Jews to make a list of principles of faith, predating Maimonides and his code of thirteen principles by two decades. One of Hadassi's principles was "To understand that the palace of the King is true, for the sanctuary of the King, great in truth, the place of the dwelling of His glory, where His indwelling is established forever." Much of his eschatological vision for the End of Days was centered on Jerusalem.[9] A fourteenth-century Egyptian Karaite, Israel ben Samuel ha-Ma'aravi, also listed the centrality of Jerusalem in his list of six principles of Judaism.[10] In contrast, Rabbanite lists of articles of faith do not include a paean to the centrality of Jerusalem.

Hadassi's mourning and his strict construction of Karaite law did not catch on among subsequent generations of Byzantine Karaites or among East European Karaites who followed the Byzantine lead in matters of law and theology. The last three significant Byzantine Karaite savants—Aaron ben Joseph (the Elder), who codified the prayer book and wrote commentaries on most of the Bible (end of the thirteenth century); Aaron by Elijah the Younger (d. 1369), who wrote a commentary on the Torah, a law code, and a philosophical treatise; and Elijah Bashyatchi (d. 1490), whose law code is still in use today—all acknowledged the centrality of Jerusalem for Jewish life, but none was a Mourner of Zion. During these centuries, Byzantine Karaism became closer to Rabbanite Judaism, perhaps under the influence of immigrants from the Iberian Peninsula, and the major differences between the two groups focused on their parallel legal systems. Attitudes toward Jerusalem and the Land of Israel did not play a significant role in Karaite-Rabbanite relations.[11]

Even when the Karaites were physically far removed from Jerusalem, the Holy City was still at the center of their aspirations. Far-flung communities sent donations to the small Karaite communities in the Land of Israel, and pilgrimage was such a major event that successful Karaite pilgrims added the title "Yerushalmi" (in Hebrew) or "Al-Qudsi/El-Kodsi" (in Arabic) to their names. We have descriptions of Karaite journeys of pilgrimage to the Land of Israel, visits that were intended, among other reasons, to bring money to the Karaite community there. One of the travelers, Benjamin ben Elijah of Crimea, who traveled to the Land of Israel in 1785–1786, reports that he was not able to eat meat in Jerusalem "according to the instructions of our sages," indicating that not all mourning customs had been abandoned by the Karaites.[12]

INTO THE MODERN ERA

Karaites arrived in Eastern Europe—Crimea, Lithuania, Galicia, and Volhynia—during the thirteenth to fifteenth centuries. They were still tied religiously and spiritually to the center in Constantinople. With the growth of the East European Karaism and the weakening of Byzantine Karaism after the Ottoman conquest, the young Karaite communities were able to produce their own intellectual leadership. They were at a far remove from Jerusalem, but memories of Karaite attachment to the Land of Israel were maintained. These Karaites saw themselves, and were considered by those around them, as part of the larger Jewish community.

In the late eighteenth century, when as a result of Russian imperialist expansions most East European Jews, Rabbanites and Karaites alike, found themselves under czarist Russian control, the Karaites looked for ways to find exemptions from discriminatory laws against Jews. They were mostly successful, but they continued to retain their Jewish identity and to be in contact with Karaite communities in the Ottoman Empire, including in Jerusalem and Cairo. At the same time as the Karaite leaders were requesting exemptions from anti-Jewish laws, they maintained their aspirations for a messianic redemption of Jerusalem.[13]

In the early twentieth century, however, East European Karaites began denying any connection whatsoever to the Jewish people, a denial that would prove lifesaving for them in the Holocaust a few decades later. This denial, however, meant that they excluded themselves from the Jewish people. That self-exclusion was so great that in the 1970s and 1980s, when only Jews were allowed to leave the Soviet Union, the few surviving Karaites did not exercise that option, remaining in their centers in Lithuania and the Crimea. Only recently have some Karaites of the former Soviet Union availed themselves of the opportunity of immigrating to Israel, but it is unlikely that their move was motivated by religious ideology.[14]

The story in Egypt was different. Karaites there had always been an integral part of the Jewish community, making up a sizable component of the Jewish population and often intermarrying with Rabbanite Jews. The Egyptian civil authorities saw both Rabbanites and Karaites as part of the same non-Muslim religious community. In the twentieth century, both groups expressed their connection to the Land of Israel through Zionist activity, including the ill-fated Lavon affair that resulted in the public hanging of two Egyptian Jews in 1955. One of them, Dr. Moshe Marzouk, was a Karaite. In the wake of the Suez campaign in 1956 and the Six-Day War in 1967, the vast majority of Egyptian Jews, including the Karaites, left Egypt.[15] While some Karaites went to Europe or the United States, most of them came to Israel and reestablished communities in Ramle, Ashdod, Beer Sheva, two Karaite *moshavim* (Ranen and Mazliah), and in a number of other cities. The first generation shared many of the trials and tribulations of other immigrants from Islamic countries, and it took a number of generations before they were firmly established economically in Israel.[16]

Despite the historic Karaite connection to the city of Jerusalem, they did not form a community in Israel's capital. Still, there was Karaite property in the Old City, which became accessible again after the Six-Day War, and some Karaites returned to their synagogue and their quarter from which the few local Karaites had been expelled by the Jordanians in 1948. Although contemporary Karaism has already given up on an ascetic Mourning for Zion, I am informed that to this day that as a sign of mourning, Karaites refrain from eating meat in Jerusalem itself.[17]

ISRAELI KARAITES AND JERUSALEM

This brings us to the Anan Synagogue and the Heritage Center. Over the years, there was usually a miniscule Karaite presence in Jerusalem. The synagogue would have Sabbath services (Karaites do not have the concept of a minyan, so that was not a problem), and it served as a point of pilgrimage for the community, especially during the holidays. As the Israeli Karaite community became more established financially, they expanded the synagogue complex and made a small museum. In 2016 they opened the Heritage Center, which is small but succeeds in telling the Karaite narrative, namely that they are the original Jews who observe the Torah as it was first given and as it was meant to be. Despite the presentation of the Karaite point of view, a short introductory film features both Karaites and academics, who give a balanced picture of the history of Karaism and its connection to Jerusalem.[18] It is now one of the recognized tourist spots in Jerusalem's Old City, visited by Jews, Karaite and Rabbanite, and non-Jews alike.[19]

The theme of the conference that is the basis of this volume was "Exile and Return." The Karaite return to Jerusalem after an exile of almost 1,000 years, the reestablishment of their religious life and communal institutions,

Karaite Heritage Center—Interior. Courtesy of the Karaite Heritage Center. Photographer: Avi Yefet.

Karaite Heritage Center—Interior. Courtesy of the Karaite Heritage Center. Photographer: Avi Yefet.

and the continuation of prayers in their Jerusalem synagogue and now the Heritage Center represent a small but not insignificant part of the larger Jewish story of exile and return.

NOTES

1. The issue of Karaite origins is very complicated and beyond the scope of the discussion here.

2. See Leon Nemoy, "The Pseudo-Qūmisīan Sermon to the Karaites," *Proceedings of the American Academy for Jewish Research* 43 (1976): 49–105. Nemoy is not totally convinced that al-Qumisi was the author of the epistle, but if he was not, then the real author had a very similar background to his.

3. For some of the issues involved in the relation between Karaism and the scrolls, see Daniel J. Lasker, "The Dead Sea Scrolls in the Historiography and Self-Image of Contemporary Karaites," *Dead Sea Discoveries* 9:3 (2002): 281–94.

4. I have described some of the differences between the two forms of Judaism in Daniel J. Lasker, "Karaism: An Alternate Form of Jewish Celebration," in *Rites of Passage: How Today's Jews Celebrate, Commemorate, and Commiserate* (Studies in Jewish Civilization 21), ed. Leonard Greenspoon (West Lafayette, IN: Purdue University Press, 2010), 141–54. Much useful material about Karaism throughout the centuries can be found in Meira Polliack, *Karaite Judaism* (Leiden: Brill, 2003). There is little basis for the commonly held belief that in the period of the golden age, Karaism was on the verge of becoming the dominant stream in Judaism; see Leon Nemoy, "Early Karaism (The Need for a New Approach)," *Jewish Quarterly Review* 40 (1950): 307–15.

5. The Hebrew term for mourners of Zion, *aveilei ẓiyyon*, is derived from Isaiah 61:3: "To grant to those who mourn for Zion; to give them a garland instead of ashes, the oil of gladness instead of mourning, the mantle of praise instead of a faint spirit; that they may be called oaks of righteousness, the planting of the Lord, that He may be glorified."

6. For important discussions about the Mourners of Zion, see Yoram Erder, *The Karaite Mourners of Zion and the Qumran Scrolls* (Turnhout: Brepols, 2017). On the Karaite community in Jerusalem and the decline of Mourning, see Haggai Ben-Shammai, "The Karaites," in *The History of Jerusalem: The Early Muslim Period, 638–1099*, ed. J. Prawer and H. Ben-Shammai (Jerusalem: Yad Izhak Ben-Zvi, 1996), 201–24.

7. For a review of Karaite relations with Jerusalem, see Daniel J. Lasker, *From Judah Hadassi to Elijah Bashyatchi: Studies in Late Medieval Karaite Philosophy* (Leiden: Brill, 2008), 229–47.

8. For Karaite origins and the assimilation of Anan and the Ananites into the Karaite movement in the Land of Israel, see Moshe Gil, *A History of Palestine, 634–1099* (Cambridge: Cambridge University Press, 1992), 777–94. See also Moshe Gil, "The Origins of the Karaites," in Polliack, *Karaite Judaism*, 73–118. As Gil has demonstrated, a number of

Anan's descendants were heads of the Jewish community in the Land of Israel, but there is no reason to assume that Anan himself was ever in the Land of Israel.

9. Hadassi's *Eshkol ha-kofer* is a compendium of all previous Karaite law and lore and much else. It is written in the form of alphabetical acrostics, and every stanza ends with the syllable *kha*. The one edition of the text (Gözleve, 1836) is quite defective. For a partial edition and English translation, see Daniel J. Lasker et al., *Theological Encounters at a Crossroads: A Preliminary Edition of Judah Hadassi's Eshkol ha-kofer, First Commandment, and Studies of the Book's Judaeo-Arabic and Byzantine Contexts* (Leiden: Brill, 2019). For Hadassi's philosophy, see Lasker, *From Judah Hadassi to Elijah Bashyatchi*, 41–59.

10. Ernst Mainz, "The Credo of a Fourteenth-Century Karaite," *Proceedings of the American Academy for Jewish Research* 22 (1953): 55–63.

11. For the changes in Karaite thought between Judah Hadassi and Elijah Bashyatchi, see Lasker, *From Judah Hadassi to Elijah Bashyatchi*.

12. For a description of these journeys, see Abraham Yaari, *Masa'ot Erez Yisrael* (Ramat-Gan: Massada, 1976), 221–67, 305–23, 459–78. The prohibition of eating meat is mentioned on p. 478. For a detailed overview of Karaite attitudes toward Jerusalem based on tombstones in the Çufut-Qal'eh Karaite cemetery in the Crimea, see Golda Akhiezer, "The Ties of the Crimean Karaites with Jerusalem and Their Reflection in *Avnei Zikkaron*," in *The Tombstones of the Cemetery of the Karaite Jews in Çufut-Qal'eh (the Crimea)* [Hebrew], ed. Dan D. Y. Shapira (Jerusalem: Ben-Zvi Institute, 2008), 300–311.

13. See Lasker, *From Judah Hadassi to Elijah Bashyatchi*, 244–46.

14. For a number of studies about the history of East European Karaites, including their connection to Jewish identity and their fate in World War II, as well as a study of the few East European Karaites who have immigrated to Israel, see the studies by Kizilov, Feferman, and Bram in Dan D. Y. Shapira and Daniel J. Lasker, *Eastern European Karaites in the Last Generations* (Jerusalem: Ben-Zvi Institute and Center for Research on the History and Culture of Polish Jews, 2011).

15. See Mourad El-Kodsi, *The Karaite Jews of Egypt, 1882–1986*, 2nd ed. (New York: n.p., 2006).

16. Although demographics are difficult to determine and many Karaites have assimilated into the general secular Israeli public, there may be between 30,000 and 40,000 Israeli Karaites today. The official website Universal Karaite Judaism is http://www.karaite.org.il.

17. Personal communication from Moshe Firrouz, chief Karaite rabbi.

18. Full disclosure: I am one of the academics who appear in the film.

19. TripAdvisor rates it as number 184 out of 315 things to do in Jerusalem (April 18, 2018). See "Karaite Synagogue," TripAdvisor, https://www.tripadvisor.com/Attraction_Review-g293983-d558452-Reviews-Karaite_Synagogue-Jerusalem_Jerusalem_District.html. On June 19, 2019, it was 187 out of 274.

Jewish Folk Songs: Exile and Return

Paula Eisenstein Baker

In an imaginary conversation between an editor and the Yiddish folk songs that he published in Vilna in 1871, the editor addresses the songs themselves in his preface to the volume: "Many years have already passed since you were born," he says to them. "You've been well-liked, and now the time has come to go be seen by the masses. Get thee out into the world!" But the worried little songs reply, "We are afraid to travel with our business out into the world. We've lived here a long time and do not know the road."[1]

But travel out into the world the songs did, thanks to this editor and others who published them. Extending the metaphor, I will argue that these songs, as employed in composing art music, did experience multiple exiles, just as they had feared, but that they also returned. I will posit that it wasn't so much their traveling out into the world that changed their status. No, as the editor may have meant—and as he probably understood—it was their appearance in print. But as we will see, their new status would be nowhere near the end of the road for them; it was part of an ongoing journey.

In this essay, I assess whether the folk song has experienced "exile and return," and I examine the effect that publishing has had on the Jewish folk song. I hope to demonstrate that the printed song and the sung song have managed to coexist in the same way that variations in the tune (and often even in the words) of any given song have always coexisted; that different versions of any tune have long been present in different communities, in different traditions, and on different continents; and that even the use of the songs as material for art music did not interfere with their lives as songs.

First, we must accept that long before any given folk song appeared in print, differences in the tune (and sometimes even in the words) already existed and that they depended on who was singing the song and where it was being sung. Interestingly, differences were also produced by the written tradition. John Spitzer has written about this phenomenon in the case of Stephen Foster's "Oh! Susanna," which was already being sung in various versions before it was published in 1848.[2] As the song became more and more popular, variations in both tune and words began to be heard—and seen—in printed versions.

Spitzer observes that "oral and written transmission sometimes overlapped. Performers orally transmitted popular songs and tunes alongside of and interacting with written transmission."[3] And in discussing the transmission of

"Oh! Susanna," he provides specific observations about the process: "as a composed and notated song moves into oral transmission, it undergoes predictable changes: its rhythms are altered to clarify the beat . . . its melody is altered . . . its pitches and rhythms are adjusted to conform to parallel passages."[4]

Are the changes introduced by oral transmission usually "inferior" to the original readings? Not necessarily. "In the case of 'Susanna,'" Spitzer writes, " the tendencies of oral transmission have evidently improved the tune. They make the rhythm clearer . . . they make the tune easier to sing and easier to remember." And, he concludes, "When composers fail to get it right the first time, perhaps singers and players have something additional and valuable to contribute to the compositional process."[5]

AN EXAMPLE FROM JEWISH FOLK SONG

As a case study, I will examine alternate versions of the words and tune for the short Hebrew folksong "Artza alinu" [We Have Ascended to the Land], which was composed in Palestine in the 1920s.[6]

The two versions below were published within two years of each other in the mid-1930s in Chicago and Berlin; neither volume provides an attribution or a date of composition for the song.[7] (There are also discrepancies in the transliteration of the Hebrew words, but these are not relevant to this discussion, and in any case, transliteration is highly dependent on the language of the country in which a song is published.)

The two tunes contain the same number of measures, and their contours are similar. Both divide neatly into three sections, each section four measures in length. The first discrepancy between them occurs in the text in measures 1 and 2: the Coopersmith version begins with the words "Artza alinu" [We have ascended to the land] in both of those measures, whereas the Schönberg version opens with the single word "Alinu" [We have ascended] in both measures. This discrepancy is heard again immediately, since the end of the fourth measure of each version has a repeat sign, indicating that those four measures are sung a second time in both versions.

The next four measures (mm. 5–8) display significant discrepancies between the two versions of the tune. In the Coopersmith version, the first two measures of this section are repeated exactly (the musical notation indicates that they are identical), and the third pitch in the first measure of the section (m. 5) is just an unimportant "passing tone" between the second and fourth pitches. In the Schönberg version, the last pitch in measure 6 connects the tune to the next measure, and the pitches in the third measure of the section differ completely from those in the first measure rather than duplicating them, the way the Coopersmith version does.

In the last four measures (mm. 9–12), the pitches in the two tunes match exactly. The only difference is the indication in the Schönberg edition that the first four measures of the tune are to be repeated following the last printed measure. All in all, there is a remarkable array of discrepancies in a tune only 16 measures long (or 20 measures if the repeat indicated in the Schönberg is honored).

OTHER ELEMENTS OF JEWISH MUSICAL TRADITION

Of course, what I have said about Jewish "folk song" does not apply only to folk song; it also applies to all the music associated with Jewish culture, of which folk song is only one element.

Another important source of Jewish tunes is our synagogue liturgy, those tunes associated with Shabbat and holiday worship, which is largely sung. There are prayer tunes: tunes associated with particular prayers that do not seem to vary much from place to place—the *Kol Nidre*, for instance, which is actually a bunch of tune fragments strung together, is invariable; it doesn't matter much where (within the Western tradition) you hear it. Then there is *nusakh*, which I am using here to refer to the style of the set of tunes for the prayers associated with a particular tradition or geographic location. We tend to adopt the *nusakh* of the group in which we are davening.

Finally, there is *trop*, the sets of tunes for chanting Torah, haftorah, and the five scrolls: *Shir haShirim* [Song of Songs], *Megillat Esther* [the book of Esther], *Eicha* [the book of Lamentations], *Koheleth* [Ecclesiastes], and *Megillat Rut* [the book of Ruth]. Tunes for the *trop* elements vary too depending on geography, but because *trop* is typically being used by one person at a time rather than a group, the elements you use are probably the ones you learned for your bar or bat mitzvah or when you first learned to *leyen*.

Returning to the question of transmission, how do tunes travel from one generation to another? The earliest stage is oral transmission: a parent sings a lullaby to a child, a person sings to his or her beloved, a leader teaches a song to a group. There are many positive aspects to oral transmission: it allows for creativity, and it is available to anyone who can carry a tune (and I have long argued that everyone can be taught to do so). People with musical talent lend their own touch to extant songs; the very talented ones invent songs. Of course, there are negative aspects too: oral transmission permits mistakes—if we can call them "mistakes," such as forgetting the tune or somehow changing it (but see above for a discussion of transmission).

BEYOND ORAL TRANSMISSION

When we move beyond oral transmission, the next mode of transmission is transcription, actually writing down the tunes; this is different than singing from memory, which allows for changes. (Transcription—and musical notation in general—came very late to the Jewish community, and for reasons unknown to me, we continue to argue about its value and importance.) But not everyone has the skill to decipher a transcribed tune—it employs a set of symbols that have to be learned, so the two options, oral and written, continue to coexist to this day.

Here, following the lead of the 1871 editor we met in the first paragraph, is my anthropomorphic analogy. The transcribed version of a song runs into an oral version that has never been transcribed. The transcribed tune says, "There's something just slightly different about you; is it the tune? Is it in the words? Maybe you repeated something in the middle?" The oral version replies, "Oh, do you like it? My singer introduced it just yesterday."

But the transcribed song was here to stay; it had several advantages. For those who do know musical notation, it simplified learning a song. It extended both the audience for the song and the number of participants in the song. One disadvantage was that transcription codified the song to some extent, but transcription has long coexisted with oral transmission, with the result that, as we have already seen, the version of a song in one collection almost always differs from the version in another. So perhaps we can say that our exiled songs never really went into exile.

One stage that followed transcribing songs was creating an accompaniment for an extant song; here I imagine one song running into another on the sidewalk: "Long time no see," says song #1. "My oh my," says song #2, "how interesting! You're on a bicycle." "Oh yes," replies song # 1, "I don't do the walking myself anymore; this conveyance supports me."

A few months later, our song #1 runs into an instrumental version. "I recognize you," says song #1, "but there's something different." "Yes, I've quit singing. I'd like you to meet Mme. Violin, it's her job." "But what about the words?" asks song #1. "Never mind the words. Have you heard Mme. Violin? Listen to her version of the song; it's really quite special."

And my last fantasy is song #1 attending a concert. He waits at the stage door to congratulate the performers, and out comes the cello. "Am I crazy," asks song #1, "or was there something about that last piece you played that sounded a little bit like me?" "You're absolutely right," replies the cello. "My composer admires you so much that he borrowed your first four measures! I was wondering whether you would recognize me! What did you think? Did you like it? Do you think other people will like it? Let me tell you about my composer!"

ART MUSIC EMPLOYING FOLK MATERIAL

And who was that composer? In this fantasy, the composer was a member of the Society for Jewish Folk Music (for "folk," think "ethnic"), founded in St. Petersburg, Russia, in 1908. The group's primary goals were composing, performing, and publishing art music based on Jewish material: folk song, *nusakh*, and *trop*.

Two major factors were responsible for the fact that the group developed initially in St. Petersburg. One factor was, quite simply, the presence of Jewish students at the conservatory there; in spite of the 3 percent quota on Jewish enrollment that governed university-level education in Russia prior to the 1905 revolution,[8] the school in St. Petersburg had always been open to both Jews and women.[9]

A second factor was that the St. Petersburg conservatory students benefited from the support and the influence of composer Nikolai Rimsky-Korsakov, who taught there until his death in 1908. Art music on Jewish themes was a logical extension of the late nineteenth-century nationalist musical style championed in Russia by the group of composers known as "the five," of whom Rimsky-Korsakov was the last active member.[10] The composer encouraged each of his students, not only by example but explicitly, to exploit his or her own ethnic heritage in composition.

Although the works published by the societies in St. Petersburg and Moscow constitute the most important legacy of this movement, the society in St. Petersburg, the group we know the most about, also organized concerts and concert tours, public lectures, and music classes. The group's concerts were presented at various secular locations in St. Petersburg, in addition to the conservatory. And over the period from 1908 to 1917, the Society for Jewish Folk Music published eighty works by its member composers.[11]

Reviews in the influential journal *Russkaia muzykal'naia gazeta* [The Russian Musical Newspaper] and in the monthly "Chronicle" issues of the journal *Muzykal'nyi sovremennik* [Contemporary Music] reported how large the audiences were and how thrilled they were by the new music. Members of the society also served on the editorial board of *Muzykal'nyi sovremennik*, and several of them published essays in its columns.[12]

The society in St. Petersburg inspired a group that was organized in Moscow about five years later. That group began as a branch of the mother organization, but after the October Revolution it was renamed the Society for Jewish Music. The Moscow group's focus was primarily on performance rather than publishing. However, as early as 1918 it began to publish works by a few of its member composers, primarily those of Joel Engel (1868–1927) and Alexander Krein (1883–1951).[13] The latest Society for Jewish Music publication I have seen bears the publication date 1919; its back cover lists eighty works.[14]

By the mid-1920s, both the St. Petersburg group and the Moscow group had ceased publishing, and many of their members had already left Russia for Europe, Palestine, or the United States. The goal of publishing had been adopted by two new groups, Jibneh and Juwal, both of which began in Berlin in 1923.[15] In 1925 those publishers were acquired by Universal Edition in Vienna, where Abram Dzimitrovsky (1873?–1943) of their Russian department handled all the music on Jewish themes.

By the mid-1930s, of course, it was clear to Universal that it would no longer be publishing or selling music by Jewish composers. In a short article published in *The Reconstructionist* in 1943, musicologist/composer Judith Kaplan Eisenstein wrote that "Dzimitrovsky salvaged every bit of music he could and sent it on to America."[16] There he reconstituted Jibneh as Yibneh and revived its activities until his death in 1943. At that point, the plates and printed sheet music were purchased by the Jewish Reconstructionist Foundation, and Judith Kaplan Eisenstein, Rabbi Mordecai M. Kaplan's oldest daughter, ran the publishing company until 1950.

ART MUSIC BASED ON FOLK MATERIAL: AN EXAMPLE

The remainder of this essay is devoted to demonstrating how Judith Kaplan Eisenstein employed Jewish tunes in a cantata, titled "What Is Torah." It was the first in a series of cantatas that she and her husband, Rabbi Ira Eisenstein, wrote and published in the 1940s and early 1950s.[17] "What Is Torah" was first performed during services for Shavuot 1942 at the Society for the Advancement of Judaism, Rabbi Kaplan's synagogue in New York, and was published the following year.[18]

The cantata is a narrative piece of music, a genre that first appeared in the late seventeenth century. It is perhaps best known from the cantatas of J. S. Bach, which were sacred vocal works in multiple movements for chorus and usually soloists accompanied either by organ or by small orchestra. The form never really died out, but it had a noticeable revival in the mid-twentieth century.[19] The musical examples that follow are drawn from "What Is Torah," the Eisensteins' earliest cantata and the only one that has been professionally recorded.[20]

"What Is Torah" demonstrates the Eisensteins' (especially Judith's) encyclopedic knowledge of Jewish music and provides an excellent example of a work that fulfilled the goals of the Society for Jewish Folk Music, the group discussed above. All the elements of Jewish music that the society wanted to employ are represented in this cantata: folk song, *nusakh*, and *trop*.

Most of the fragments and entire examples heard in a performance of "What Is Torah" would have been familiar to listeners in 1942, if not to today's audiences, and many of the sources for the musical material are listed in a foreword to the volume. However, there are a few pieces of material that are not identified; there are also fragments that may not be obvious, and I have identified those. For the sake of completeness and for performers and audiences in future generations and/or other cultures, I have listed all the fragments as they appear in the work and as they are described in the authors' foreword. I further identify any that were not thoroughly identified, and I add several that were not listed.

The opening motive is a simplification of the shofar call *tekiah* [a single blast]. The authors write only that "The trumpet call is derived from the Shofar calls." This motive is used throughout the cantata to begin a new section, just as shofar calls are used in the synagogue to announce a new year. And every time the motive is heard, it is followed by a solo speaking voice inquiring "What is Torah?" Only twice does the motive vary: in measures 263–265, the final pitch is extended by one measure, and in measures 373–375, close to the end of the cantata, the opening fifth is heard three times, perhaps to recall the shofar call *shevarim* [three short blasts] rather than the *tekiah*.

The body of the cantata opens with the *akdamut* tune, the melody for a lengthy Aramaic *piyyut* [Jewish liturgical poem] that is traditionally chanted prior to the first aliyah on the morning of Shavuot. (The same tune is heard in the kiddush for Shavuot as well as for Sukkot and Pesach.) About this, the authors write simply that "the opening song, 'In the Wilderness', [is derived] from the chant of 'Akdamut,' associated with the Shabuot festival." The tune is presented initially in its nonmetric original (mm. 2–5) but is then expanded into a metric song for chorus (mm. 6–25), labeled in the foreword to the volume as "The opening song: 'In the Wilderness.'"

With hardly a pause (indicated only by a fermata over the previous note), the chorus then launches into "Zemer l'simchat yisrael" [A song of (taking) joy in Israel], which the authors describe as "from a song by Joel Engel, its text taken from a medieval poem in the Simchat Torah service." Unidentified in the foreword, Engel (1868–1927) was an important figure in the early twentieth-century movement to compose art music on Jewish themes, although he was not himself a member of the St. Petersburg Society for Jewish Folk Music mentioned earlier. This song first appeared in Engel's volume *Shirei yeladim* [Songs for Children], and the words are from the second stanza; the text of the first stanza is identical except that it begins with the words "Hitkabtsu malachim [Gather, angels]."[21]

A long episode of dialogue follows in which the text is assigned first to individual voices in an unaccompanied question-and-answer format and then to half the chorus (m. 42) in unison over piano accompaniment. Next we hear the last sentence of the Torah account of the sixth day in the story of creation sung by the chorus. But the normal *trop* for the end of an aliyah is replaced by the "festive" *mercha tipcha mercha sof pasuk* [a series of prescribed tune elements], which is also the tune used for *hazak, hazak* [be strong, be strong] sung when the scroll is lifted on reaching the end of a book of the Torah. This is described as follows in the preface: "'Vay'hi erev,' and all other cadences using this melody, from the coda verses in the cantillation of the Pentateuch."

That tune segues directly into the beginning of the kiddush for Friday night to match the text, sung by the chorus and labeled only "'Vayehulu,' from the Friday evening service." The tune is regularized rhythmically and provided with a piano accompaniment; after the first six measures, the choral singing is overlaid by spoken narration describing Shabbat.

Following the next trumpet call (mm. 77–78), the chorus sings "Lamidbar" [To the desert], which the foreword describes only as "from a Yemenite song." The tune has been identified as a folk melody;[22] the words, however, are from a poem by Alexander Pen (often Penn) (1906–1972), a poet born in Russia and active in communist circles in prestate Israel.

After a repetition of the *hazak hazak* tune (mm. 96–99) and a long interlude (mm. 99–125), we hear "Ashirah ladonai" [Let us sing to the Lord], described in the foreword only as "from an eastern oriental melody." That "oriental melody" was found and arranged for four voices with piano accompaniment by composer and musicologist Erwin Jospe (Berlin, 1907; Ramat Ha-Sharon, 1983) when he was music director at the Anshe Emet Synagogue in Chicago; it was first published in 1947.[23] The version of the melody in "What Is Torah" assigns the soprano line to the chorus; the piano accompaniment is very simple.

"Ashirah ladonai" ends without a ritard in measure 131 and is followed by a shofar call and three measures of busy piano accompaniment, pianissimo behind dialogue (mm. 133–135). That pattern breaks off, and a measure later the piano switches to a progression of chords in which the top pitch moves upward by half steps (with the exception of mm. 142–143), beginning on D sharp and ending on B natural. Against this background, the chorus recites a series of commandments (printed in capital letters in the text), drawn from the "holiness code" in Leviticus 17–26 and from the Ten Commandments.

In the midst of that recitation (m. 144), the chorus chants (in English) "Remember: you were slaves in the land of Egypt" to a tune fragment resembling elements of *trop*. The fragment is not identified in the foreword, and I have so far been unable to identify it. The recitation then continues, ending in measures 157–163 with the words "Ye shall be holy," followed by the chanting of the Shema ["Shema Yisrael" (Hear O Israel), a declaration of faith] to the tune used for Rosh Hashanah and Yom Kippur.

After another repetition of the question "What is Torah?" the piano accompaniment becomes denser, with steady triplet chords on all four beats, initially in both hands, through measure 170. At that point, the triplets are restricted to the left hand in the piano, and for a few measures the accompaniment is less intense. The triplets are replaced (in m. 175) by sixteenth notes with accents, initially on every beat in the left hand and then on every beat in both hands. That pattern continues through measure 179 and switches to just the first beat in measure 180. In measure 182, the chorus breaks in with what the foreword refers to as "*V'natan lanu* [and He gave us], from the folksong *Baruk* [sic] *elohenu*" [Blessed is our God].

The musical unit that appears next (mm. 198–205) is identified only as "a lament from a Yemenite song." And measures 209–211 provide a rare instance of a musical motive for which the cantata mentions no source at all. That motive is an almost exact quotation of the first two measures of the folksong "Oyf'n pripetchik" [On the Hearth], with words by Russian Jewish poet Mark Warshavsky (1848–1907). Warshavsky published the song in Warsaw in 1900 in an anthology titled *Judische Volkslieder*, where it is labeled "Der Alef Bejss" [The Alphabet].[24]

That quotation from "Oyf'n pripetchik" introduces a three-measure motive (mm. 211–213) based on the *lernsteiger* [study chant] featured in a song by Moise Mil'ner (1882–1953). The authors identify the motive and describe it as "'Kometz alef oh' [the letter aleph with the vowel kametz (is pronounced) "oh"] from the famous song by Milner." The song, known either as "In heder" [In School] or "Der alef-beis," was originally published by the Society for Jewish Folk Music in St. Petersburg in 1914. The two motives, one from "Oyf'n pripetchik" and the other from "In heder," continue to alternate, brilliantly intertwined, through measure 232.

The next piece of motivic material is drawn from what the authors identify as "the Kabbalist's chant, from a Hasidic melody used by Engel in his incidental music to the Dybbuk." The motive is first heard in the third measure of the first violin part of the first movement, "Mipneh Mah" [Wherefore?], of Joel Engel's *Suite aus der Musik zu der dramatischen Legende von An-ski "Hadibuk"* (opus 35).[25] In measures 234–249 of "What Is Torah?," it is hummed by the chorus as background to spoken text and continues behind the text, slightly altered, in the piano through measure 253.

At measure 254, the chorus sings "Vos is die beste schoire? Yankele vet lernen Toire" [What is the best stuff? Yankele is going to study Torah]. In the foreword, the authors cite the first phrase of the text as the song's title and refer to its source only as "a Yiddish lullaby," and in measure 254 the score says "like a lullaby." The tune is actually the first phrase of a lullaby that begins with those words, although they also appear in several other lullabies.[26] In the cantata, that phrase is followed by the chanting of the text "That the spirit of knowledge may blossom and flourish," employing the tune for *hazak hazak*. A shofar call and the question "What is Torah?" follow. The piano continues, segueing into an accompaniment for the text "It is the Temple site," chanted to "the cantillation of the Book of Lamentations, used on Tish'a B'Ab."

The next piece of musical material is another example not mentioned in the foreword. It is "Eliyahu hanavi" [Elijah, the Prophet], a song from the Pesach seder that often concludes the short service marking the end of Shabbat. In the cantata, it is sung only once (beginning in m. 296), and even that instance is background for a recitation. According to at least one musicologist, the song we know by that name was actually the refrain that followed individual stanzas now rarely sung; it was well known in America by at least the beginning of the twentieth century and among East European Jews probably earlier than that.[27]

The chorus sings again beginning at measure 316: the text there is "La-avodah ve-la-melakah" [to work and to labor], which is both the refrain and the title of what the authors describe as "a modern Palestinian song." It is now credited, by Motti Regev and Edwin Seroussi, as a setting by Nahum Nardi (1901–1977) of a children's poem by Hayim Nachman Bialik (1873–1934).[28] The authors refer to Nardi as an "urban" (as opposed to a "kibbutz") composer, and they describe the song as "a classic Eretz Yisraeli song that praises hard work and labor as the cornerstones of the Zionist project."

That song is the last one identified in the preface. However, three more pieces of music are sung before the cantata ends. The authors may have felt that identification was unnecessary because the pieces were so familiar, but citations are provided here for the sake of completeness and for the benefit of those in future generations or other communities or countries.

In measures 342–350, the chorus sings the opening verse of the well-known African American song "Go Down, Moses," first published by the Jubilee Singers in 1872. Although the song is now usually considered a spiritual, it began—according to one account—as early as 1862 as an anthem for the "contrabands" (escaped slaves or others who identified with the Union forces during the American Civil War).[29]

At that point, a two-measure transition leads into the first verse of "America the Beautiful," a song whose words were written in 1895 by Katharine Lee Bates (1859–1929), later a professor of English at Wellesley College.[30] And although its tune, composed by Samuel Augustus Ward (1848–1903), a church organist and composer, now strikes us as indivisible from the poem, until 1926 Bates's words were sung to various tunes including "Auld Lang Syne"!

Following the *teruah* shofar call in measures 373–375, the piano reprises—behind dialogue (mm. 376–384)—the unmetered *Akdamut* tune from measures 2–5 that followed the shofar call opening the work. The cantata ends with the *hazak, hazak* tune underlying the text, "For it is our life and the length of our days," followed by the complete Hebrew quotation, "*hazak, hazak, ve-nithazek*" [be strong, be strong, and let us be strengthened].

EXILE AND RETURN

As I hope I have demonstrated, one of the wonderful aspects of music is that tunes do not ever get "used up"—they get shared. They can coexist in many different incarnations: the little tunes we met on the first page were nervous about

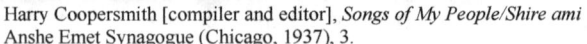

Two versions of Hebrew folksong "Artza alinu."

appearing on the world stage, but their wares turned out to be of interest to many. Even better, they were not obliged to give up their wares: they both kept them and shared them. As a result, they continued to exist both in their original form and in multiple other forms, and they continue to be available not only to those of us who sing them but also to the composers who employ them.

In conclusion, I return to my initial contention that the tunes addressed by the editor in 1871 went into exile initially as the result of appearing in print and subsequently by being adopted by composers. As we have seen, the story is far more complicated than that. I have come to think of the use of the tunes by composers as both an exile and a return, just as the title of this volume suggests, albeit unwittingly.

ACKNOWLEDGMENTS

Miriam Eisenstein was extremely helpful in identifying some of the elements that appear in *What Is Torah*. I am grateful to Robert S. Nelson for creating the musical example.

NOTES

1. Peysakh-Eliyahu Badkhn, *Kanaf renanim oder zeks folkslider* [Songbird, or Six Folk Songs], quoted and translated in James Loeffler, *The Most Musical Nation: Jews and Culture in the Late Russian Empire* (New Haven, CT: Yale University Press, 2010). A similar image appears in Loeffler's description of Yiddish writer Y. L. Peretz's visit to St. Petersburg in 1910. On the use of folk songs in art music, Peretz is said to have observed "But on the long road to cold Petersburg the songs will freeze a little bit" (Loeffler, *The Most Musical Nation*, 171).

2. John Spitzer, "'Oh! Susanna': Oral Transmission and Tune Transformation," *Journal of the American Musicological Society* 47, no. 1 (Spring 1994): 90–136.

3. Spitzer, "Oh! Susanna," 102. Spitzer's abstract (146) ends with "oral and written aspects were mixed in the transmission of 'Susanna.'"

4. Ibid., 117.

5. Ibid., 132.

6. Data abut the song's 1920s origin appears at "Artza Alinu—We Went Up to Our Land—Song Lesson—Shmuel Navon," All Readable, http://www.allreadable.com/dd8eKlJD.

7. The tune labeled "Coopersmith" appeared in Harry Coopersmith, comp. and ed., *Songs of My People/Shire ami* (Chicago: Anshe Emet Synagogue, 1937), 3. The tune labeled "Schönberg" appeared in Jakob Schönberg, *Shire erets Yisrael* [*Songs of the Land of Israel*] (Berlin: Hotsa'at Yudisher Ferlag, 1935), 8–9.

8. See, e.g., Mikhail Beizer, *The Jews of St. Petersburg* (Philadelphia: Jewish Publication Society, 1989), 81.

9. *Usloviia priema v S.-Peterburgskuiu konservatoriiu imperatorskago russkago muzykal'nago obshchestva i izvlechenie iz pravil konservatorii* [Conditions of Admission to the St. Petersburg Conservatory of the Imperial Russian Music Society and Excerpts from the Rules of the Conservatory] (St. Petersburg: "Russko-frantsuzskiia" typographiia, 1914–1915), 9.

10. The other four composers were César Cui, Aleksandr Borodin, Mily Balakirev, and Modest Mussorgsky.

11. Most sources—e.g., Albert Weisser, *The Modern Renaissance of Jewish Music* (1954; reprint, New York: Da Capo, 1983), 68, G. V. Kopytova, *Obshchestvo evreiskoi narodnoi muzyki v Peterburge-Petrograde* [The Society for Jewish Folk Music in Petersburg-Petrograd] (St. Petersburg: n.p., 1997), 68—attribute eighty-one works to the society, but the work listed as no. 81—a version for cello and piano by Solomon Rosowsky (1878–1962) of his *Hebraische (Chssidische) Melodie* [Hebrew (Chasidic) Melody] published for viola or English horn and piano as no. 79—does not appear to have been published. The Solomon Rosowsky Collection (Archives, Jewish Theological Seminary of America) includes several manuscript drafts but no printed copy of a work for cello and piano with that title.

12. More about the history of the society and its composers appears in Loeffler, *The Most Musical Nation;* Klára Móricz, *Jewish Identities: Nationalism, Racism and Utopianism in Twentieth-Century Music* (Berkeley: University of California Press, 2008); Jascha Nemtsov, *Die neue Jüdische Schule in der Musik* (Wiesbaden: Harrassowitz, 2004); Weisser, *The Modern Renaissance of Jewish Music.* An early (and brave!) discussion of the society appeared in M. I. Vainshtain, "Obshchestvo Evreyskoy narodnoy muzyki kak faktor kul'turnoy zhizni Peterburga nachala XX v." [The Society for Jewish Folk Music as a Factor in the Cultural Life of St. Petersburg in the Early 20th Century], in *Etnografiya Peterburga-Leningrada: materiali yezhegodnikh nauchnikh chteniy* [Ethnography of St. Petersburg–Leningrad: Material from the Yearly Academic Conference], ed. N. V. Yukhnyova, (Leningrad: Nauka, 1988), 29–38. The career and works of one composer, Leo Zeitlin, is treated by Paula Eisenstein Baker and Robert S. Nelson, in *Leo Zeitlin: Chamber Music* (Middleton, WI: A-R Editions, 2009), and *Leo Zeitlin Palestina: An Overture for the Capitol Theatre, New York* (Middleton, WI: A-R Editions, 2014).

13. Loeffler, *The Most Musical Nation,* 194.

14. Jascha Nemtsov, "From the History of the New Jewish School," Musica Judaica, http://www.musica-judaica.com/history.htm, asserts, however, that hundreds of works were composed during the period 1923–1929.

15. A more detailed history of these two publishers can be found in Jascha Nemtsov, "History of the Publishing Houses Jibneh and Juwal," trans. Eliott Kahn and Verena Bopp, *Musica Judaica* 18 (2005–2006): 1–42. My response to his article, which corrects some mistakes and provides further history, appears in "Yibneh-New York: 1940–1950" [Russian], in *Iz istorii evreiskoi muzyki v Rossii* [On the History of Jewish Music in Russia], Vol. 3, *Obshchestvo evreiskoi narodnoi muzyki v Peterburge (1908–1921): Stoletie spustia* [The Society for Jewish Folk Music in St. Petersburg, 1908–1921, 100 Years Later] (St. Petersburg: Jewish Community Center and Russian Institute for the History of the Arts, 2015), 129–44.

16. Judith K[aplan] Eisenstein, "Music Notes," *The Reconstructionist* 8, no. 3 (March 20, 1942): 19. It is my impression that Judith thought Universal had given Dzimitrovsky not only the entire stock of published works on Jewish themes but also the plates for reprinting the works. But he may have purchased the material. An English-language document on the letterhead of Associated Music Publishers, Inc., in New York, dated September 2, 1941, and signed by Hugo Winter, the former managing director of Universal in Vienna, states that the publishing house had sold "The Jibneh Edition" to "Mr. A. Dzimitrowsky [sic]" in April 1933 (this letter is in the possession of the author). That date is confirmed by a letter written in 1938 in which cellist and composer Joachim Stutschewsky indicates that Jibneh became the property of "a friend of ours" in 1933; it seems clear that he is referring to Dzimitrovsky. The letter, addressed to Salli Levi, the prime mover in the World Centre for Jewish Music in Palestine, appears in Philip V. Bohlman, *The World Centre for Jewish Music in Palestine, 1936–1940: Jewish Musical Life on the Eve of World War II* (Oxford, UK: Clarendon, 1992).

17. Ira Eisenstein and Judith Kaplan Eisenstein, *What Is Torah: A Cantata for Unison Chorus and Piano* (New York: Jewish Reconstructionist Foundation, 1943). The other cantatas were *Our Bialik* (New York: Jewish Reconstructionist Foundation, 1945), *The Seven Golden Buttons* (New York: Jewish Reconstructionist Foundation, 1947), *Reborn* (New York: Jewish Reconstructionist Foundation, 1952), and *Thy Children Shall Return* (New York: Reconstructionist Press, 1954). In his autobiography, Eisenstein refers to the cantatas but does not name them. Ira Eisenstein, *Reconstructing Judaism: An Autobiography* (New York: Reconstructionist Press, 1986), 171.

18. Judith Kaplan Eisenstein subsequently composed at least two more cantatas independently: *The Sacifice of Isaac: A Liturgical Drama* (New York: Reconstructionist Press, 1972) and *Shir Hashahar: Song of the Dawn* (New York: Transcontinental Music Publications, 1974).

19. Among the best-known American cantatas from that period are John Latouche and Earl Robinson, *Ballad for Americans* (New York: Robbins Music,1940); John Latouche and Jerome Moross, *Susannah and the Elders* (New York: Chappell, 1949), composed in 1940 but unpublished until 1949 as one of the *Ballet Ballads* (Howard Pollack, e-mail, September 22, 2018; Howard Pollack, *The Ballad of John Latouche* (New York: Oxford University Press, 2017), 273; George Kleinsinger, Paul Tripp, and Rose Marie Grentzer, *Johnny Stranger* (New York: Bourne, 1950).

20. WorldCat lists three professional recordings of "What Is Torah."

21. Joel Engel, *Shirei yeladim* (Berlin: Jibneh Edition Jerusalem, Agency for the Disapora, n.d.), 8–11. Edwin Seroussi, director of the Jewish Music Research Centre, Department of Musicoloogy, Jerusalem, identified the Engel volume in which this song appears (e-mail, September 13, 2018).

22. See "To the Desert" [Hebrew], Zemereshet, https://www.zemereshet.co.il/song.asp?id=629&artist=183.

23. Erwin Jospe, "Sing unto the Lord/Ashira Ladonai" (New York: Transcontinental Music Corporation, 1947). See David Berger, "Lost & Found: Ashira Ladonai (Sing unto the Lord), Arranged by Erwin Jospe," American Conference of Cantors, April 8, 2018, https://www.accantors.org/lost-found-ashira-ladonai-sing-unto-lord-arranged-erwin-jospe. None of the sources I consulted indicated what city Jospe died in; the information was provided by a nephew, Raphael Jospe (e-mail, September 16, 2018).

24. For more information about "Oyf'n pripetchik," see "Oyfn Pripetchik," The National Library of Israel, http://web.nli.org.il/sites/NLI/English/music/daily_song/Pages/deralephbet.aspx. Some sources claim that Warshawsky was also the composer.

25. Tel Aviv (Palestine)/Berlin: "Juwal," Verlagsgesellschaft für Jüdische Musik, 1926. The work is scored for clarinet, string quartet, string bass, and percussion.

26. Ruth Rubin, *Voices of a People: Yiddish Folk Song* (New York: A. S. Barnes, 1963), 37–38, provides this text and indicates that the tune appears in Yehuda Leib Cahan, *Yidishe*

folkslider hit melodies (New York: Yiddish Scientific Institute, 1957), no. 339. However, that volume does not include a tune for that text.

27. Neil W. Levin, "Liner Notes/Variations on 'Eliahu Hanavi,'" Milken Archive, https://www.milkenarchive.org/music/volumes/view/intimate-voices/work/variations-on-eliahu-hanavi/.

28. Motti Regev and Edwin Seroussi, *Popular Music and National Culture in Israel* (Oakland: University of California Press, 2004), 158.

29. L. C. Lockwood, *Oh! Let My People Go: The Song of the Contrabands* (New York: Horace Waters, 1862), 5, cited at "The Song of the 'Contrabands' 'O Let My People Go: Words and Music Obtained through the Rev. L. C. Lockwood, Chaplain of the Contrabands at Fortress Munroe/Arranged by Thomas Baker," The Library Company of Philadelphia, https://digital.librarycompany.org/islandora/object/Islandora%3A9540#page/2/mode/1up.

30. "America the Beautiful," Library of Congress, https://www.loc.gov/item/ihas.200000001/.

Is Zionism a Movement of Return?

Haim Sperber

Mainstream Zionist historiography tends to describe Zionism as a movement of return. Early Zionism (1881–1917) is portrayed as a political movement composed of two distinct subgroups: religious Zionism and secular Zionism. Both groups are described as having the same objective: creating a Jewish state in the Land of Israel.[1] This essay offers another perspective regarding Zionism. I shall focus our attention here on one question: was Zionism a movement of return from its outset, or did it become one in a later stage?

Conventional historiography offers the following periodization of early Zionism (before 1914):

- The Lovers of Zion [Hovevei Zion] phase (1881–1896), focusing on immigration to Zion. This constitutes the First Aliyah period.[2] The movement operated mainly in Eastern Europe.[3]
- The Zionist Organization movement, which was the Herzlian phase (1897–1904). In this period the focus was on international politics. It was Theodor Herzl who made Zionism an international Jewish movement, not just an East European one.
- Post–Herzlian Zionist organization (1904–1914), which focused on immigration to Zion. This was the period of the Second Aliyah.

In this essay I claim that early Zionism (1881–1914) was not aiming at returning[4] to Eretz-Israel and reestablishing the Third Temple [Beit Ha-Miqdash Ha-shlishi], a popular term for Zionists after 1967. Why did this change? I offer here an alternative interpretation of the development of Zionism: only in 1967 did Zionism become a movement of return. I also claim that the roots of the post-1967 division in Israeli society respecting the rule of the whole Land of Israel [Eretz Israel Ha-Shlema] derive from a change in the ways the Zionist objectives were set.

My main claim is that the Zionist movement was in fact a political union of two different movements aiming at two different objects: (1) re-creating the old kingdom of the Jewish people in the Land of Israel or in other places (cultural-ethnic nationalism) and (2) creating a new political Jewish nation (political nationalism).

Asher Ginsberg [Ahad Ha'am][5] offered a similar claim by distinguishing between those aiming at solving the Jewish question and those concerned with the Jews question. In my view, these two movements reflect two different kinds of nationalism—the Jewish question: cultural-ethnic, and the Jews question: political. Ahad Ha-am and his bitter rivals, the religious Zionists, reflected the first; Herzl reflected the second.

In this essay I investigate the difference between the various attitudes and claim that at the end of the nineteenth century, both movements came to the conclusion that establishing a united political organization was a must but did so for different reasons. The decision to form a united political organization blurred the difference between the two. Only after the Six-Day War in 1967 did the issue emerge again; it continues to influence Israel until now.

In my view, there are three periods during which the idea of return changed: 1897–1917, 1917–1967, and 1967 onward. Only since 1967 has the idea of return become important.

1897–1917

Dichotomy was part of Zionism, as it is part of any other political movement. Nationalism covers but a part of the whole range of political activities.[6] People were religious, socialist, etc. and at the same time were Zionists.

My suggestion here is that in addition to those differences, there was a basic dichotomy in the Zionist organization between cultural-ethnical nationalism and political nationalism.[7] The first emphasized the cultural aspects of nationalism; the second emphasized the territorial aspects.[8] These variations in nationalism were not confined to Zionism.

For Ahad Ha'am, cultural Zionism was part of a trend emphasizing cultural autonomies. This trend was created by Ahad Ha'am's close friend, the historian Simon Dubnov.[9] Jewish territorial nationalism had other variations as well.[10] Late nineteenth-century Zionism was composed of two different variations of nationalism. Herzl represented one point of view; Ahad Ha'am presented the other.

It was Herzl who understood the importance of political unity within Jewish nationalist movements and created the Zionist movement in Basel in 1897. The difference between the two versions of nationalism brought Ahad Ha'am to publish, a few months after the first Zionist Congress (in October 1897), what I believe was his most important piece, *Medinat Ha-Yehudim Ve-Tzarat Ha-Yehudim* [The Jewish State and the Jewish Problem]. (*Jewish State* was also the title of Herzl's famous book.)

Here Ahad Ha'am claimed that the East European Lovers of Zion movement represented a totally different version of Zionism, a movement dealing with the daily problems of Jewish Life, "the real Jewish Problem." Herzlian Zionism was, according to Ahad Ha'am, a political movement. It believed that creating a Jewish state would solve the Jewish problem, which, according to Herzl, was antisemitism.

Ahad Ha'am was a great rival of the religious groups in Lovers of Zion [Hovevei Zion or Hibat Zion], the forerunner of the Zionist movement in Eastern Europe. However, I claim that he had much more in common with them than with Theodor Herzl.

Herzl's perspective was very different. He disregarded the cultural identity issue and was concerned only with the political one.[11] His point of view was based on two assumptions: (1) the need to combat antisemitism[12] and (2) assisting European powers in the colonialist project.[13] Herzl did not convince Ahad Ha'am to join his organization but did persuade East European members of the earlier Lovers of Zion movement to join him.[14]

Yossi Goldstein rightly claimed that

> The conflict between Herzl and Ahad Ha'am encapsulated the cultural divide that separated the two, as well as it reflected the political and ideological rift separating East from West. The Eastern bloc wished Zionism to maintain strong ties to a sense of Jewish continuity (if not necessarily to traditional Jewish practice). The Western one was more cosmopolitan and assimilationist in its bent. From the first Zionist Congress onward, Ahad Ha'am assumed the role of Herzl's chief opponent. At first, he was a voice crying in the wilderness, but within seven years, he headed a united front whose members sought to remove Herzl or at least force him into a minority. The point of no return was reached in a clash known as the "Alteneuland Affair,"[15] whose personal side was as strong as its other aspects, if not more so. For after this episode concluded with his defeat and Herzl's victory, Ahad Ha'am bowed out of all active Zionist political life.[16]

I claim that the Ahad Ha'am–Herzl conflict was much deeper than Goldstein portrays it. It reflected the gap between the two brands of nationalism described above.

1917–1967

In 1904 Herzl died, and Zionist leaders decided to concentrate on working within Jewish communities, especially in Eastern Europe, and creating more settlements in Palestine. There was no chance to create a Jewish state soon, they believed.[17] However, until 1917 Zionism was a very small and unsuccessful political movement. We must remember that until 1917 almost nobody could have known that Zionism would emerge as the leading and most successful Jewish nationalist movement. Before 1917 the socialist Bund, established the same year as the Zionist organization, was the most powerful nationalist organization among Jewish youths in Eastern Europe.[18]

The publication of the Balfour Declaration in 1917 (by the way, it was Ahad Ha'am, living at that time in London, who translated the Balfour Declaration into Hebrew) and the emerging possibility of establishing a Jewish state in Palestine further blurred the differences of ideology. The success of Zionism and the establishment of a Jewish state empowered political Zionism and blurred even more these differences. Novelty rather than nostalgia was the main issue.

The new state symbolized the Jewish future (not the Jewish past). Greatness was now, not in antiquity.[19] The Jewishness of Israel had to do with its ability to be a safe haven for Jews and become a focal point for the Jews of the world. Return to the holy places was a very neglected issue in the prestate and early state history of Israel.[20] The question "who is a Jew?" was much more important than reoccupying the whole Land of Israel, as was the theme of conquering the dessert.[21] The Six-Day War in 1967 changed that.

1967 ONWARD

It is commonly accepted that the idea of returning to the land of the fathers was mainly conceived by the more religious groups within Zionism.[22] Those groups stated that Eretz Israel [the Land of Israel] was much more important than Medinat Israel [the State of Israel].[23] But we tend to forget that the founders of the movement called the Whole Land of Israel [Eretz Israel Ha-Shlema] included secular socialists such as Haim Guri and Nathan Alterman.[24] Since 1967, the differences between the two perceptions of Zionism have become obvious and are getting clearer and clearer.

Thus, only in 1967 did the topic of Zionism as a movement of return became common in Israel. Until 1967, there were ways in which the collective memory of Israeli relied on the past. The Bible played an important role in this.[25] Israeli and international competitions on knowledge of the Bible are good examples. However, in 1967 many "holy sites" related to the Bible were occupied by Israel. This was a turning point in making Zionism, for many in Israeli society, a movement of return instead of a movement of creation.

NOTES

1. Dimitry Shumsky recently analyzed the Zionist thought of Leon Pinsker, Theodor Herzl, Ahad Ha'am, Vladimir Ze'ev Jabotinsky, and David Ben-Gurion and suggested that not all Zionist thinkers had a common goal: establishing a Jewish state in Palestine. Dimitry Shumsky, *Beyond the Nation-State: The Zionist Political Imagination from Pinsker to Ben-Gurion* (New Haven, CT: Yale University Press, 2018).

2. See Yossi Goldstain, "The Beginnings of *Hibbat Zion*: A Different Perspective," *AJS Review* 40, no. 1 (April 2016): 33–55.

3. On the complex relation between the terms "nationalism" and "diaspora" in Jewish Eastern Europe, see Joshua Shanes, *Diaspora Nationalism and Jewish Identity in Hapsburg Galicia* (Cambridge: Cambridge University Press, 2012).

4. See Amnon Raz-Krakotzkin, "Exile, History, and the Nationalization of Jewish Memory: Some Reflections on the Zionist Notion of History and Return," *Journal of Levantine Studies* 3, no. 2 (Winter 2013): 37–70.

5. Steven J. Zipperstein, *Elusive Prophet: Ahad Ha'am and the Origins of Zionism* (London: Peter Halban, 1993), esp. chap. 3, "A Spiritual Center."

6. Benedict Anderson, *Imagined Communities: Reflections on the Origin and Spread of Nationalism*, rev. ed. (London: Verso, 2006), esp. chap. 3, "The Origins of National Consciousness."

7. Similar analysis was suggested by David H. Weiss, "A Nation without Borders? Modern European Emancipation as Negation of Galut," *Shofar* 34, no. 4, (2016): 71–97. Though I agree with his assumptions, I do not accept his argument that the debate already existed during the process of emancipation in the late eighteenth and early nineteenth centuries. For a different view, see Evyatar Freisel, "Zionism and Jewish Nationalism: An Inquiry into an Ideological Relationship," *Journal of Israeli History* 25, no. 2 (2006): 285–312.

8. Yitzhak Conforti, "Searching for a Homeland: The Territorial Dimension in the Zionist Movement and the Boundaries of Jewish Nationalists," *Studies in Ethnicity and Nationalism* 14, no. 1 (2014): 36–54.

9. The best summary on the relations between the two is still Alexander Orbach, "Jewish Intellectuals in Odessa in the Late Nineteenth Century: The Nationalist Theories of Ahad Ha'am and Simon Dubnov," *Nationalities Papers* 6, no. 2 (1978): 109–23. On Dobnov's theory regarding Jewish nationalism, see Simon Rabinovitch, *Jewish Rights, National Rites, Nationalism and Autonomy in Late Imperial and Revolutionary Russia* (Stanford, CA: Stanford University Press, 2014), esp., chap. 1, "Jewish Autonomy Imagined and Remembered." See also Brian Horowitz, " S. M. Dubnov's Ideological Challenge in Emigration: Autonomism and Zionism, Europe and Palestine," *Scripta Judaica Cracoviensia* 11 (2013): 11–20.

10. The most famous was the Jewish Territorial Organization. See Gur Alroey, *Zionism without Zion: The Jewish Territorial Organization and Its Conflict with the Zionist Organization.* (Detroit: Wayne State University Press, 2016).

11. Gideon Shimoni and Robert S. Wistrich, *Theodor Herzl: Visionary of a Jewish State* (New York: Herzl, 1999).

12. Shlomo Avineri, *Herzl: Theodor Herzl and the Foundation of the Jewish State* (London: Weidenfeld & Nicholson, 2013), esp. chap. 2, "Emancipation and Its Discontents."

13. See Axel Stähler, "Zionism, Colonialism, and the German Empire: Herzl's Gloves and Mbwapwa's Umbrella," in *Orientalism, Gender, and the Jews: Literary and Artistic Transformations of European National Discourses*, ed. Ulrike Brunotte, Anna-Dorothea Ludewig, and Axel Stähler (Berlin: De Gruyter Oldenbourg, 2015), 98–123.

14. Yossi Goldstein, "The Development of the Zionist Movement in Russia, 1881–1917" [Hebrew], in *Hitpathuta shel Ha-Tnuaa' Ha-tzionit Be-Russia, 1881–1917* [*The History of the Jews in Russia;* in Hebrew, *Toldot Yehudi Russia*], Vol. 2, ed. Ilia Luria Jerusalem: Merkaz Zalman Shazar, 2012), 289–319.

15. See Eran Kaplan, "Herzl, Ahad Ha'am and the *Altneuland* Debate: Between Utopia and Radicalism," in *The Individual in History: Essays in Honor of Jehuda Reinharz*, ed. ChaeRan Y. Freeze, Sylvia Fuks Fried, and Eugene R. Sheppard (Waltham, MA: Brandeis University Press, 2015), 42–54.

16. Yossi Goldstein, "Eastern Jews vs. Western Jews: The Ahad Ha'am–Herzl Dispute and Its Cultural and Social Implications," *Jewish History* 24 (2010): 355–77. For a different narrative, see Yitzhak Conforti, "East and West in Jewish Nationalism: Conflicting Types in the Zionist Vision?," *Nations and Nationalism* 16, no. 2 (2010): 201–19.

17. Goldstein, "The Development of the Zionist Movement in Russia," 310–319.

18. Yossef Gorny, *Converging Alternatives: The Bund and the Zionist Labor Movement, 1897–1985* (Albany: State University of New York Press; 2006), chap. 1, "Between Class and Nation: The Bund in Russia, 1897–1917."

19. On the effect of the Balfour Declaration, see Ophir Yarden, "The Balfour Declaration: From Imagining a State to Re-Imagining Majority-Minority Relations in Jewish Thought and the Jewish State," in *Religious Imaginations: How Narratives of Faith Are Shaping Today's World*, ed. James Walters (Chicago: Chicago University Press, 2018), 57–81.

20. David Ellenson provides a good summary of the Jewishness of Israel in "'Jewishness' in Israel: Israel as a Jewish State," in *Essential Israel: Essays for the 21st Century*, ed. S. Ilan Truen and Rachel Fish (Bloomington: Indiana University Press, 2017), 263–79.

21. Yael Zerubavel, "Desert and Settlement: Space Metaphors and Symbolic Landscapes in the Yishuv and Early Israeli Culture," in *Jewish Topographies: Visions of Space, Traditions of Place*, ed. Julia Brauch, Anna Lipphardt, and Alexandra Nocke (Aldershot, UK: Ashgate, 2008), 201–22.

22. Avi Sagi and Dov Schwartz, *Religious Zionism and the Six Day War: From Realism to Messianism* (London: Routledge, 2018), esp. chap. 2: "Real History and Sacred History"; Aviad Rubin, "Bifurcated Loyalty and Religious Actors' Behaviour in Democratic Politics:

The Case of Post-1967 Religious Zionism in Israel," *Religion, State and Society* 42, no. 1 (2014): 46–65; Gideon Aran, "A Mystic-Messianic Interpretation of Modern Israeli History: The Six Day War as a Key Event in the Development of the Original Religious Culture of Gush Emunim," in *Studies in Contemporary Jewry* 4 (Oxford: Oxford University Press, 1988), 263–75.

23. Yaacov Yadgar, *Sovereign Jews: Israel, Zionism, and Judaism* (Albany: State University of New York Press, 2017).

24. Dan Laor and Moshe Tlamim, "The Last Chapter: Nathan Alterman and the Six-Day War," *Israel Studies* 4, no. 2 (1999): 178–94.

25. Anita Shapira, "Ben-Gurion and the Bible: The Forging of an Historical Narrative?," *Middle Eastern Studies* 33, no. 4 (1997): 645–74.

The Jew in Situ: Variations of Zionism in Early Twentieth Century America

Judah M. Bernstein

"There is no bridge between Washington and Pinsk." So lectured Chaim Weizmann, president of the Zionist Organization, to the delegates at the annual American Zionist convention in Cleveland in June 1921.[1] Weizmann was presenting a stark choice to American Jews who wished to support Zionism. On the one side stood the core principles of Zionism as they were first pronounced in Europe, in "Pinsk"—Jews everywhere wallow in exile, and Zionism is the only viable answer. On the other side was, in Weizmann's schema, an Americanized and therefore deracinated Zionism, that of "Washington," which viewed America as home and construed Zionism as a philanthropic mission to aid Jews suffering elsewhere. Even at this early stage in Zionist history, the prospects for building a Jewish state in Palestine were inextricably linked to the construction of Jewish identity in America and closely associated with questions of Jewish authenticity.

In making his distinction between an authentic Jewish nationalism with roots in Europe and a deracinated Jewishness situated in America, Weizmann formulated a dichotomy that would come to characterize the way scholars have interpreted Zionism's or Israel's impact on American Jews for decades. In this essay, I question the historicity of this dichotomy. Both kinds of Zionism—the Zionism of "Pinsk" and "Washington"—had their intellectual purveyors among Zionist leaders in early twentieth-century America. One kind was endorsed by a cohort of prestigious figures, first among them Louis Brandeis. The other kind found exponents among an array of more obscure writers and thinkers, and I analyze three of the most important and, to my mind, largely neglected. Neither version of Zionism was more germane to early twentieth-century America than the other, and both were shaped by historical forces at play in America at the time. Such an examination will question the presumption of an exclusive authenticity as it applies to American Zionism and American Jewish identity and will reveal how both versions reflected attempts to square a commitment to Jewishness with prevailing American intellectual currents and concerns.

THE AMERICANIZATION PARADIGM

Taking for granted the exceptionalism of the American Jewish experience, historians have claimed that in order for American Jews of all backgrounds to embrace the Zionist cause, Zionism had to shed its European characteristics. In its European form, Zionism conceived of all Jewish life outside of Palestine as *golus* (exile). Antisemitism, European Zionists contended, would always afflict Jews across the diaspora until the majority of them moved to Palestine and founded a state of their own. This axiom made sense to European Zionists, who had experienced firsthand the frustrations of emancipation or the depredations of antisemitism. Finding in America economic opportunities, political liberties, and a benign social order that Europe apparently lacked, America's Jews could never adopt the notion, so the argument has gone, that America constituted exile, as did Europe. Zionism in America therefore had to be adapted to America's unique conditions.

The leaders of American Zionism, scholars have repeatedly pointed out, departed from their European colleagues by seeking to demonstrate how Zionism reinforced rather than undermined the place of Jews in American life. They maintained that the Zionist project of rescuing diaspora Jewry from the clutches of exile did not apply to America's Jews. Zionism for American Jews instead came to represent another philanthropic venture whereby American Jews collected large funds to save Jews who lived elsewhere. In asserting that America, and not Palestine, was their home, American Zionists constructed a Zionism that perfectly cohered with good Americanism. The extent to which immigrant Jews began to adopt this version of Zionism suggests the extent to which they had become "American" as well.[2]

Scholars found confirmation of this view in the biography of perhaps the foremost leader of American Zionism in the early twentieth century, Louis Brandeis. Brandeis, an attorney with extensive experience in progressive causes who in 1916 became the first Jew to serve on the U.S. Supreme Court, applied his American progressivist commitments to the philosophy of Zionism he propounded while operating as nominal or de facto leader of the movement from 1914 to 1921.[3] Brandeis devoted most of his public utterances and writings about Zionism during these years to the task of reconciling Zionism and Americanism, the goal of which was to establish that people could support one without compromising on the other. Brandeis's embrace of Zionism and his argument that Zionism in America meant saving the Jews of Europe, some have argued, demonstrated to the masses of immigrant Jewry that one could indeed be a good Zionist and a good American, thus leading to the popularization of Zionism in the United States during the war.

How could one back an enterprise that demanded loyalty to a foreign political cause without at the same time jeopardizing one's allegiance to America? Brandeis's answer to this question was twofold: (1) American acculturation did not require a complete rejection of old world commitments, and (2) American and Jewish values intersected so seamlessly that supporting the latter via Zionism in fact reinforced rather than tainted the former. Brandeis rejected the melting pot theory of American identity, which demanded that America's many immigrant groups shed their old world attachments and ethnic markers to produce a new, homogeneous American nation. Instead, Brandeis endorsed "cultural pluralism," or the premise shared by an influential cohort of American intellectuals, Jewish and non-Jewish, that America was and would continue to be a nation composed of many ethnic groups, or as Brandeis called them "nationalities," all united in their loyalty both to their own cultures and to fundamental American principles.[4] Each ethnic group had its special contribution to make to American civilization, and therefore each should work to preserve its heritage. At the same time that immigrant groups shared their gifts with a broader American society, they would adopt core American principles and become part of a greater American whole, loyally devoted to America as well as to their old homes.

For Brandeis, no ethnic group was more capable than America's Jews of realizing the cultural pluralist vision, so thoroughly did Brandeis believe that Jewish and American principles coincided. "Jews," he declared, "were by reason of their traditions and their characters peculiarly fitted for the attainment of American ideals."[5] Brandeis maintained that Jews inherited from the Bible a devotion to democracy, social justice, and truth and had nurtured these values over the course of their long exile.[6] America therefore offered an inviting, almost natural environment for Jewish achievement, as Brandeis argued in one key essay in 1915. "The ability of the Russian Jew to adjust himself to America's essentially democratic conditions . . . lies mainly in the fact that the twentieth century ideals of America have been the ideals of the Jew for more than twenty centuries."[7]

Brandeis maintained that those Jewish ideals, and in turn the project of American-Jewish synthesis, could be actualized best by a strong commitment to Zionism. According to Brandeis, the furtherance of the Jews' biblical-cum-American values in Palestine—which Brandeis considered to be the overarching purpose of Zionism—would strengthen the innate Jewish attachment to democracy, social justice, and the like within America itself.[8] Brandeis expected Zionism to implement in Palestine such quintessential American concepts as the "brotherhood of man," "social justice," and "effective democracy," which were all forged in the crucible of Jewish history and enshrined in Jewish law.[9] For this reason he frequently referred to the first Zionist settlers of Palestine as "Jewish Pilgrim Fathers" or "Palestinian Pilgrim Fathers."[10] Famously emphasizing the intersection of Zionism and Americanism at an address at a regional assembly of Reform rabbis in 1915, Brandeis averred that "Loyalty to America demands rather that each American Jew become a Zionist. For only through the ennobling effect of its striving can we develop the best that is in us and give to this country the full benefit of our great inheritance."[11] Zionism, in other words, brings to the fore pristine Jewish values that are quintessentially American. In supporting the Zionist program, Jews will share those values with the greater American society as well as actualize them in Palestine, thus fulfilling the mechanics of cultural pluralism. In turn, Jews will become better Americans themselves.

The essential point here is that Brandeis believed that Jews were not just perfectly at home in America but that America facilitated the expression of core Jewish values in a way that no other country could. America was the natural domicile of modern Jewry, and Palestine would be its laboratory, a home for East European Jews built in the American image. Exile, or *golus*, America was not. Brandeis's Americanism-Zionism synthesis captured the thinking of a number of other leading Zionist figures of the period, such as Julian Mack, Stephen Wise, and Felix Frankfurter, all of whom revered Brandeis and considered him the unrivaled leader of the movement. It would be a mistake to conclude, however, that Brandeis's philosophy ruled the day or that its alternatives, while deviating from Brandeis's version of good Americanism, were not themselves a fusion of American and Jewish concepts or influenced by American intellectual and social currents.

THE TRUE JEW

Between November 1924 and February 1925 *New Palestine*, the Zionist Organization of America's (ZOA) English-language weekly, ran a symposium on the question of what the role of religion in the future Jewish Palestine should be. Leaders from across the political and religious spectrum of American Jewish life weighed in on the topic. Regardless of their answer, the majority agreed that an authentic Jewishness that had been stifled by centuries of exile could reemerge only in Palestine.[12] Arguing that Americans should refrain from making demands on how Palestine's Jews organized public life, Maurice Samuel insisted that "Palestine is going to produce, or reproduce, the true type of Jew, which we in the Diaspora have forgotten. . . . We are not fit to pass on the question. Let Palestine work itself out."[13] Another symposium participant, Abe Fromenson, disagreed with Samuel. Fromenson countered that the observance of Jewish law must be a nonnegotiable component of Palestinian public life, averring that "In Eretz Yisroel we hope to achieve our aspirations for a complete Jewish life in a completely Jewish environment, with a physical and psychological background of Jewish history."[14]

Yet despite their differences, Samuel and Fromenson agreed that only Palestine could allow for the emergence of an authentic or "complete" Judaism, however defined. This is not to say that Samuel and Fromenson called on all Jews to leave America for Palestine. They and others articulated an alternative American Zionism, one more ambivalent about Jewish life in the United States yet just as germane to interwar America as Brandeis's. This section explores the conceptual worlds of Maurice Samuel and two of his colleagues, Samuel Melamed and Ludwig Lewisohn. All journalists and men of influence in Jewish letters (if not wider American letters in the case of Lewisohn), they adhered to the view that Jewish life in America was somehow under assault, flawed, and incomplete and could survive only through the emergence of a superior Jewishness in Palestine.[15]

Maurice Samuel's Zionism was rooted in assumptions about America, diaspora, and nationalism that differed substantially from Brandeis. Abandoning any sort of Jewish practice for socialism while attending university in England, Samuel embraced Zionism as a young man and worked for the ZOA after World War I as a propagandist and administrator. A prolific author, he achieved notoriety for his third book, *You Gentiles*, published in 1924. *You Gentiles* ruminated on the differences between Jews and non-Jews, rejecting in the process the central premises of Brandeis's philosophy.[16] In that book, Samuel described "Gentile" and "Jewish" types, arguing that the two were immutable and irreconcilable. There would always be frictions between them, Samuel claimed. Jewish assimilation of any kind was impossible and, moreover, was a cause of rather than a solution to pervasive intergroup frictions.

Doubting the possibility of the harmonious exchange of different groups' gifts or the benefits of any sort of synthesis of American and Jewish values,

Samuel instead limned a portrait of persistent tension punctuated only by moments of fleeting quiet. "With the best will on both sides, successful adaptation to each other will always be insecure and transient," he wrote. "We shall delude ourselves . . . with the belief that we have bridged the gulf."[17] Samuel therefore rejected the notion that America's Jews must accommodate themselves to American life and culture. "These are two ways of life, each utterly alien to the other," wrote Samuel. "Each has its place in the world—but they cannot flourish in the same soil."[18]

Considering America to be foreign soil, it is not surprising that Samuel lauded with frequency Jewish life in Palestine while construing life in America as a cheap replacement, forever incomplete. Zionism, Samuel wrote in another article that appeared in *New Palestine* in 1923, "is about transplanting into our lives, as far as possible, those vital forces which we would inherit naturally if we lived in the Jewish homeland."[19] In this Samuel revealed his romantic-nationalist interpretation of Zionism, an outlook that assumed an organic connection between nations and the territories that birthed them. No matter how committed to Zionism, there must always remain, in Samuel's view, something "artificial" about American Jewish life, divorced as it is from Palestine, the putative birth land of the Jewish people, and submerged as it is in a "Gentile" environment anathema to the "Jewish" essence. Whereas a foreign land such as America militated against the full expression of the Jewish spirit, Palestine, the Jews' natural domicile, naturally generated it, a point that Samuel elaborated upon in *I, the Jew*, a book published in 1927 that received more positive acclaim.

In *I, the Jew* Samuel reiterated the idea that Jewish life could be complete only in Palestine.[20] According to Samuel, the topography of Palestine produced essential Jewish tendencies, such as the Jews' paradoxical proclivity for abstractions and an attention to material concerns, that endured for thousands of years. Traveling across the Jezreel Valley in Palestine, for example, Samuel exclaimed, "The same concentration of infinity in the image of daily life occurs again in the Valley of Yizreel [*sic*]. All life's problems are reproduced here . . . but the answer that will be given will be as remote from the spirit of the western world as the answers given more than twenty years ago."[21] Insisting that Zionism must transcend the mere need to find a refuge for persecuted Jews, that Zionism was about Jewish spiritual well-being rooted in the land as much as the Jews' physical security, he wrote that "if there is any meaning at all in an hereditary culture, in the forces which move among us to make us something more than the brute, then we can base our claim on something greater than the need of the individual—the need of a spirit which cannot live itself out except in the place of its birth."[22]

Perhaps no better example of an American Zionist intellectual who expressed grave doubts about the possibilities of acculturation in America and stressed the imperatives of reviving Jewishness in Palestine is offered by Samuel M. Melamed. Born in Russian Lithuania, Melamed came to America in 1914 and served as writer or editor under several major Yiddish and English newspapers. By the 1920s he was a regular contributor to *New Palestine*, and by 1927 he was running his own journal of Jewish opinion, *Reflex*. Infamous among other American Jews for his underhanded journalistic practices and his libelous editorial polemics, Melamed emerged as the gadfly of American Jewish letters in the interwar years, consistently denouncing American Judaism as overly materialistic, culturally vapid, and altogether irredeemable.[23] In one article he wrote for *New Palestine* in December 1923, for example, he proclaimed that life in America and the rest of the diaspora corrupted the Jewish personality to such an extent that American Jews had devolved into "mental cripples." They had become souls "clothed in garments foreign to it," concealing indefinitely the soul's true nature. "The Jew in countries of the diaspora is not a pure Jew, that is to say, he is not typically Jewish as the Germans are typically German . . . but is partly the Jew and partly the product of his environment, his education," Melamed pontificated. Only in Palestine, he claimed, would a "real Jew" emerge: "A normal and well-balanced life will produce a normal and well-balanced Jew. This normal and well-balanced Jew will be the typical Jew and the real representative of the Jewish 'species.'"[24]

In this Melamed advanced a thesis similar to Samuel's that he would repeat throughout the interwar period: the emergence of a robust, authentic, and complete Jewish culture was impossible outside of a Jewish Palestine. The creation of a complete Jewish culture was linked to Melamed's trenchant denunciation of all forms of Jewish religion, which he viewed as an illegitimate by-product of the diasporic condition. Because Jews lived among other peoples and were constantly under threat, Melamed argued, Jewish religion and law had become calcified, leading to centuries of "frozen culture" that had produced nothing worthwhile since Maimonides's *Guide to the Perplexed* and had failed to stem the tides of Jewish dissolution to boot.

In Melamed's imagined Palestine, Jewish law would be adjudicated by secular courts, Jewish religious praxis would evolve organically, rabbis would become unnecessary, and an authentic Jewish "civilization" would emerge unimpeded by a repressive system of religious observance. "All the 'fences' established around the Jewish fundamental laws will be done away with, because these 'fences' . . . have been established for the purpose of preserving the Jewish religion. . . . In Palestine there will be no need" for them, Melamed concluded.[25] Though he focused more on critiquing Jewish religion than did Samuel, the same assumptions about diaspora and homeland that drove Samuel's thinking undergirded Melamed's.

Ludwig Lewisohn's critique of assimilation in the 1920s resembled Samuel's and Melamed's in key ways. Even before Lewisohn declared himself a Zionist, the then arts editor of *The Nation* had published in 1922 a memoir, *Up Stream*, in which he despaired of the possibilities of cultural pluralism in America. In *Up Stream* Lewisohn detailed his difficulties securing a teaching position in a university upon graduating from Columbia with a PhD in English language and literature. He identified the ingrained anti-Jewish animosity that worked to limit his employment opportunities in the academy, notwithstanding the fact that he was a converted Christian and, by his own account, thoroughly assimilated.[26]

Lewisohn attributed his personal travails to a larger postwar American reaction against all those deemed outside of the Anglo-Saxon mainstream, a trend that he felt had become more severe by the time of his publishing of his first open statement of support for Zionism, the travelogue *Israel*, in 1925.[27] In *Israel*, Lewisohn countered nativist demands for "one hundred percent" loyalty, assimilation, or intermarriage, arguing that "Aryans" and "Jews" constitute diametrically opposed types. Any kind of accommodation between them, Lewisohn felt, was futile, for Jews in America who sought to acculturate would always face the antagonism of non-Jews who perceived them as different, and Jews, conversely, would always feel the buried yet continuously throbbing impulse that they in fact were.[28]

Lewisohn dramatized the impossibilities of assimilation and the importance of staying true to one's self in his most celebrated piece of writing from the 1920s, the novel *The Island Within*, published in 1928. The protagonist, a son of German Jewish parents who seeks to escape his Jewishness through professional success and intermarriage, ultimately discovers that there is no outrunning his background and that he must return to his people. The protagonist's father offered this comment about the impossibilities of rapprochement between Jew and non-Jew upon learning of his son's marriage to a non-Jewish woman, the daughter of a Protestant minister, words that would prove prescient when his son's marriage ends in divorce. These words articulate the thrust of the novel:

> Dey hate us. Dey all hate us.... It voild be all right if dey vere bet people. But some det hate us most are fine ent honest people in every odder vay. Ent it vould be all right if ve vere bet people ent deserved to be hated. But ve are a good people, honest ent hartvorking ent kin tent charitable ent en educated people.... Ent dey hate us.... [E]very *Goy* in der vorld hes a little bit of det hate in him. He cen't help it.... But det little bit of hate betveen men ent vife—Vell, I said too much already.[29]

In *Israel* and *The Island Within*, Lewisohn offered two solutions to the plight of the Jew living in the West and chafing against the twin expectations to assimilate but to remain apart, excluded, and despised. As the title suggests, *Israel* would seem to argue that only in Palestine can Jews free themselves from the burdens of exile. Explaining the decision of a group of young women to work as pioneers in a colony in Palestine, Lewisohn wrote in *Israel* that they had not fled pogroms or other physical violence but instead had sought to transcend the kinds of pressure with which any American Jew was forced to contend: "They have escaped the false position, the moral discomfort, the thousand restraints and inhibitions and subtle injustices of their old lives. Here they stand upon their own earth; they are among their own folk. Life takes on a new freedom and naturalness, a new spontaneity."[30]

Yet, Lewisohn differed from Samuel and Melamed in the extent to which he acknowledged that Jews could reconstruct an authentic Jewishness outside of Palestine. "Every Jew can find himself. I have done so. Not everyone need go upon so long a pilgrimage," Lewisohn wrote in *Israel*.[31] Lewisohn believed that the Jews of the diaspora could actively choose to spurn assimilation, to proudly embrace their Jewishness, to create a thick Jewish culture and social life devoid of the impulse to conform to non-Jewish mores and pressures. In so doing, they would be counteracting the forces of reactionary and belligerent nationalism that demanded the dilution of all minority groups in the name of Anglo conformity. Lewisohn believed that such chauvinism, the opposite of a distinctly Jewish "spiritual nationalism," had caused World War I and was polluting the world. Choosing Jewishness, in other words, was Lewisohn's antidote for postwar reaction.[32]

This Lewisohn's protagonist in *The Island Within* accomplishes after undergoing great psychological hardship, deciding to divorce his non-Jewish wife, abandon his job at a clinic for work at a Jewish hospital, provide his son with a rigorous Jewish education, and embark on a medical mission to assist the persecuted Jews of Romania but not to move to Palestine. Lewisohn thus differed from Samuel and Melamed, both of whom did not allow for the possibility of a compelling and fulfilling return to Jewishness outside of Palestine. Yet in his idealization of a Jewish turning inward, in his search for a free and complete kind of Jewishness insulated from any sort of "Americanism," and in his trenchant critique of assimilation, Lewisohn parted ways with Brandeisian concerns about synthesizing Americanism and Zionism.

Thus, their differences notwithstanding, Samuel, Melamed, and Lewisohn operated with a shared set of assumptions that militated against Brandeis's views. According to these three, Jews constitute a racial type separate and distinct from other types among whom they live. Any kind of acculturation to American norms is a fool's errand at best, a perversion of one's race consciousness at worst. America, no matter how hospitable it may appear in comparison to Europe, exerts the same corrosive effects on Jewish life as does any other diasporic society, and Jews are just as alien to the American environment as they are to that of any in Europe. Finally, and more along the lines of Samuel and Melamed than Lewisohn, the only possibility for discovering and fostering authentic Jewishness could occur in Palestine, the land of the Jews' birth and the natural climate of the Jewish race as well as a habitat unsullied by the foreign influences and pressures of the diaspora.

MODERNISM AND NATIVISM

Current historiography has drawn a sharp division between the "American" Zionism of Brandies and his circle and the sort of "immigrant" Zionism that stressed the ubiquity of antisemitsm, the perils of assimilation, or the notion of America as *golus*. This schema has been employed to categorize the views of Samuel, Lewisohn, and Melamed as remnants of a European Zionist legacy that percolated in American Zionist circles in the early decades of the twentieth century but eventually lost any allure and disappeared as Jews Americanized.[33] Yet Samuel, Lewisohn, and Melamed had all lived in America for a decade or more by the interwar years. They hailed from German as well as East European backgrounds; they all possessed thorough modern educations, either acquired as students or autodidacts; and they all wielded considerable influence in Zionist affairs and American Jewish letters. Instead of marginalizing their views as "immigrant" or "foreign," it is worth considering how two competing interwar trends germane to American intellectual life, cultural nationalism and nativism, shaped their thinking.

On the one hand, Zionism in America during the interwar period must be situated within larger developments in American modernism that spurred a reconsideration of notions of race, culture, and nation.[34] Following the war, a number of prominent white and black American writers and artists began to call for an American renaissance that would provoke a break between America, a land of progress and promise, and Europe, the site of reaction and world war.[35] They sought out America's authentic cultural wellsprings, such as black folk songs, and hoped to undo what they saw as American culture's thoroughgoing Puritanism, which they deemed a backwards vestige of European culture.[36] These intellectuals placed great value on what they saw as America's racial or ethnic diversity and transnational makeup, seeing this as a key source of American cultural vitality and the path to re-create what it means to be American. They were therefore fiercely critical both of the nativist demands for cultural assimilation into a homogenous and insipid American type and of the dissemination of lowbrow urban culture marred by materialism.[37]

In their publicist and journalist activities, all three men interacted in one way or another with the circles of non-Jewish intellectuals who embodied this sort of modernist cultural shift in American arts and letters. Lewisohn was an editor at *The Nation*, one of the premier outlets that advanced the new cultural nationalism and engaged in a thorough criticism of American race relations. Samuel's two books, *You Gentiles* and *I, the Jew*, were published by Harcourt, Brace, and Co., a publishing house renowned for giving voice to American critics, black writers, and translations of European modernist works. And Melamed's journal *Reflex* was a patent imitation of *American Mercury*, H. L. Mencken's organ of trenchant opinion that advanced the cultural nationalism of the interwar period.[38]

Samuel, Lewisohn, and Melamed, in turn, all employed elements of the interwar modernist critique of American life in their own writings on Zionism and American Jewish life. Samuel's emphasis on the connection between soil and nation repurposed modernists' adulation for an American folk culture rooted in the American South or the American frontier. Melamed's vilification of Jewish religion as a mummified and unproductive form of Jewishness invoked modernist critiques of Puritanism as an impediment to American renaissance, mirroring the language of figures such as Mencken. Lewisohn's depiction of Zionism as a "spiritual nationalism" echoed modernist opposition to the nativism of the period. In sum, all three exemplified interwar cultural nationalism in decrying assimilation, advocating for a Jewish cultural revival unmoored from traditional religious practices and beliefs, and seeking to locate an "authentic" source for Jewish life.

Conversely, Samuel, Lewisohn, and Melamed adopted the very nativist categories and modes of logic that cultural nationalists at the time so vehemently opposed. Nativists in the interwar years insisted that Jewishness and Americanness inherently disrupted each other—in other words, that one could not be a Jew and at the same time be "one hundred percent" American.[39] In many of their public writings, American Zionists countered that there was no predominant American type; rather, America was composed of many nationalities, each with its own contributions to American life and culture. However, not unlike contemporary black intellectuals who both polemicized against but could also sometimes adopt the nativism that targeted them, Samuel and Melamed exhibited the inverse of the nativist logic in their argument that one could be a complete Jew only in Palestine—that America, in other words, undermined one's "one hundred percent" Jewishness.[40]

With his argument that one could return to a form of authentic Jewishness outside of Palestine, Lewisohn remained more committed to the cultural pluralist vision. But even he adopted nativist notions of immutable racial types and nativist criticisms of hybrid identities, arguing as he did that Jews could thrive in America only if they resisted blending with their larger environments and mingling with non-Jews and instead stayed true to some sort of Jewish essence. The fixation of these three thinkers on notions of racial essence and completeness, along with their hostility to cultural exchange and synthesis, bespeaks the subtle ways that American nativism, the scourge of Jews and other minorities in interwar America, influenced their thinking.

CONCLUSION

Samuel, Melamed, and Lewisohn disagreed with Brandeis about not only the imperatives of amalgamating Americanism and Zionism but also what it meant to be an authentic Jew. For Brandeis, it entailed a merger of Jewish and American values, with Zionism as a way for Jews to actualize purely American—and purely Jewish—principles. America therefore offered the penultimate home for Jews. For Samuel, Melamed, and Lewisohn, it meant the expression of an uncorrupted Jewish essence, with Zionism serving as the path to discovering a Jew's "island within." This task was made difficult if not impossible in America.

Scholars have tended to reify the differences between Brandeis and Samuel, Melamed, and Lewisohn, seeing the former as an articulation of Americanized Jewishness and deeming the latter as the final gasps of a Pinsk-oriented Zionism in an immigrant Jewish community rapidly acculturating. Yet, both drew from the American cultural universe in which American Jewish intellectuals were situated. Neither could claim a monopoly on "authentic" Jewishness or Americanized nationalism; instead, both sought to integrate prevailing ideas about America, race, culture, and nationalism into their own interpretations of what Zionism signified.

Historians of American Jewry ought to reckon with the fact that some leading intellectuals of American Zionism, all of whom wielded significant cultural influence in American Jewish letters and organizational influence in the ZOA in the 1920s, expressed open doubt about the notion of America as a special home. That this chorus became more intellectually sophisticated and grew louder in the 1920s suggests that American Zionists did not move easily or simply from an "immigrant" to an "American" mentality, much as immigrant Jews at large did not blaze a simple path from foreigners to full-fledged, confident, and secure Americans.

The America that Jews encountered in the early twentieth century was a land of contradictions, not a place of unvarnished freedoms. It no doubt offered its Jewish citizens unprecedented economic opportunities and political liberties and largely shielded them from the violence that had become emblematic of life in imperial Russia and then war-torn Eastern Europe. But this was also a country where Jews faced dire questions about the maintenance of Jewish culture and the durability of Jewish sociological boundaries. It was a place where antisemitism was expressed freely in the popular press, prejudices against Jews ran rampant in universities and professional spaces, and nativism was debated openly in Congress. Jews of all religious and political persuasions had to negotiate this confusing American blend of tolerance and exclusion. Some American Zionists embraced Brandeis's progressive-inspired optimism, while others resorted to the nativist-inflected pessimism of Samuel, Melamed, and Lewisohn.

NOTES

1. See Maurice Samuel, ed., *Report of the Proceedings of the 24th Annual Convention of the Zionist Organization of America* (New York: ZOA, 1921), 145.

2. In my view, aspects of this narrative characterize the current scholarship on American Zionism. For a number of prominent examples, see Melvin Urofsky, *American Zionism*

from Herzl to the Holocaust (New York: Anchor, Doubleday, 1975), 2, 89–91, 118, 148–50; Yonathan Shapiro, *Leadership of the American Zionist Organization, 1897–1930* (Champagne: University of Illinois Press, 1971), 180–204; Naomi Wiener Cohen, *American Jews and the Zionist Idea* (New York: Ktav Publishing House, 1975), xvi, 17; Allon Gal, "Aspects of the Zionist Movement's Role in the Communal Life of American Jewry (1898–1938)," *American Jewish History* 63 (1985): 140–55.

Only a few scholars have advanced critiques of what one could call the Americanization paradigm. Maier Bryan Fox found significant divergences between Brandeis's views and that of the "masses" and rejected Shapiro's argument of wholesale assimilation in the 1920s. Few have taken note of the significance of Fox's contributions. See Maier Bryan Fox, "American Zionism in the 1920s" (PhD diss., George Washington University, 1979), I–V. Evyatar Freisel questioned Urofsky's premise that Brandeis was most responsible for the growth of Zionism during World War I, arguing instead that many of the major ideological and organizational underpinnings of the ZOA's growth were in place years before Brandeis became president of the Provisional Executive Committee of General Zionist Affairs. See Evyatar Freisel, "The Influence of Zionism on the American Jewish Community: An Assessment by Israeli and American Historians," *American Jewish History* 2, no. 22 (1985): 132–33, 144. In *Zionism and the Roads Not Taken: Rawidowicz, Kaplan, Kohn* (Bloomington: Indiana University Press, 2010), Noam Pianko surmised that American Jewish historians' emphasis on the non-European character of American Zionism reflected those historians' wish to portray integration and synthesis as a resounding success. Pianko, in contrast, found in the thought of the three intellectuals he studied profound feelings of "unrootedness" and the ongoing influence of European theories of nationalism. See 22, 122, and especially 129, where he differentiates Mordechai Kaplan's conception of American Zionism from that of Brandeis.

3. Some, such as Urofsky, lauded Brandeis's "Americanization" of Zionism, seeing it as one of his signal intellectual achievements and a main reason for the rapid growth of Zionism during the war years. Others, such as Jerold Auerbach, argued that it eviscerated American Zionism of some sort of authentic Jewish content and spurred bickering within different factions of the ZOA through the 1920s. See Urofsky, *American Zionism,* 126–27; Jerold S. Auerbach, *Rabbis and Lawyers: The Journey from Torah to Constitution* (Bloomington: Indiana University Press, 1990), chap. 6; Jonathan D. Sarna, "'The Greatest Jew in the World since Jesus Christ': The Jewish Legacy of Louis D. Brandeis," *American Jewish History* 81, no. 3 (Spring–Summer 1994): 354–59; Philipa Strum, *Brandeis: Beyond Progressivism* (Kansas: University of Kansas Press, 1993), 107–9. In my view, both Urofsky's interpretation and Auerbach's critique reify dichotomies between Americanized and authentic Jewishness/Zionism that the historical actors themselves utilized to tar their opponents. In the process, both miss an opportunity to properly contextualize the various factions in early twentieth-century American Zionism.

4. Louis D. Brandeis, *Brandeis on Zionism: A Collection of Addresses and Statements by Louis D. Brandeis* (New York: ZOA, 1942), 19. Brandeis most likely embraced these views due to the influence of Zionist thinker and university professor Horace Kallen, a pioneer

of the cultural pluralist school of thought. See Sarah Schmidt, "The Zionist Conversion of Louis D. Brandeis," *Jewish Social Studies* 37, no. 1 (Winter 1975): 18–34; Shapiro, *Leadership of the American Zionist Organization*, 71–72.

5. Brandeis, *Brandeis on Zionism*, 63.

6. Ibid., 22, 44, 49.

7. Ibid.

8. Ibid., 28–29.

9. Ibid., 29.

10. Ibid., 27–28, 63.

11. Ibid.

12. See *New Palestine* for the following figures' views on the question: Emmanuel Neumann (November 14, 1924), Maurice Samuel (November 14, 1924), Simon Bernstein (November 28, 1924), Oscar Leonard (December 5, 1924), M. Pollak (December 12, 1924), A. H. Fromenson (December 19, 1924), Sol Rosenbloom (December 19, 1924), J. Mitchell Rosenberg (December 25, 1924), Morris Lazaron (January 9, 1925), Bernard Drachman (January 27, 1925).

13. Maurice Samuel, "Where Jews *Are* Jews," *New Palestine*, November 14, 1924.

14. A. H. Fromenson, "Jewish Fundamentals," *New Palestine*, December 19, 1924.

15. Of the three, Lewisohn, a writer for the respected American journal *The Nation*, a professor at a major university, and a well-published author, carried the most prestige. Samuel may have been the most well-traveled ZOA propagandist of the 1920s, addressing thousands of Jews across the country on various topics related to Zionism as well as his books. See, e.g., *New Palestine*, June 26, 1925. Along with publishing frequently in *New Palestine* and running his own journal of opinion, *Reflex*, Melamed played a large role both in Chicago Zionist and national Zionist affairs. See, e.g., "Conference of Chicago Zionists," *New Palestine*, January 25, 1924).

16. For the opprobrium it provoked among Jewish pundits, see, e.g., Abram Lipsky's review in *New Palestine*, January 30, 1925; David Phillipson's review in *American Israelite*, November 13, 1924; and the editorial in *Jewish Exponent*, October 31, 1924). See also Samuel Schulman's review in *Jewish Exponent*, November 21, 1924. For Samuel's response to some of his critics, see his article "You Critics of 'You Gentiles,'" published in *American Israelite*, January 22, 1925, among other venues.

17. Maurice Samuel, *You Gentiles* (New York: Harcourt, Brace, 1924), 24.

18. Ibid., 36–37.

19. Maurice Samuel, "Zionism as an Art," *New Palestine*, July 27, 1923.

20. Though not without its detractors, *I, the Jew* was received more favorably by critics in Jewish and non-Jewish publications and attracted far less controversy. See, e.g.,

Louis Finkelstein's review in *New Palestine*, May 20, 1927, which explicitly draws a sharp contrast with *You Gentiles*, as well as the favorable review in the *New York Times*, April 24, 1927.

21. Maurice Samuel, *I, the Jew* (New York: Harcourt, Brace, 1927), 197.

22. Ibid., 210.

23. For reminiscences that reveal Melamed's brash approach as well as his lowly reputation, see Meyer Weisgal, *So Far . . .* (New York: Random House, 1971), 70–71, as well as Marie Syrkin's impression, discussed in Carole Kessner, *Marie Syrkin: Values beyond the Self* (Waltham, MA: Brandeis University Press, 2008), 177.

24. S. M. Melamed, "The New Jew," *New Palestine*, December 28, 1923.

25. S. M. Melamed, "Zionism," *New Palestine*, November 6, 1925. For other examples, see his articles in *New Palestine* (December 7, 1923; January 29, 1926; June 25, 1926; January 7, 1927) as well as his editorials in his journal of opinion, *Reflex*.

26. Ludwig Lewisohn, *Up Stream* (New York: Boni and Liveright, 1922), 89, 120, 123, 149.

27. Ibid., 231–35; Ludwig Lewisohn, *Israel* (New York: Boni and Liverirght, 1925), 69–71, 277.

28. Lewisohn, *Israel*, 38, 42–46, 260. Lewisohn cited with esteem Samuel, *You Gentiles*, whose Gentile-Jew dichotomy and critique of assimilation Lewisohn recognized as similar to his own (260).

29. Ludwig Lewisohn, *The Island Within* (New York: Harper & Brothers, 1928), 236.

30. Lewisohn, *Israel*, 174–75. See also 196–97.

31. Ibid., 280.

32. Ibid., 109, 236, 249–52, 278.

33. For an example of this interpretation as it relates to Samuel and Lewisohn, see Shapiro, *Leadership of the American Zionist Organization*, 228.

34. The discussion that follows is based on Roderick Nash, *The Nervous Generation* (New York: Ivan R. Dee, 1990); Lynn Dunemil, *The Modern Temper* (New York: Hill and Wang, 1995); Ann Douglas, *Terrible Honesty: Mongrel Manhattan in the 1920s* (New York: Farrar, Straus and Giroux, 1996); George Hutchinson, *The Harlem Renaissance in Black and White* (Cambridge, MA: Harvard University Press, 1997).

35. Douglas, *Terrible Honesty*, 4; Hutchinson, *The Harlem Renaissance*, 12–14, 96–102.

36. For some examples, see Hutchinson, *The Harlem Renaissance*, 96–107, 210–11, 319.

37. Nash, *The Nervous Generation*, 43; Dumenil, *The Modern Temper*, 165–69; Hutchinson, *The Harlem Renaissance*, 211.

38. See Hutchinson, *The Harlem Renaissance*, 215, for Lewisohn as well as his chapters on *The Nation*, the *New Republic*, the *Mercury*, and black writing and modernist American publishing; Douglas, *Terrible Honesty*, 81; Dumenil, *The Modern Temper*, 152.

39. See, e.g., John Higham, *Strangers in the Land* (New Brunswick, NJ: Rutgers University Press, 2002), 255–78.

40. See, e.g., Barbara Foley, *Spectres of 1919* (Champagne: University of Illinois Press, 2003); Kevin Gaines, *Uplifting the Race* (Chapel Hill: University of North Carolina Press, 1996), esp. chap. 9; Hutchinson, *Harlem Renaissance*, 91.

Returning to Jewish Theology: Further Reflections on Franz Rosenzweig

Jean Axelrad Cahan

INTRODUCTION

There is presently a considerable amount of discussion In North America and Western Europe about the relationship between the humanities and the sciences and, by implication, what this might mean for religion. For those of us in Jewish studies, it may be helpful to consider an earlier version of debate on this topic to see what kinds of arguments were being made or visions were being put forward and what might still be relevant. In particular, I am interested in reconsidering some of Franz Rosenzweig's ideas on a possible return to Jewish theology. While at least one important commentator on Rosenzweig, Hilary Putnam, estimated that Rosenzweig was not greatly disturbed by or interested in historical and scientific critiques of Judaism,[1] I believe that this was a central preoccupation of his, and indeed his account of revelation was intended to displace or overcome precisely that type of critique.

In an afterword, composed in 1930, to Rosenzweig's *Stern der Erlösung* (*Star of Redemption,* 1921), Gershom Scholem sought to provide an intellectual context for his friend's largely incomprehensible but highly acclaimed work.[2] Scholem concurred with Rosenzweig's conviction that contemporary theology, both Jewish and Christian, had been enormously weakened by overinvolvement with philosophy, especially German Idealism. Philosophical thought had become the style and the standard for theology and religious thought, which should instead have been working with their own resources and materials.[3] The historical disciplines of the *Wissenschaft des Judentums* as well as of psychology and sociology had emptied [*entleert*] the world (George Steiner would later say "disenchanted" it). Traditional notions and experiences of God's creativity and divine-human relations had been replaced by lifeless abstractions. Rosenzweig responded through narration and display in the *Stern* of his own experience of divine revelation, love, and creativity. He sought to found a new way of philosophizing as well as a new theology, both of which would speak about lived experience of the divine and in which language itself took on a new type of importance.

Scholem's own reaction to Rosenzweig's work was that in addition to Kabbalah and the writing of Franz Kafka, it amounted to a last best hope for creative Jewish religiosity. Like Rosenzweig, Walter Benjamin, Martin Buber, Franz Kafka, and other contemporaries, Scholem was dismayed by the "embourgeoisement" of modern Judaism. On the other hand, he was repelled by nineteenth-century Orthodoxy and had limited patience for Reform movements. He also thought that modern physics had rediscovered the possibility of miracles. Along with Kabbalah, this was an important counter in the argumentative context in which all these thinkers and writers were working.[4]

Scholem's view of Rosenzweig came to have a considerable influence. It was carried forward in Robert Alter's work on Kafka and literary modernism, in Hilary Putnam's essays on Judaism as a way of life, and in some postmodern discussions of ethical responsibility. While this work is very interesting, in my view it oddly does not quite do Rosenzweig justice. As is evident from Rosenzweig's work, his return to Jewish theology, which turned especially on his idea of revelation, was motivated by a constant effort to regain the footing that Judaism—and religion more generally—had lost in the face of scientific cosmology and other sciences. Although many commentators have noted the importance of Rosenzweig's theory of revelation, they rarely provide a detailed account of it and therefore fail to show Rosenzweig's persistent engagement with the problem of how the divine world relates to the natural one.[5] In this essay I therefore seek to describe Rosenzweig's theory of revelation in somewhat more detail than is usual. In this way, I hope that his preoccupation with the implications of modern science will become more apparent.

THE INTELLECTUAL CONTEXT OF ROSENZWEIG'S WORK

Traditional metaphysics—a foundational subdiscipline of philosophy—contributed to many diverse theological conceptions of the origins of the universe and of humanity. In this way it helped fulfill one of the main functions of religion identified by the sociologist Emil Durkkeim: the representative function. For Durkheim (1858–1917), whose work was very much "in the air" as Rosenzweig was writing, religion has several functions. On one level it provides practices and ideas that enable individuals and groups to live and adapt to circumstances. On a theoretical level, it provides a set of representations of the world. The practical functions would always be required, according to Durkheim; they are an essential and permanent aspect of human life and should not or could not be dismantled. But the "speculative," representative functions would outlive their usefulness and disappear.[6]

That Rosenzweig was very much aware of the representative function of religion—and of a loss of legitimacy in this regard—can be seen in writings outside of the *Stern*. For example, in "Die Wissenschaft von der Welt" (The Science of the World), a series of lectures delivered at the Freies Judisches Lehrhaus between April and June 1922, he posed the question of how the many different worlds of art, law, faith, and nature relate to one another and whether it makes any sense to ask the further question of which one of these worlds has the most reality or truth.[7] Rosenzweig begins to answer these questions by stating, first, that these are not only worlds but also worldviews [*Weltanschauungen*]; each purported world is actually a set of representations in someone's mind.

Indeed, in the case of the World, unlike God and Man (the other main elements in Rosenzweig's ontology), we must ponder whether the World is anything other than, or beyond, its representations. Rosenzweig was inclined to think not. For him, representations of the natural world are no more mind-independent or objective than any other representations. Even the systematicity and law-like aspects of these representations do not make them any less "relative" to the thinking subject than any others.[8] In fact, Rosenzweig holds that art and law display more order and necessity than nature. To the implicitly anticipated objection that it is difficult to see how anything could be more necessary or orderly than, say, the laws of mechanics, he replies that art and law are more necessary than the natural world because they have orientation. The world of nature and of material things has no orientation, meaning it has no *Mittelpunkt* [centerpoint]. We will see better the significance of orientation and the *Mittelpunkt* in the next section. Rosenzweig here wishes to emphasize that the world of natural things is in a sense indiscriminate: it "knows no *havdalot*," distinctions or separations, no center and periphery.[9]

A world of representations, however, is not the same as a world of spirit [*Geist*]. Rosenzweig is at pains to point out that spirit, such as Hegel's Absolute Spirit, is constructed or created, even as it too constructs and creates. Spirit as conceived by Hegel is an objective entity: it "realizes itself and thereby destroys the world" and it subordinates everything human to itself.[10] Spirit is not a creative force; it is something itself created or constructed and seeks to dominate the world. Spirit is also to be distinguished from the soul, which is truly creative.

Rosenzweig then puts forward (though not in a very clear way) a further argument as to why the natural world known by science cannot be the most real or ultimate world: if the natural world were the most real, it would serve as the standard or measure of reality. But a standard for all realities and representations of realities cannot itself be either a world or a representation. It must be something absolute, beyond all our other representations. Moreover, if the standard is something beyond all representations, its existence does not presuppose a person, personality, mind, or soul, holding that particular representation or person who puts it into effect.[11] Nonetheless, the existence of such a standard would be a possible metaphysical proof for the existence of an Absolute, or God in Spinoza's sense, which is the ground and measure of all representations.[12] At this point Rosenzweig does not proceed to deny the existence of such a Spinozistic God, probably because he has already conveyed an alternative in the *Stern der Erlösung*.

Rosenzweig's argument is confusing. A standard does not have to be a separately existing entity outside of anyone's mind or separate from the things for which it is the standard. The standards of theoretical coherence, evidence, and mathematical certainty expressed through or embodied in physics are not somehow beyond the theories themselves, the representations in physicists' minds, or the concrete expressions of those representations (in material equipment, journal articles, etc.). In addition, it is difficult to see how a standard could be equivalent to a god, even of the Spinozistic type. A benevolent interpretation of Rosenzweig's notion would be that by "standard" he means "ideal," and an ideal, such as an ethical one, should have or does have some sort of substantiality. But Rosenzweig does not state or explain this explicitly.

THE IDEA OF REVELATION

Rosenzweig was not concerned only with the challenges to the intellectual or representative functions of religion. He also wanted to renew traditional Judaism as a living experience and a living religion and thereby to evade the increasingly technological, stultifying world of material things and processes. Unfortunately, in the *Stern der Erlösung* his method, if there was one, was to assert his passion rather than provide coherent trains of theological or philosophical reasoning that others could follow. Rosenzweig's avoidance of metaphysical argument on key philosophico-theological questions, such as that of revelation, has often been noted.[13] Scholem himself harshly described certain sections of Part Two of the *Stern*, which contains the theory of revelation, as relying on "the ragged clothing of scandalous allegory and confused drivel" [*Lumpengewand skandaloser Allegorie und verwirrten Geschwatzes*].[14] It is in any case a seemingly indiscriminate mixture of religious vision, theology and philosophy.

Of the many concepts that a persuasive theology must treat, the concept of revelation is perhaps the most important. In most theologies, historically supported by a philosophical apparatus, revelation is both the metaphysical link between the divine and the human and the foundation for religious ethics. Certainly Rosenzweig held this to be so: "[What is needed is a renewal of] the offensive thought of revelation" and "[an] intrusion of the spirit into the nonspirit."[15] He therefore devoted a complex section to revelation in Part Two of the *Stern der Erlösung* and referred to it quite frequently elsewhere.

In general, the *Stern*'s *i*deas on any topic begin from the unit of individual lived experience rather than elements of a traditional ontology, such as a First Cause, Substance, or Absolute Spirit. Thus, in the section on revelation in Part Two of the *Stern,* Rosenzweig begins by reiterating some ideas already presented in the first section of the book (on metaphysics): God himself, or itself, initially transforms itself from nothingness, nonbeing, into a something, a something that creates and affirms the world. This transformation occurs in a momentary [*Augenblicklich, nicht verhängt von uran*] manner.[16] This is also a sign of difference from the gods of mythology, who are static. They have never had the experience of moving from a condition of hiddenness to one of revealedness.[17]

Rosenzweig suggests here as well that the movement toward creation, which is simultaneously a movement of revelation, is also a mark of difference between believer and unbeliever: the unbeliever has never experienced the hiddenness of God. For the pagan, a god may be visible and yet not revealed; for the true believer, there must be an experience of hiddenness.[18] The movement of divine creation-revelation is irreversible; it contains a force of "infinite breath," a force that "breaks forth directly from the depths of divine hiddenness" and "secures the revelation within creation," preventing the condition of revealedness from reverting to one of hiddenness and secrecy.[19] Beneath the neoplatonic or stoic references to breath, light, and fate, we have a metaphysical claim about the nature of God as a self-creating being, a being that creates other things, such as the natural world, and has the capacity to reveal itself in some instances.

From here Rosenzweig proceeds to a denial that God possesses attributes or properties such as love. Love is not a basic, unchanging property of God [*unveränderliche Grundform*] but instead is a fugitive quality that occurs only momentarily.[20] Moreover, God's love is not universal or total; it is given or directed only to the individual. As Rosenzweig describes it, God's love is capricious, arbitrary: "God always loves only whom and whatever it loves" and always only in the present [*Sie (die Liebe) ist immer im Heute und ganz im Heute*]. Paradoxically, however, past and future loves are bound up with present ones, as they are "devoured" [*verschlungen*] by present love. Rosenzweig is here retaining the Hegelian notion of sublimation; he is in effect saying that past loves are sublimated [*aufgehoben* in Hegel's terminology] in present ones. But since Rosenzweig is trying to get away from German Idealism and Hegelian language in particular, he uses another term. On the other hand, he also differs from Hegel in that future loves, not just past ones, are also somehow sublimated in the present. This does not fit the Hegelian pattern of sublimation. Be that as it may, Rosenzweig insists that God's love is the eternal victory of love over death [*Diese Liebe ist der ewige Sieg ueber den Tod*].[21]

But how is God's love received by the individual, and what has this got to do with revelation? Individuals must prepare themselves to receive divine love, light, and revelation, which are all entwined, by learning to see them. They does this by passing through stages of doubt and defiance. As I have argued elsewhere, for Rosenzweig defiance is a critical stage in both arriving at and maintaining faith, a process that he describes in earlier sections of the *Stern*.[22] At a certain point, having become open to divine love and revelation, individuals aquire the "pride of defiance" [*Stolz des Trotzes*]. This defiance does not undermine their faith; on the contrary, it gives individuals the strength to withstand doubt and misfortune. This type of proud defiance is like a body of deep, still water in which individuals are immersed and feel supported and protected by it. It is a defiance that is humble as well as proud. Overall, individuals now feel sheltered and that no power can take this feeling away from them.[23]

Rosenzweig understands the defiance of the individual also as a means of arriving at a strong sense of self (he uses the phrase "emphatic self," or *betontes Ich*). This is not important in itself but is important because an emphatic self is required for an I-You relation within God, between God and an individual, and between human beings.

Revelation begins, for Rosenzweig, in the dialogue of God with himself [*Selbstgespräch Gottes*], in which God is, as it were, self-separated into an I and a You. God is not a self-contained, independent being but instead is a being that asks after the whereabouts of the You. The same is true for human beings. In the very posing of the question "Where are You?" (meaning where is another self), the self discovers itself, the individual discovers him/herself. Therefore, a prophet cannot be an intermediary between God and Man; rather, Man hears the voice of God and the question "Where are You?" directly.[24] God's own self strives to avoid becoming an entity referred to only in the third person, to become an It, and achieves this by commanding "love Me." The God posited and experienced by the individual who feels loved, who hears the commandment to love, and loves God in return is the true God and truly exists.[25] This is the revealed God, as opposed to a merely independently existing God (the god of the philosophers), and comes into being only through the recognition and love of human beings.[26] A philosophical argument for the existence of God is therefore precisely what is not needed.

Revelation is the sphere of love between an I and a You, but it is also the sphere of language. Thus, prayer is the completion of revelation. Language in this sphere exists in contrast to language in the sphere of creation, which is determinative, narrative, reifying, and conditional.[27] Moreover, creation-as-such is to be contrasted with creation-as-revealed. Created things, as in nature, are always in the past, but creation-as-revealed is always n the present. Human individuals are the paradigm of entities that are creation-as-revelation. They have highly individualized names, and whatever has its own name cannot be seen merely as part of a species or merely as one thing among other things. More importantly, its particular location in space-time is in a certain sense nonexistent or irrelevant: it carries its "here and now" around with it.[28]

At first glance this last statement is not only bewildering. It seems to threaten the very historicity, the veracity, the importance, even if temporary, of an individual life. But this may be precisely Rosenzweig's intention, namely to provide a form of consolation for mortality and even for misfortune. If one carries one's own here and now around with one, then externalities of natural existence, which include whatever may be inflicted by biological or sociopolitical processes, are not important. As Rosenzweig wrote in the lecture described in the previous section, "[Political] power wants to conquer everything. But there are things that are unconquerable."[29] I shall return to this theme below.

The self with a proper name seeks orientation, a centerpoint for its experiences. It cannot survive in the undifferentiated juxtaposition of things and representations. It requires an ordering that is nonetheless grounded in an external order,[30] which it can carry around with it. Such an orientation is acquired through acknowledgment of one's dependence on God, by naming and addressing God.[31] It is important to note this ground provided by the external order. While Rosenzweig does not explain exactly what he means, we may infer that he is not out to either assert or deny the existence of the external, natural world in any simple way. As we saw above, he assumes the natural world to have the ultimate status of a mental representation or construct. On the other hand, as we see here, he is not prepared to deny it all reality or significance; on the contrary, he is assigning it an ordering or grounding function. This places him closer to the Idealist tradition that he seeks to criticize rather than the existentialist one in which he is usually placed.

But Rosenzweig also maintains in these pages of the *Stern* that his conception of revelation puts creation in a different light. It is no longer creation as understood by the German Idealists, a constructed totality. The categories of that school have been transcended by his own understanding of creation, which is inextricably linked to revelation as described above, and is part of a threefold process: creation-revelation-redemption. Idealism was not able to go beyond the first stage, creation. Through its constructions of totality, of the Absolute and the All, Idealism sought to rival theologies of creation but remained limited, its notions of revelation and redemption weak or nonexistent. Disconcertingly, Rosenzweig then adds that battles between differing concepts about existence, and indeed for existence, are decided by power alone.[32] It is not clear exactly what he means by this. He could be thinking of political power, such that concepts that "win" in a society and become dominant are the end result of a struggle for political power among different groups with their different ideas and conceptions. More likely Rosenzweig is thinking of explanatory power, for he says "When concepts prove to be powerless over against others, they cede their categorical character to those others."[33] To have the character of a category, a concept has to be directly related to existence, not mediated by some other entity or circumstance, such as experience.[34]

Whatever Rosenzweig may mean by "direct relation to existence, not mediated by experience," his aim is to emphasize the revealed character of things in the world. Creation and revelation are synchronous, equally original, neither preceding the other. A thing revealed, through being named and loved, is simultaneous with its creation and creator [*Das Werk ist genau so alt wie sein Urheber*]. Rosenzweig holds that while philosophy was for centuries, up to the beginning of the nineteenth century, preoccupied with the distinctions between immanence and transcendence, it was also known that this distinction is vitiated in and through language. The Song of Songs, for Rosenzweig, is an instance of direct communication between God and Man, "a genuine spiritual love song about God's love for the individual person."[35] This form of communication is what Rosenzweig seeks to achieve through his own philosophical theology of revelation, the "speaking language of revelation" [*sprechende Sprache der Offenbarung*], the I-You language of revelation, which Martin Buber also described.

The loved-named individual, who has been opened to revelation of divine love, has for Rosenzweig ontological, conceptual, and emotional primacy over the merely natural human being. The natural human being falls victim to all-overcoming death, the "deathly coldness and rigidity of objects in their perishing," but nonetheless remains within the warmth of eternal divine love. This is presumably what Rosenzweig means by the phrase, cited above, that love is stronger than death (though referring mainly to divine love, it would not preclude the remembering love of human beings with whom one has also been in an I-You relation).

Rosenzweig simply does not address, in any traditional philosophic or theological way, the conceptual issues that this view of revelation and the God-Man relation raise. For example, how does God speak directly to humans? Is a voice heard? The Song of Songs is a written text as well as a sung-heard piece of language: how did that text come into being, if not through the mediation of a person, precisely what Rosenzweig does not wish to admit? For philosophers of a traditional analytical stripe, this is frustrating. But I think it is unfair to conclude that Rosenzweig has simply failed to make a case. By passionately laying out a vision, however unsystematic and unclear, he has defiantly presented an alternative conception of belief in the existence and love of God; the sheer force of assertion is intended to reinforce the doubter's potential or hesitant movement toward being open to divine love and to help avoid getting bogged down in logical, abstract back-and-forths.

Rosenzweig maintains that his understanding of God's love is and revelation is *gefühlsmässig klar;* that is, it is clear to and through the emotions.[36] He contrasts this with mere conceptual or empirical clarity. Goethe and Herder, however great their own poetry, reduced the Song of Songs to mere worldly, human love, not taking it as an expression of divine love: "The goal was always to change the lyrical, the I and You of the poem, to an epic-intuitive Him and It." Theirs was a conception of revelation that was uncanny, disturbing [*unheimlich*], and a result of the entire mind-set of the late eighteenth and nineteenth centuries, a mind-set that sought to make everything objective and to purify language. "[W]ith no other book of the Bible has there been such a critical drive to such extensive transformations, indeed overturning of traditional texts."[37] But removal—through misinterpretation by European poets and by science—of the feeling of being in a relationship with God through the divine word has ended only in a dead relation with some sort of objective, impersonal entity.

Surprisingly, Rosenzweig continues, science itself contained the seeds of a solution to this dismal process of humanistic reinterpretation of religious speech. It was discovered (presumably by anthropologists) that just as in the Song of Songs, in Syria it is still the case that a shepherd who marries is seen and sees himself as a king. The significance of this is not that the "humanistic" interpretation (by Herder, Goethe, and others) is confirmed. Rather, it shows, as does the Song of Songs, that love (whether to God or a human being) cannot be "purely human."[38] The peasant or shepherd transcends his lowly status through his self-image, albeit temporary, as a king. Similarly, the human individual transcends his contingent, worldly status through experiencing, believing that he experiences, divine love. Love transcends empirical conditions, just as language brims with a divine transcendence [*Übersinn*]. Love is empirical-transcendent [*sinnlich*-ü*bersinnlich*]. Thus, the image or metaphor of a king in the Song of Songs is not a decorative accessory but instead is essential, because it expresses this idea of transcendence.

The Song of Songs, for Rosenzweig, is the ultimate articulation of how an individual human self becomes an "emphatic self" and of a love that is stronger than death. In this text creation shifts into and is overcome by revelation. It is the *Kernbuch der Offfenbarung*, the core text of revelation.[39]

We see, then, that despite the often murky language, the struggle between scientific or secular (humanistic) interpretations of the Bible was in the forefront of Rosenzweig's mind as he wrote this portion of the *Stern*.

THE PROBLEM OF HISTORICISM

A topic that is closely linked to the science/theology theme—and concomitantly to revelation—is that of historicism. Roughly, this is the problem of how historical thinking and investigation have undermined many grounds of traditional religious belief, such as the Exodus experience of the Jews and the divinity of Jesus for Christians. As is well known in broad terms, Rosenzweig sought to overcome this problem by separating Judaism from history, claiming that Jews and Judaism are somehow beyond history. This topic has been extensively analyzed by Amos Funkenstein and David Myers, among others. Both also show how various other Jewish thinkers responded to this problem.[40] However, while Myers describes Rosenzweig as refusing to accept "the corrosive effects of historical time" on Judaism, the role of Rosenzweig's conception of revelation in this view of history is left largely unexplicated, and Rosenzweig's answer to the question of "the possibility of co-habitation of critical historical science and faith" is not entirely clear from Myers's essay.[41]

We have seen that Rosenzweig was very much aware of the crisis posed for theology and religious thought more generally by scientific developments, especially in the nineteenth century. Along with the natural sciences, the disciplines of history, archaeology, the *Wissenschaft des Judentums,* and sociology tended to undermine long-held beliefs. Myers shows that Rosenzweig's work was part of a wider antihistoricist effort to counter historical reductionism. It was an effort both Jewish and non-Jewish, both philosophical and theological. Rosenzweig's views on history were shaped, according to Myers, not only by philosophical debates about the nature and meaning of history, in which Hegel and Rosenzweig's own teacher Friedrich Meinecke were preeminent, but also by contemporary discussions within Christian and especially Protestant theology. The Jewish antihistoricists included S. R. Hirsch and S. D. Luzzatto; non-Jewish exponents included Dilthey, Windelband, Rickert, and Heidegger.

We saw above that Rosenzweig maintains in the *Stern* that the self carries its own space-time around with it. Whatever this might mean exactly, a logical consequence would be that events in either natural or historical space-time are of secondary importance. So whether, for example, Abraham existed or not or some other historical fact mentioned in the Bible is or is not a fact within a scientific representation of the world would not matter to the individual's possible experience of divine love and capacity to reciprocate that love. A further consequence would be that returning to theology does not mean, for Rosenzweig, denying the truth of scientific representations; it means regarding them as inessential to the main process within the individual soul or self, namely becoming open to revelation. For the purposes of the historicist/antihistoricist debate, this would mean that theology and modern scientific scholarship can coexist because they deal with different sets of representations, as Rosenzweig would put it. It is in this sense, I believe that Jews and Judaism remain *übergeschichtlich,* beyond history, for Rosenzweig.

However, this assessment—that Rosenzweig arrived at a stance of compatibility, if not reconciliation, between theology and the sciences, both natural and social—may be too weak. In the section on miracles that precedes the main section on revelation, Rosenzweig makes a bolder claim. After a dizzying survey of Western intellectual and religious history and the role of different moments of enlightenment (up to and including the Enlightenment of the eighteenth century), Rosenzweig states that science is too one-dimensional in form to be able to explain or cope with the variegated experiences and ideas of humanity. Nor, as he says often, is German Idealist philosophy, for all its pretensions, able to do any better. On the other hand, Nietzschean sujective perspectivism is also inadequate.

There is only way forward from the philosophical and existential dead end that seems to have been reached, one way out of the multiplicity of *Weltanschauungen* on all things, within a single individual as well as within German and Western society. Philosophy, both as a generalizing discipline, with some claim to be objective or scientific, and as a discipline that has come to see the importance of a new thinking that begins with individual existence (Rosenzweig's and others' own contribution) must accept the entrance of theological ideas on creation and even more so on revelation. Philosophy, if not science, needs theology. Philosophy "must hold fast to its new starting point and perspective, that of the subjective, extremely personal, more, the incommensurable self that is submerged in itself, and yet arrive at the objectiovity of science."[42]

There follow some very unclear passages as to how Rosenzweig thinks a bridge between the intensely subjective and the objective is actually formed. He is in general very resistant to precise methodological prescriptions, holding that they can come only after the labor toward something has been done. The account of the bridge seems to come down to the role of language. It would take us too far afield to explore this topic in detail, but the main idea is that spoken language is the binding element between human beings and humanity as a whole. The whole grammar of different languages embodies creation, revelation, and redemption.[43] Language is the "organon" of revelation, and all of humanity orders itself along this "thread" of language. What we can take from these passages, which contain many mixed metaphors as well as reflections on prelinguistic thought and the origins of the cosmos, is that language provides a medium for intersubjective thinking. It is this intersubjectivity that provides the exit from pure subjectivity, the self concentrated on itself and on God's love, and provides a transition into communal existence, into history, and the possibility of redemption. Philosophy and history (as a science or discipline with pretensions to objectivity) are thus not merely reconciled in the sense of coexisting peaceably; they become entwined with one another through the processes of creation-revelation-rededmemption. But the starting point must always be the individual reception of revelation.

Rosenzweig had adumbrated his ideas about historicism and revelation before writing the *Stern* in the essay "Atheistische Theologie" [Atheistic Theology] in 1914. This essay is often understood as expressing Rosenzweig's concern about the consequences of historicism and the incompatibility of historicism and religion. Indeed, that theme is strongly present. But another principal concern is the constructed quality of contemporary theology. Thus, the problem is not only that historical evidence throws doubt on many aspects of Jesus's life, for example, or many events in Jewish history. The underlying problem is the assumption that certain ideas, such as ideas of God, can only be the result of human projections or constructions and that God, or the divine, is not an independent Other that has broken through from its realm of infinite otherness to the human world.[44] Rosenzweig is completely unwilling to accept this assumption.

Rosenzweig is therefore at pains to distinguish the explanation of myth formation from true revelation. Scholars, especially historians, says Rosenzweig, describe myths as the accretion of certain ideas around historical persons, events, or peoples and reduce the features of their objects of study to purely human terms. Thus, myth is understood as the superhuman product of a human creation process [*das Übermenschliche als Ausgeburt des Menschlichen*], and revealed religions are understood as mere myths.[45] But, Rosenzweig maintains, precisely here lies evidence for the power of revealed religion: while the fact that myths are accretions of legends and fantasies around historical persons and events shows that they (the myths) are in an uninteresting sense untrue, it also shows that the same persons and events have an actuality, a historicity, that too can be captured by faith and revealed religion.[46] Through its theories of human projection, historicism seeks to eliminate the vast difference between divine and human as well as the seemingly humiliating idea of revelation. But once a historical moment occurred in which the thought or experience of revelation was actually present, the shadow of this experience can never be entirely removed. Try as they may, human beings, and especially Jews, cannot escape from revelation as the central idea of faith.[47]

CONCLUSION

Rosenzweig did not present a clear, unified definition of the scope and methods of Jewish theology, as at least some of his contemporaries sought to do or as some of the principal Jewish philosophers in the past had done.[48] Indeed, it is not evident that he was doing theology at all.[49] Nor did he put forward any kind of detailed engagement with modern science (as Maimoinides and others had sought to do), despite living in an era that saw great innovation in both the natural and social sciences, including Einstein's theories of relativity and

Durkheim's theories of society. He was aware of developments in the latter two sciences and yet was brusquely dismissive of them, relegating them to a realm of "unimportant truths."[50] Ultimately his central concern was to assert, rather than argue for, the primacy of the revelation of God's love to the individual over everything else.

This religious vision, though supported only intermittently by philosophical arguments, is nonetheless reminiscent of some earlier Jewish thinkers. The vision of the individual open to divine love recalls Maimonides's conception of providence in the *Guide for the Perplexed*:

> The providence of God, may He be exalted, is constantly watching over those who have obtained this overflow, which is permitted to everyone who makes efforts with a view to obtaining it. If a man's thought is free from distraction, if he apprehends Him, may he be exalted, in the right way and rejoices in what he apprehends, that individual can never be afflicted with evil of any kind. For he is with God, and God is with him.[51]

It may also call to mind Bahya ibn Pakuda's concepts of devotion and trust in God. However, in both of these cases the overflow of divine love is constant, not momentary or instantaneous and seemingly arbitrary, as it is for Rosenzweig. Nonetheless, both of these theories have a strong neoplatonic coloration, as does the *Stern*; they are permeated by images of overflowing light and love.

Rosenzweig's return to theology is in many respects problematic for the contemporary post-Holocaust reader. The supremacy of revelation over natural and sociohistorical processes as he describes it is difficult to accept. Divine love, in Rosenzweig's characterization, is so fugitive and arbitrary and the processes of political and physical destruction is so great in the time since his death that one cannot see how one might attain to or retain such love. Yet the thought that one is somehow bathed in divine love, no matter what, is consoling. Ultimately for many readers, philosophical and scientific skepticism in regard to Rosenzweig's conceptions of revelation and of a return to theology may remain in the foreground, the vehemence of his assertions notwithstanding. But as Rosenzweig's own fortitude in the face of historical and biological misfortune shows, that is probably our loss.

NOTES

1. Hilary Putnam, *Jewish Philosophy as a Guide to Life: Rosenzweig, Buber, Levinas, ittgenstein* (Bloomington: Indiana University Press, 2008), 2.

2. Gershom Scholem, "Nachwort," in Franz Rosenzweig, *Der Stern der Erlösung*, Mit einer Einfuhrung von Reinhold Mayer und einer Gedenkrede von Gershom Scholem (Frankfurt am Main: Suhrkamp Verlag, 1993).

3. Ibid., 532.

4. Ibid., 533. I take the phrase "argumentative context" from Ivan Strenski, *Durkheim and the Jews of France* (Chicago: University of Chicago Press, 1997), 55.

5. Relatively more detailed treatments of Rosenzweig on revelation can be found in Stephane Moses, *Systeme et Revelation* (Paris: Seuil, 1982); Amos Funkenstein, "Franz Rosenzweig and the End of German-Jewish Philosophy," in *Perceptions of Jewish History* (Berkeley: University of California Press, 1993); Alexander Altmann, "Theology in Twentieth-Century German Jewry," *Leo Baeck Institute Yearbook* 1 (1956).

6. Marcel Fournier, *Emil Durkheim, 1858–1917* (Paris: Fayard, 2007), 699.

7. Franz Rosenzweig, "Die Wissenschaft von der Welt," in *Zweistromland:Kleinere Schriften zu Glauben und Denken,* Hrsg. Von Reinhold und Annemarie Mayer (Dordrecht: Martinus Nijhoff Publishers, 1984), 655.

8. Ibid., 658.

9. Ibid., 661.

10. Ibid.

11. Ibid., 662–63.

12. Ibid.

13. The point has been especially well made by Peter Eli Gordon, "Rosenzweig Redux: The Reception of German-Jewish Thought," *Jewish Social Studies*, new series, 8, no. 1 (Autumn 2001): 1–57.

14. Scholem, "Nachwort," 532.

15. Franz Rosenzweig, "Atheistic Theology," cited in N. N. Glatzer, "Foreword," in *The Star of Redemption*, trans. William W. Hallo (New York: Holt, Rinehart and Winston, 1970), xiii.

16. Franz Rosenzweig, *Der Stern der Erlösung*, Mit einer Einfuhrung von Reinhold Mayer und einer Gedenkrede von Gershom Scholem (Frankfurt am Main: Suhrkamp Verlag, 1993), 178.

17. Ibid., 176.

18. Ibid.

19. Ibid., 179.

20. Ibid., 183.

21. Ibid.

22. Jean Axelrad Cahan, "Rosenzweig's Dialectic of Defiance and Critique of Islam," *Journal of Jewish Thought and Philosophy* 9 (1999): 1–20.

23. Rosenzweig, *Stern*, 187.

24. Ibid., 198.

25. Ibid., 202.

26. Ibid., 203.

27. Ibid., 207.

28. Ibid., 208.

29. Rosenzweig, "Die Wissenschaft von der Welt," 660.

30. Rosenzweig, *Stern*, 208.

31. Ibid., 209.

32. Ibid., 210.

33. Ibid.

34. Ibid.

35. Ibid., 213.

36. Ibid., 222.

37. Ibid., 223.

38. Ibid., 224.

39. It is surprising that Hilary Putnam, who devoted an entire chapter to Rosenzweig on revelation, did not mention this lengthy discussion of the Song of Songs. Instead, Putnam quite artificially (as he himself recognized) brought in an analysis of Abraham and Genesis. See also Putnam, *Jewish Philosophy*, 43–45.

40. Amos Funkenstein, *Perceptions of Jewish History* (Berkeley: University of California Press, 1993); David N. Myers, *Resisting History: Historicism and Its Discontents in German-Jewish Thought* (Princeton, NJ: Princeton University Press, 2003).

41. Myers, *Resisting History*, 87.

42. Rosenzweig, *Stern*, 117–18.

43. Ibid., 123.

44. Rosenzweig, "Atheistische Theologie," in *Zweistromland*, 692.

45. Ibid., 692–93.

46. Ibid., 693.

47. Ibid., 697.

48. Apart from the classics of Jewish theology and philosophy, a contemporary of Rosenzweig's, Alexander Altmann, produced a cogent essay: Alexander Altmann, *Was ist judische*

Theologie? Beitrage zur judischen Neuorientierung (Frankfurt am Main: Verlag des Israelit und Hermon G.M.B.H., 1933).

49. Franz Rosenzweig, "Das neue Denken," in *Zweistromland*, 152.

50. Ibid., 159.

51. Moses Maimonides, *The Guide of the Perplexed*, with an introductory essay by Leo Strauss, trans. Shlomo Pines (Chicago: University of Chicago Press, 1963), Part III, chap. 51, p. 625.

Exile and Return: Indian Jews and the Politics of Homecoming

Joseph Hodes

On May 14, 1948, Israel became a nation and opened its doors to Jewish immigrants from across the globe. Between May 1948 and December 1951 the tiny nation absorbed 684,000 people, doubling its Jewish population in three years. Never before in recorded history had so much ethnic, linguistic, and cultural diversity come to such a small geographical entity in such a short time to form a new collective. This essay documents how the Bene Israel, a Jewish community from India, came to Israel during this period of mass absorption, were dissatisfied with Israel, returned to India, and then once more left India and returned to Israel.

The Bene Israel, whose own tradition maintains that they have lived in India for more than 1,800 years, is the largest of the three major Indian Jewish communities, which also include the Cochin and Baghdadi Jews. The Bene Israel, numbering 20,000 at the height of their population in India, began to immigrate to Israel in 1948. By 1960, approximately 8,000 community members lived in Israel. Today, there are 75,000 Bene Israel in Israel and approximately 10,000 in India, mostly in Mumbai.[1] For centuries, they lived in villages on the Konkan coast in the state of Maharashtra and self-identified as both Indian and Jewish. In India, Jews have lived primarily under the hegemony of Hinduism, one of the oldest religious traditions in the world, with over 1 billion adherents.[2] Hinduism has existed almost exclusively in India, but in the modern period its adherents can be found throughout the globe.[3]

The experience of Jews in India is unique. Jews in the diaspora lived almost exclusively in the Christian and Islamic worlds. Of all the religious traditions in the world, only two—Christianity and Islam—claim that the only way to salvation is through them. Neither Judaism, Hinduism, Buddhism, Shinto, Sikhism, nor any other religion holds that nonadherents cannot find their own religious path. In both the Christian and Islamic worlds, Jews were subject to the hardships of antisemitism to varying degrees. Under Hindu hegemony in India, Jews had an 1,800-year history free of antisemitism. This was due primarily to the traditional Hindu understanding of conversion whereby one could not convert to Hinduism.[4] A person was either born a Hindu or was not Hindu. One was welcome to live according to Hindu norms and attend

Hindu celebrations but could be a Hindu only by birth.[5] Consequently, Jews never experienced any pressure to convert, and Judaism too is traditionally a nonproselyting religion. Jews never asked the Hindus with whom they lived in the villages and later the cities of India to convert, and thus Hindus did not see Jews as a threat. Jews lived peacefully with their Hindu brethren in India, and their religion was never perceived as detrimental to their lives.[6]

Indeed, under British colonialism in the modern era, Jewish religious identity became a benefit. The British used a divide-and-conquer policy to control India.[7] The British pitted Hindus against Muslims and ruled from above, running the colony with the assistance of two small minority groups, Jews and Parsis (Zoroastrians). By the turn of the nineteenth century, the Bene Israel held key positions[8] as doctors, lawyers, civil engineers, civil servants, and high-ranking military personnel.[9] Although India is not often associated with Judaism, under British rule Jews were instrumental in state affairs. In August 1947, however, nine months before Israel became a nation, the British left the subcontinent, the Republic of India was born, and Hindus once again became the hegemonic force. Jews did not fear for their safety, but they did wonder whether the Hindu majority would allow them, a tiny minority, to maintain their prestigious societal positions. The overwhelming belief was that the Hindus would not. When Israel became a state in 1948, many Jews in India, fearing not for their safety but instead for their lifestyle, decided to immigrate to the new nation. When they arrived in Israel, however, it was not at all what they had envisioned.

HOMECOMING

Israel's early years were ones of great struggle. In fact, as late as 1956, Israel was regarded in many diplomatic circles less as a state than a kind of besieged refugee camp, frantically seeking to organize and defend itself amid awesome economic, social, and military difficulties.[10] The sheer number of immigrants who had to be absorbed during the first three years far exceeded what the new nation could accommodate. To begin, there was nowhere to house the massive influx of people. Initially, army barracks left behind by the British were used. Barracks that in January 1949 housed 28,000 people accommodated 90,000 by December 1949.[11] From there the nation turned to tents, and tent cities bloomed. This was not a long-term solution, so *mahabarot*, or transitional settlements, were created. Although envisioned as temporary housing, many *mahabarot* housed immigrants for years.[12] The *mahabarot* were shacks made of tin, corroborated steel, and plastic with no running water or electricity; food was cooked on kerosene stoves.[13] They were little better than the army barracks.

The new nation also had to deal with grave social strife. The Jewish immigrants coming from almost every nation in the world did not yet share a language. Most immigrants did not know Hebrew and had to learn it. Conflict between communities arose as in the barracks, tent cities, and *mahabarot;* and Middle Eastern and North African Jews lived alongside European Jews.[14] German Jews, who came from one of the most technologically advanced nations, lived with Yemenite Jews, who had never seen a clock or a watch before. The social strife became dire, and the communities eventually had to be separated as the cultural clashes became more pronounced. Ashkenazi Jews felt that Sephardic and Mizrachi Jews were backward, while Sephardic and Mizrachi Jews felt that Ashkenazi Jews were too cerebral, slavish to their watches and schedules, and the purveyors of terrible food.[15]

Due to overcrowding, food shortages became severe and led to illness throughout the nation. In some of the reception camps, many children became ill.[16] At one point, it was reported that 200 of 370 children in the Raanana camp were ill.[17] During the winter of 1951, a visiting United Nations expert on nutrition stated unequivocally that he had encountered more cases of malnutrition in Israel than anywhere else in the world.[18] One Bene Israel immigrant interviewed for this study (who wished to remain anonymous) recounted that his family moved to Israel with a healthy child, who became ill and died in a barracks reception camp.[19]

With a lack of housing and nutrition also came a lack of jobs and schooling. In the first three years many immigrants sat idle, waiting for employment opportunities to emerge and schools to become functional. Often when jobs did emerge, they were only part-time or far from the homes of the immigrants. Sometimes the new immigrants had to travel far to work slept in other cities or locations, only returning to their families on the weekends. Giora Josepthal, the director of the Jewish Agency's Absorption Department, was kept up at night by the conditions and scrambled against all odds to find solutions but claimed that there was "nothing to be done but quietly cry."[20]

RETURN TO INDIA

By 1951 some of the Bene Israel, who had an India free of antisemitism to return to, felt a strong desire to return to the subcontinent. Their conditions had become quite dire by that point. They lacked jobs, good housing, education, and food (until 1952, rationing made both food and clothing scarce). Many in the Bene Israel community felt that the Zionist enterprise had made false promises. One letter found in the Central Zionist archives complains about the situation at the time: "we were informed [in India] that there was no shortage of work and that all were profitably employed on land and other projects. Now with errors of back pay, up to two to three months' pay are overdue."[21] Although not politically organized, the Bene Israel community began to stage protests and strikes in front of the Jewish Agency offices in Jerusalem seeking to be repatriated to India.[22]

By late 1951 many Bene Israel children lived in a wretched state, undernourished and with few winter clothes due to the rationing that lasted until early 1952. To rectify this situation, the community held peaceful sit-ins on their kibbutzim and at the offices of the Jewish Agency, inspired by Gandhi's *satyagraha* [nonviolent civil disobedience] movement in India. On November 21, 1951, 150 Bene Israel, including children, 7 pregnant women, and a nine-day-old baby, held a hunger strike outside the Jewish Agency offices in Tel Aviv.[23] A second protest at the same spot in March 1952 demanded repatriation to India.[24] On May 11, 1952, the Bene Israel again demonstrated outside the office seeking repatriation. Protests recurred in 1954, once more demanding either repatriation or an immediate solution to housing, employment, and education issues.

While these protests by the Bene Israel always remained peaceful, the police, who were handling many different protest groups in Israel, did not always react peacefully. Physical violence during these protests came to a head in April 1956 at another peaceful sit-in outside the Jewish Agency office over unmet housing, work, and educational needs. Dr. M. Young of the Jewish Agency promised that the demonstrators' needs would be met and asked them to disperse. The protesters disbanded and went to the offices of those who could make good on Dr. Young's assurance, where they were told that the Jewish Agency did not intend to meet his promises. After appealing to every available government agency for help, the community resumed its peaceful protest. The official complaint report issued by the community records that the police battered all those present, including the elderly, the infirm, and children. A woman five months pregnant who was beaten by a police officer was taken to hospital, where she miscarried.[25] Despite the violence, the protest continued. During the night more police arrived, assaulted the protesters more severely, forced them into police vans, and dumped them on the side of a road far from the Jewish Agency office. One young man was arrested and sentenced by a magistrate to a month's imprisonment. Some community members became too scared to protest for fear of violence.

The government of Israel, though, acquiesced and began the process of assisting the Bene Israel's return to India. The government did pay their repatriation costs, and on April 2, 1952, an initial group of 115 flew back to India.[26] Shortly thereafter, the Israeli government helped more Bene Israel return to India. The government would help the Bene Israel return to India throughout the 1950s. Upon arrival, however, the Bene Israel found that the situation in India was not as it had been.

When India became a republic on August 15, 1947, it did so under duress. In order to leave, the British partitioned the subcontinent into two nations, India and Pakistan. The partition of British India was a great trauma for the subcontinent leading to mass migration and mass communal violence and bloodshed. The trauma of partition—much like the trauma of the partition of British Mandate Palestine in the Middle East—was a great wound whose legacies and politics are still being played out today. (While Israel and Jews saw the partition of Mandate Palestine and the creation of modern-day Israel as the ultimate redemption after the Nazi Holocaust, for the Arab world that partition and its results are known simply as *al nakba* [the catastrophe]. The Israelis and Arabs would fight three major wars over the partition in one generation, followed by many smaller yet no less brutal military campaigns.)

The partition of British India was no less traumatic for India and led to incredible violence as Muslims, Hindus, and Sikhs who had lived side by side in villages for centuries found themselves on different sides of the political divide. Violent episodes occurred sporadically until 1946, when violence in what is referred to as the direct day of action erupted and spread across northern India in some of the largest communal violence in the twentieth century.[27] The direct day of action began on August 16, 1946, after talks between the British (led by Viceroy Mountbatten), Hindus (led by Mahatma Gandhi and Jawaharlal Nehru), and Muslims (led by Muhammad Ali Jinnah) failed to produce amicable results concerning the independence of India from British rule, especially in Jinnah's view. In reaction to the breakdown in talks, Jinnah, speaking from his home in Bombay, called for protests, and events quickly escalated beyond what anyone could have foreseen.[28] Muslims marched into the Hindu quarter of Calcutta and begin killing, looting, and raping. The Hindus responded in kind by marching into the Muslim quarter escalating the violence.[29] The killings set off a chain of violence throughout North India that lasted until after the British left India on August 15, 1947.

The trauma of partition, however, did not remain limited to to violence leading up to Independence from British rule. The main trauma came after independence. On August 15, 1947, the British left India, setting borders and recognizing Pakistan as a Muslim home on the Indian subcontinent. Amid the violence set off by the direct day of action, people began to move en masse—the largest human migration in recorded history, with an estimated 10 million–20 million people moving.[30] Hindus and Sikhs who lived in what had become Pakistan moved by the millions to India, and millions of Muslims, primarily in northern India, moved to the newly formed nation of Pakistan.[31]

Neither side completely anticipated this migration. India's Prime Minister Nehru expected some refugees coming from Pakistan to India—but not 4.7 million people pouring into the new nation.[32] Pakistan's government, led by Jinnah, while also anticipating some movement, never envisioned its doors opening to millions of Muslims throughout the subcontinent. Moreover, the Pakistani government never expected the majority of its Sikhs and Hindus to leave. Consequently, the unanticipated migration happened in a state of disarray. On foot and by donkey and oxcart, people simply fled the villages where their families had lived for centuries.[33] They set off on many roads in two columns, one heading into Pakistan and the other heading into India. The migrants marched in the brutal August heat with no accommodations for basic needs. There were no toilet facilities, there was nowhere to sleep, and there was almost no access to water or food. Arial footage of this migration shows columns stretching out for fifty miles, followed by another fifty-mile column only a few miles behind.

Both India and Pakistan became independent during a transition from colonial to postcolonial rule at a moment of intense crisis, and their handling of the refugee crisis either bolstered or undermined the new states' legitimacy. India built refugee camps and devoted time and attention to rehabilitation, creating among other organizations the Refugee Protection Society and the All India Refugee Welfare Association.[34] However, the core principle of refugee rehabilitation in India was self-rehabilitation. The Indian government distinguished between the experience of being dislocated and the ability to survive in one's new home without the government's help. To achieve the latter, the government adopted the official stance that every able-bodied adult refugee had to find gainful employment, and no one willing to work could be denied the opportunity to earn a living.[35] It was understood that the infirmed and the majority of women were not part of this enterprise, but a narrative of shame regarding able-bodied men who did not work developed. Mohanlal Saksena, who served as minister of rehabilitation from 1948 to 1950, promoted the idea that if one had the energy and courage to accomplish the very difficult task of packing up all of one's belongings and leaving home to move to a completely foreign nation, then surely that person, once arrived, had the ability to work for a living and help establish the new state.[36] Those who still received financial assistance from the government after the initial period of settlement were seen as lazy, and the receipt of government aid became a disincentive and a demoralizing act. A refugee became a full member of the new state through the capacity for self-sufficiency.[37]

Many refugees to India and the majority of the Indian population before partition were villagers and farmers. Most refugees quickly started to cultivate the land they were allocated. In addition, the areas newly populated with refugees needed communal work to function: canals had to be dug, roads had to be created or widened, and all the other infrastructure that the new population needed had to be constructed. Even as farmers worked their lands, they built much-needed canal systems to facilitate the growth of their land. Today there are no refugees from the partition in India. There are those who were refugees and the descendants of refugees, but they have all been absorbed.[38]

In the aftermath of the partition, India sought to unify and become a state with a national identity based on secular and democratic principles. The constitution they created drew from the politically liberal states of the West and promised to "promote the welfare of the people by securing and promoting . . . a social order in which justice, social, economic, and political, shall inform all institutions of national life."[39] The constitution stipulated that no citizen should be discriminated against on the grounds of religion, race, caste, sex, or place of birth. The constitution guaranteed freedom of conscience and the right to profess, practice, and propagate religion, subject to the public order and morality. No institution supported by federal funds could offer religious instruction. While the constitution was a thoroughly modern document, India was plagued with an illiteracy rate of 86%, making its implementation challenging, if not impossible, in rural areas. The Bene Israel, if not aware of details of the new state's laws, would have understood the challenges to a secular democracy in India, which had always prioritized religious identity. However, despite the trauma of partition and the challenges of implementing the new constitution and creating a secular liberal democracy, the transfer of power from British colonial rule to the new Indian government was peaceful.

The Congress Party led by Jawaharlal Nehru took power with the governmental apparatus remaining in place. The most important aspect of this government, certainly in the early years of India's independence, was the Indian Civil Service (ICS), which changed its name to the Indian Administrative Services shortly after partition. This service oversaw the operation and functioning of what was to become the world's largest democracy, including the revenue, railways, customs, income tax, foreign service, and state-level services, such as medical, health, education, and police. Second in importance to the newly formed nation was the highly disciplined and experienced Indian military, which had fought for the British in Afghanistan, Ethiopia, Burma, Abyssinia, and Yemen as well as in both world wars.

Before moving to Israel, the Bene Israel had been very important players in both the ICS and the Indian military under colonial rule. Indeed, in the military the Bene Israel had enlisted in almost all of the native regiments in the Bombay presidency (a province that included what is today Gujarat, two-thirds of Maharashtra, northwest Karnataka, and parts of Pakistan) and held almost all the staff appointments and nearly half the native officers of each regiment for a century and a half. In the ICS, the Bene Israel had held key administrative posts and trusted positions as train engineers. However, in the new India, Hindus held these positions. The newly formed nation had done away with British rule, which had imposed a divide-and-conquer policy and prohibited Indians from rising to top positions. In the new India top spots were highly competitive and open to Hindus, who quickly filled them. Also, many Bene Israel who left their jobs to move to Israel found that during their absence, those positions had been filled by Indians who had remained in India. Thus, the Bene Israel who returned to India from Israel found their jobs and livelihoods gone. Finding the same type of high-ranking positions in the new India was extremely difficult.

It is worth taking a moment to underscore that the Bene Israel's loss of positions was due not to any anti-Jewish sentiment but rather to a new situation where competition for the jobs they had vacated was fierce. An example of the absence of anti-Jewish sentiment can be clearly seen in the case of one Indian Jew who had remained and never moved to Israel. Jack Jacob was a member of the Baghdadi Indian Jewish community, not the Bene Israel community. Born in Calcutta in 1923, he rose to become a lieutenant general in the Indian Army. He is best known for commanding India's Eastern Army in its victory over Pakistan in 1971 in a war that saw Bangladesh separate from Pakistan to become its own sovereign nation. Jacob served as governor of the Indian states of Goa and Punjab. The difference between Jacob and the Bene

Israel was that after India's independence, he never left or gave up his position in the military and later, through hard work and the absence of antisemitism, rose in the ranks.[40] In India, he is remembered as a national hero.

RETURN TO ISRAEL

As the Bene Israel who returned to India found that their jobs were no longer available and that the communities they left were no longer intact (many of their members had also moved to Israel), the returnees began to discuss going to Israel once again.[41] They were not the only participants in this discussion. The Indian press developed an interest in the leaving and return of the Bene Israel. Picking up the story, the Indian national press portrayed Israel in a very negative light.[42] In 1952 and 1953 during the repatriation of the Bene Israel community, the Indian press published articles accusing Israel of being a racist state. The claim of the *Times of India* and the *Bombay Chronicle* that "Indian Jews weren't up to the mark"[43] painted a picture of a racist Israeli state that would not accept the Bene Israel due to their skin color. The Bene Israel seeking to return to Israel fought these allegations, and by May 1953 the journals retracted their accusations in articles such as "Indian Jews Back Israel—Discrimination Denied."[44] Reprinted in many newspapers across India, this article reported that "Neither at work, nor socially, was there any trace of discrimination on account of color or origin. It is indeed contrary to the very spirit which inspired the creation of the state of Israel."[45]

The articles denying racism in Israel came after Lakshmi Menon, deputy minister of external affairs in Nehru's cabinet, declared in the Indian parliament that "one of the reasons which prompted the Indian Jews to return from Israel to India was the colour bar."[46] A prompt response to the Indian government signed by fifty-eight Bene Israel returnees on May 17, 1953, denied any trace of discrimination in Israel on account of color or origin:

> We regret the controversy which attended our return to India — it was a confession of failure to come up to the high standards demanded by a pioneering country. As you are fully aware, there are many of us today who would like to be given another chance to take part in the great work of reconstruction that is in place there. Had we the means, many of us would have already been in Israel today. If the Jewish Agency gives us another opportunity and pays for our passage again, we would today be all going to Israel with a greater determination to make good. In the interest of truth, we would like

you and hereby authorise you to convey this letter to all concerned. We feel that the good name of Israel should not be sullied by unjustified criticism of its government or people.[47]

The Bene Israel community was dependent on the Jewish Agency, because most could not afford to reimmigrate on their own. Due to the cost to the Israeli government, their repatriation was not a high priority for the Jewish Agency. Over the next several years, however, most of the repatriated Bene Israel who sought to return were brought back at Israel's expense, along with additional Bene Israel *olim* [immigrants to Israel]. On their return to Israel, housing, education, and work remained problematic, even if they felt that these issues did not result from racial discrimination.

While the challenges that Israel faced persisted for the Bene Israel as well as all Israelis, the situation had changed for the better by the mid-1950s, and there were signs of continued improvement. Production was on the rise due to a new economic policy implemented in 1952 and fresh infusions of foreign capital into the new state. Finance Minister Eliezer Kaplan understood that the newcomers' plight was so acute that without economic growth, it would be impossible to transform them into committed citizens. This would require more government spending and economic infusions from abroad. To achieve these, the government took advantage of many economic opportunities from abroad, including reparations from Germany and economic ties to the United States. This economic assistance took many forms, including grants, soft currency loans, and Export-Import bank loans as well as technical assistance.[48] From the early 1950s onward, this amounted to between $40 million to $60 million annually. Financial assistance from Jews abroad proved to be even more substantial than government loans. Charitable contributions from Jews abroad to institutions, such as the Hebrew University of Jerusalem, Technion, the Weitzman Institute, and Hadassah Hospital, exceeded US$750 million from 1949 to 1961. By the late 1950s, life was still difficult but no longer grim.

CONCLUSION

One of the experiences that Jews share is being an oppressed minority. Most Jews grew up in homes where the stories of one's family were often stories of persecution or nearly escaping persecution. This was almost a universal Jewish community experience. If you didn't hear those stories in your own home, you were informed of them by the community you lived in. For many, they weren't stories but a grim reality of life. There were and are, of course, many positive shared experiences of the Jews, but the story of oppression is a common thread. In the first generation of Israelis, these stories and the memory of the Holocaust were acute. The Bene Israel, however, did not have that in common with their Jewish brethren in Israel. With the absence of antisemitism in India, the Jewish identity formation there would have been quite different. Indian Jewry did not go to Israel to escape persecution; they went for other reasons. Because they did not come to escape persecution, they would have had, as a group, less reason to endure the hardships of the early years.

Israel was in many ways created as a safe haven for a persecuted minority scattered throughout the globe. The Bene Israel were not persecuted. Also, with a hospitable India to return to, it would have been for many of them an obvious choice to return. The situation on the ground in Israel during the first few years was so dire that many communities vocalized the sentiment that if they had a place to return, they would. Most Jews, however, had no place to return to. Many of those who did, left. Many Jews who could go to Canada, the United States, England, and Australia left Israel in the early years, feeling that life in Israel was too challenging.

Jews from what had been Nazi-occupied Europe felt that they could not return, and many did not have anywhere to return to. In the aftermath of the Holocaust, over 250,000 concentration camp survivors were left in those camps after the war. The camps were turned into Red Cross refugee camps, but those people hoped and waited for Israel to become a nation so they could leave the camps and go to a new home.

For the Bene Israel, their options were very different. They had a place to return to, so it is not surprising that many of them did. When they returned to India and realized that they would rather be in Israel, they came back to Israel, this time with a much better understanding of the challenges the state was facing. Upon return to Israel, the Bene Israel have entered almost every field, have been a great addition to the state, and are Israeli in every way.

NOTES

1. Nissim Moses, "Bene Israel Genealogy Program," Private archives of Nissim Moses, Petah Tikva, Israel.

2. "Current World Population," Worldometers, http://www.worldometers.info/world-population/.

3. Alex Michaels, *Hinduism: Past and Present* (Princeton, NJ: Princeton University Press, 2004), 4.

4. Gavin Flood, *An Introduction to Hinduism* (New York: Cambridge University Press, 1996), 7.

5. Ibid., 8.

6. Samuel Haeem Kehimkar, *The History of the Bene Israel of India* (Tel Aviv: Dayag, 1937), 14.

7. Bipan Chadra, *India's Struggle for Independence* (New York: Penguin Books, 1989), 28.

8. Joan Roland, *Jews in British India* (London: Brandeis University Press, 1989), 24.

9. Ibid., 24.

10. Howard Sachar, *A History of Israel from the Rise of Zionism to Our Time* (New York: Knopf, 1996), 395.

11. Ernest Stock, *The Chosen Instrument: The Jewish Agency in the First Decade of the State of Israel* (New York: Herzl Press, 1988), 75.

12. Sachar, *A History of Israel*, 395.

13. Ibid.

14. Dvora Hacohen, *Immigrants in Turmoil* (New York: Syracuse University Press, 2003), 134.

15. Tom Segev, *1949: The First Israelis* (New York: Free Press, 1986), 119.

16. Ernest Stock, *The Chosen Instrument: The Jewish Agency in the First Decade of the State of Israel* (New York: Herzl Press, 1988), 112.

17. Ibid.

18. Ibid.

19. Joseph Hodes, interview with multiple Bene Israel community members, June–August 2008, Israel.

20. Stock, *The Chosen Instrument*, 95.

21. Central Zionist Archives, S6/6147.

22. Shalva Weil. "Bene Israel Indian Jews in Lod Israel: A Study of the Persistence of Ethnicity and Ethnic Identity" (PhD diss., University of Sussex Graduate School, 1977), 70.

23. Ibid.

24. Ibid.

25. Central Zionist Archives, S42227.

26. Ibid.

27. Bipan Chadra, *India after Independence, 1947–2000* (London: Penguin Books, 2000), 112.

28. Vazira Fazila-Yacoobali Zamindar, *The Long Partition: The Making of Modern South Asia* (New York: Columbia University Press, 2007), 98.

29. Ibid.

30. Ibid.

31. "Pakistan Demographics Profile," Index Mundi, 2018, https://www.indexmundi.com/pakistan/demographics_profile.html.

32. Cyril Henry Philips, *The Partition of India Policies and Perspectives, 1935–1947* (London: Aberdeen University Press, 1970), 254.

33. Penderel Moon, *Divide and Quit* (Los Angeles: University of California Press, 1962), 118.

34. Fazila-Yacoobali Zamindar, *The Long Partition*, 103.

35. Ibid.

36. Philips, *The Partition of India*, 256.

37. Ibid.

38. Ibid.

39. Ibid.

40. Raoul Wootliff and JTA, "Jack Jacob, Indian Jewish War Hero, Dies at 92," The Times of India, January 14, 2016, https://www.timesofisrael.com/jack-jacob-indian-jewish-war-hero-dies-at-92/.

41. Central Zionist Archives, S6/6327.

42. Ibid.

43. Ibid.

44. Ibid.

45. Ibid.

46. Ibid.

47. Central Zionist Archives, S6/6149.

48. Sachar, *A History of Israel*, 424.

Against the Sabra Current: Hanokh Bartov's *Each Had Six Wings* and the Embrace of Diasporic Vitality

Philip Hollander

MEETING EXPECTATIONS: HANOKH BARTOV AND HIS APPROACH TO ISRAELI IMMIGRANT ABSORPTION

When the State of Israel proclaimed its independence on May, 14, 1948, its provisional government justified the state's establishment by pointing to the Holocaust: "The catastrophe which recently befell the Jewish people—the massacre of millions of Jews in Europe—was another clear demonstration of the urgency of solving the problem of its homelessness by re-establishing in Eretz-Israel the Jewish state, which would open the gates of the homeland wide to every Jew and confer upon the Jewish people the status of a fully privileged member of the community of nations."[1]

While Israel's role as a sanctuary enabling Jews to pursue "their right to a life of dignity, freedom and honest toil" should not be diminished, Israel's provisional government asserted a more expansive vision.[2] Declaring that "the State of Israel will be open for Jewish immigration and for the Ingathering of the Exiles," it drew on the traditional Jewish rhetoric of exile and return to communicate the momentous nature of what they perceived to be taking place.[3] Even though the second clause proves largely synonymous with the first, the strong resonance that it has among Jews led to its introduction. First referenced in Deuteronomy 30:3 and later developed by the former prophets, the concept of ingathering of the exiles [*kibbutz galuyot*] became entrenched in the weekday Jewish liturgy. The tenth blessing of the Eighteen Benedictions reads "sound the great shofar to herald our freedom, raise high the banner to gather our exiles [*lekabetz galuyotenu*]. Gather us together from the four corners of the earth."[4] This prayer expresses the idea that God will return the scattered Jewish people to their ancestral homeland and improve their lives when they repent for their sins. Subsequently, the medieval Jewish scholar Moshe ben Maimon (1135–1204) connected the exilic ingathering to the messianic age.

The State of Israel's founders secularized the idea of the ingathering of exiles and employed its rhetorical force to convey the idea that the state would radically transform and better Jews' lives. Consequently, they created expectations for the State of Israel that far surpassed those assumed by other postcolonial nation-states that emerged after World War II. During the first years of Israeli statehood hundreds of thousands of Jews, whose expectations had been influenced by the proclamation of independence's ideas and tone, made their way to Israel. Its population doubled in four years, and the need to integrate these immigrants into Israeli society was widely recognized as the most significant challenge facing the new state.[5]

Hebrew writers were pushed to depict this transformative event and to provide guidance to the coalescing nation.[6] Although not an immigrant who arrived in Israel during statehood's first years, Hanokh Bartov took up the challenge of portraying early state period Jewish immigration to Israel. His novel *Shesh kenafayim le-echad* (*Each Had Six Wings*, 1954) numbers among the first depictions of immigrant absorption in Israeli literature; its groundbreaking nature earned it widespread acclaim. Subsequently, it was adapted for the stage and published in multiple editions.

Each Had Six Wings has long received scholarly consideration. By and large, critics have asserted that it directs immigrants to temper their expectations and let elements of their diasporic pasts wither so they can emerge reborn in the Israeli melting pot.[7] Recently, scholar Batya Shimoni challenged this reading when she asserted that the novel expresses disappointment with mainstream Zionist ideology and a yearning for connection to the Jewish past and tradition offered by diasporic Jewish life.[8]

Building on Shimoni's reading, this essay highlights *Each Had Six Wings'* promotion of an Israeli culture actively drawing on diasporic Jewish culture as necessary for more effective realization of the Zionist vision—something that sets it apart from other contemporary Israeli works and differentiates its author from his Israeli literary counterparts. Born in the small agricultural community of Petakh Tikvah and socialized in Palestine's incipient modern Jewish community, Bartov (1926–2016) numbers among the first Sabras, or native-born Israelis. Yet he stood apart from most native-born Israelis and immigrant youths who cleaved to Sabra norms and characteristics. He did not see it as necessary to uncritically assume these characteristics and adopt these norms to highlight the difference between diaspora Jews and himself. Raised in a traditionally oriented settlement by East European immigrants who arrived in Palestine the year before his birth, Bartov implicitly understood and accepted his connection to the diaspora and did not view it as wholly negative. Furthermore, his encounter with Holocaust survivors in Europe immediately after World War II while he served in the Jewish Brigade drove home his sense of Jewishness. Consequently, the idea of exilic ingathering resonated strongly with him. He expected that the new state and its veteran citizens would dedicate their time and resources to new immigrants' integration into their society.

Bartov unexpectedly found veteran Israelis, including those who served alongside him in the 1948 war and expressed their commitment to the Jewish collective by putting their lives on the line to guarantee national survival, abandoning the utopian dreams that fueled the Zionist project. Solipsistically, they turned a blind eye to Holocaust survivors' unspeakable losses and the sacrifices made by Jews from Arab lands who left everything behind to pursue their Zionist aspirations. Instead, they myopically focused on the heavy losses that they and other young Israelis suffered during the 1948 war. Consequently, when resources were scarce, veteran Israelis proved ready to use force to ensure that limited resources went to them.[9] While veteran Israelis supplied immigrants with resources and opportunities, these went primarily to immigrants, especially immigrant youths, ready to abandon Jewish traditions and aspects of the Jewish past. Rather than viewing this as the best or most just form of resource allocation, Bartov viewed it as a waste of the tremendous resources brought to Israel by immigrant Jews whose values, norms, and social structures primed them to contribute effectively to the advancement of communal needs in difficult times with limited resources. Rather than having immigrants transform themselves to adapt to their new surroundings, Bartov turned to native-born and veteran Israelis and called upon them to learn from the new immigrants and alter their ways to better advance Jewish Israelis' shared vision.

THE PROLOGUE'S PRESENTATION OF THE DOMINANT ISRAELI FRAME OF REFERENCE

The prologue of *Each Had Six Wings* presents widely accepted early state period Israeli views about diaspora Jews and Sabras and the possibility of transitioning from one group to the other.[10] While critics have interpreted this as confirmation that Bartov shared these views and believed in the dominant paradigm for immigrant acclimation to Israeli society, he rejected this interpretation both immediately after the novel's publication and decades later.[11] In fact, Bartov introduces the dominant Israeli frame of reference for understanding the fictional world of the novel and the Israeli reality that it reflects to highlight this narrative frame's inadequacy. He saw the need to work toward the creation of a more balanced frame of reference acknowledging immigrants' abilities and the resources they brought with them from the diaspora.

Indeed, the prologue appears to support the view of diaspora Jews as "uprooted, cowardly and manipulative [and] helpless and defenseless in face of persecution" and the individual acting in accordance with Sabra norms and values "as young and robust, daring and resourceful, direct and down-to-earth, honest and loyal, ideologically committed and ready to defend his people to the bitter end."[12]

Nonetheless, the prologue presents the view that diaspora Jews could transform themselves into Israelis through adherence to the Zionist Conversion Paradigm.[13] This conversion process, symbolically initiated by the diaspora Jew's assumption of a Hebrew name after arrival in Israel, brought about individual rebirth through the shedding of one's diasporic traits and features and the assumption of a native-Hebrew identity considered to exist at the core of every Jew's being. Viewing the world in accordance with this widespread Zionist frame, the Sabras constituted a faultless ideal type that everybody, especially immigrant males, should unhesitatingly endeavor to emulate, since nothing about diasporic Jewishness proved authentically Jewish or worthy of retention.

The prologue opens with a description of a displaced persons (DP) camp in postwar Germany and presents the dominant early state period Israeli view of diasporic existence as fragile and unsustainable and those who reside in the diaspora as defenseless and morally suspect:

> The camp—the same camp. The square of red buildings, brick buildings, stood in its place. The asphalt square—the same square. The long barracks, the black barracks with their smell of tar, forests, and urine-soaked sheets—the same barracks. The barbed wire. The guard towers. Even the large Gothic letters in the workshop. Only the gates were removed and absent. Only the road that headed out from here and merged into the main road was open to all. People came and went as they pleased, but the camp was not emptied. People now came freely, or could it be that the same fear haunted them? People crossed borders, people walked in the rain, and people hung on as they travelled by train. Now the camp was open to the world, but the world was still closed before the camp.[14]

Rather than stressing diasporic Jewish life's improvement following Nazi forces' defeat and the end of systematic efforts at European Jewry's extermination, this description promotes the idea that diasporic Jewish life has not changed at all. Element after element accentuates continuity. Even the description of the concentration camp gates torn off of their hinges serves this theme. Instead of voicing the arrival of liberation and freedom, it communicates diasporic Jewish insecurity. Like millions of other contemporary European refugees, Jews are on the move. Yet they do not have a tangible home to which they can return. Throughout Europe, survivors returning to locations they previously considered their homes are not welcomed. Even those who survive frequent anti-Jewish violence, such as the Kielce pogrom, feel dispossessed.[15] Consequently, the former camp turns into a voluntary ghetto. For all intents and purposes, the surrounding world is closed off to Jews. Little hope for improvement is visible.

Three nameless teenage boys soon appear and come to personify the camp's ghettoized Jews. As convoys head west and east, they remain immobile. They await a man with whom they will share a pilfered bottle of rum. These youths' act of theft and their daytime drinking and inactivity intimate how exilic life erodes Jews' moral character and inhibits their ability to better their lives.

The prologue's presentation of the possibility of individual transformation and a better Jewish future's realization through return to the ancestral homeland contrasts sharply with its linkage of exilic Jewish life with a bleak future. Amnon, the messiah-like figure awaited by the boys, embodies this brighter future. Even though he spent his first fifteen years in the diaspora and still speaks fluent Yiddish, immigration to Palestine and kibbutz membership have transformed him. He drinks a toast with the three boys to honor them, but rum is not his preferred beverage. He and the other kibbutz members drink vitamin-rich Palestinian-grown orange juice and live healthy, productive lives. The three boys yearn for physical contact with Amnon and are drawn to his stories about kibbutz life. Hinting at their ability to transform themselves from consumers of sweetness to its producers through mimicry of his lifestyle, Amnon enlists the boys to distribute candies to the camp's other children while he narrates additional kibbutz tales. All three boys yearn for the ancestral homeland's sweetness, but Amnon clarifies that their transformation into Sabras requires that they leave their diasporic past behind. Hence, he forecasts that this transformation will be easier for the two orphaned youths free from a parental yolk than it will be for the third boy, who resides in the DP camp with his parents and young sisters.[16]

SIDELINING THE ZIONIST CONVERSION PARADIGM

After arriving in Israel together with his family, Menasheh Klinger, the third boy featured in the prologue, abandons it, settles on a kibbutz, and pursues Zionist conversion. Had Bartov intended to promote the Sabra as a faultless ideal type that all Israelis should unhesitatingly endeavor to emulate, it would have been easy for him to draw upon experiences from his four-year membership on kibbutz Eyn ha-Horesh to portray Menasheh's Zionist conversion on the kibbutz. Yet following his journey to the kibbutz, Menasheh almost completely disappears from the novel. Bartov's decision to forgo this opportunity points to his disinterest in confirming mainstream Zionist beliefs and views. Viewing the Sabra as an illusory social construct with little basis in reality, he deconstructs it to more realistically portray emerging Israeli life.

Rather than looking upon the Jewish diasporic experience as something that could be sloughed off like a growing snake's constricting skin that it must molt to survive, Bartov believed that it was necessary to engage with Jewish diasporic experience and address its significance for his whole generation. As he explained in his Ussishkin Prize acceptance speech in 1954, "when I started to narrate, I already knew that I was not just telling the story of strange immigrants. I was telling my story, my memory of my childhood, my parents' home from when it was the home of new immigrants, the story of my generation that allegedly distanced itself 500 parasangs from the world referred to as the Second Israel."[17] To even indirectly tell his story, Bartov needed to present his disinterest in exclusive pursuit of the idealized and unrealizable norms of his generation and his belief that such disinterest was not shameful. Initially, this proved difficult. Yet decades later he succinctly explained, "I do not pass the entrance exam for mythological sabraness. As a real flesh and blood Sabra, that simply isn't me."[18]

Since serious engagement with the complex legacy of diaspora Jewishness proved fundamental to the form of Israeliness that Bartov considered truly authentic, he used it as one of the central threads from which he wove his novel. He offers the following description:

> The attitude of a native-born Israeli to diaspora Jewry, to that whole way of life that we refer to as the diaspora. This attitude would subsequently be defined as a feeling of guilt, and the character of this feeling is such that when it found voice it expressed itself in divergent ways. On the one hand, it was hatred of this origin and all that it involved, and, on the other hand, it was a yearning for roots, a

genealogy, and paternal tradition. Initially, shame that they preserve diasporic implements in father's home, and, in the end, a feeling of absence and a search after what is missing.[19]

When Menasheh abandons his family's home and escapes to the kibbutz, he fulfills his novelistic function by voicing the hatred of the diasporic past described above. Bartov does not keep the novel focused on Noah and Gitl Klinger's home and the immigrant community that organically forms around it in Jerusalem's imaginary Bik'at Zayit neighborhood to communicate this sentiment or to serve as an indirect vehicle for advancement of kibbutz ideals and the Zionist conversion paradigm.[20] Bik'at Zayit proves important to Bartov because it serves as a point of contact between the diasporic Jewish way of life and Israeli society. It enables him to draw on his childhood memories, the literature he read in his youth, material gleaned during his studies at the Hebrew University, and his experience living in a Jerusalem immigrant neighborhood in 1949 and 1950 to convey the rich inheritance that contemporary Israelis could attain from diaspora Jewry if they just made an effort. In this way, Bartov proved able to convey the full complexity of the native-born Israeli's relationship to the diaspora.

THE DIASPORIC JEWISH COMMUNITY STRIKES ROOT IN ISRAEL'S ROCKY SOIL

The opening chapter of *Each Had Six Wings* intentionally disrupts the frame of reference presented in the prologue. It does so by demonstrating how maintenance of one's diasporic character, rather than its jettisoning, offers a way to succeed in Israel. After journeying by boat to Israel and a three-month stay in a coastal transit camp, the Klinger family finds itself loaded on the back of a truck with other new arrivals and their meager possessions. While fifteen-year-old Menasheh and the children on board orient themselves by hanging out of the back of the truck or peering through tears in the tarpaulin enclosing the truck's back end to see what is before them, the adults, who can only orientate themselves by looking at where the truck has already gone, view the future through the prism of the past. Attention to Gitl and Noah Klinger's responses following their arrival at their destination enables one to observe the continuing usefulness of employing earlier strategies to guide one's movement into the future.

When the truck stops toward nightfall on the Jordanian border in what will soon be revealed to be one of Jerusalem's abandoned formerly Arab neighborhoods, Gitl and other adults, whose eyes are "well-versed in disappointment," find an earthly Jerusalem radically divergent from the heavenly Jerusalem of their imaginations: "The well-known sights, the sights that stalk them. Again, spread out before them were desolate landscapes, rocky fields, and olive trees with dust-covered canopies. And, again, ruins—barbed wire, sandbagged windows."[21] Therefore, it would prove unsurprising if Gitl, who has experienced tremendous heartache, including having a child die of starvation in her arms, refused to get off the truck and wallowed in self-pity. Yet she chooses to take control of her situation through language: "If you asked me, more than this is a city, it is a cemetery whose dead are sleeping in it."[22] By presenting her perception of reality, Gitl shakes off her discontent and finds a way to soldier on and care for those who need her.

In contrast, Noah endeavors to optimistically seize hold of any opportunity to improve his life and the lives of those around him by not lingering too long on past and current disappointments. This is what enabled him to remain alive and allowed him to care for his family after the war broke out. When it was still possible, Noah escaped from Poland with his family. In the Soviet interior, he found sanctuary and security for them in the forests, where he and Gitl fought as partisans. After months in a transit camp, whose inhabitants await infrequent prospects for resettlement in Tel Aviv, Noah decides to take another chance to try to better his life and those of his family. When presented with the opportunity for permanent housing and the prospect of supporting his family through work as a shoemaker, he jumps at it. Consequently, he looks past the destruction of war visible in Jerusalem to see a "a great city for the Lord."[23] Noah recognizes that it has tens of thousands of residents who can provide him with a decent living making and repairing shoes. Therefore, he displays little reticence when he gets off the truck.

Soon Noah starts noting what will be necessary to strike root and starts doing these things. His family has been given the right to reside in part of an unoccupied Arab house rendered barely habitable by war, looting, and lack of upkeep. Nonetheless, while holding the hand of his five-year-old daughter, whom he has just lifted out of the truck, Noah immediately "surveyed what stood before him with a calm experienced eye."[24] A lockless front door, shattered windows, an absence of furniture, a filthy interior, a broken-down stone courtyard wall, a dislodged entrance gate, and a lack of running water soon get placed on a prioritized mental to-do list. After feeding his young children and eating something, Noah starts working with Gitl and Menasheh to transform the house into a home. Significantly, when Menasheh comes back with a foraged lock mechanism, Noah immediately installs it in the door and supplements it with boards nailed to the door's interior and exterior surfaces to cover over a large hole. In contrast with the DP camp, where residents were vulnerable to external threats, the installation of the lockable door creates a boundary between the outside world and the home's interior and establishes a nurturing familial space.

Then, with a wandering Jew's help, Noah and Menasheh repair a malfunctioning pump and ensure that the family will have a reliable water supply. While the Sabra truck driver condescendingly portrays new immigrants as dependents waiting for veteran Israelis to do everything for them, the Klingers display independence, initiative, and an ability to systematically address the issues at hand. These are not attributes that they acquired in Israel. Instead, they brought them from the diaspora. It will be this diaspora legacy that will guide the family's acclimation to Israel and their ability to anchor communal development in the Bik'at Zayit neighborhood.

MENAKHEM-MENDL AND SHEYNE-SHENDL ASCEND TO ISRAEL

Critics have noted a connection between *Each Had Six Wings* and East European Jewish literature, but the novel's connections to Sholem Aleichem's literary work, both large and small, remain unexplored.[25] Although Sholem Aleichem (1859–1916) composed most of his fiction in Yiddish, his son-in-law Yitzhak Dov Berkowitz (1885–1967) spent decades translating it into Hebrew, and his translations assumed a prominent position in the Palestinian Hebrew literary polysystem. Thus, Palestinian Jewish children such as Bartov were quite familiar with Sholem Aleichem's work and his portrayal of East European Jewish life.[26] Two explicit references to Sholem Aleichem's work in *Each Had Six Wings* demonstrate this. When he denigrates Bik'at Zayit's East European immigrant residents by comparing them to the frequently foolish residents of the shtetl Kasrilevke, where many of Sholem Aleichem's stories are set, the immigrant physician Theodore Stern references Sholem Aleichem's work. Similarly, the schoolteacher Rakefet, the novel's most prominent Sabra figure, refers to Sholem Aleichem's work when speaking with her vacuous native-born friend Iyya. When Iyya delays communication of the most important details of the story she is telling, Rakefet compares her storytelling technique to that of Sholem Aleichem's famed protagonist Menakhem-Mendl, who saves the most significant things he has to say for epistolary postscripts.[27]

This reference's presence in a largely realist novel conveys Bartov's sense that Sholem Aleichem's fiction constituted a cultural touchstone for both diaspora Jews and native-born Israelis.

More significantly, awareness of Sholem Aleichem's influence on Bartov's fiction enables one to recognize that Bartov draws on the figures of Menakhem-Mendl and Sheyne-Shendl from Sholem Aleichem's epistolary story cycle *Menakhem-Mendl* when he depicts Noah and Gitl Klinger. In so doing, Bartov creates more positive archetypal representatives of diaspora Jewry.

When Menakhem-Mendl encounters financial difficulties, he is forced to leave Kasrilevke to retrieve his invested dowry to use in support of his wife Sheyne-Shendl and their children. Striking out on his own for the first time, Menakhem-Mendl does not get the whole dowry back. Nonetheless, he finds his newfound freedom invigorating and optimistically tries to make back the lost money by investing in the stock exchange. Unfortunately, after earning a great deal on paper, he loses his money. Yet rather than despairing, he picks himself up, optimistically pursues another get-rich scheme, and fails again. This cycle repeats itself over and over. Throughout his adventures, Menakhem-Mendl writes to Sheyne-Shendl to communicate his successes, but over and over he is forced to acknowledge failures.

Meanwhile, Sheyne-Shendl, who lacks her husband's optimism and proves unable to envision a genuine improvement in the family's situation, writes to Menakhem-Mendl to convince him to come back to Kasrilevke. At the very least, he could help her shoulder the burden of raising their family. Sheyne-Shendl finds it incredibly frustrating that Menakhem-Mendl does not listen to her. She wants him to accept that the world will continue on as it always has and put aside his quest for material success. As her anger and helplessness mount, she peppers her letters with proverbs and idiomatic expressions that draw on the accumulated folk wisdom of East European Jewry in an unsuccessful effort to convey her message.[28]

Despite the tenuousness of their relationship, reflected by their exclusively epistolary connection, Menakhem-Mendl and Sheyne-Shendl combine to give archetypal expression to early twentieth-century East European Jewish society. Menakhem-Mendl conveys its belief in modernization, progress, and a better future; Sheyne-Shendl presents its deep conservatism, its connection to Jewish wisdom of the past, its fatalistic approach to the world, and its ability to endure hardship and suffering to ensure the survival of future generations of Jews.

Drawing on the model provided by Menakhem-Mendl and Sheyne-Shendl, Bartov intends for Noah and Gitl to represent the yin and yang of

East European Jewish society; he draws on his studies in East European Jewish history and culture to breathe life into this representation and advance a more positive attitude toward diaspora Jewry than the one offered by Sholem Aleichem. Bartov expresses gratitude to Ben-Zion Dinur (1884–1973), who taught Jewish history at the Hebrew University and served as president of the Yad Vashem Holocaust Remembrance Center between 1953 and 1959, for teaching him about East European Jewish history.[29] Bartov fondly recalls two seminar papers that he wrote for Dinur. While researching one of them, Bartov spent months reading East European Jewish folktales, folksongs, and proverbs written in Yiddish and Hebrew. Later, he explains, "I transplanted the treasures of folk wisdom that I had copied on to index cards into the speech of the characters of *Each Had Six Wings*."[30] These treasures serve as the basis for Gitl's snappy Yiddishized Hebrew retorts and evoke Sheyne-Shendl's letters.

Cognizant of a strong anticapitalist and antispeculative bias that would have made it difficult for him to model his desired archetypal East European modernizer and optimistic forward thinker too closely on Menachem-Mendl, Bartov drew on knowledge of the East European Jewish labor movement acquired during his studies with Dinur and sociologist Arye Tartakower (1897–1982) to construct a diasporic figure better able to garner contemporary Israeli readers' sympathy and identification.[31] Making Noah a shoemaker enables Bartov to employ him to advance progressive values such as equality and justice frequently identified with the East European Jewish labor movement.[32]

Finally, Bartov delicately depicts Noah and Gitl's sex life to communicate their strong and fruitful bond, as well as Jewish diasporic experience's vitality and its ability to nourish Israeli society:

> As he stood there, half-dressed and caught up in thought, he turned to Gitl's bed and sat on its edge.
> "Gitl," he whispered.
> "What's going on?"
> "Gitl, I'm telling you, it will be good here yet."
> "My heart's fluttering with joy. Now let me go to sleep."
> "We've already been through more difficult days and we came out whole. Gitl . . ."
> "A type of desolate exile, without people, without livelihood. . . . Get your hands off me, Noah."
> "We'll make a good living yet. I have two healthy arms."
> "Get out of here, Noah. Even without you, I am warm. You're already having problems sleeping?"

"People settled here too. Just have some patience. The day isn't far off."

"Beggars and fools like you."

"On the contrary," his naughty giggling voice expanded in the darkness. "The more fools there are, the more beggars there will be. The more beggars there will be, the more they will need to mend their old shoes . . . Gitl."

"Stop yourself, you evil beast. You're going to wake the kids."[33]

In contrast with Menakhem-Mendl and Sheyne-Shendl, whose relationship is constantly on the verge of disintegration, Noah and Gitl live together peacefully and only rarely allow their differences in worldview to drive a wedge between them. These differences are part of what attracts them to each other, keeps them together, and enables their success through performance of complimentary tasks.[34] Even if Gitl is a full-figured woman who might not be attractive to everybody, her husband finds her sexually arousing. Aware of her husband's optimism, Gitl does not make pessimistic statements to convince him. Instead, she wants him to persuade her with more than words. The couple's increasingly playful debate of the future is merely a form of verbal foreplay, likely accompanied by actual foreplay initiated by a half-naked Noah. The sexual pleasure that Gitl begins to feel overwhelms her fatalism and brings her to embrace the moment.

When Gitl tells her "evil beast" that he is going to wake the kids, she has already consented to his advances and just wants him to be a bit quieter during intercourse. The couple's five-year-old daughter Haya'leh, conceived and born during the war, and their two-year-old daughter Tzipi, conceived and born in the DP camps, hint that they have had a healthy relationship with an active sex life for a long time. It is what has enabled them to weather devastating traumas such as the loss of a child. Their relationship's health and Gitl's fertility allude to the ability of the diasporic worldview they collectively represent to contribute to Israeli society's development.

FROM HOUSEHOLD TO COMMUNITY: THE EXPANDING REALM OF DIASPORA JEWISHNESS

Although the novel's first chapter replaces the prologue's antidiasporic narrative frame with a more positive image of diaspora Jewishness and the presentation of diasporic Jewish characteristics' ability to aid immigrants in building their lives in Israel, this worldview still finds voice in a single family. Consequently, its ability to serve a larger population looking to find their way in Israel remains in doubt. In subsequent chapters, this diasporic worldview takes hold among the residents of the Bik'at Zayit neighborhood and enables them to come together as a community. Noah's charismatic leadership proves critical to this worldview's spread, because his actions express its central elements. His interventions in neighborhood life initially appear rather insignificant, but they gradually spread his worldview throughout the neighborhood and pave the way for its political empowerment.

After a decade of war and upheaval, it would have proven perfectly reasonable if Noah had retreated into his own private world once he ordered his home and opened his shoe shop for business. Yet when he consciously forgoes this option, he begins to emerge as Bik'at Zayit's charismatic leader. During the previous decade, Noah inhabited a world where animalistic self-interest, rather than social ties and the types of behavior they dictate, governed individual behavior. Yet as the assistance Noah receives with the water pump on his first night in the neighborhood makes clear to him, reestablishment of broader social ties would enable him, as well as the neighborhood's other residents, to accomplish more. By working to reproduce the type of productive social ties that Jews previously shared in Eastern Europe, he and other survivors, who numbered among Bik'at Zayit's first postwar residents, could start putting the Holocaust behind them.

Furthermore, if they did not begin to think more broadly, Bik'at Zayit's residents would remain a disconnected hodgepodge of people. Moral action, grounded in consideration of collective needs, as well as the particular needs of others, could create trust between neighborhood residents, develop social ties, and transform these residents into a community. As Bik'at Zayit gradually fills with newly arrived immigrants from Europe and North Africa, the need to forge communal bonds that transcend the ethnic, political, and economic differences that divide the neighborhood's residents becomes increasingly pressing.

When Noah adopts Tzirkin, his efforts to forge broader social ties begin. Wounded in the chest during the Independence War, after being drafted upon arrival in Israel, Tzirkin proves his worth according to native-born standards, and the government rewards him with a place to live. Consequently, when he is released from the hospital after eight months, he arrives to take up residence in a bedroom allocated to him in the Arab home inhabited by the Klingers. A five-member family, the Klingers usurped his room when nobody arrived to claim it. Interested in keeping it, Gitl tries to get him to leave by arguing that he is in the wrong place. Even after Tzirkin explains "I am not one of the

Hebrews" and makes clear that he is also a Yiddish-speaking East European Jew who suffered a great deal during the war, Gitl ignores his fragile physical condition and evident need. Instead, she actively works to best prioritize her family's needs.[35]

While Noah also wants to keep Tzirkin's room, he proves unable to keep Tzirkin at a distance. After learning about Tzirkin's injuries, how he has lived on his own since World War II broke out, and how he survived the war in the Soviet Union like the Klingers, Noah feels compelled to give him his rightful room. Yet unlike the government, Noah recognizes that this solitary young man needs more than a room and, consequently, looks to provide him with the intimacy and community that he lacks. This effort starts small when Noah invites Tzirkin, who lacks relatives and friends, to share his modest Shabbat table. Tzirkin recognizes and appreciates Noah's concern for him. The two men soon become close friends. Due to Noah's overtures, Tzirkin cedes the large room to which he is entitled, cognizant of the Klinger family's greater need for space, and takes a smaller one.

Similarly, Noah repeatedly puts aside self-interest to promote collective interests and communal bonds that transcend the immigrants' divergent origins. Government failure to allocate sufficient resources and opportunities to the new immigrant community prompts two important examples of this. Despite the neighborhood's location far from most employment sites, only one bus serves it; even when it arrives, it arrives at irregular times and is frequently full. Consequently, those repeatedly thwarted in their efforts to make it into town to work or apply for work grow frustrated. Extended waits combine with summer heat and the condescending attitudes of the bus drivers, who look down on the neighborhood's North African immigrants, to bring things to a boil. A group of immigrants denied access to transportation start rioting. Looking to vent their frustration, they pick up stones and prepare to attack a bus driver and destroy his bus. Regardless of the immediate satisfaction that destruction and violence will provide the exasperated immigrants, the end result will likely be further curtailment of their transportation options that will hurt all neighborhood residents.

Noah has little need for public transportation, because his shoe repair shop is found on the neighborhood's main artery. Yet when he sees the riot beginning, he immediately acts in the neighborhood's best interest. While he uses physical force to subdue the rioters, who attempt to inflict bodily harm on him and even stab him, Noah remains calm and does not let interethnic prejudice inflame him. Instead, he empathizes with the frustrated rioters.

When the disheveled mother of one of the rioters curses him for injuring her son and physically strikes him, Noah does not raise his hand to hit her and lets her continue until she tires. He has no personal agenda. Order needs to be maintained in the neighborhood so that the residents can, as Menasheh explains, "live like people live."[36] While Gitl pleaded with Noah not to get involved, she recognizes the importance of what he accomplishes. She takes pride in it and the status it gives her in the neighborhood.

A second and pivotal instance of Noah advancing collective interests and forging communal bonds that transcend the immigrants' divergent origins occurs when he brings the neighborhood's residents together in support of Glik, one of its neediest figures, and his family. Initially, when viewed through Gitl and Tzirkin's critical eyes, Glik's masculinity is attacked and his unsuitability for Israeli life is emphasized. The stark contrast between diaspora Jews and more veteran Israelis found earlier in the novel reproduces itself with Gitl and Tzirkin in the role of veteran Israelis.

When Glik borrows a chair from Tzirkin's barbershop so that his pregnant wife can sit comfortably in the shade while he purchases chicken at the neighborhood butcher shop, he becomes a conversation topic for Gitl and Tzirkin. Glik is a bald nearly sixty-year-old man with a Polish-style handlebar moustache, and his wife is decades younger than him. On its surface, their union proves difficult to comprehend. Gitl, who forgoes inquiry into its origin, finds "the bridegroom's" impregnation of his wife laughable.[37] Incapable of controlling his sexual desire, a senior citizen, who should know better, knocks up a younger woman. Then, rather than owning up to the absurdity of a man his age raising a newborn, he acts like a besotted eighteen-year-old.

Tzirkin and Gitl, who find it shocking that "this grandpa" has attained such a young woman, or *pargit,* for a wife and view it at the last flickering of his potency, employ Glik's efforts to attain a young chicken, or *pargit,* to ridicule him.[38] To satisfy its citizenry's dietary needs, the young state established rationing.[39] Even when individuals had ration cards, they could not always exchange them for foodstuffs. With meat one of the most difficult foods to attain, the neighborhood women push and shove to get a chicken before the supply runs out. Consequently, Glik fails to secure a place in line. Successive waves of exiting women push him back. Unlike the neighborhood's capable housewives who get chickens for their pots, Glik remains outside the store wiping streams of perspiration from his face and neck. When he finally enters the store, Tzirkin employs double entendre and calls out approvingly "penetrated and entered."[40] Gitl follows up with a faked groan of sexual pleasure.

They find Glik's impotence humorous, certain that his penetration of the store's door is the only successful penetration that he can now perform. This impotent "diaspora" Jew is contrasted with virile Israelis like them.

Rather than taking pleasure in ridiculing Glik from a distance, Noah recognizes his inherent value and looks for a way to help him contribute to the community and strengthen it. Therefore, he works to bridge the gap between Glik and other community members. Noah searches Glik out. When he learns where Glik lives, he goes with Tzirkin to visit him. They find him outside his ramshackle one-room apartment and explain to him that he is not alone. All of the neighborhood's residents are "new [to Israel] and they need to help each other."[41] Indeed, Glik and his wife Masha do their best to make do with limited material support. Yet the couple does not make enough to eat properly; Masha, whose pregnancy is advanced, finds it difficult to ascend to the rooftop, where the apartment received from the Jewish Agency is situated alongside water tanks and clothes lines. Even though he has thirty years of experience as a pastry chef and baker, Glik cannot find work in his profession or outside it. Recognizing Glik's professional experience and his ability to contribute to the community, Noah looks for a way to help him help himself and others.

Initially, Noah makes use of a personal resource to aid Glik, but his individual effort fails. Noah splits the space he has attained for his shoe repair shop to provide a location where Glik can open a bake shop. This enables Glik to get a loan for necessary equipment and supplies. Yet as the birth of Glik's child approaches, his efforts to open the bakery hit a brick wall. The municipal authorities refuse to grant him permission to open the bakery.

Rather than accepting the municipality's rigidness, Noah organizes the neighborhood's residents to get it to permit Glik to support his family to the best of his ability. Noah recognizes that "the veterans will not help."[42] Nonetheless, he refuses to allow them to impede mutual immigrant aid. Recognizing the community's right to have its voice heard and honored by the institutions purported to represent it, Noah and scores of community members head to the mayor's office to lodge a protest and demand that the city permit Glik to open the bakery.

When the protesters arrive, they are met by bureaucrats less interested in justice or equality than promoting the needs of veteran Israelis, including themselves. Noah turns to the clerk who greets the protesters at the entrance to the mayor's office and respectfully requests to speak with the mayor as a representative of the Bik'at Zayit neighborhood's residents. The clerk ignores him because he speaks in Yiddish. Consequently, Noah turns to the native Hebrew speaker Rakefet, who teaches in the neighborhood school and whose empathy for the immigrants has led her to participate in their protest, to act as the group's spokesperson. She requests to see the mayor in fluent Hebrew, but the clerk ignores her too. He then tries to turn away the protesters by telling them that they can meet with the mayor only by appointment. When they refuse and say they will wait to speak with the mayor, the clerk rejects this idea out of hand. Instead of granting the protesters the access they desire, the clerk spirits the mayor out of his office and calls the police to disperse the protesters.

Noah, his co-organizer Vidal (a Bulgarian-born communist), and Rakefet decide that they will not be moved until they get a permit that will allow Glik to open his bakery. They begin to shout the three Hebrew syllables for mayor to make their voices heard:

> The three of them were already calling out rhythmically—a weak, embarrassed rhythm. The people in their places were perplexed, but very quickly they recognized that an innovation had been made, that a new stage had begun, that they would no longer sit like beggars at the door. One by one they joined in, repeating it and coming together with these three rhythmic syllables. And already the voice of one was blended with the voice of the general public, attracted to and drawn forth by the general public, and the voice of the general public is nothing but the echoed voice of one amplified and strengthened a hundred fiftyfold, rolling and echoing through the halls.[43]

When the neighborhood residents, who barely understand each other and might not even understand what they are shouting, join Noah, Vidal, and Rakefet in their protest chant, they demonstrate that the callous clerk's reference to them as a mob proves incorrect. They are no longer willing to act like beggars ready to accept whatever crumbs the Israeli government sends their way. They constitute a unified group of Israelis who demand that the democratically elected government act justly and serve the common good.

Unfortunately, native-born and veteran Israelis refuse to heed the protesters' poignant call for justice and democracy. Labeling the protest "illegal assembly, amidst disruption of public order and the municipality's proper function," the callous clerk ignores the protester's democratic right to free expression and calls on the police to disperse the "Communist" protest.[44] Even after Rakefet reiterates the group's motivations, when she explains that "we demand justice and this is the only chance we have of getting it," the police commander refuses to accept the protest's legitimacy.[45] Soon policemen freely wield their batons, beat the steadfast protesters, and arrest their leaders.

Rakefet and Benzion, the police commander sent to disperse the demonstrators, are mutual acquaintances who served alongside Rakefet's fallen boyfriend Gabi in the Independence War. Their acquaintance enables Bartov to employ their confrontation immediately prior to the protest's violent suppression to present Rakefet's embodiment of the ideals for which Gabi died and Benzion and other native-born Israelis' betrayal of them. Struggling with how best to honor Gabi's memory, Rakefet commits herself to educating the immigrant children attending Bik'at Zayit's neighborhood school and helping them acclimate to Israeli life. She sees it as inevitable that Israeli society will assume the character that they and their parents give to it. Consequently, by aiding them in building a democratic country committed to justice and equality, she finds a way to transcend her personal loss, voice her dead beloved's ideals, and join a new community offering her a more meaningful existence.[46]

In contrast, Benzion embraces a legacy of injustice and suppression of the popular will when he dons a former British Mandatory Police uniform—something that foreshadows his men's indiscriminate use of batons against other Jews, including Holocaust survivors. When Benzion ignores the legitimacy of the protesters' claims and explains to Rakefet that he is just following orders, his betrayal of Gabi's legacy is further amplified. Benzion's justification proves identical to the one employed years earlier by Germans to explain their participation in the Final Solution.

To better realize the ideals she identifies with Gabi's legacy, Rakefet distances herself from veteran Israelis who do not live in accordance with them and aligns herself with the newcomers, whom she sees as their actual guardians. Cognizant that Benzion needs to make a living and that his police service is his livelihood, she does not attack him and tells him to just do his job. Nonetheless, she refuses to step aside and make it easier for her former comrade-in-arms to act in opposition to her beliefs. If he and his underlings want to employ indiscriminate and illegitimate force against protesters, they will need to beat her too and suffer the pangs of conscience. Noah and the other immigrant protesters understand that Rakefet is committed to the same values as they are and looks to join their community. Therefore, when two policemen grab her and push her to the floor, they rush to defend her.

While the protest does not immediately bear fruit and the dropping of charges against the jailed protesters and the acquisition of a permit for Glik's bakery are attained only through intervention of native-born Israelis, the protest points to Noah's transformation of the immigrant neighborhood into a community that embodies higher ideals.[47] Rather than promoting the Zionist Conversion Paradigm, the novel calls on native-born Israeli Jews to reengage with the diasporic Jewish experience. This will require that they acknowledge their society's most vulnerable Jewish members, yoke their fate to that of the newly arrived immigrants, and work to satisfy the needs of all Jewish Israelis.

THE IMPENDING INTERRUPTION OF THE DIASPORIC JEWISH LEGACY'S TRANSMISSION

Despite the community's unification around its commitment to caring for its least fortunate members' needs, the novel points to native-born culture as a potentially insurmountable obstacle to positive diasporic Jewish values' effective transmission. It appears that immigrant children, native-born Israelis, and children of immigrants will encounter difficulties when trying to employ these values to aid in Israeli state and society's productive development.

While Noah's charismatic leadership catalyzes community development and elevates his status among Bik'at Zayit's residents, Menasheh finds little value in his accomplishments and moral stature. As long as Menasheh stays close to home, these perceptions go unvoiced. Yet when Menasheh discovers a completely different world inhabited by native-born and veteran Israelis, his anger about his father's failure to adequately support the family and his father's failure to integrate into Israeli society by attaining Hebrew fluency rise to the surface. Menasheh still dreams of the utopian world that Amnon promised him and a mature sexual relationship that he envisions at the heart of it. While his father can guide Menasheh toward attainment of a mature sexual relationship, his father cannot offer his son a path free of pain and difficulty. Consequently, when his friend Shimi tells him that he can attain the type of life he desires by leaving home and jettisoning his family, Menasheh heads off to realize his dream on a kibbutz with little regret.

When Menasheh accepts a neighborhood boy's invitation to go out to the movies at his expense, he takes an important step forward. To mature, he needs to think about what elements of his previous socialization and which standards of his new country he will ultimately adopt. Yet when Menasheh observes veteran and native-born Israelis wearing nice new clothing, going out to cafés, and viewing films at the cinema, he is overwhelmed. He begins to wonder if the sacrifices his father requires him to make for his values are worth it. Money suddenly seems more important to Menasheh. It would enable him to dress appropriately and take part in the types of dating activities that could help him find a partner. When Menasheh tries to get around his lack of money by placing his palm on that of a girl he meets at the cinema, she rebuffs his advances. Lacking self-confidence and being reticent to turn to his father for help, he does not see a way of furthering this relationship. Consequently, recollection of a traumatic experience that occurred years earlier, when he ran away from a girl who took a fancy to him in the DP camp and dragged him to a secluded forest location for sex, leads Menasheh to view himself as sexually deficient.

Noah tries to help Menasheh deal with the negative feelings that his sense of sexual inadequacy produce, but Menasheh shuts him out. Menasheh finds it hard to talk with his dad about the discomfort his relationship difficulties makes him feel. Nonetheless, when Menasheh complains about his lack of money and the inability to do things that other teenagers do, Noah does what he can and gives him money. Menasheh uses it to take the girl he met earlier out on a date. Fearful that she will dump him once his poverty is exposed, Menasheh feels that he must bed her before it is too late. He takes her to a secluded spot—something that recalls his earlier forest encounter. As he prepares to have his way with her, he forcefully undresses the girl and caresses her upper body. Yet when he kisses her face and tastes salt, he recognizes that she has been crying and becomes aware that his unchecked sexual desire has almost led him to rape the nonconsenting girl. Menasheh stops what he is doing, takes the girl home, severs his relationship with her, and represses the incident.

Menasheh overhears his parents having sex and is likely aware that their experiences have not prevented them from maintaining a healthy sexual relationship, but he proves reticent to expose himself to them and chooses to forgo their aid. When Menasheh meets Shimi, a former acquaintance from Germany, he is presented with a solution that will not require him to consider the connection between his past experiences and the difficulties he encounters developing a mature sexual relationship. Shimi asserts that Menasheh can find happiness by just abandoning his childish idealism.[48] While Shimi's sister lives in Jerusalem and pressures him to live with her to preserve what remains of their shared past, Shimi finds his sister and brother-in-law's urban bourgeois life monotonous. Once he learned Hebrew, Shimi easily integrated into kibbutz life. He finds it more pleasurable to live together with other young people on the kibbutz than to struggle to repair frayed familial ties. If Menasheh learns Hebrew and ceases to let his family hold him back, Shimi prophesies that he too will find an enjoyable life on the kibbutz. Eventually Menasheh gets his parents, who feel guilty about their limited ability to care for him, to allow him to try kibbutz life. By acquiring the new language and embracing the new culture at the expense of his exilic heritage, Menasheh looks to finally start afresh.

While Menasheh's short-term future might look bright, his abandonment of his family foreshadows the difficulties impeding exilic values' ability to impact either Israeli society or Menasheh and the problems that will likely result. Menasheh is blind to Noah's heroic community-building efforts and how adoption of the ethos that he embodies can advance Israeli society. On a personal level, he fails to comprehend the significance of Noah's ability to balance his pursuit of the communal good with a pleasurable relationship with Gitl that includes an active sex life. It seems unlikely that Menasheh will learn how to achieve this balance on the kibbutz and that his relationship problems will cease.[49] Furthermore, when Menasheh leaves his family behind, he only makes it more difficult for his father to support it and lead the community. Without a clear heir, things might soon descend into chaos in the immigrant neighborhood and destroy everything his father worked to build.

The implosion of Rakefet's engagement with Theodore Stern points to an additional obstacle to positive diasporic Jewish values' employment for Israeli society's productive development. As the novel opens, Rakefet mourns her dead boyfriend Gabi and their lost future together. When she comes to perceive her efforts to aid new immigrants in creating the best possible Israel as the best way to honor his legacy, however, she finds a way forward. Consequently, she dives into her work at the neighborhood school and actively participates in the protest. This motivation also makes her the native-born character most sympathetic with the new immigrants, most open to what they can contribute to the emerging nation, and best prepared to integrate into the community they are creating.

Rakefet consents to a date with Theodore Stern, an immigrant doctor studying Hebrew language with her friend Iyyah, seeing it as an additional way to link her fate with that of the new immigrants and transcend her loss. Despite how different Stern is from Gabi, Rakefet learns to appreciate and love him. Their engagement bodes well for the possibility of veteran Israelis absorbing the best of what exilic Jews bring to Israel and immigrants embracing the best of what the native-born can offer. Yet when Masha Glik is revealed to be Theodore's wife, whom he has presumed dead, veteran Israelis and new immigrants' ability to build a better future together by putting their personal traumas behind them comes into doubt. Theodore recognizes that he still loves Masha and wants to be with her. Yet she is married to another man, who has fathered her child. Theodore cannot resurrect his past. Simultaneously, a new future with Rakefet seems increasingly unlikely. If Theodore cannot move beyond his relationship with Masha, he likely will be unable to help Rakefet put aside her lingering feelings for Gabi. Their relationship looks doomed to fail.

Finally, the novel concludes as Bik'at Zayit's residents head from a synagogue, where a baby-naming ceremony for Glik's daughter has just occurred, to a rooftop celebration outside Glik's apartment. While previous scholars have accepted Glik's assertion that assignment of the name Rakefet, linked to both an indigenous flower and a virtuous native-born woman, will enable the baby to leave behind the trauma of the Holocaust and integrate into Israeli life, the novel's ending before the celebration proves significant.[50] The fact that the girl is the product of an adulterous relationship between a married woman and a man who is not her husband further emphasizes this abrupt ending's noncelebratory character.

While the neighborhood's largely secular character and its residents' casual religious observance likely mean that they would not ostracize the girl like devout Jews, who would bar her and ten generations of her descendants from marrying ordinary Jews, Bartov's assignment of the status of *mamzerah* [bastard] to the girl belies her parents' desire to give her a fresh start. Ultimately, their well-intentioned efforts to cover over the events of the Holocaust will fail. The baby will never truly be able to transcend what they endured. She will likely attempt to rebel against this familial past and the liminal status it will cause her to inherit. Reinvention, such as what Menasheh undertakes, will likely drive her, but only active engagement with the diasporic past will ever allow Baby Rakefet to draw positive elements from it and move forward happily as an Israeli. From a humanistic perspective, she is the product of years of mutual support under extreme conditions and a love that gradually develops. If Baby Rakefet and those around her can embrace this diasporic legacy, the deferred celebration will indeed arrive.

CONCLUSION

While the first-generation of native-born Palestinian Jews are traditionally viewed as maintaining a condescending attitude toward diaspora Jews and their exilic lives, *Each Had Six Wings* reflects a more equivocal attitude to diasporic Jewish life maintained by Bartov that many other young native-born Israelis likely shared. Rather than believing in the inherent superiority of the culture that he took part in creating, the Holocaust and the trauma of the 1948 war brought home that culture's limitations to him. Looking to incorporate productive elements of exilic life into Israeli culture to strengthen it for Israeli society's benefit, Bartov strove to provide a more balanced view of diasporic Jewish life. Despite the setbacks that they encountered, most immigrants to Israel displayed a surprising vitality, and many looked to use their energies to restore the organic bonds of community typical of diasporic Jewish life prior to the Holocaust.

Indeed, the legacies of the Independence War and the Holocaust made it difficult for veteran Israelis and new immigrants to appreciate this vitality and draw on diasporic communal forms to develop Israeli society in a way that benefited the whole Jewish population. Nonetheless, by the early 1950s Israeli writers such as Bartov, who attempted to shape the national response to mass immigration, asserted the value of such efforts. Unfortunately, veteran Israelis interested in an end to national mobilization and the opportunity to finally live a "normal life" put their personal interests first. Not enough was done to bring Israeli Jews together as one people. While wholly understandable, the high expectations set by the idea of ingathering of the exiles were never met. Consequently, many internal Jewish cleavages were introduced. After more than seventy years of statehood, they remain unrepaired.

NOTES

1. "Provisional Government of Israel's Declaration of the Establishment of the State of Israel," Knesset, cdli: https://www.knesset.gov.il/docs/eng/megilat_eng.htm.

2. Ibid.

3. Ibid.

4. Jules Harlow, ed. and trans., *Siddur Sim Shalom: A Prayerbook for Shabbat, Festivals, and Weekdays* (New York: Rabbinical Assembly & United Synagogue of Conservative Judaism, 1985), 113. In non-Ashkenazic traditions, the second cited line concludes "to our Land."

5. Tom Segev, *1949: The First Israelis* (New York: Henry Holt, 1998), 96.

6. Dan Laor, "Mass Immigration as 'Content and Subject' in Hebrew Literature in the First Years of Statehood" [Hebrew], *ha-Tzionut* 14 (1989): 161–62.

7. For a scholarly treatment of the novel that addresses its early reception, see Avner Holtzman, *The Heart's Key: The Literary Art of Hanokh Bartov* [Hebrew] (Jerusalem: Mossad Bialik, 2015), 67–84. For a scholarly discussion that contextualizes the novel in the literature of its time, see Laor, "Mass Immigration as 'Content and Subject' in Hebrew Literature in the First Years of Statehood," 161–75; Gershon Shaked, *Hebrew Fiction, 1880–1980* [Hebrew] (Tel Aviv: ha-Kibutz ha-Me'uhad, 1977–98), 4:70–71;

Nurit Gertz, "Zionism, the Kibbutz, and the Shtetl: The Struggle for the Souls of New Immigrants in Hanokh Bartov's 'Each Had Six Wings'" [Hebrew], *Iyunim bi-tekumat Yisrael* 8 (1998): 498–521; Oded Nir, *Signatures of Struggle: The Figuration of Collectivity in Israeli Fiction* (Albany: State University of New York Press, 2018), 87–93.

8. Batya Shimoni, "The Place to Which the Heart Yearns: The Kibbutz, the Neighborhood, and the Shtetl in 'Each Had Six Wings' by Hanokh Bartov" [Hebrew], *Dapim le-mehkar be-sifrut* 16–17 (2008–2009), 294–310.

9. For more on this phenomenon, see Moshe Naor, "The 1948 War Veterans and Postwar Reconstruction in Israel," *Journal of Israeli History* 29, no. 1 (2010): 47–59.

10. Yael Zerubavel, "The 'Mythological Sabra' and Jewish Past: Trauma, Memory, and Contested Identities," *Israel Studies* 7, no. 2 (2002):118.

11. Hanokh Bartov, *Each Had Six Wings* [Hebrew] (Tel Aviv: Ma'ariv Readers' Club, 1988), 264–71; Hanokh Bartov, *To Grow Up and Write in the Land of Israel* [Hebrew] (Or Yehudah: Zemora-Bitan, 2008), 132–42.

12. Zerubavel, "The 'Mythological Sabra' and Jewish Past," 116.

13. Ibid., 117.

14. Hanokh Bartov, *Each Had Six Wings* [Hebrew] (Merhavyah: Sifriyat po'alim, 1954), 7.

15. On the Kielce pogrom, see Jan Gross, *Fear: Anti-Semitism in Poland after Auschwitz; An Essay in Historical Interpretation* (New York: Random House, 2006).

16. For a similar reading, see Shimoni, "The Place to Which the Heart Yearns," 297–99.

17. Bartov, *To Grow Up and Write in the Land of Israel*, 68.

18. Ibid., 134.

19. Bartov, *Each Had Six Wings* (1988), 265–66.

20. Gertz, "Zionism, the Kibbutz, and the Shtetl," 512–13.

21. Bartov, *Each Had Six Wings* (1954), 15.

22. Ibid., 12–13.

23. Ibid., 13.

24. Ibid., 18.

25. For assertion of East European Jewish literature's influence on this work, see Gertz, "Zionism, the Kibbutz, and the Shtetl," 498–99; Shimoni, "The Place to Which the Heart Yearns," 305.

26. On the influence of Sholem Aleichem's fiction and Berkowitz's translation on Bartov, see Bartov, *To Grow Up and Write in the Land of Israel*, 67–70.

27. Bartov, *Each Had Six Wings* (1954), 116, 121.

28. For more on Sholem Aleichem's *Menakhem-Mendl* and its structure, see Dan Miron, *The Image of the Shtetl and Other Studies of Modern Jewish Literary Imagination* (Syracuse, NY: Syracuse University Press, 2000), 157–78.

29. Bartov, *Each Had Six Wings* (1988), 270.

30. Ibid.

31. Ibid.

32. Marxist scholar Oded Nir categorizes Noah and the other craftsman who open shops in Bik'at Zayit as members of an emerging petit bourgeoisie critical to the novel's political unconscious. This, however, does not invalidate the claim that Bartov strove to depict Noah as the embodiment of the East European Jewish labor movement. See Nir, *Signatures of Struggle*, 87–93.

33. Bartov, *Each Had Six Wings* (1954), 33.

34. This scene challenges Nurit Gertz's claim that Gitl is linked to desolate land, death, and infertility in the novel. Gertz, "Zionism, the Kibbutz, and the Shtetl," 305.

35. Bartov, *Each Had Six Wings* (1954), 59.

36. Ibid., 54.

37. Ibid., 143.

38. Ibid., 144.

39. On rationing in the earlier state period, see Anat Helman, *Becoming Israeli: National Ideals & Everyday Life in the 1950s* (Waltham, MA: Brandeis University Press, 2014), 47–67.

40. Bartov, *Each Had Six Wings* (1954), 144.

41. Ibid., 215.

42. Ibid., 219.

43. Ibid., 279.

44. Ibid., 281.

45. Ibid.

46. Holtzman asserts that the novel's polyphonic nature, which leads it to present the interior worlds of various characters and not just Sabra ones such as Rakefet, gives it a "democratic" spirit. Holtzman, *The Heart's Key*, 81.

47. Laor, "Mass Immigration as 'Content and Subject' in Hebrew Literature in the First Years of Statehood," 170.

48. Bartov, *Each Had Six Wings* (1954), 175.

49. Careful attention to Menasheh's psychological problems contradicts earlier reference to him as a realization of the Israeli dream. Laor, "Mass Immigration as 'Content and Subject' in Hebrew Literature in the First Years of Statehood," 169.

50. Shimoni, "The Place to Which the Heart Yearns," 307; Holtzman, *The Heart's Key*, 77.

Shylock and the *Ghetto*, or East European Jewish Culture and Israeli Identity

Dror Abend-David

INTRODUCTION

Israeli playwright Yehushua Sobol is a well-recognized contributor to Holocaust drama.[1] His plays are not only an important contribution to the animated discussion about the holocaust in Israeli society but have also legitimated and enabled a public conversation about the holocaust in Germany since the 1980s.[2] And Sobol's work is certainly an important source when wishing to either teach or discuss the genre of Holocaust drama in general.[3] However, literature can be surprising—and a play is not always exclusively dedicated to the historical period and events that it describes. *Ghetto*,[4] the earliest and best known of Sobol's Holocaust plays, was originally written in Hebrew. It features a number of characters whose political ideologies reflect a number of contemporary social, economic, and political facets of Israeli society.

This is not to say that the play has nothing to do with either the Holocaust or East European Jewish society. On the contrary, the play is based on real historical characters of the Vilna Ghetto that have been recorded in the diary of the ghetto librarian Herman Kruk.[5] These characters represent political movements and social factions that were a part of Jewish East European society before World War II. But these characters and ideologies receive a new meaning on the Israeli stage toward the end of the twentieth century, as the playwright draws direct comparisons to Israeli society. This is a striking representation in the context of a society that believes it has re-created itself in a manner that is radically different from the culture of prewar diaspora Jews.

Moreover, Sobol uses an additional literary device that might provoke the sensitivities of Israeli Jews. He uses the Shakespearean character of Shylock, the Jewish moneylender in *The Merchant of Venice*, and creates three characters that embody, in different ways, a number of the stereotypes that have been attributed to Shakespeare's ghetto Jew during some four hundred years. To Israeli Jews, who believe that they have outgrown both Jewish East European culture and antisemitic stereotypes of the type that the Shylock character represents, the play suggests that they must recognize and come to terms with unresolved issues that are related both to the trauma of the Holocaust and to East European Jewish identity.

WHAT DOES "GHETTO" MEAN IN HEBREW?

During World War I, many Jewish towns in Eastern Europe were displaced. Men were drafted, and many died or were wounded. Families were separated and fell into poverty, and many were struck by illness and were the victims of violence. Many of those who were young, healthy, and of some means immigrated elsewhere. Even before World War II, the Jewish population in Eastern Europe was in great social, economic, and cultural decline.[6] In some places (and notably in the United States) this situation met with compassion, nostalgia for traditional Jewish life before the war, and sometime even a sense of guilt.[7] But this was not the case in Palestine. And even in Israel after World War II, the plight of Jewish East European Jewry was met with sorrow but was also taken as proof of the superiority of Zionist ideology. In a society that established itself on *Shlilat HaGalut* [the rejection of Jewish diaspora], the ghetto—whether in the horrifying context of the Holocaust or as a reference to traditional Jewish East European life—has become a symbol of past practices, ideologies, religious and popular beliefs, traditions, and social norms that should not be emulated by a Zionist society. The latter believed that it purified itself through physical labor, military formation, and moral fortitude.

There are many ways in which this attitude has become more subtle, compassionate, and reasoned over time—and Sobol's play is certainly a part of this process. However, in much of the rhetoric either by Israelis or about Israel, the "ghetto" still appears as a negative expression, one that stands for Jewish attitudes and practices that should be eradicated from modern Jewish life.

Writing in *The Atlantic* on September 29, 2016, Jeffrey Goldberg mourns the death of Shimon Peres, whom he refers to as "Israel's greatest visionary, a man who understood that it would never be morally or spiritually sufficient for the Jews to build for themselves the perfect ghetto and then wash their hands of the often-merciless world." He adds, "He understood that Jewish optimism and Jewish innovation and Jewish achievement were all predicated on Jewish survival. But he also dreamt of a better world, and told Israelis that the age of the ghetto was over."[8]

Writing more than a year later in *Haaretz* on June 9, 2017, Israeli writer Doron Rosenblum ties the culture of the ghetto with Jewish fundamentalism: "It's easy to forget that even before the territories, Israel was—beneath the secular mannerisms—a sort of theocratic *ghetto;* an unfinished national structure. It's easy to forget that even the secular, open-collared among our leaders had been carrying from the start the seeds of messianism."[9] And writing more recently on October 25, 2018, in *Yediot Aharonot*, Meir Shalev observes that "Israel . . . is not a villa in the jungle[10] but rather a shtetl [East European Jewish town] in the *Kasbah* [the citadel of a North African city]."[11] These, among many other references, provide a strong sense that when it comes to Israeli culture, the heritage of the Jewish diaspora is, more often than not, seen as synonymous with pettiness, lack of vision, religious fundamentalism, and a provincial and selfish attitude. As late as 2018, any implication that Israelis are continuing the culture of the shtetl can only be perceived as harsh criticism of those who failed to embrace the superior vision of Zionism.

SHYLOCK AND THE GHETTO

It is probably easiest to recognize the relationship between *The Merchant of Venice* and Sobol's *Ghetto* when looking at the production of the play in Germany. In Germany, *Ghetto* was first directed in 1984 by Peter Zadek, who is well known for his productions of *The Merchant of Venice* between 1961 and 1993. The German production of *Ghetto* also marks a "*Merchant* renaissance" of productions and adaptations of *The Merchant of Venice* after the play has been unofficially boycotted since the end of World War II. And as Alan Bern, the musical director in two of Sobol's German productions of *Ghetto*, records, the ending scene of the 1992 production included the recitation of Shylock's monologue.[12]

In an Israeli context, it is easier to recognize the relationship between *Ghetto* and *The Merchant of Venice* after recognizing the role of *The Merchant of Venice*—and the character of Shylock in particular—as a quintessential mark of the Jewish diaspora. Shylock, the "Ghetto Jew," is accepted on the Israeli stage begrudgingly and in most cases as a sign of warning about the way Jews should not behave. This interpretation has been largely consistent and can be traced back to the beginning of the Zionist theater. By the beginning of the twentieth century, when Palestinian Jews took their first steps on the Hebrew stage, one could choose from a wide array of images of Shylock's character and had the option to regard him as either a positive or a negative character. Shylock's character—often the impediment as well as the motivation for Shakespearean performance in the Jewish theater—has been attributed many stereotypes over some four hundred years. He has been represented as greedy, vengeful, rigid, cruel, hateful, and nationalistic, but also as courageous, moral, self-sacrificing, and caring about his only daughter. Shylock has been represented as a positive character, mostly in modern productions. He is often depicted as a victim who scores a moral victory by standing up to the antisemitic court, even when he formally loses in the trial against Antonio. In the Yiddish theater, most famously in Jacob Adler's production in 1901 and Maurice Schwartz's production in 1947, Shylock is presented as a moral hero whose moral victory is the victory of the Jewish people and a vindication of Jewish ethics.

This is not the case in the Israeli theater, where the earliest production of *The Merchant of Venice*, in 1936, was contextualized by a debate as to whether the play is appropriate for the Zionist stage and whether William Shakespeare should be rejected as an antisemite. Director Leopold Jessner appeased public opinion prior to the performance by publishing an article in which he promised to mount a production that would reject diaspora culture and uphold proper militant Zionist values:

> My reference here is to *Habima*, which rejected, from the very time of its inception, the character of an establishment of entertainment, in favor of the nobler mission of expressing the *Eretz-Isareli* [Jewish-Palestinian] worldview, to serve, in this capacity, as a vehicle of propaganda[13] for the *Eretz-Isareli-an* conception. . . . A "Shylock of consciousness" . . . the consciousness of a Diaspora Jew . . . cannot be useful for *Habima*. . . . It therefore presents this legend, along with the significant character of Shylock. However, it does not present a tolerant Shylock, but Shylock the warrior.[14]

The theme of "a militant Shylock" was expressed in 1936 through a translation, a musical score, and interpretive acting that turned Shylock into the main and most powerful character in the play; first appearing docile and bent over, but later walking up straight and speaking with confidence, undergoing the redemptive growth that the Zionist theater would wish for all diaspora Jews.

To some extent, every Israeli production of the *The Merchant of Venice* was plagued by concern about the play's antisemitism on the one hand and the need to respond to Shylock, the quintessential diaspora Jew, on the other. But one performance that is particularly fraught with the tensions between Jews, non-Jews, and diaspora Jews is Tyrone Guthrie's production in 1959. Guthrie directed the play in Germany in 1957, featuring German Jewish actor Ernst Deutsch in the role of Shylock. Deutsch's performance was criticized in the Israeli press as demeaning to Jewish identity,[15] and Guthrie was rejected when he first offered to direct the play in Israel. When he was finally invited to direct *The Merchant of Venice* in Israel, Ari Vorshber, the art director of the Habima national theater, was asked why Guthrie was rejected in the first place.

In response, Vorshber said, "It seem that we still have not freed ourselves from a Diaspora-like mentality." [16] The decision to finally allow the production was presented by Vorshber, in comparison, as the cosmopolitan and liberal choice of Israeli Jews, who are better educated, converse with non-Jews on equal footing, and are free of inferiority complexes and a paralyzing fear of antisemitism. In short, the decision to invite Guthrie freed Israelis from "a Diaspora-like mentality." In reality, however, the meeting between the Irish director, who was trained to follow the Anglophone interpretation of the play, and the local production of the Israeli National Theater, served to demonstrate the extent to which the play has been changed by Zionist ideology. The comedy, featuring three love stories and the Jewish moneylender as a minor character, had turned into a political tragedy in which Shylock, who lends his name to the play, is presented as the major character. Guthrie, who had to contend with a complete subversion of his production for the benefit of a nationalist Jewish interpretation, left Israel unhappy, offering some choice complements for the "national egotism" of Jews who rewrote Shakespeare's "masterwork." [17]

And, as Y. Saa'roni writes in relation to Guthrie's production, the only justification for a production of the *The Merchant of Venice* in Israel is the rejection of Shylock, "a Jew of this sort," who can only be viewed by more sophisticated Israeli Jews as "pure parody":

> To present Shylock as pure parody, as a distant folk legend, while stressing our negative attitude to a Jew of this sort—is an artistic and theatrical Israeli project; an original and refreshing contribution to the interpretation of Shylock's chapter in Shakespearean dramaturgy.[18]

THE RETURN OF THE REPRESSED

In opposition to the prevailing Israeli rejection of East European Jewish culture, Sobol's 1984 play *Ghetto* (directed by Gedalya Besser for the Haifa Municipal Theater) is in many ways the "return of the repressed," as the stereotypes of East European Jewry, the reminders of an uneasy past, are brought back to the Israeli stage and made uncomfortably relevant to contemporary Israeli culture. As in *Hamlet*, where the ghost of Hamlet's father lingers because it must attend to unfinished affairs, the conjuring of the literal ghosts of the Vilna Ghetto (as the play is based on real characters) suggests that their experience, uncomfortable as it might be, is not altogether irrelevant. By doing so, *Ghetto* offers an opportunity to explore the development from traditional Jewish European life in the diaspora/exile to contemporary Israeli culture, and the remnants of European History that are still—and in contradiction to Zionist ideology—an important part of Jewish and Israeli identity.

In *Ghetto*, Sobol presents a complex relationship between his play and *The Merchant of Venice*. Like Philip Roth in his novel, *Operation Shylock*,[19] Sobol divides the character of Shylock into a number of characters that exemplify some of the stereotypes that are associated with him: being vengeful, cruel, unscrupulous, and greedy. He presents three characters: a vengeful librarian, the cruel head of the Jewish ghetto, and an unscrupulous merchant. Rather than denying these stereotypes, Sobol creates situations in which these stereotypes might contain a grain of truth. And by awarding these stereotypes to different characters, he is able to examine them in depth, understand the context of certain behaviors, and even exonerate them. These characters, based on actual prisoners of the Vilna Ghetto, are presented as complex characters who react to the complex reality of Nazi occupation and genocide. The Israeli audience, trained to criticize the social passivity, lack of sophistication, and unchecked materialism of diaspora Jews, leaves the theater with some understanding of their historical circumstances and perhaps considers that these characters are not very different from their Israeli descendants.

A VENGEFUL SHYLOCK

The character of Herman Kruk is based on the ghetto's librarian, whose surviving diary provides the historical basis for the play. Kruk portrays Shylock's alleged vengefulness and dislike of non-Jews and objects vehemently to any form of collaboration with the Nazis, even when such collaboration might save lives. In fact, Kruk does not care at all about saving lives, including his own. He not only protests against the administration of the ghetto that collaborates with the Nazis, but also protests against the ghetto theater (although he changes his mind later on), and any form of normalizing the life in the ghetto. He initially supports the armed resistance in the ghetto, but he later concentrates on scoring a moral victory rather than a military one: Kruk is interested in practicing passive resistance by sustaining Jewish culture and keeping a record of Nazi atrocities. This is not to say that he is not vengeful. As he explains to Dr. Paul, a Nazi officer who engages Kruk in an intellectual debate, the Nazis are destined to destroy themselves by their own aggression, while Kruk's nonviolence will ensure the survival of Jewish culture even if he and other Jews will be killed:

PAUL: Do you know what your Freud says about the origins of aggression?

KRUK: Yes, that it is caused by our death instinct.

PAUL: German aggression indicates, therefore, that we possess a strong death instinct?

KRUK: Death-o-mania.

PAUL: What?

KRUK: You must know this better than I do.

PAUL: And the lack of aggression on your part indicates a lack of a death instinct in the Jewish soul, explaining the principle of "*Netzakh Israel* [the eternity of Israel]!"

KRUK: Maybe.

PAUL: You don't seem excited about my theory, although it should please you as a Bundist[20] and anti-Zionist.

KRUK: How is this related?

PAUL: I don't know whether you would be happy or unhappy to hear this, but the Jews in Palestine are nothing like you. They organize a military network. . . . Is this the death instinct that we have been able to deliver from our souls into the Jewish soul?[21]

Sobol includes in the dialogue more than a slight goading of militant Zionist culture as he presents to the Israeli audience a facet of Shylock's character (and of diaspora Jewry) that they are not familiar with: of sustaining dignity and resistance from a position of weakness. In fact, the very choice of the Vilna Ghetto as the location for the play takes a deliberate exception to the popular Israeli myth of the Warsaw Ghetto that is known for its active militant resistance against the Nazis. The Vilna Ghetto represents a different myth: a myth of a group of Jewish intellectuals and researchers known as "the paper brigade," who labored to save books and texts, including Kruk's ghetto diary. This perspective, of passive resistance and a moral victory, provides a completely different point of view to a Zionist dogma that criticizes the alleged passivity Holocaust victims who "went like sheep to slaughter." In addition, Kruk's intellectual character provides an important perspective for most Israelis, who know very little about secular, intellectual, literary, and artistic creation by East European Jewry.

A CRUEL SHYLOCK

The character of Jacob Gens is based on the Jewish head of the Vilna Ghetto. There is no denying that Gens behaves cruelly. He collaborates with the Nazis on a daily basis while sending Jews to their death. He instills in the ghetto a reign of terror and uses the methods of the Nazis in suppressing any opposition to his authority, including sentencing Jewish prisoners to death. It is therefore with no small measure of irony that Gens is presented as a committed Zionist who calls for the abandonment of Yiddish in favor of Hebrew in the ghetto schools. He is blamed by Kruk for adopting both the methods and the frame of mind of his Nazi supervisors. In the spirit of Kruk's conversation with Dr. Paul, Gens is blamed by Kruk for destroying the eternal nature of Jewish culture by destroying the language of the Jews and their historical tradition of nonviolence. This grave charge can also be read as an accusation against Zionist society, which ostracized Yiddish and adopted a military culture. And this charge is even more unsettling when it is coupled with the accusation of adopting the culture and methods of the Nazis.

But the accusations against Gens—and by implication against Israeli society—are not completely justified. Gens abhors his task and uses every opportunity to negotiate with the Nazis the number victims, taking every opportunity he can to save men, women, and children. He risks his own life to give prisoners fake work permits that might save their lives, and when he is ordered to remove children from any family that has more than two offspring, he appends the remaining children to families that have only one child. Secretly, while formally persecuting and oppressing the armed resistance against the Nazis, he provides the resistance with some assistance. In a moving statement, he says that he is dirtying his own soul in order to save as many Jews as possible. Here, Sobol exposes the audience to the complexity of Jewish collaboration with the Nazis and the difficulty of judging those who put themselves in harm's way to save as many people as possible. The irony, however, is that Gens fails. Everyone must die, Gens included. He burdens himself with terrible guilt to no avail. And as Kruk predicts, only Kruk's diary survives to tell the story of passive resistance and cultural sustainability in the Vilna Ghetto.

SHYLOCK, THE GREEDY MERCHANT

The character of Weisskopf (no first name) is based on a young Jewish gangster who used his criminal experience to obtain a position of power and profit in the Vilna Ghetto. In Sobol's play, the muscular gangster is transformed into a cunning merchant so as to fit even better the stereotype of a greedy Shylock. In different ways, Weisskopf is both the most obvious and most complex character in the play. He is an obvious character because, as Bern writes, he is easily recognized as a "kind of contemporary Über-Shylock, a Jewish fat cat businessman seen through Nazi eyes."[22] He is also a complex character, because like Shylock (and most of Shakespeare's antagonists), he has a compelling case to make and his own form of integrity.

At first, Weisskopf seems to have few redeeming qualities. Unlike Gens and Kruk, who come to appreciate each other to some extent, Weisskopf is never completely redeemed. However, even he appears to possess his own method of resistance to Nazi oppression. Weisskopf presents the ability to appear and to behave in a way that is similar to non-Jews—displaying money and property as they are translated into social currency—as an act of revenge, one that is perhaps more effective than mere violence. The successful Jewish schemer is therefore resisting non-Jewish oppression by beating non-Jews at their own economic game. And to a great extent, this method is not very different from Shylock's attempted revenge in the Venetian court, which is based on his capital and his contract with Antonio.

In a speech that can be compared with Shylock's own speech in act 3, scene i, of *The Merchant of Venice*, Weisskopf addresses (with some interruptions) a group of Jews who are preparing a banquet. During the banquet, which Weisskopf is funding, he hopes to convince the Germans to open a launderette in the ghetto. In Weisskopf's speech, Sobol uses a binary opposition to present the servicing of the German soldiers with food, flowers, and sex as revenge. The Jews are presented as respectable, while the Germans are referred to a pigs:

> WEISKOPF: Flowers! More flowers! Fill the place up with flowers! *He snaps at an actor who puts roasted chicken on the table.* No! This table is for cold cuts. The chicken goes over there. Put it next to the gravy. Where's the *cholent*? *He looks around and panics.* Where's the *cholent*!? *He sees an actor carrying the cholent.* Bring it here, you idiot! . . . No, not now. When? When the guests arrive?! Drinks over here. Wait! Wait! Don't scatter the drinks all over the place. Make them easy to reach. Open up all the bottles. Don't worry about what's left. Whatever's left will be sent tomorrow to the poor house. So the poor will also have some fun. We'll show them how the Jews can throw a party. We'll show those pigs. . . . Don't save me money you *shmock*! Is this your money? I give the money, so don't you start saving me Money! I am going to make a deal that is worth ten times as much. A hundred times! . . . The band is here! Sit down. Tune up

your instruments so they don't squeak. We should have good music. Where is the stage? . . . What?! Is this how you decorate a stage?! More flowers!! Make it look beautiful. Yes! More flowers! Don't spare the flowers. Show them what the Jews can do. Let their eyes pop out and drip into their mouths. May they suffer Pharaoh's afflictions and Job's scabies. . . . Make the beef look nice. Let them eat. Let them choke on it. May they stuff their bellies and never empty them again, so that they will be blocked on both ends when Titus's worm will climb into their heads. Put the rice here! May they be constipated so their entrails will pop out of their asses and wrap around their necks. *The actresses walk in. They look gorgeous with new dresses and make up.* Heeey! Look at the Girls! Not bad. . . . *He lays his hand on LJUBA's behind and she smacks him.* Hey! Hey! Don't forget why you're here. Don't worry if you get a little dirty. Everything will be washed away in our new launderette.[23]

The stress here is on external appearance, assuming that the mere appearance of the place will overwhelm the Germans: "Don't spare the flowers. *Show* them what the Jews can do. Let their *eyes* pop out and drip into their mouths." The description of the Germans as pigs is negated by the description of the Jewish women, again placing the issue of external appearance as a vehicle of power. Beautiful flowers, food, and women are translated into a new launderette that will make money, employ Jews, and perhaps even save their lives. Corporeality (demonstrated acutely through the sexual services that the Jewish women award the German soldiers) is therefore presented as an essential characteristic that Jews during the war (and in the postwar era) have to adopt in order to survive in a non-Jewish world. Of course, this imagined power is short-lived, and Weisskopf loses both his dignity and his life. But for a brief moment, his ability to impress his enemies makes him their equal and perhaps even their superior.

THE RECONCILIATION OF THE SHYLOCKS

In comparison with Kruk, the two characters of the profiteering Weisskopf and the militant Gens are presented as shortsighted realists who are unable to recognize the loss of Jewish culture that results from their actions. The motivations of Gens and Weisskopf are different. Weisskopf wants to make money, while Gens's only interest is in saving Jewish lives. But in the long run, Gens can rule the ghetto only through violent methods that he learns from the

Germans and an empty nationalist rhetoric that stifles the alternative voices in his community.

At the same time, Gens sees in Kruk an image of a diaspora Jew who is proud, nationalistic, intellectual, and utterly impractical. Ironically, Kruk's staunch ethical code seems immoral when it precludes saving victims with fake work permits, making deals with the Nazis, and establishing a corrupt ghetto economy that sustains Nazi atrocities. From Gens's perspective, it is more ethical to corrupt his own soul by accomplishing these tasks with the purpose of saving Jewish victims.

Before the end of the play, Gens and Kruk meet and share their point of views, understanding and forgiving each other. Weisskopf, a man of few words and even fewer thoughts, is not extended the same courtesy. At times it seems that the uneducated, lower-class *unterveltnik* [criminal element] is equally despised by the Nazis and by his own people. But before Weisskopf is executed by the Nazis, Gens tries to save him, to no avail. Before Weisskopf is humiliated and put to death, the viewer recognizes that Weissopf has his own moral code and internal sense of integrity. And by the end of the play, all three characters embody tragic attempts to respond to impossible circumstances with the limited means at their disposal, using what Edith Wharton wisely refers to as "the arts of the enslaved."[24]

AN ISRAELI PERSPECTIVE

In Germany, the 1984 production of *Ghetto* was a catalyst for a much-needed public discussion about the Holocaust. Opening during the same year in Israel, *Ghetto* was clearly a play about the Holocaust as well. But the significance of the play had more to do with the characterization and culture of the victims. Forty-nine years after the Holocaust, in a society that believes that it has long done away with a "diaspora-like mentality," the play presents psychological phenomena that are ingrained and perpetuated in modern Jewish culture long after the physical walls of the Jewish ghetto have been dismantled.

The first hint that Sobol provides to this effect is the name of the narrator, Srulik, based on the actual character of Israel Segal, a Holocaust survivor and the artistic director of the theater in the Vilna Ghetto. The nickname, however, is also the namesake of an allegorical character in caricatures from the 1950s drawn by Kariel Gardosh. In Gardosh's work, Srulik [short for Yisrael] is a character that symbolized Israeli society. The implication is that the entire State of Israel is an allegorical Holocaust survivor who is trying to recover from a traumatic past. The ghetto, by implication, is a microcosm in which various Jewish identities are made to coexist.

One certainly recognizes the character of Gens, the Zionist pragmatist, whose strength and talent are in the realm of action, a character of few words but deep sentiments and commitment to Jewish interests. But Gens also carries the memories of war and persecution, and his reactions are often exaggerated, unnecessarily belligerent and hostile. Gens means well, and we understand his motivation, but his pragmatism also seems impractical at times, marred with bitterness and contempt toward do-gooders and intellectual critics, left-wing activists (or nonactivists) the likes of Herman Kruk. Gens's rhetoric of distrust, of a lack of choice, and of impending genocide and annihilation can sometimes be traced to the belligerent foreign relations of a posttraumatic Jewish state. And like Gens, who hangs the members of the Jewish resistance, it is sometimes the feeling of Israeli officials (and members of the Israel public) that in trying times of existential catastrophe, one cannot afford to be tolerant of dissenting voices. And of course, times always seem to be marred by an impending existential catastrophe. If Gens's dialogue sounds at times uncomfortably familiar, it is perhaps because the existential crisis, deeply rooted in the Jewish ghetto, is extended indefinitely and seems to turn into a way of life.

It is a little more difficult to recognize the character of the Israeli Weisskopf, as he symbolizes everything that Zionist culture aimed to eradicate: the Jewish speculator, profiteer, *luftmentsch* [hustler], and petty *ganef* [thief]. This character has been criticized in Hebrew literature, starting with G. Shofman and going all the way to Doron Rozenbloom.[25] As late as the 1960s, the Israeli government was still waging war against small businesses, self-employed merchants, and those who had the tenacity to own a private vehicle. Praise was reserved for organized labor and, of course, large corporations and multimillionaires. The Weisskopfs waited patiently and reemerged in the 1980s in a flashy and fashionable exterior that corresponded to their notion of dignity and power. Now they are *yazamim*, initiators and electronic-age entrepreneurs. They create, sell, underwrite, go into bankruptcy, and re-create apps and services ranging from launderettes to small colleges, hiring and firing people with actual skills who are surprised to find themselves at the lower end of the Israeli food chain. As in Sobol's play, we can understand the motivation of the new glitzy Weisskopfs: they carry not only the historical insult of antisemitism but also the more recent insult by Israeli politicians who let small businesses fuel the Israeli economy but denigrated and exploited small business owners. Who cannot understand their joy when they address a crowd of skilled employees to announce that they are "going out of business" and retiring to an extended vacation in the Caribbean? But while their motivation is understandable, even Sobol sends Weisskopf to his death at the first available opportunity. Is the unstable Israeli economy able to contain the *luftgesheftn* or, in their glitzy new nickname, "the economic bubble"?

The least familiar of the three Shylocks is the author of the diary that inspired the play. The character of Kruk, the scholar, liberal, and pacifist, is missing from the Israeli recollection of East European Jewish culture, as it is missing from Israeli society in general. In the Israeli school system, the phenomenon of Jewish enlightenment is tied exclusively to Hebrew creation, with as little reference as possible to original language and geographical locations. Moreover, the Israeli audience would find it difficult to locate an equivalent to Kruk's character in contemporary Israeli society. In opposition to an extreme right-wing conservative elite, an Israeli opposition can be largely defined as a moderate right-wing faction that still contextualizes ideas of tolerance and civil rights within principles of Jewish supremacy and Orthodox religious politics. Radical liberals, anti-Zionists and conscientious objectors exist in Israel mostly within the rhetoric of right-wing politicians. In reality, they are limited to a very small minority of ostracized activists and intellectuals who are the victims of administrative persecution and public violence.[26] Kruk's abilities to curb violence and to make decisions according to his individual ethics within a context of scholarly knowledge and a wide historical perspective are a challenging proposition to an Israeli audience. If Sobol means to imply that the facet of East European Jewish culture that Kruk's character represents has endured in contemporary Israeli society, he is surely incorrect. But it is possibly Sobol's intention to imply that Kruk's character is exactly what is missing from Israeli society, as it could use the perspective of a more substantial liberal opposition.

The captivating quality of *Ghetto*, however, is that it does not make a univocal statement. The audience meets the three Shylocks and understands and even identifies with their circumstances. As they know the three characters better, the viewers come to the inescapable question: "What would I do?" At times they would like to believe that they would have acted like Kruk, and at other times like Gens, or even like Weisskopf. Most importantly, the Israeli viewers are able to identify with Sobol's Shylocks and perhaps even to accept them as part of their heritage and as cultural legacies that deserve serious reflection rather than scorn and rejection.

CONCLUSION

Our understanding of the phenomena that Kruk, Gens, and Weisskopf represent in contemporary Israeli society can be relabeled by the more contemporary term "post-traumatic stress disorder." But particularly in some of the more philosophical dialogues of *Ghetto*, Sobol hints that the culprit might be a loss of balance. Each character can be understood and identified with. And yet, each of them behaves in an extreme fashion and with complete intolerance of other views. In the same manner that Shmuel Niger blames the loss of linguistic balance between Hebrew and Yiddish on a national traumatic amnesia that followed World War I,[27] Sobol is blaming World War II for a loss of cultural and political balance. To the Israeli audience that associates the ghetto only with the memory of the Holocaust, and diaspora Jews with the image of Holocaust victims, the character of Kruk holds a surprise: a millennium of deep thought, literature, poetry, drama, social activity, and ethical thought, a culture that extends across Eastern Europe and reaches every academic and creative field.

To early Zionists, the world of ideas that Herman Kruk represents must have been a greater ideological threat than the profiteering of Weisskopf. While Weisskopf, the "Über-Shylock," served as an easy target for the denigration of diaspora Jews, the cultural offering of Jewish intellectuals could present an actual opposition. And in a world in which Yiddish culture has been eradicated and in which many of those who still speak Yiddish are Ultra-Orthodox Jews who do not care about secular Yiddish culture, a great deal of Jewish thought, creation, and historical perspective have been lost in the likes of Herman Kruk. In *Ghetto*, Gens and Kruk must negotiate and perhaps even complement their differences. And while they both die, Kruk leaves behind a legacy of Jewish passive resistance and moral courage that withstood Nazi oppression. Sobol chooses the myth of Vilna, of saving books and documenting Jewish history over the militant legacy of the Warsaw Ghetto Uprising of 1943,[28] to suggest that there is more than one manner in which to consider Jewish courage and strength of character.

To the Israeli audience, Kruk's conversation about passive resistance, a moral legacy, and the rejection of the German "death wish" are intellectual innovations. They know little about the culture of diaspora Jews before the Holocaust, as the achievements of this culture have been denigrated and forgotten. Walking out of the theater into a reality in which moral leaders such as Noam Chomsky,[29] Zeev Sternhell, and Yeshayahu Leibowitz are considered pariahs and a perversion of Jewish nationalism, the audience might consider whether something is missing; whether in a Zionist society that allows little opposition we find ourselves as a Gens or a Weisskopf who lacks the moral leadership of Herman Kruk.

More importantly, the audience might consider that without the legacy of Jewish intellectualism, Zionist society lacks a legacy the makes Jewish culture unique. In the relentless struggle, as Jeffrey Goldberg writes, for "Jewish survival," Israelis abandoned "Jewish optimism and Jewish innovation and Jewish achievement"—and they have done so not because they failed to abandon the ghetto, but because they did abandon the most important part of diaspora culture.

NOTES

1. Yehushua Sobol, *Ghetto* [Hebrew] (Israel: Or-Am, 1984); Yehushua Sobol, *Adam* [Hebrew] (Syracuse, NY: Syracuse University Press, 1996); Yehushua Sobol, *Ba-Martef* [In the Basement] (Israel: Or-Am, 1990); Yehushua Sobol, *Moshel Polin* [Governor of Poland] [Hebrew/German], theatrical performance, Vienna, 1995.

2. See Kerstin Mueller, "Normalizing the Abnormal: Joshua Sobol's *Ghetto* in West Germany," *Journal of Germanic Studies* 45, no. 1 (2009): 44–63; Alan Bern, "Who Is Weiskopf? Joshua Sobol's *Ghetto* on East & West German Stages," lecture printout, The 2003 Dorit and Gerald Paul Lecture, The Robert A. and Sandra S. Borns Jewish Studies Program, Indiana University, 2004.

3. See, among many other anthologies, Irene Watts, ed., *A Terrible Truth*, Vol. 1, *Anthology of Holocaust Drama* (Toronto: Playwrights Canada, 2004).

4. Sobol, *Ghetto*.

5. Herman Kruk, *Togbukh fun vilner* geto [Diary of the Vilna Ghetto] (New York: YIVO Institute of Jewish Research, 1961).

6. For a thoughtful description of East European Jewish society after World War I, see Shmuel Yosef Agnon, *Guest for the Night*, trans. Misha Louvish (New Milford, CT: Toby, 2014).

7. A famous example: Jacob Gordin, *Mirele Efros: A lebens bild in fir akten* [Mirele Efros: A Life's Picture in Four Acts] (Warsaw: Self-published, 1911).

8. Jeffrey Goldberg, "The Unbearable Smallness of Benjamin Netanyahu," *The Atlantic*, Sepetember 29, 2016, https://www.theatlantic.com/international/archive/2016/09/shimon-peres-benjamin-netanyahu/502319/ (my emphasis).

9. Doron Rosenblum, "The Wind Would Have Yellowed Anyway," *Haaretz*, June 9, 2017, https://www.haaretz.com/opinion/.premium-the-wind-would-have-yellowed-anyway-1.5482049 (my emphasis).

10. This expression is used often in Israeli politics to present Israel as a privileged European persence in the Middle East.

11. Meir Shalev, "Mashber Emuna" [A Crisis of Faith], *Yediot Aharonot*, October 25, 2018, https://www.yediot.co.il/articles/0,7340,L-5027131,00.html. Where not indicated, the translation is my own.

12. Bern, "Who Is Weiskopf," 9.

13. The word "propaganda" is a cognate and is used in the original. However, at the time, the word did not carry a negative connotation.

14. Leopold Jessner, "Of the *Eeretz-Israeli* [Palestinian] Theater and Its Purpose" [Hebrew], *Bamah*, May 1936, 3, 6.

15. Y. Aviel, "A Jew Performs in the Role of Shylock in Germany" [Hebrew], *Haboker*, December 27, 1957, 8.

16. Anonymous, "Director Guthrie Will Direct Shylock at *Habima*" [Hebrew], *Davar*, December 27, 1957, 6. Vorshber actually said "a Diaspora-like psychology." The word "psychology" is sometime interchangeable in spoken Hebrew with "mentality," which is the term that most likely expresses what Vorshber meant to say in this context.

17. Annoymous, "Guthrie Attacks Shylock Myth," *Jerusalem Post*, February 24, 1959, 3.

18. Y. Saa'roni, "The Shylocks and Us" [Hebrew], *Moznaim: A Monthly Periodical of the Hebrew Writer's Association in Israel* 8, nos. 5–6 (April–May 1959): 469.

19. Philip Roth, *Operation Shylock: A Confession* (New York: Simon & Schuster, 1993).

20. The Bund, a Jewish socialist movement, called for the formation of independent cultural autonomies in Jewish communities around the world rather than for a migration of Jews to Palestine.

21. Sobol, *Ghetto*, 92.

22. Bern, "Who Is Weiskopf," 2.

23. Sobol, *Ghetto*, 69.

24. Edith Wharton, *The Age of Innocence* (New York: Windsor Editions, 1920), 308.

25. G. Shoffman, *Selected Stories* [Hebrew] (Tel Aviv: Am Oved, 1994); Doron Rosenblum, *Israeli Blues* [Hebrew] (Israel: Am Oved, 1995).

26. The Israeli press provides a long list of incidents, both of administrative persecution and public violence, against political dissidents. A recent example of administrative persecution is the decision of the Israeli science minister to block the appointment of a leading Israeli brain researcher to a joint Israeli-German scientific committee because she signed a petition in support of soldiers who refused to serve in the occupied West Bank. See Asaf Ronel, "Israeli Minister Blocks Top Brain Researcher Because She Protested the Occupation," *Haaretz*, July 10, 2018, https://www.haaretz.com/israel-news/.premium-israeli-minister-blocks-top-brain-researcher-because-she-protested-the-occupation-1.6248809. For an example of violence, see Jonathan Ofir, "After Mob Attacks Alternative Memorial

Day Ceremonies, Israeli Education Minister Criticizes Ceremonies, Not Mob," *Haaretz*, May 4, 2017, https://mondoweiss.net/2017/05/alternative-ceremonies-criticizes/.

27. Smuel (Charney) Niger, *Bilingualism in the History of Jewish Literature* (Lanham, MD: Universtiy Press of America, 1990), 87.

28. Not to detract from the courage and sacrifice of the participants in the Warsaw Ghetto Uprising.

29. See Amira Hass, "Noam Chomsky Denied Entry into Israel and West Bank," *Haaretz*, May 16, 2010, https://www.haaretz.com/1.5121279.

Exile and Zionism in the Writings of Rav Shagar

Shlomo Abramovich

WHO WAS RAV SHAGAR?

The term "Zionism" can be understood in many ways. However, for the most part, it refers to the connection to Zion and Israel. Whether this notion leads to an actual attempt to move to Israel or stays as an amorphous ideology, the place and the land have significant roles in Zionism. As we will see, many Zionist thinkers also added to it a negative attitude toward the exile and diaspora. Some negate the actual living outside of Israel, and others also refer to the exile as philosophical and existential, which contradicts the essence of Zionism.

Therefore, finding a Zionist thinker with a positive approach to the exile is exceptional. In this essay, I present Rav Shagar's ideas on such an approach and examine his unique position on Zionism.

Rav Shagar should definitely be described as an exceptional thinker; his writings challenge the conventional religious perceptions in religious Zionism. He was born in 1949 to Holocaust survivor parents and grew up in the Religious Zionist educational system: high school yeshiva in Jerusalem and Hesder yeshiva [combining Talmud study with military service] in Yavne. He fought in the Yom Kippur War in 1973, where he lost many of his friends and was badly injured. This tragic experience deeply affected him and brought him to ask existential and philosophical questions leading him to develop his concepts.[1] He took part in the creation of several unusual yeshivot and religious educational institutions, and in 1997 he established his own yeshiva, Yeshivat Siach Yitzhak, where he taught and developed his unique ideas. In 2007 he passed away from cancer.[2]

Most of Rav Shagar's writings were published posthumously by his followers, who are still working on publishing his varied writings. This causes methodological difficulties in the attempt to examine and summarize his ideas. Among his books, different ideas and approaches can be found that were written in separate times and connotations. Also, the fact that his writings are still being published requires a certain amount of carefulness in claiming definite arguments about his ideas. Therefore, in this essay I focus only on the ideas presented in the sources discussed, and any general determination about Rav Shagar's attitudes will refer only to the way it is expressed in the sources.

The books published until now are varied in style and context. Homilies to the Jewish holidays, interpretation to the Talmud, and discourses about Chasidism are only part of Rav Shagar's prolific works. However, Rav Shagar is mostly known for his philosophical writings and especially his unique approach to postmodernism. In the past years, his writings are being discussed in academia especially since the publishing of his first book in English, which also focuses on his approach to postmodernism.

I will not attempt to summarize Rav Shagar's whole complex approach. However, as an introduction to further discussion, I will present some of his main concepts in this field. I focus on ideas that contribute to the main discussion about the positive meaning of the exile.

A POSTMODERNIST RABBI

In his writings, Rav Shagar describes the loss of faith in grand narratives under postmodernism: "People lost faith in the idea of a cohesive world, with a single, comprehensive meaning, a world governed by a clear and consistent set of principles."[3] The postmodern deconstruction, which describes the entire reality as a human construct, aims to shatter the basic ideologies and concepts.

These ideas are usually described as a critical threat to the religious world, which is based on strict principles and ideologies. However, Rav Shagar shows that these notions not only have deep sources in the Jewish thought but also create an opportunity for spiritual renewal.

Rav Shagar finds the roots for his ideas in the Kabbalistic theory about the shattering of the vessels. This theory describes the creation of the world as a process of destruction due to the divine influence that meets the physical world, that is, the vessels. They could not stand it and therefore shattered. However, this deconstruction is not the final level and allows man to reconstruct the world differently. This Kabbalistic notion refers to the creation of the world but also gives man the ability and obligation to become a creator, using the shards of the world to create a new one. The purpose of this process is to "purify the vessels" and to create a new world that can hold a higher level of the divine influence.[4]

This description provided Rav Shagar with the ideological basis to accept the postmodern mode of life. The loss of faith in the grand narratives and the postmodern deconstruction are another step in the process of the shattering of the vessels, which frees them from their limitations and opens them to divine and infinite influences. As mentioned, this will create new opportunities for a deeper and higher way of living and understanding the world. Rav Shagar points to the connection between postmodernism and the New Age movement and shows how it leads to mysticism.[5] This is an example of opening new options after the destruction of old concepts, among them modern rationality. In his writings he even predicts the next step in this process and describes a mental revolution, when mysticism will lead to the developing of new spiritual abilities and to the revival of prophecy.[6]

Postmodernism is also identified with relativism and skepticism, as Rav Shagar shows from writings of different thinkers. If everything is only a social construction, then everything is also subjective and should not be accepted as absolute truth. These ideas, instead of being a threat to religion and faith, which is usually based on total acceptance of clear religious principles, are the basis for Rav Shagar in creating a unique view about faith in the postmodern world.

In a personal and intimate essay titled "My Faith," Rav Shagar described the new phase of faith that should be adopted in this era:

> It is a path of choice, of creativity. Its point of departure is not identity but freedom. . . . It stems from a postmodern consciousness that denies the self and authenticity posited by the existentialists. Here faith is a choice in the full sense of the word: establishing, rather than abiding by, the rules of the game.[7]

This is a different view of faith than the common rational one. Instead of proving faith, a person should choose it; instead of seeking for certainty, a person should learn to live with the unknown, as in of Rav Shagar's essay titled "Living with the Nothingness."[8] These ideas require a deeper and longer discussion, but we can see how the postmodern terminology and ideas were used by Rav Shagar to describe the religious experience. Skepticism is turned into a faith that is based on choice, and the deconstruction is a process of purifying and elevating our understanding of the world beyond its previous limitations.

Rav Shagar compared his attempt to deal with postmodernism to Rav Kook's approach to modern ideologies. Rav Kook searched for the religious roots of ideas such as nationalism and secularism and described the opportunities they opened to religious life and thought. Rav Shagar sees it as the mission of rabbis and thinkers of our time that they should not avoid or be afraid to deal with.[9]

The ways Rav Shagar chose to deal with postmodernism have been described by different scholars. Hoanoch Ben Pazi, for instance, presented two approaches that can be found in Rav Shagar's writings. The first is as an attempt to help and guide the confused religious intellectual who faces postmodernism and is feeling confused and threatened. Rav Shagar then provides guidelines on how to cope with the dangers of postmodernism to religious thought and what postmodernism might contribute to religious thought. At the same time, Ben Pazi shows how sometimes Rav Shagar is not an outside adviser who is dealing with postmodernism but instead a postmodernist rabbi who is creating a new way of thinking, living postmodernism from within and giving it a religious connotation.[10]

As said above, this brief introduction to Rav Shagar's attitude to postmodernism does not attempt to present a whole picture of his unique ideas but instead is intended to give a short glimpse of it that will be the basis for the main discussion about his perspective on exile and Zionism. Before I get to it, I will discuss the idea of negating the diaspora, which was common among many Zionist thinkers, in order to emphasize the uniqueness of his ideas.

SHLILAT HA-GOLAH: THE NEGATION OF THE DIASPORA IN ZIONIST THOUGHT

In order to evaluate the uniqueness of Rav Shagar's positive attitude toward the exile, I will present the role of the idea about the negation of the diaspora in Zionist thought and the criticism of it in recent years.

David Ben-Gurion was a proud supporter of the idea of negating the diaspora. Of course, he was not the first to present the idea, but his important role in shaping Israel made him a powerful promoter of this ideology, which was rooted in the nature of the country. In 1957 at the National Zionist Congress, he described the exile as a "poor and miserable experience that we should not be proud of."[11] In many ways, the Proclamation of Independence of Israel, which Ben-Gurion had a significant influence on, also presents these ideas in its opening words:

> The Land of Israel was the birthplace of the Jewish people. Here their spiritual, religious, and political identity was shaped. Here they first attained to statehood, created cultural values of national and universal significance and gave to the world the eternal Book of Books.[12]

The next paragraph describes the forcible exile and the striving to go back to the Jewish homeland and then skips to aliyah and Zionism. Thousands of years of life in the diaspora, with all its cultural and social achievements, do not appear in the core text of the modern State of Israel. This is a clear example for negating the diaspora and even erasing it from Jewish history.

This view was part of the Zionist perspective of many leaders and thinkers. Ahad Ha'am, also known as Asher Zvi Hirsch Ginsberg, for example, wrote about it and described in depth his theories about the exile. Yosef Gorani pointed at other figures as well, such as Ze'ev Jabotinsky, Yosef Haim Brenner, and Abba Kovner, who in their writings about creating a new model of a proud Zionist Jew also displayed a negative view of the exile.[13]

There are different aspects in the idea of negating the diaspora. Its basic understanding refers to the actual demand to leave the land of exile and move to Israel. However, this view became weaker as the Jewish communities outside of Israel became stronger. Even radical supporters of this ideology, such as Ben-Gurion, realized that even after the establishment of Israel, the diaspora was not going to disappear in the near future; therefore, actual negating of it would not be practical and productive. Ahad Ha'am also rejected the idea that the diaspora was not appropriate to the Jews and that therefore they must physically move to Israel as soon as possible, a notion that he defined as the "objective negation." He claimed that this idea was harmful and could cause hopelessness and lead to assimilation.

More common is the ideological negation of the exile. In this view, the exile is described as a negative way of living with harmful effects on the nature of the Jewish people. The focus is not on actually living outside Israel but instead is on the values coming along with it. Ben-Gurion, for example, in his speech in 1957 mentioned above, used Shylock, in *The Merchant of Venice*, as an example of a negative result of the exile, as the Jews became identified with nonproductive occupations. He was very careful not to blame the people who were living in the diaspora, including Shylock, for their way of life. However, Ben-Gurion was very clear and used harsh words in his criticism of the negative moral and ideological results of the exile, which created characters such as Shylock.[14]

Hence, Rav Shagar's ideas about positive ideological influences of the exile were exceptional. As a proud Israeli Zionist, his focus was not the actual exile and living outside of Israel but rather its philosophy that, he found, contributed important additions to Zionism.

The ideology of negating the diaspora was much criticized in recent generations and in many ways is considered not politically correct. One of the reasons for that change is the effect it has on the relationship between Israel and the Jewish communities outside of the country. Negating the diaspora might create a feeling of superiority of Israelis over Jews in the diaspora, and as the Jewish communities in other countries became stronger and more confident in themselves, especially in the United States, this kind of relationship could not last.

Criticism of this ideology came from American Zionist thinkers who described in different ways how being a Zionist did not contradict being strongly identified with American society. Jonathan Sarna shows a few examples of this perspective and quotes writers such as Louis Brandeis and Israel Friedlaender. Sarna also explains why historically due to their different experiences in gaining emancipation and equal rights, an ideology of negating the diaspora could not develop in American Zionism compared to the struggle of the Jewish communities in Europe.[15]

The rejection of the idea of negating the diaspora demands a new definition of the role of Israel. Even among Zionist writers who do not accept the idea of negating the diaspora, a difference can be found between Israeli and American writers. An example of this can be found in the argument between Gorani and Sarna. Gorani, in his view of the current relationship between Israel and the Jews in the United States, emphasizes the role of Israel as the center of the Jewish nation due to its uniqueness as a Jewish state.[16] Sarna disagrees and describes an equal relationship between Israel and the Jews in the United States. He calls for a free market and a friendly competition between all the Jewish communities around the world so that each place will seek to create a better environment for Jews and Judaism for the benefit of all people.[17]

Criticism of the idea of negating the diaspora from a different angle comes from postmodernists and post-Zionists. The criticism of this idea became a symbol for criticism of Zionism. The adoption of the ideology of negating the diaspora by Ben-Gurion and the other founders of Israel was blamed by post-Zionists for causing various moral and social injustices in Israel, particularly the discrimination against Mizrachi Jews and Palestinians. Arrogance and aggressiveness are part of the characteristics of the Zionists as portrayed by post-Zionists, who claim that negating the diaspora caused a negating of any sector that did not fit into the new Israeli model that was created.[18]

The criticism of the negation of the diaspora came with a positive, romantic perception of the exile. In contrast to the Zionists mentioned above, who describe the negative ideological and moral effects of the exile, the post-Zionists describe the important contributions of the exile to Judaism, as it creates a better society with equal rights and social justice for minorities.[19] Some post-Zionists even describe the exile as the original nature of the Jews and as "the most important contribution that Judaism has to make to the world," even more than monotheism.[20]

The historical and ideological discussion about the ideology of negating the diaspora is part of the argument about the nature of Israel, as some of the critics call for defining Israel as a multicultural country. The Israeli-Palestinian conflict is part of this discussion because it is part of the results of these arguments. The exile is a model of life without a country, a nation without a place and with no need for one—the opposite of the modern notion of nation-state. If the exile is the desirable and natural way of life for the Jewish people, then the conclusion is that Israel should be defined not as a Jewish state, since Jews do not need a country of their own, but instead as a state defined by its own citizens, with equal rights for the Palestinians.

In some cases, the basis for the post-Zionist criticism is postmodernist ideas, as some of the writers who describe the positivity of the exile use clear postmodernist terminology.[21] This leads us back to Rav Shagar, whom I titled earlier as a "postmodernist rabbi." As we will see, he adopted some of the terms and ideas used by the post-Zionist critics in regard to negating the diaspora as part of his postmodernism in general. His view should also be defined as criticism of this ideology but from a different angle. Rav Shagar is not post-Zionist but has a unique definition of Zionism, as I will show in the end of this essay. He is also not motivated by the developments and changes in the Jewish communities in the diaspora and their relations with Israel, like the American Zionists. Rav Shagar was a proud Zionist, was rooted in Israel, and believed in the importance of adding the exile to Israeli Zionism.

MIRACULOUS NATIONALISM

In his discussions about the exile, Rav Shagar used postmodern terminology and quotes and based his views on current thinkers. As mentioned, it was part of his ideology, as he saw the integration of postmodernism into religious thought as part of the challenges demanded from thinkers and rabbis at this time. Therefore, the easiest way to define his view about the exile is to relate it to the ideas mentioned above of the postmodern criticism of negating the exile. However, I claim that despite the similar terminology and his usage of postmodern ideas, he is coming to this topic from a totally different angle.

The postmodern sympathy of the exile is part of a larger view about modern nationalism. The basis for the postmodern sympathy emerges from ideas about nationality as a human construct and nations as "imagined communities."²² The rejection of nationality leads to the rejection of the nation-state, and the result might be to admire the exile as a preferred way of living. According to this view, the Jews should not seek an ancient homeland but instead should live among the other nations, because keeping their own separated nationality is insignificant. These ideas might not be accepted by all types of postmodern thinkers, but they are the common explanation for the appreciation of the exile among many of these writers.

Rav Shagar had a similar conclusion; he described the exile as "the ideal Jewish condition."²³ However, this is not because of the insignificance of nationality and nation-state but instead is due to the uniqueness of the Jewish people as a nation: "its place is beyond geography, and its identity transcended the constricted boundaries of nationhood."²⁴ The Jews are in the exile, spreading among other nations, because of their divine nationality. They do not allow themselves to be limited to the structure of a specific place and country. Rav Shagar compared the uniqueness of the Jews to the unity of God, as in both cases it cannot be limited to a confined space, but "the whole earth is full of His glory."²⁵

In Rav Shagar's view, nationalism is not rejected as a whole but exists in other nations. He was not denying the distinctions between nations and does not refer to nationalism as a human imagination. To the contrary, his view was based on the essential difference between the Jews and the other nations. Nationality is real, and the nation-state is the natural way of life to all the nations except for the Jews, who are beyond these limitations and definitions. The exile fits the Jews due to their unique spiritual identity. The people who gave the world the Book of Books cannot be limited to a single land and country.

In describing the unique existence of the Jews, Rav Shagar used the writings of Franz Rosenzweig and Slavoj Žižek.²⁶ Žižek writes about "'the part that is no part,' not simply a nation among the nations, but a remainder, that which has no proper place in the 'order of nations'"; Rosenzweig describes the Jews as a nation that "was seized by the river of the world and driven off . . . remains standing on the shore." He portrayed the Jewish existence as having "the universe entirely in itself." Rav Shagar gives to these philosophical ideas a Jewish religious connotation and describes the Torah as the "heterotopic space in which the Jew resides." The devotion to the Torah, the divine law, is what alienates the Jews from the natural order of the world and from the other nations. Rav Shagar is using the writings of traditional Jewish thinkers to base his ideas, particularly the Maharal of Prague.

It should be noted that there is a difference between the presenting of these ideas by the Maharal and by Rav Shagar. When the Maharal, who lived in

Prague in the sixteenth century, was talking positively about the exile, it might sound apologetic: as a way to comfort himself and his followers. He explained that the Jews were in the exile only because of their greatness and because they were beyond the need of an actual land. But when Rav Shagar was saying the same ideas at the end of the twentieth century while living in a sovereign Jewish state, it had a different meaning. In spite of the modern state he was living in and of which he was a proud citizen who even fought as a soldier to protect the country in the 1973 war, he found the exile to be the desirable way of life for the Jews. His unique view about the State of Israel is based on the difference between theory and reality and on an unusual definition of miracle and nature.

In Rav Shagar's view, the settlement of the Jews in an actual country was a miracle. The Land of Israel represents the physical world, the human natural order, which is unnatural for the Jews. They were forced to have a country of their own, to get involved into politics, to have a government, a flag, and all other characteristics of a modern country. This was not a matter of necessity but rather a divine requirement, a miracle performed by God: the rootless nation has its own place in the world.[27]

This is a unique definition of Israel, different from the common Zionist narrative as presented in the Proclamation of Independence of Israel. The proclamation explained that the establishment of the state is "the natural right of the Jewish people to be masters of their own fate, like all other nations, in their own sovereign State."[28] According to Rav Shagar, having a country of their own is not natural to the Jews, and they are not like the other nations. Having the State of Israel is a demand from God, and its existence is a miracle because it contradicts the nature of the Jewish people.

According to this view, living in Israel is an unusual existential experience. The Jews are expected to be citizens in a modern country but should know that deep inside of them, it is not their natural way of life. Jews should not feel too comfortable in their life as members of a modern state[29] but instead should participate in it, without fully belonging, due to their divine nature. Life according to this split existence has various implications in actual life in Israel, as Rav Shagar describes, and I will present a few aspects of them in politics and Israeli society.

BEYOND THE RIGHT-LEFT DICHOTOMY

Rav Shagar was a Religious Zionist, right-wing in his political affiliation, and he established his yeshiva in the West Bank. He opposed the Oslo Accords, criticized the way the peace process with the Palestinians was negotiated, and was against the Israeli withdrawal from the Gaza Strip. However, he also resisted the dichotomy of the Right and Left and presented a unique political vision, which was partly based on his view about the exile discussed in this essay.

Although he wrote about political issues and referred to current events in his writings, Rav Shagar was not a political figure, and his main interest was the philosophy behind the politics, as Shaul Magid wrote: "The Realpolitik does not concern him, what concerns him is the soul of the people."[30] The basis for Rav Shagar's political ideology and his attitude toward the Israeli-Palestinian conflict was his religious and philosophical concepts. In this essay, his political statements will serve as actual implications of the ideological ideas presented above.

In his writings, Rav Shagar criticized his own political sector and described the danger of rigid ideology and strict nationalism that existed on the Right. He was afraid of aggressiveness and lack of sensitivity to the other that often accompanied this type of ideology. He claimed that Religious Zionists' absolute confidence in the natural right to inherit the Land of Israel and the strong feeling of connection to the place and the nation might cause disregard for the suffering of the Palestinians.

Rav Shagar also pointed to the experience of the Jews in exile as a possible basis for these reactions: "The exiled nation . . . becomes sovereign over a defined territory. . . . Must its collective historical memory of Diaspora and defeat compel it to treat the other residents of the land with contempt and hostility?"[31] Rav Shagar's response to his rhetorical question is clearly negative. In his view, the exile should have a positive effect on the nature of the Jews and should bring them to ethical behavior toward the other nations.

Rav Shagar claimed that the memory of the exile should make the Jews more sensitive to others. The Torah commands the Jews to remember not only the Exodus and the heroic victory over the Egyptians but also their suffering and poverty in Egypt to "foster sensitivity and awareness of the other's tenuous plight, and to prevent condescension toward him,"[32] as Rav Shagar explained.

Nonetheless, the effect of the exile goes beyond that. It is not only the memory of the past, which teaches how not to behave in the present. In Rav Shagar's vision, the exile is also part of the Jewish existence even after inheriting their land and establishing a Jewish state: "The insecurity of the Diaspora must deeply inform our confidence as the inheritors of the land. Otherwise, confidence will degenerate into hubris, into the sense that all is due to "my power and might of my hand."[33]

As I described above, in Rav Shagar's vision, the exile represents the divine and unlimited existence of the Jews. The Land of Israel is a Jewish heritage due to a command from God, and the Jews are called to live in this duel being as the inheritors of the land and as a nation beyond the limitations of place. This complex existence creates a modest nationality, a sense of belonging to the place with the notion that the Jews do not have a natural homeland. This should prevent feelings of arrogance and rigidity, which often accompany the notion of "this land belongs to us." The biblical promise of Israel to the Jews was described by Rav Shagar as requiring the Jews to have a sense of modesty in their nationality and in the building of the country, as the land was not their natural or legal right. This modesty should affect their attitude to other nations, including the Palestinians.

Rav Shagar does not offer any actual solutions to the Israeli-Palestinian conflict and does not express a clear position regarding current practical questions. However, he calls for a change of the Right and Left dichotomy and challenges the Right, his sector, to adopt some of the values traditionally identified with the Left. Compassion and sensitivity toward the Palestinians and the unceasing desire for peace, said Rav Shagar, should not contradict the strong nationalism of the Right.[34]

Magid compares Rav Shagar's view of Zionism to Rav Menachem Froman's and presents it as the ideological basis for the new generation of settlers he describes in his article.[35] Rav Froman was an exceptional figure, an Orthodox rabbi of a settlement in the West Bank who constantly tried to promote an alternative path for peace and met many times with Palestinian leaders, including Yasser Arafat. Rav Froman also tried to create a dialogue between religious leaders, both Jewish and Muslims, as a basis for future peace between the nations.[36]

Rav Shagar was not involved in similar political actions but believed that peace can and should come from the national Right. His view of soft nationalism, affected by the exile as a source of ethical values, can be a basis for real cooperation between the nations. A true peace, wrote Rav Shagar, will rise not by neglecting the connection to the land and weakening national identity but instead by adding the humility and boundlessness of the exile.[37]

CONFLICTS AND EDUCATION

The positive attitude to the exile in Rav Shagar's thought is the basis for other issues he discussed about the Israeli society, and I will present two of them.

The first will be the conflicts and tensions between different sectors in Israel. In an essay he wrote for the Yom Ha'atzmaut [Independence Day] celebration in 1986, Rav Shagar described the feeling among many people that Israeli society was falling to pieces due to the hatred between the different groups. He described how those feelings might lead to the conclusion that the idea of a state for the Jews cannot last, and maybe the right place for the cosmopolitan Wandering Jew is in the exile, spreading among the nations.[38]

Rav Shagar's response to this conclusion was complex. He agreed that the unique nature of the Jews is the reason for the separation into different sectors and for the clashes between them, and he also ascribed this nature to the identification of the Jews with the exile. As mentioned above, in his view, the exile is natural to the Jews because of their divine and infinite nature, which is beyond any limited place. The infinite nature of the Jewish people is being expressed in the many ideologies and sectors comprising it. The holy Jewish identity cannot be limited to a single way of expression but instead has to have multiple faces. This is another example of the comparison that Rav Shagar made between the nature of the Jews and divinity, which also has endless ways of expressions due to its infinite nature.

In addition, the divine nature of the Jews gives each sector the feeling that its ideology is extremely important, and therefore it should not compromise with the other groups but should fight for its beliefs. Rav Shagar did not criticize the reality of the divided Israeli society; instead, he gave it a religious justification. According to his view, the Jews are fighting with each other and do not get along together because of their greatness and their divine nature.

However, there is a light at the end of the tunnel. Rav Shagar's conclusion is not that the Jews should go into exile but instead should bring the exile into their life in Israel. He said, similar to what we saw above about the Jewish nationality, that Jewish unity and solidarity is a miracle. Naturally, they cannot live in one place and cannot get along with each other, but they are forced to do so, and the way to do it is by understanding their miraculous existence.

In order to explain the miraculous existence of the Jews, we should go back to his view of Jewish nationalism. Rav Shagar said that the Jews should have a universal nationalism, based on the postmodern universalism rather than the modern type. He explained that from a modern point of view, universalism is based on the idea of the equality of all human beings. If everyone is equal, there should not be any difference between the nations. However, according to the postmodern view, universalism is based on the otherness of all human beings, which creates a different type of cooperation: when each individual or nation is essentially different, there should not be any tensions or conflicts, since they are not competing with each other. That can create a unity between the nations, even though each nation is keeping its own unique identity.

Rav Shagar finds the roots for these ideas in Jewish thought. He explains that in addition to the uniqueness of the Jews as the chosen people, there is another view of all the nations as God's creations when each nation has its own role in the divine plan. According to this view, all nations are equal, including the Jews, despite their separate identities, as they are all doing their role. This is the universal nationality of the Jews: they should keep their own identity, should practice their own religion, and should not involve themselves with the other nations, but at the same time they should have a wider perspective and see themselves as part of all humanity, fulfilling their role just like all the other nations.[39] He even quotes Rav Kook, who explains that this level of existence, where the Jews are equal to the other nations, is a higher level of existence, as part of God's creation, above the unique nature of the Jews.[40]

Similarly, Rav Shagar explains how the different sectors among the Jewish people can coexist together. He calls on them to accept the differences between the sectors and to appreciate the other sectors, as they are also sparks of the divine nation. This means that each sector should fight for its own beliefs and must keep its own identity but also should realize that in a wider perspective the other sectors also have their own justification. This is more than just a pluralism of "live and let live"; it is based on the idea that human limited understanding cannot hold the whole infinite Jewish identity, and therefore one sector cannot represent all the Jewish nation. From a divine perspective, all sectors have a role and should be respected, but at the same time each sector should keep and express its own view.[41]

We can easily find in these ideas Rav Shagar's religious postmodernism. The idea of faith based on choice, which he describes as a result of postmodern deconstruction and the opening of new spiritual options, is one of these structures. The Jews and every sector should keep their own identity from a place of choice, despite the idea that all nations and all sectors also represent divinity and have their own role in the world.

The faith in the divine infinite, as expressed in the kabalistic notion of *ayin*, or nothingness, should lead to openness to the other and to true tolerance to opposite ideologies.[42] Magid describes Rav Shagar's view in this way: "The celebration of nothingness holds the potential for truth to come from every corner, the Arab and the Jew, the homeland and the Diaspora, Israel and the world.[43]" Particularism and choice in one's own way should not lead to the negation of the other. The idea of an infinite divinity, when expressed in different ways, is the basis for this concept. Thus, each part should keep its own identity, as it is a spark from divinity, but at the same time should give space to the other, as it is also an alternative spark out of the infinite. These ideas lead to the last implication of Rav Shagar's positive attitude to the exile in his writings about the proper education for religious Zionists.

In his writings, Rav Shagar criticized the common religious Zionist educational system in Israel, which he finds irrelevant to the postmodern era, and he claimed that it cannot last anymore.[44] He said that the typical religious Zionist belongs to multiple cultures and is exposed to different values and therefore needs to learn how to live a coherent life in this reality. Rav Shagar claimed that the existing system failed to do this and does not prepare its members for the current world. He suggests alternative methods. I will not present all his suggestions[45] but will focus on one idea, which is based on his theories about the exile and the ideas discussed in this essay.

Rav Shagar calls for the shaping of an educational environment that combines domesticity and exile. On the one hand, the system must educate based on its own core values, to present its beliefs to the students and give them a feeling of belonging to a deep and rich tradition. On the other hand, the idea of the exile, as unlimited divine existence, will give students a sense of skepticism and curiosity and present them with a space to choose. There should not be any negation of the other; instead, there should be an open space where different and opposite ideologies can coexist without competing with each other. This kind of atmosphere will enable students to develop a rooted identity with confidence; in this way, they can choose from the options that exist in this world. Students will also create a diverse identity, with different worlds that coexist separately and without competition and fake harmonization of the differences.[46]

We can see how Rav Shagar was using the same structure and teaching that different approaches and ideologies should not contradict each other, as each is representing a spark of the divine infinite. Even religious education, which traditionally is not open to the competition of other ideologies, should let the students have the space to choose. This means that religious education should educate the students according to its own values, but it should not do so through negating other ideologies, as they also have a role in the divine infinite universe.

The idea of the exile adds a sense of complexity and diversity to Rav Shagar's philosophy. The rootlessness, as an expression of the infinite divinity, enables the openness to the other and the accepting of different ideologies. Rav Shagar was describing a duel existence, when the idea of the exile is added to a strong nationalism and to identification of each sector with its own beliefs.

WAS RAV SHAGAR A POST-ZIONIST?

Post-Zionism is being discussed recently in Israel both in the public and the academy. Usually, the attitude toward this term is dependent on the social affiliation of the writer, with some groups badly criticizing it, while others adopt it or at least will discuss its relevance to their ideology. Therefore, it is surprising to find that Rav Shagar, as a right-wing Orthodox rabbi, writes very positively about post-Zionism, which he views as an important development of Israeli society. The question becomes whether Rav Shagar should be defined as post-Zionist, especially according to his ideas about the exile as presented in this essay.

Obviously, it is a matter of definition, as post-Zionism was defined in so many ways and was used to identify different types of ideologies. Uri Ram presents a broad overview of different definitions of this term. One definition he presents is that critics of the idea about negating the diaspora are post-Zionists. According to another definition, processes of Jewish revival are connected to post-Zionism, as it emphasizes a different center to Jewish identity other than the traditional national Zionism.[47] According to these views, Rav Shagar should be defined as post-Zionist, based on his writings presented in this essay. Ram also writes about the tension between post-Zionism and neo-Zionism; he identifies neo-Zionism as an emphasis of the Jewish aspect of Israel over its democratic-civilian one.[48] According to this view, Rav Shagar should be defined as neo-Zionist.[49]

As mentioned before, when dealing with Rav Shagar's ideas, it is important to separate theory and reality. When Rav Shagar writes positively about the exile and calls it the desirable way of life for the Jews, he does not call for Jews to emigrate from Israel but instead talks about the values that the exile carries as an idea. In this sense, Rav Shagar is definitely Zionist and a proud Israeli. His Zionism is deeply religious when he identifies the land and the state with terms such as "holiness" and "redemption."[50] However, at this point, his religious Zionism is taking him away from traditional Zionism. His postmodern religiosity, as presented at the beginning of this essay, leads him to see the positive in post-Zionism.

Rav Shagar believed that the emergence of post-Zionism is the beginning of a new era, which he identified with the messianic era and the end of days.

Post-Zionism in his eyes is part of the process of shattering the vessels, which will open new opportunities and lead the Jewish nation to its next step beyond the limitations of the place and nation.[51] Here again I should point out the difference between theory and reality: Rav Shagar did not talk about the post-Zionists as actual people and movements that will probably disagree with the way he defines them. He talks about their ideologies and the meaning he finds in their appearance in the course of Jewish history.

These ideas do not move Rav Shagar from his identification with Zionism. Just as he calls to add the exile into the life in Israel, as seen above, he also calls to add the ideas of post-Zionism and the new options it is opening to the Zionist ideology. In his view, the postmodern deconstruction is leading men to reconstruct the world differently, and the purpose of shattering the vessels is to purify them. This is the basis for Rav Shagar's complex thought, whereby opposites such as Zionism and post-Zionism or exile and Israel can coexist together.

NOTES

1. Rav Shagar publicly presented his thoughts about the war, maybe for the first time, in a meeting of yeshiva student soldiers who fought in the Yom Kippur War ten years after the war. Warriors of Yeshiva, "Discourses of Warriors, a Decade after the Yom Kippur War" [Hebrew], Daat—Jewish and Spiritual Studies, 1986, http://www.daat.ac.il/he-il/tsava-imilhama/maamarim/sih-lohamim.htm.

2. Avichai Zur, "Holy Deconstruction: Introduction to Rav Shagar's Thought" [Hebrew], *Akdamot: The Journal for Jewish Thought* 21 (2008): 111–12.

3. Shimon Gershon Rosenberg, *Faith Shattered and Restored: Judaism in the Postmodern Era*, trans. Elie Leshem (Jerusalem: Magid Books, 217), 86.

4. Shimon Gershon Rosenberg, *The Remainder of Faith* (Tel Aviv: Resling, 2014), 30–32.

5. Ibid., 173–75; Rosenberg, *Faith Shattered and Restored*, 118–29. The importance of this change is described in other places when he defines his religiosity as based on mysticism. Shimon Gershon Rosenberg, *Tablets and Broken Tablets: Jewish Thought in the Age of Postmodernism* [Hebrew] (Tel Aviv: Miskal, 2007), 437.

6. Shagar, *Tablets and Broken Tablets*, 177–79.

7. Shagar, *Faith Shattered and Restored*, 34

8. Ibid., 85

9. Shagar, *Tablets and Broken Tablets*, 430

10. Hanoch Ben Pazi, "Rav Shagar and the Ethical Challenge of Postmodernism" [Hebrew], *Akdamot: The Journal for Jewish Thought* 29 (2014): 203–8.

11. Yosef Gorny, "The Attitude to the Diaspora: Between Negation and Acceptance" [Hebrew], *Zmanim: A Historical Quarterly* 59 (1997): 104.

12. Provisional Government of Israel, "The Declaration of the Establishment of the State of Israel," Knesset, May 14, 1948, https://www.knesset.gov.il/docs/eng/megilat_eng.htm.

13. Gorny, "The Attitude to the Diaspora," 104–5.

14. Ibid.

15. Jonathan D. Sarna, "Response: The Question of Shlilat Ha-Galut in American Zionism," in *Beyond Survival and Philanthropy: American Jewry and Israel*, ed. Allon Gal and Alfred Gottschalk (Cincinnati, Hebrew Union College Press, 2000), 59–60.

16. Gorny, "The Attitude to the Diaspora," 108.

17. Sarna, "Response," 62.

18. A fascinating discussion about it, with a wide range of sources, can be found in an article of Daniel Gutwein, presented also in his website: "Criticism of 'Negation of the Diaspora' and the Privatization of Israeli Consciousness" [Hebrew], in *The Jews in the Present—Gathering and Dissemination: In Recognition of Yosef Gorni*, ed. Eliezer Ben-Rafael et al. (Jerusalem: Yad Izhak Ben-Zvi, Tasht, 2009), 201–19, https://danigutwein.wordpress.com/2009/01/01/44/.

19. Daniel Boyarin and Jonathan Boyarin, "Israel Has No Motherland," *Theory and Criticism* 5 (1994): 100–101.

20. Daniel Boyarin and Jonathan Boyarin, "Diaspora: Generation and the Ground of Jewish Identity," *Critical Inquiry* 19, no. 4 (1993): 723.

21. Rav Shagar, for instance, presents the ideas of Ilan Gur Zeev. Shagar, *Tablets and Broken Tablets*, 209–17.

22. As presented, e.g., in Benedict Anderson, *Imagined Communities: Reflections on the Origin and Spread of Nationalism* (London: Verso, 1983).

23. Shagar, *Faith Shattered and Restored*, 182.

24. Ibid., 181.

25. Ibid., 189.

26. Ibid., 187–88.

27. Shimon Gershon Rosenberg, *Bayom HaHu* [Hebrew] (Alon Shevut: Institution for the Advancement of Rav Shagr's Writings, 2012), 194–95.

28. Provisional Government of Israel, "The Declaration of the Establishment of the State of Israel."

29. Magid finds in these ideas a basis for new types of settlers, who rejected the philosophy of Rav Kook and replaced it with Rav Nachman's. Saul Magid, "The Settler Nakba and the Rise of Post-Modern Post-Zionist Religious Ideology on the West Bank," *Tablet*,

September 19, 2017, http://www.tabletmag.com/jewish-arts-and-culture/245084/settler-nakba-post-zionist-religious-identity.

30. Ibid.

31. Shagar, *Faith Shattered and Restored*, 184.

32. Ibid., 185.

33. Ibid.

34. Shagar, *Tablets and Broken Tablets*, 144–45; Shagar, *Bayom HaHu*, 132–33, 328–29.

35. Magid, "The Settler Nakba."

36. Douglas Martin, "Menachem Froman, Rabbi Seeking Peace, Dies at 68," *New York Times*, September 9, 2013, https://nyti.ms/2FnYMHy.

37. Shagar, *Bayom HaHu*, 330–32.

38. Ibid., 193.

39. Shagar, *Tablets and Broken Tablets*, 130–32.

40. Ibid., 128–29.

41. Shagar, Bayom *HaHu*, 194–99.

42. Shagar, *Tablets and Broken Tablets*, 152–57.

43. Magid, "The Settler Nakba."

44. Rav Shagar has many other comments about religious Zionist education. For example, he claims that it is "too ideological" and creates insincerity among its members, but these arguments are beyond the interest of this essay.

45. For example, he calls to create a deeper connection between the schools and the community. Shagar, *Tablets and Broken Tablets*, 193–95.

46. Ibid., 202–7, 222.

47. Uri Ram, "Post-Zionism: The First Decade," in *Society and Economy in Israel: Historical and Contemporary Perspectives*, Vol. 1, ed. Avi Bareli et al. (Sede Boqer: Ben-Gurion Institute, 2005), 812.

48. Ibid., 819.

49. However, Rav Shagar does not fit with the ethnic neo-Zionism that Ram mentioned earlier in his article (Ram, "Post-Zionism," 805), as seen in his ideas about universalism.

50. Shagar, *Bayom HaHu*, 128–30.

51. Shagar, *Tablets and Broken Tablets*, 326–29, 337–49.

The Role of the Temple Mount Faithful Movement in Changing Messianic Religious Zionists' Attitude toward the Temple Mount

Mordechai (Motti) Inbari

The Temple Mount is the most sacred site of Judaism and the third most sacred site of Islam, after Mecca and Medina in Saudi Arabia. The sacred nature of the site has made it one of the main foci of tension and friction in the context of the Israeli-Arab conflict.

The year 1996 marked an important milestone in the world of religious Zionism. The Committee of Yesha Rabbis (a group of Orthodox rabbis from the settlements in Judea, Samaria, and the Gaza Strip) ruled that Jews are permitted and even encouraged to enter the Temple Mount. The committee imposed restrictions regarding specific areas where entry is permitted and urged visitors to undertake special ritual purification before doing so. Nevertheless, every rabbi was encouraged "to go up [to the Temple Mount] himself, and to guide his congregants on how to do so in accordance with all the constrictions of *Halacha* (Jewish religious law)."[1] Since 2003, when the Temple Mount was reopened to Jewish visitors after a three-year closure due to the Al-Aqsa Intifada, this ruling has been put into practice. Every day, dozens if not hundreds of Jews, mainly students from the nationalist yeshivas, visit the Temple Mount and engage in solitary prayer.[2] According to Israel Police records, some 25,000 religious Zionist Jews visited the mount in 2017.[3]

The ruling by the Committee of Yesha Rabbis is contrary to long-standing religious edicts, to the position of the leaders of the Mercaz Harav Yeshiva, to the position of the Chief Rabbinate, and to the opinion of the majority of Haredi rabbis. All of these authorities argue that it is a grave religious transgression for Jews to enter the Temple Mount. According to halacha, all Jews are considered to be impure due to contact with the dead, since they have come into contact with deceased persons or with others who have at some point been in such contact. During the temple period (536 BCE–70 CE), Jews were cleansed from the impurity of the dead by virtue of the "sin water"—the ashes of the red heifer mixed in water. Since the destruction of the Second Temple, red heifers have not been available. Moreover, the precise dimensions of the temple have been lost, including the location of the Kodesh Kodashim [Holy of Holies]—the most sacred site—identified as the dwelling place of the Shechina, the Divine Presence. Entry into this section was absolutely prohibited with the exception of the high priest (who was cleansed with the sin water before performing his sacred duties) on the Day of Atonement.

Since the location of the Second Temple is no longer known and since red heifers are unavailable, it was ruled that Jews are prohibited from entering the entire Temple Mount area even though this area is known to be bigger than that of the temple itself. Accordingly, a person who enters the Temple Mount area incurs the (theoretical) penalty of *karet* [the divinely imposed death penalty]. This position that prohibits Jews from entering the Temple Mount has been supported in numerous halachic rulings.[4]

Until the Six-Day War (June 1967), when Israel had conquered the site, the question of Jews entering the Temple Mount was purely theoretical. Since the thirteenth century, Jews had not on the whole entered the Temple Mount both because of the rabbinical prohibition and because those controlling the site, and particularly the Muslim authorities, did not permit Jews to enter. From the thirteenth century, the Muslim authorities ruled that non-Muslims were not allowed to enter the site, and the death penalty was enacted for disobeying the rule.[5]

After the Arab-Israeli War (1948) the Temple Mount was left under Jordanian control, and Jews were not allowed to enter the old city of Jerusalem. The status of the site changed only after it was taken by the Israel Defense Forces (IDF) in June 1967.

Since the 1967 war, Israeli governments have always sought to mitigate the tension raised by this subject, allowing the Muslim *waqf* to maintain its control of the Temple Mount. The status quo arrangement that was introduced by Israeli security minister Moshe Dayan following the occupation of the holy sites, who stated that the Temple Mount would continue to serve as a Muslim place of prayer, while the Western Wall would be a Jewish place of prayer. Under this arrangement, Jews and Christians are permitted to visit the site. As a security measure, the Israeli government has agreed to enforce a ban on non-Muslim prayer on the site. In 1968, the Israeli Supreme Court decided not to intervene in the question of Jewish prayer on the Temple Mount, ruling that this was a political rather than a judicial matter. The court permitted the Israel Police to establish procedures for entry into the Temple Mount on the basis of security considerations.[6]

Since the occupation of the Temple Mount by IDF troops in the Six-Day War, however, a number of groups within Israeli society have demanded a change in the passive approach of the Jewish religious establishment and the Israeli government on the question of the site. These groups advocate action to end Muslim control of the site and to start a process that will lead to the establishment of the Third Temple. The restoration of the Davidic kingdom and the rebuilding of the temple are the zenith of Jewish messianic expectations. The return of the Jews to their homeland with the rise of the Zionist movement, the establishment of the State of Israel, and the conquest of the Temple Mount in the Six-Day War of 1967 opened speculation for the possibility of rebuilding the temple.

The Temple Mount Faithful movement is the oldest of the groups devoted to the Temple Mount and the temple. Gershon Salomon, the leader of the movement, has an international reputation due to his indubitable rhetorical capabilities that have kept his actions on the public agenda over a period of almost four decades. The Temple Mount Faithful was the first significant group to demand the removal of the mosques from the mount and the transformation of the mount into a Jewish center, and the movement drew together most of the activists in this field. Its supporters came from the maximalist circles of the Movement for the Greater Land of Israel, including veterans of the Lechi and Etzel underground movements in the preindependence period, and also from adherents of the messianic Religious Right. Over time, however, the movement lost its prestige, and a number of key activists left and founded other frameworks that gradually grew in strength, such as the Movement for the Establishment of the Temple, which was created from the religious faction in the Temple Mount Faithful. Today, only a handful of activists remain in the Temple Mount Faithful, attending the regular demonstrations held several times a year. This movement, which is not specifically Orthodox in character, seems to have lost its appeal and to have been reduced to a marginal status among the Temple Mount groups.

Although much of Salomon's power and prestige has declined, there is a significance to his movement and the ideas it has manifested over time. In this essay, I examine the impact of the Temple Mount Faithful on the changing attitudes of the messianic religious Zionist movement regarding the Temple Mount. In order to understand the magnitude of change among religious Zionists over the question of the Temple Mount, I start my discussion with the opinions that prohibited Jewish presence on the Temple Mount.

THE ZIONIST ORTHODOX ESTABLISHMENT AND THE TEMPLE MOUNT DILEMMA

THE CHIEF RABBINATE

After the Six-Day War in June 1967 and the occupation of the Temple Mount under Israeli sovereignty, the Chief Rabbinate decided to continue the passive tradition on the question of the Temple Mount. In other words, Jews were to confine themselves to the reintroduction of prayers at the Western Wall.

Just a few hours after the Temple Mount came under the control of the Israeli forces on June 8, Israel Radio issued the warning by the Chief Rabbinate not to enter the site. At the first convention of the Council of the Chief Rabbinate after the war, Chief Rabbis Nissim and Unterman continued to argue that Jews must not be permitted to enter the site.

The rabbinate's announcement was drafted by Rabbi Bezalel Jolti, who was invited to the meeting even though he was not a member of the Council of the Chief Rabbinate: "Since the sanctity of the site has never ended, it is forbidden to enter the Temple Mount until the Temple is built."[7]

The minority position in the meeting was represented by Rabbi Chaim David Halevy, then rabbi of Rishon Lezion, who proposed that the question of entering the Temple Mount be left to the local rabbis, who would issue their edict to those following their authority. Shaul Israeli (a prominent teacher at Mercaz Harav Yeshiva) sought to prepare a map identifying the permitted areas on the Temple Mount. Despite the minority position, the Council of the Chief Rabbinate ruled that the entire Temple Mount area was out of bounds. Yitzhak Abuhatzeira, rabbi of Ramle, was the first rabbi to demand that warning signs be placed at the entrance to the site forbidding Jews to enter.[8]

MERKAZ HARAZ YESHIVA AND THE TEMPLE MOUNT

The Six-Day War (June 1967) created a new reality in the Middle East. In the course of the war, Israel occupied the West Bank, the Gaza Strip, the Golan Heights, and the Sinai Peninsula. The Israeli victory in the war created fervent hope among the younger generation of religious Zionists. The dominant school within this population, the graduates of Mercaz Harav Yeshiva in Jerusalem, headed by Rabbi Zvi Yehudah Hacohen Kook, propagated the perception that the Israeli victory in this war reflected God's will to redeem His people. The postwar era therefore represented a higher stage in the process of redemption. The Gush Emunim mass settlement movement, established in

1974 and led by the graduates of the yeshiva, aimed to settle the territories occupied by the IDF in order to establish facts on the ground and to settle the biblical Land of Israel with Jews. They saw settlement as a manifestation of God's will to redeem His people.

On the issue of the Temple Mount, however, Rabbi Kook continued to view the Temple Mount as out of bounds. Kook signed the declaration issued by the Chief Rabbinate immediately after the occupation of the site, prohibiting Jews from entering the Temple Mount.

Indeed, Kook felt compelled to oppose in the fiercest possible terms the idea of Jews entering the Temple Mount area in order to pray.[9] He ruled that the sanctity of the Temple Mount was so great that it was prohibited even to place one's fingers inside the cracks in the Western Wall. Kook fiercely opposed the demand to undertake archaeological excavations on the Temple Mount, since it "is surrounded by a wall. We do not pass this wall and we have no need for [the site] to be studied."[10]

It should be emphasized that the principled position of Kook against Jews entering the Temple Mount was not intended to weaken the demand for Israel to demonstrate its sovereignty on the site. He argued that the Jewish people enjoyed "property ownership" of the area of the Temple Mount. However, he explained that the State of Israel had not yet attained a spiritual level permitting Jews to enter the area of Mt. Moriah. Only after the state has been built in the spirit of the Torah, in both the practical and spiritual realms, he said, would it be possible to enter the holy site.

OPPOSITION TO THE MAINSTREAM: RABBI SHLOMO GOREN

Despite the firm ruling of the assembly of the Chief Rabbinate prohibiting entry to the Temple Mount, there have been chief rabbis who, in a personal capacity, have permitted Jews to enter. Most famous among them was Rabbi Shlomo Goren.

Goren was chief rabbi of the IDF at the time of the Six-Day War. This biographical fact constitutes a key point in the development of his personal approach and his vigorous campaign to open up the Temple Mount. After the war, he initiated the mapping of the site by soldiers from the Engineering Corps in order to identify areas prohibited to Jews, since the Temple Mount site of today is considerably and indisputably larger than the original dimensions of the First and Second Temples. When he realized that his initial expectation that the Islamic presence would be removed would not materialize and that the mosques were to remain, Goren sent a confidential memorandum to Prime Minister Levi Eshkol demanding that entry to the Temple Mount be closed to both Jews and Gentiles, but this was rejected.

After the war, Goren established his office on the Temple Mount. On Tisha B'Av (a day of mourning to commemorate the destruction of the First and Second Temples), the rabbi and a group of his supporters brought a Torah scroll, an ark, and prayer benches to the Temple Mount, where they prayed Mincha [the afternoon service]. After the prayer, Goren announced that he would also hold Yom Kippur (Day of Atonement) prayers on the site. His plans were thwarted by the intervention of Minister of Defense Moshe Dayan and Chief of Staff Yitzhak Rabin.[11]

In 1972, Goren was appointed the Ashkenazi chief rabbi of Israel. In this capacity, he attempted to change the position of the Chief Rabbinate on the subject of Jewish prayer on the Temple Mount. He initiated a discussion in the plenum of the rabbinate and at two sessions in March 1976 lectured at length on his research. Despite his vigorous demand, the council refrained from making any changes to its original decision while nonetheless urging Goren to publish his studies. They later added that when his recommendations were presented in writing, it would be possible to convene a broader forum than the Council of the Chief Rabbinate. This served as a pretext for removing the issue from the agenda.[12] At the same time, Goren's efforts in the political arena to persuade Prime Minister Menachem Begin to ease the government position regarding Jewish prayer on the Temple Mount also failed.[13]

In the absence of political and rabbinical support, Goren was unable to issue an official and public permit allowing entry to the Temple Mount. Moreover, the question of the entry of women was one of the aspects that deterred him from issuing an independent declaration opening the Temple Mount to all Jews. Goren believed that women must not be permitted to enter the Temple Mount area due to the question of ritual impurity and was afraid that a sweeping permit for Jews to enter would also result in women entering the site.[14]

TEMPLE MOUNT FAITHFUL

Gershon Salomon is the founder and unchallenged leader of the Temple Mount Faithful movement. He comes from a well-known family of rabbis who settled in Jerusalem in 1811 out of messianic motives. He is also descended from Yoel Moshe Salomon, one of the founders of Petach Tikva and one of the

Gershon Salomon, head of Temple Mount Faithful (portrait). National Photo Collection, Moshe Milner photographer.

earliest Zionist pioneers in Palestine. In 1958 as the commander of an infantry unit, Salomon was involved in combat action on the Golan Heights. During the course of the fighting an IDF tank run over him, causing severe injury to his legs. After spending a year in the hospital he managed to recuperate, and after a long struggle with the military authorities he returned to his previous unit and served as an operations officer. Salomon never completely recovered from the injury and suffers from a severe limp. Despite his injury, Salomon marches on demonstrations alongside the other members of his movement, although this is visibly a strain for him. As a soldier, he also participated in the battle for Jerusalem in the Six-Day War.

The connection between Salomon's disability and his activities in the Temple Mount Faithful is explicit and direct. Salomon claims to have experienced divine revelation on the day he was injured. When the Syrian soldiers came to kill the IDF soldiers lying in the field, they suddenly fled in fear after thousands of angels circled above him, protecting his injured body. Since then, he reports, he has become an agent of God bearing the message of the reconstruction of the temple. Salomon states that since this event he has regularly experienced divine revelation and that his ongoing efforts for the Temple Mount are the product of this direct connection.[15]

Salomon established the Temple Mount Faithful movement at the end of the 1960s. The movement is essentially one of protest, and the activities are arranged according to the Hebrew calendar. In the period leading up to the Jewish festivals—and particularly festivals that have a connection with the ancient rituals on the Temple Mount, such as the three pilgrim festivals, Hanukkah, and Tisha B'Av—a demonstration takes place in the form of a pilgrimage including elements from the rituals performed on the Temple Mount as related in Jewish tradition. At the festival of Sukkot [Tabernacles], for example, the procession passes through the Siloam tunnel in order to create a symbolic water-related element recalling the ritual pouring of water and the joy of the water libation ceremony. At Hanukkah the marchers carry torches, and at Shavuot [Pentecost] the first harvest offerings are brought to the mount. Similar demonstrations also take place on Zionist occasions such as the Memorial Day for Fallen IDF Soldiers and Jerusalem Day.

Having participated in several of these demonstrations, I can report that they have a uniform character. The event effectively begins a few days before the march, when Salomon asks the Israel Police for permission to hold a prayer service on the Temple Mount on the given date. After receiving a negative response, as is invariably the case, Salomon petitions the High Court of Justice. The judicial ruling that has become established is that the court permits the Temple Mount Faithful to enter the site but not to pray there. Entry is conditioned on the professional opinion and discretion of the Israel Police, which in practice invariably determines that such entry is not to be permitted due to the security situation.[16] This situation has its origins in the status quo arrangement introduced by Moshe Dayan following the occupation of the holy sites, which stated that the Temple Mount would continue to serve as a Muslim place of prayer, while the Western Wall would be a Jewish place of prayer.

The police always reject Salomon's requests to enter the Temple Mount. Accordingly, the demonstrative procession of the Temple Mount Faithful stops at the entrance to the Temple Mount, on the embankment leading up to the Mograbi Gate. The following is a description of one such procession that takes place every year at Hanukkah. The Temple Mount Faithful gather in Jerusalem and travel together to the tombs of the Maccabees near Modi'in. This location was chosen due to the connection between the festival and the movement's demand to end the Muslim administration on the Temple Mount. Salomon

Gershon Salomon, head of Temple Mount Faithful, wearing a bag as an act of mourning for the destruction of the Temple on the 9th day of Av. The picture was taken at the Western Wall plaza. National Photo Collection, Moshe Milner photographer.

delivers a speech by the side of the Maccabean tombs reviewing the history of the Hasmonean family, which rebelled against the Greeks and purified the Temple Mount from idol worship—a process he compares to modern-day reality, urging the prime minister of Israel to learn the lesson of Hanukkah and remove Islam from Mount Moriah. A symbolic torch race to Jerusalem the takes place; a number of individuals begin to run in the direction of Jerusalem, carrying torches, and after covering a certain distance they board busses and continue their journey to the capital.

After arriving at the Jaffa Gate at the entrance to the Old City, the group carries signs, flags, and a symbolic model made from cardboard and intended to denigrate the emblems of Palestinian nationhood (such as a coffin for Yasser Arafat or a Palestine Liberation Organization flag). The group marches toward the plaza inside Jaffa Gate so as to enable the press photographers to record the procession. Here Salomon stops and makes a speech (in Hebrew followed by English) demanding the removal of the Muslims from the Temple Mount. He also addresses current affairs in Israel, emphasizing his hawkish views on various issues relating to Israel and the Arab world. He then proceeds to take the cardboard model and tear it to shreds, sometimes also burning it, as the media cameras flash away. Salomon then holds an impromptu press conference, answering questions from the reporters.

The group then continues toward the entrance to the Temple Mount, where it is stopped at the Mograbi Gate by dozens, if not hundreds, of police officers. There is a glaring discrepancy between the number of demonstrators, which is sometimes as few as twenty individuals, and the number of police personnel securing the demonstration, which is sometimes as high as three hundred. Salomon again makes a speech, quoting extensively from the Bible. The pilgrimage ends at the gates of the Temple Mount with a sense of pain and disappointment. Salomon urges the government to open the mount and bemoans what he considers its weak and defeatist behavior. The event ends with "Hatikva," the Israeli national anthem, and with words of thanks to the Israel Police for protecting the demonstration.

The application for police permission, followed by the petition to the High Court of Justice, as well as the words of thanks to the police and the singing of "Hatikva" all reflect that Salomon is essentially a Zionist. He views the Temple Mount as a national symbol that should be the home of the national institutions; the military ceremonies that currently take place in the plaza by the Western Wall should properly be held on the mount itself. It is his Zionist perspective that leads Salomon to request a permit for the demonstrations and to contact the official bodies of the Israeli state (the police and the courts). He is extremely careful to ensure that members of the movement observe the legal instructions and refrain from confronting the police. The same approach leads him to thank the police for their protection.

Salomon does not lead illegal action; he refrains from entering the Temple Mount without permission and repeatedly files requests with the authorities. Although he has received a negative response for almost fifty years, this has not led him to despair or anger, and he has steadfastly maintained his position. Indeed, his movement publicly condemned the plan by the Jewish Underground, led by Yehuda Etzion, to blow up the mosques on the Temple Mount. "The Temple Mount Faithful Youth announced that while it supports any action to end the disgrace on the Temple Mount, it believes that independent actions of this type can at present only damage the struggle, since there

Gershom Salomon, head of the Temple Mount Faithful, presents a model of the Third Temple next to the Mugrabi Gate of the mount during the movement's demonstration. National Photo Collection, Moshe Milner photographer.

can be no greater disgrace than for the Israeli government to rebuild with its own hands the mosques on the Temple Mount."[17]

Although Salomon ensures that his movement does not engage in any illegal or violent activities, its central message—the removal of the mosques from the Temple Mount—may be perceived as conveying an aggressive message for Islam and, accordingly, may cause serious conflicts on the mount between Muslim worshippers and the Israeli law enforcement agencies. In 1987, for example, thousands of Muslim worshippers, throwing stones at the Western Wall plaza, protested against entry into the site of the Temple Mount Faithful. This incident ended after intervention by the mayor of Jerusalem at the time, Teddy Kollek. In October 1990, however, during the height of the First Intifada, mediation efforts were to no avail, and a demonstration by the Temple Mount Faithful led to a bloodbath. The incident occurred during the festival of Sukkot, when the *waqf* exploited the announcement by the movement of its intention to lay the cornerstone for the temple (an announcement lacking any real substance) in order to incite passions, calling on the Muslim masses to come in person and defend the holy sites of Islam. The clarifications by the police that Salomon would not be permitted to enter the Temple Mount and that there was no intention of laying a cornerstone for the temple were of no use. Thousands of Muslims gathered at the site and were incited by slogans called by the muezzin in the Al-Aqsa Mosque.

A mistake by an Israel Border Guard policeman, who accidentally dropped a gas grenade close to the plaza by the Dome of the Rock, led to a mass riot. Protracted clashes erupted between the police and the crowd, and the Muslims managed to take control of the police station on the Temple Mount, forcing the police officers to retreat from the site. The police action to retake the mount resulted in seventeen killed and several hundred wounded on the Palestinian side and thirty-four injuries among the Israel Border Guard police and Jewish worshippers at the Western Wall. This incident is considered the most serious on the Temple Mount since the site was conquered by Israel in 1967.[18]

THE MOVEMENT FOR THE ESTABLISHMENT OF THE TEMPLE

As noted above, the Temple Mount Faithful was once the central grouping of temple activists. During its early years the movement was joined by right-wing maximalists, both religious and secular, and managed to include the divergent perspectives within a single framework. As time passed, however, it became impossible to maintain this combination, and the Orthodox circles left the movement. Yosef Elboim, a Jerusalemite and a member of the Belz Chasidic movement, initiated the crisis. In a personal interview, Elboim explained to me that the purpose of the split was to increase the number of people involved in the Temple Mount issue. He claimed that after a number of activists from the settlement of Kiryat Arba, near Hebron, refused to remain in the Temple Mount Faithful because of Salomon's "secular" approach, he realized that there was no alternative but to establish a new Orthodox group.[19] While for Salomon the Temple Mount was a Zionist and national symbol, for Elboim the site held first and foremost a religious and ritual importance. Accordingly, Elboim and his friends felt that the Temple Mount Faithful could not meet their needs, since Salomon attached less significance to the religious function embodied by the temple.

Yosef Lerner and Israel Ariel joined Elboim, and in 1987 they founded the Movement for the Establishment of the Temple. This breakaway group did not consider itself bound by the approach taken by the Temple Mount

Faithful and anticipated that the divisions would increase the number of people involved in the field by creating alternative frameworks for different target populations. A further reason for the division, as noted by Elboim and Lerner (and by other activists I spoke to during my research), relates to Salomon's forceful personality and his centralized approach to leadership.

A further point of disagreement between the Temple Mount Faithful and the Movement for the Establishment of the Temple related to the question of the ideal of rebuilding the temple. During its early stages, the Temple Mount Faithful did not include the construction of the temple as a practical objective; its messages focused on the national aspects of sovereignty over the mount. For example, the movement's "Declaration of Allegiance" included the following:

> I declare allegiance to the Temple Mount, the sacred national and religious center of the Jewish People and the Land of Israel, and I undertake to act with all my strength for the return to the Jewish People of this national symbol of the resurrection of the Jewish people in its Land.
>
> I shall bear allegiance to Jerusalem, the eternal capital of Israel.
>
> I shall be proud to serve as a soldier in the IDF in all the liberated sections of the Land of Israel, and to carry the message of the Temple Mount wherever I may go.[20]

This declaration does not state that the movement seeks the rebuilding of the temple; neither does the name of the movement embody this objective. Another declaration by the movement demanded the "removal of the disgrace" and the opening of the Temple Mount to the Jewish people in order "to transform it into the national, religious, and spiritual center of the Jewish People and to remove our alien enemies from it."[21] Once again, these publications do not mention the rebuilding of the temple. Accordingly, the breakaway faction decided to emphasize its distinct identity in the name it chose—the Movement for the Establishment of the Temple—and by positioning this objective as its central operational goal.

THE IMPACT OF THE OSLO ACCORDS ON MESSIANIC RELIGIOUS ZIONISM

The messianic school of religious Zionism was profoundly shaken after the disclosure of the Oslo process (1993), which was based on an attempt to secure a compromise between Israel and the Palestinians regarding the territories of

Judea, Samaria, and Gaza, within the framework of a political process, and was expected to culminate in a further compromise on the Temple Mount. While the followers of the approach of Mercaz Harav Yeshiva believed wholeheartedly in a determinism that is leading the Jewish people and the State of Israel toward complete redemption, the emerging reality showed precisely the opposite position—the State of Israel seemed, in some respects at least, to be growing more secular, and its governments were leading a political process founded on painful concessions of parts of the Land of Israel in return for a partial peace agreement. The establishment of the Palestinian Authority and Israel's recognition of this body inevitably challenged the vision of the Greater Land of Israel. In the background, there was also concern that the Temple Mount would be lost and handed over to Palestinian control. Thus, the zenith of messianic expectation—the anticipated establishment of the temple as the peak of the messianic process—now faced a grave danger due to the gradual surrender of sovereign territory.

In this situation, an increasing number of religious Zionist authorities, including leading elements of the settlement movement, began to express positions that interpreted the Israeli withdrawal from territories in Judea and Samaria as divine punishment for the lack of Jewish attention to the Temple Mount, due to the rabbinical prohibition against entering the site. For example, Dov Lior, rabbi of Kiryat Arba and one of the leading spiritual leaders of contemporary religious Zionism, stated:

> We, who believe in reward and punishment and in Divine providence, must know that one of the main reasons why we are suffering torment is the profound apathy among large sections of our people concerning the Temple Mount in general and the construction of the Temple, in particular.[22]

The fear of further concessions led to practical measures designed to thwart any such developments. In 1996 during the high point of the opposition to the Oslo process among the settlers, the Committee of Yesha Rabbis issued a bold ruling urging all rabbis who held the position that it was permissible to enter the Temple Mount to "ascend the Mount themselves, and to guide their congregants in ascending the Mount within all the limitations of *Halacha*." The argument behind the ruling was that the lack of a Jewish presence on the Temple Mount, due to the halachic prohibition against entering the site, had led the Israeli governments to see the site as one that could easily be relinquished. Accordingly, if masses of Jews began to enter the Temple Mount in order to pray, it would be harder for the Israeli government to transfer sovereignty over the site to the Palestinian Authority.[23] This decision also constituted an expression of defiance vis-à-vis the Israeli Chief Rabbinate, challenging its repeated rulings.

THE OPENING OF THE TEMPLE MOUNT IN 2003

The Temple Mount was closed for Jewish visits during 2000–2003 due to the Al-Aqsa Intifada. As soon as the Temple Mount reopened, dramatic changes were observed regarding visits to the site. During the first three months after the Temple Mount reopened for Jewish visitors, some 4,000 Jews entered the site.[24] This trend has continued, and almost every day Jewish religious communities, sometimes numbering hundreds of people, come to pray on the mount.

The journalist Nadav Shragai has reported, based on police records, that there is a growing trend among religious Zionists to visit the Temple Mount. Thus, in 2009 there were 5,650 visits, but in 2015 the number doubled to 10,770. In 2016 the number rose to 14,050 visits, and in 2017 the estimation was of about 25,000 visits. Shragai also observed that hundreds of rabbis, including leading rabbis, permit these visits.[25]

Thus, if in the past yearning for the Temple Mount was the obsession of a marginal, ostracized (sometimes violent) minority within the religious Zionist public, today it has become one of the most significant voices within that community. Scholar Tomer Persico quoted in his research a survey conducted in May 2014 among the religious Zionist public, according to which 75.4% said that they favor "the ascent of Jews to the Temple Mount," compared to only 24.6% against. In addition, 19.6% said that they had already visited the site, and 35.7% said that they had not yet gone there but intended to visit. In response to the question "What are the reasons on which to base oneself when it comes to Jews going up to the Temple Mount?," 39.2% said that the ascent is needed in order "to witness the special site," 54.4% thought that a visit should be made in order to carry out "a positive commandment [*mitzvat aseh*] and prayer at the site," 58.2% claimed that the ascent "will raise awareness about the Temple and its meaning," and fully 96.8% replied that visiting the site would constitute "a contribution to strengthening Israeli sovereignty in the holy place." Apparently, concluded Persico, for the religious Zionists who took part in the survey, the national rationale in ascending the Temple Mount was far more important than the halachic grounds. "Ethnocentric consciousness is replacing halachic sensibility."[26]

CONCLUSION

In this essay, I observed how the religious Zionist movement has changed its attitude toward the Temple Mount. In Jewish traditions, the reestablishment of the temple is perceived as the zenith of the messianic process. In the Jewish eschatological vision, when Jewish exile would end, the return of the Jews to their homeland would take place as promised by God, and the reconstruction of the temple as a place of worship for God would be one of the heights of redemption. However, Jewish tradition learned to put restraints on messianic expectations, and Jews were banned from entering the Temple Mount or doing anything active to hasten the End of Days.

After the Six-Day War in 1967, the attitude of religious Zionism toward the Temple Mount remained according to tradition, and many authorities banned Jews from entering the site. However, this ban has weakened, and since the 2000s most religious authorities are actually encouraging their followers to visit the Temple Mount. As Tomer Persico has shown, overwhelmingly a majority of religious Zionists see the visits to the Temple Mount from the perspective of promoting the site as a national symbol.

In the essay, I recorded a dispute that took place during the 1980s among activists, followers of the Temple Mount Faithful. These followers, who came from Orthodox background, were unhappy with Salomon's concentration on the Temple Mount as a national symbol; they wanted to focus on the site as a place of worship. The splitting movement called itself the Movement for the Establishment of the Temple in order to sharpen these differences.

Over the years, the Orthodox branch has gotten stronger, while Salomon's power has weakened. The Movement for the Establishment of the Temple was able to bring new energies into the advocacy of the Temple Mount, and one of its major successes was influencing the decision of the Yesha Rabbis, discussed above, to permit Jews to enter the site. Salomon was left behind, and his movement became marginalized.

However, from the survey quoted above, it is clear that among religious Zionists the idea that the Temple Mount should serve as a national symbol is much more prominent than that the site should serve as a place of worship. Here we can see how Salmon's ideas have gained prominence and influence.

Although as a leader he was disregarded, his message has gained much impact on Israeli society especially among the sector of religious Zionism.

Note: Sections of this essay were previously published in Motti Inbari, *Jewish Fundamentalism and the Temple Mount* (SUNY Press, 2009), 79–89.

NOTES

1. *Decision of the Committee of Yesha Rabbis* [Hebrew], 8 Shevat 5756 (February 7, 1996).

2. This figure is mentioned in a letter from Minister Tzahi Hanegbi published in *Yibaneh Hamikdash* [Hebrew] 206, no. 7 (2005): 9.

3. Nadav Shragai, "The Permited Mountain," *Israel Hayom,* July 30, 2017, http://www.israelhayom.co.il/article/493403.

4. For further discussion of the prohibition of *Karet*, see *The Talmudic Encyclopedia* [Hebrew] (Jerusalem, 1972) 7, 14:553. On the halachic debate concerning entering the Temple Mount, see *The Oral Law* [Hebrew] 10 (1967); Shaul Sheffer, *The Temple Mount—Crown of Our Glory* [Hebrew] (Jerusalem: Self-published, 1968), 61–68. A list of thirty halachic rulings prohibiting Jews from entering the Temple Mount was collected by scholars at Ateret Cohanim yeshiva and collated in the booklet *Iturei Cohanim* [Hebrew] 16 (1985). The list includes the ruling issued by the Chief Rabbinate in 1967. In a groundbreaking step, the leaders of the Haredi public at the time added their names to this ruling, as did Rabbi Zvi Yehudah Hacohen Kook, head of Mercaz Harav yeshiva.

5. Shmuel Berkowitz, *The Wars of the Holy Places: The Struggle for Jerusalem and the Holy Sites in Israel, Judea, Samaria and the Gaza Strip* [Hebrew] (Or Yehuda: Hed Artzi, 2000), 11–13.

6. Shmuel Berkovitz, *The Temple Mount* [Hebrew] (Jerusalem: Jerusalem Institute for Israel Studies, 2001).

7. For his detailed reasoning, see Bezalel Jolti, "The Prohibition on Entering the Temple Mount in These Times" [Hebrew], *Oral Law* 10 (1967): 39–45.

8. A summary of the meeting held on 1 Sivan 5727 (June 11, 1967) can be found in Yoel Cohen, "The Chief Rabbinate and the Temple Mount Question" [Hebrew], in *The Israel Chief Rabbinate—Seventy Years since Its Foundation* II, ed. Itamar Warheftig (Jerusalem: Heikhal Shlomo Publishers, 2003), 769.

9. Zalman Koren, "Memorandum concerning the Position of the Chief Rabbinate through the Generations on the Question of the Temple Mount" [Hebrew], *Iturei Kohanim* 201 (2000): 27–32.

10. Shlomo Aviner, *Lemikdashcha Tov* [Hebrew] (Jerusalem: Hava Library, 1999), 12–13.

11. Nadav Shragai, *Mount of Dispute* [Hebrew] (Jerusalem: Keter Publishers, 1995), 29–35.

12. Cohen, "The Chief Rabbinate," 772–73.

13. The correspondence between Goren and Begin is quoted in Shlomo Goren, *The Temple Mount* [Hebrew] (Tel Aviv: Sifrei Hemed, 1991), 32–33.

14. Ibid., 460–502.

15. From a movement publication.

16. With the exception of one occasion in April 1981.

17. *El Rosh Hahar* [Hebrew] 2 (1985): 1.

18. Shragai, *Mount of Dispute*, 340–63.

19. Motti Inbari, interview with Yosef Elboim, September 2, 2004, Jerusalem.

20. *Kol Ne'emanei Har Habayit* [Hebrew] 3 (1988): 3.

21. The declaration was published on 1 Ellul 5748 (1988) and appears in *Yibaneh Hamikdash* [Hebrew] 14 (1989): 16.

22. *Yibaneh Hamikdash* 111–12 (1996): 4.

23. *Decision of the Committee of Yesha Rabbis*, 18 Shevat 5766.

24. *Hatzofe*, February 2, 2004. This figure is based on information from the Israeli Police.

25. Shragai, "The Permitted Mountain."

26. Tomer Persico, "The End Point of Zionism: Ethnocentrism and the Temple Mount," *Israel Studies Review* 32, no. 1 (2017): 104–22.

www.ingramcontent.com/pod-product-compliance
Lightning Source LLC
Chambersburg PA
CBHW061436300426
44114CB00014B/1707